PREPARING SPIRITUALLY
for
HARD TIMES

A COMMENTARY ON I PETER

Dennis L. Allen

The Lockman Foundation has graciously given me permission to include the entire text of I Peter and parallel passages in this commentary. I hesitate to include the entire text in my commentaries because reading a passage in its context is critical to sound exegesis. Most interpretive mistakes are due to ignoring the context of the passage, and I do not wish to encourage bad habits in my readers.

However, I include the full text because some readers may be able to acquire this commentary who do not have access to a Bible. I am also aware of the reader's tendency not to look up cross references, missing out on the best commentary of the Bible, which is the Bible. This commentary is written in a form that can be read like any other book, if desired. Nevertheless, this commentary will be most helpful to those who have open Bibles before them.

Preface

The age in which we live is the worst time in church history for the persecution of Christians. Americans may not know this because the worst persecution is mostly overseas. But we are seeing the tide of anti-Christian sentiment rising even in the land of the free. The Bible tells us that as we near the end of the age we should expect persecution of believers to grow more widespread and severe. Even people with no spiritual interest see that hard times are coming and many are becoming "preppers."

Hard times in general and persecution in particular challenge us most, not physically or mentally, but in the spiritual dimension of our life. Man was created to be primarily a spiritual being with a physical body. Our spiritual condition takes the lead in deciding whether the difficulties we face turn out to be a net gain, as God intends, or a loss.

Peter knew firsthand about persecution. And he could see the storm approaching as the Roman emperor Nero was blaming Christians for the fire that he had set in Rome. So Peter wrote to tell believers how to prepare so that they could be victorious through hard times. The whole Bible is relevant to our times. But understanding the message of I Peter and incorporating it into our own way of thinking is especially so at this point in history.

In my study and teaching I have used the *New American Standard Bible* since 1974. Having labored over my own translations of parts of the Old and New Testaments while in seminary, I found the NASB to be the most accurate and literal translation from the original Greek and Hebrew. For all its grammatical accuracy, the NASB is very readable and dignified, as befits the word of God.

The translators knew what they were doing. The original authors (human and divine) were very precise in their grammar and choice of words, even to number, gender, case ending, verb tense, the use of articles, choice of synonyms, and so forth. The Bible is very precise in everything it says and is precisely correlated. A good translation preserves all this as much as possible. Our interpretation and the doctrines we draw from Scripture should also be precise and accurate.

The value of commentaries is to give us understanding of things that aren't so obvious. That's why I don't skip over the difficult parts. This takes a lot of research and a lot of deep thought (not to mention education and experience). One must read and re-read the passage in its context until the logical flow of thought (which always exists) reveals itself. The Biblical author, being carried along by the Holy Spirit (II Peter 1:20f), planned his work and followed an outline as he wrote. We can discern his outline if we work at it. I don't feel that I have figured out the passage and am ready to teach it until I know the original author's outline and intentions. Then I employ his outline to teach what he intended to teach. In my commentaries I always want to follow the logic of the authors' argument through the whole book.

I interpret the Bible by the literal (grammatical), cultural, historical method. This is the normal way to interpret any literature. And, more importantly, it is the method the Bible uses whenever it interprets itself. It does this quite often, providing us with authoritative examples of how God expects us to interpret His word. The literal method of interpretation lets God speak for Himself. Any other approach is to change God's revelation. It doesn't add light to God's word. Rather, it darkens counsel (Job 38:2).

Transliterated Greek words in this commentary will be rendered in italics. The long vowels e and o, _eta_ and _omega,_ are underlined to distinguish them from the short vowels, *epsilon* and *omicron* (for example, *agape, epignosis).* All Biblical quotations are from the *New American Standard Version,* 1977 edition, and are rendered in bold type. I retain the formatting of the *NASV.* If capital letters appear in the middle of sentences, they show that the passage quoted is poetic in form with the capitalized letter starting a new line in the Old Testament passage.

It is my intent that this commentary be exegetically sound and complete, not skipping over any difficult passages. Most of the Bible is not difficult to understand if one is prepared to study it with determination, honesty, and a

4

readiness to obey. I have labored to show the theological ramifications of the text and have taken a more extensive biblical look at a few of the more controversial doctrines found in I Peter. These include showing why the atonement is unlimited in scope but limited in application and why the doctrine of baptismal regeneration is not biblical. The doctrines of predestination and eternal security, so essential to a biblical understanding of salvation, are also covered in some detail. The basis for hope in the midst of hard times is certainty of our salvation. So Peter has made sure that we have a thorough understanding of the biblical doctrine of salvation.

This commentary is written with a view to teaching the reader how to study and interpret the Scriptures on his own. So it includes comments on Bible study methods and principles of interpretation. It also shows how logic is applied to the understanding of the Bible.

Finally, I have followed Peter's purpose by teaching why it is good and smart to take the long view, as God does. This book is all about the hope we find in total devotion to the Lord. Half-hearted devotion will not work in a world where difficulties abound. The extensive applications in these pages will help the reader to understand the principles and to make good use of them.

About the author:

The author has been a Bible teacher and speaker since 1974. After six years with Campus Crusade for Christ (now Cru), he attended Talbot Theological Seminary, earning a master of divinity degree in 1984. He was a middle and high school teacher for 20 years. As an exegetical theologian he is known for making difficult or complex Biblical passages and their related doctrines understandable without being simplistic. His commentaries are adapted from his sermon notes and reflect his commitment to the perfect integrity and infallibility of the Bible as the word of God. He and his wife Karen live in central Ohio and have two grown sons. The author has also written *Colossians: Complete in Christ* and *Revenge at Ravenna.*

Contents

Chapter 1

1:1-2, Peter's Guide to Spiritual Survival

¹ Peter, an apostle of Jesus Christ, to those who reside as aliens, scattered throughout Pontus, Galatia, Cappadocia, Asia, and Bithynia, who are chosen
² according to the foreknowledge of God the Father, by the sanctifying work of the Spirit, that you may obey Jesus Christ and be sprinkled with His blood: May grace and peace be yours in fullest measure.

Most of us have gone through hard times. And all of us have hard times in our future. You've probably noticed a survivalist mindset growing, because Christians aren't the only ones who see the disintegration of society.

Some segments of our society, and many of its institutions, are becoming bolder, more energetic, and less restrained by law in their antagonism against Christianity. Some countries in the world are actively persecuting Christians with torture, confiscation of property and children, enslavement, and murder.

In America, Christianity has not been heavily persecuted because of the country's Christian history. But that background is being actively erased from the collective memory. We can expect to continue on that course as our society continues to reject God and pursue evil. I see the value of being prepared mentally and physically for whatever we are about to face. Scripture cites the ant as encouragement to stock up for the future (Prov. 6:6). But survivalists haven't analyzed what people will need the most as society turns nasty. The Apostle Peter did because he had already been through it. So he wrote a *spiritual* survival guide.

It should be evident that much of the suffering we face does not have its source in any kind of persecution. Suffering is a part of life in a fallen world. Peter's words will help us there as well. We can also bring suffering upon ourselves by our poor choices (see 4:15). But Peter will be addressing primarily the suffering that comes from following Christ.

Man is primarily a spiritual being. When the spiritual dimension suffers deficiency, the other dimensions are negatively affected. So the spiritual aspect of being prepared for hard times is the most important. The purpose of Peter's first epistle is to prepare Christians spiritually for expected persecution. We could entitle his book *Successful Suffering*.

As such, this letter is as relevant to Christians of every century as it was to the original recipients. The situation we face is the same, only more so, and we must meet the same challenges. **The whole world lies in *the power of* the evil one,** according to I John 5:19. So Christianity has almost always faced opposition and persecution, usually subtle, but occasionally severe. We represent God in a world that wants to eliminate all reminders of God's existence. If we are prepared to face persecution victoriously, then the regular hard times will be less of an issue.

For a book dealing with suffering, I Peter is a very encouraging and practical guide, even if you are not currently facing trials. The principles for being victorious through suffering turn out to be the same that lead us to victorious living in general. I hope you will internalize the principles now, before the really hard times hit. It's a foolish man who waits until he gets hungry to plant his corn: "Foresight!? I don't see a need for it."

Peter's opening salutation gives us the basis for the encouragement of the whole letter. We are chosen by the Father, sanctified by the Holy Spirit, and sprinkled with the blood of the new covenant inaugurated by Jesus Christ.

The Personal and Historical Context of I Peter

To understand the Bible correctly and to get the most out of it, we need to know the historical setting, the author, the recipients and their situation, the purpose, and so forth. Commentators call these introductory matters.

Author

The author of this epistle is Peter, of course. That has never been seriously challenged, although some have expressed the mistaken opinion that an uneducated Galilean fisherman could not have written such a finely crafted work as I Peter. But the term *uneducated* in Acts 4:13 simply meant that Peter had not been formally trained in the rabbinic tradition. Jesus hadn't either, as far as we know, yet Jesus was recognized as a brilliant rabbi.

By the time he wrote this letter, Peter had been speaking publicly and arguing the case for the gospel for over 30 years. Experience like that will teach a man to organize his thoughts and to express them in a way that produces understanding and forestalls objections. But even at the beginning of his ministry, in Acts 4:13, where the rulers and elders of the Jews remarked on his lack of formal education, they recognized that Peter had ability far beyond his training. Apparently, he learned more from *his* rabbi than they learned from theirs. Plus Peter had the Holy Spirit revealing truth to him. We must never lose sight of the fact that, ultimately, the Bible is the word of God revealed by the active work of the omniscient Holy Spirit.

Peter operated a fishing business in **Galilee of the Gentiles**, as Isaiah 9:1 called it. So he had to be conversant in Greek. In I Peter 5:12 Peter wrote, **Through Silvanus, our faithful brother (for so I regard him), I have written to you briefly.** This was Silas, short for Silvanus, who accompanied Paul on his second journey, in Asia Minor, and now serves as Peter's secretary in the writing of this letter. Peter gives him more validation than would be expected for an amanuensis who simply wrote from dictation.

In ancient times, secretaries had considerable input. So Silas could have smoothed Peter's expressions to some extent, if that were necessary. Silas was a Gentile and would be fluent in Greek. Furthermore, he may have been known to the recipients. And he had the gift of prophecy, according to Acts 15:32.

We are quite familiar with Peter, the leader and spokesman of the 12 Apostles. Peter was married and his wife apparently traveled with him in his missionary work, at least some of the time (I Corinthians 9:5). He was initially brought to Christ by his brother, Andrew. His original name was Simon, but Jesus changed his name to *Cephas* (in the Aramaic language), which is translated *Petros* in Greek. His name means *rock*, as in a large rock outcropping. And Peter strikes us as a guy who might be named Rocky. This was the first known use of *Petros* as a name.

Peter writes this epistle so the gates of hell shall not overpower the church. So it's appropriate to look at Matthew 16:15-19:

**[15] He [Jesus] said to them, "But who do you say that I am?"
[16] And Simon Peter answered and said, "Thou art the Christ, the Son of the living God."
[17] And Jesus answered and said to him, "Blessed are you, Simon Barjona, because flesh and blood did not reveal *this* to you, but My Father who is in heaven.
[18] "And I also say to you that you are Peter, and upon this rock I will build My church; and the gates of Hades shall not overpower it.
[19] "I will give you the keys of the kingdom of heaven; and whatever you shall bind on earth shall be bound in heaven, and whatever you shall loose on earth shall be loosed in heaven."**

Jesus reminded Peter that He had changed his name when they first met. This was a significant thing to do--Jesus was claiming authority over Peter. And Simon Peter took the name, indicating his acceptance of the Lord's authority over him. Peter, as the spokesman, represents all the Apostles. And the church is **built upon the foundation of the apostles and prophets**, Ephesians 2:20. The foundation of the church, then, is the revelation (the New Testament) that was given by God through the first century Apostles and prophets. And the central and most basic truth of that foundation is this confession that Peter just received from the Father, **"Thou art the Christ, the Son of the living God."** This is logically the first of the "Three Great C's": the Great Confession (Mt 16:16), the Great Commandment (Jn 13:34), and the Great Commission (Mt 28:18-20) that serve as the outline for all the church is to do.

These Three Great C's are found in each of the gospels and in the book of Acts, as well as in several epistles. Peter develops all three of these in this letter.

The Roman Catholic Church claims that Peter was the first pope, although there is no indication that Peter ever was a bishop in the Roman church or that the Roman bishops succeeded Peter in any meaningful way. And there is certainly no indication in God's word that the Roman church, or any church, was to boss the others. Jesus is the head of the church (Eph. 5:23; Col. 1:18). The office of Apostleship was a one-time function. (I sometimes use the upper case A when I need to distinguish Christ's Apostles from other apostles, "sent ones," who were not of the twelve and didn't have the designated authority of the twelve. One of the canons, or standards, for inclusion into the New Testament was that the work had to have Apostolic authority.) No one who wasn't an eye witness of Christ's resurrection can meet the qualifications for Apostleship given in Acts 1. So obviously, when the Apostle John died, that was the end of the Apostles.

But God had a plan of succession ready. According to Ephesians 4:11, the ones who succeeded the Apostles and built upon that foundation for the rest of the church age were evangelists, not another generation of Apostles. The keys of the kingdom have already been used by Peter to open the door of the kingdom to Jews first, then to Samaritans, and then to Gentiles. That includes everyone; there are no more doors to open. So the keys are no longer needed.

Recipients

The original recipients of this letter were scattered throughout five Roman provinces in northern Asia Minor, north of the Taurus Mountains and south of the Black Sea (now part of Turkey). This letter would go to churches that Paul founded in Lystra, Derbe, Colossae, Ephesus and the other six churches addressed by letters in Revelation, etc. Peter may have founded some of the churches in Bithynia, Pontus, and North Galatia. If so, that could explain why the Holy Spirit prohibited Paul from going there (Acts 16:7), since He had already assigned that area to someone else.

These recipients are referred to as **aliens**, sojourners, living in a foreign country, even if they were born there. Aliens often don't have the same rights and privileges as everyone else. It's better to be an alien in one's native country than an alien to God's eternal kingdom. Judging from comments in the epistle, the recipients were mostly Gentiles, although some were Jews. Refer to 1:14; 2:10; and 4:3. Even the Gentile believers would have been taught from the Old Testament, since that was the only Bible they had at the time.

These Christians were already suffering various trials, but Peter anticipates an increase in the severity of the persecution. The provinces apparently did not inflict any official persecution (that is, government-mandated) until the early second century, but people in the provinces usually copied what they saw in Rome. And in Rome, Peter sees government-sanctioned persecution increasing.

Place and Time

According to 5:13, Peter is writing from Rome, which he refers to cryptically as Babylon. We might wonder why Peter is in Rome, where Paul, the Apostle to the Gentiles, has already been (although not free to move about the city). Peter and Paul were not at odds, as some have portrayed.

The little confrontation in Antioch 30 years earlier (Galatians 2:11) was a one-time thing, and doctrine was not the issue. Peter and Paul both got their doctrine from the Holy Spirit, so the doctrine is identical. Compare Peter's salutation to Paul's words in II Thessalonians 2:13. **But we should always give thanks to God for you, brethren beloved by the Lord, because God has chosen you from the beginning for salvation through sanctification by the Spirit and faith in the truth.** We find several parallels between Peter's letters and Paul's letters to the Thessalonians. And Silas was involved in those as well.

Neither was a clash of personalities the issue. Peer pressure from some bigoted Jewish Christians from Jerusalem had intimidated Peter into altering his behavior toward the Gentile believers in Antioch, and Paul corrected him on it (as Gal. 6:1 directs). That doesn't make them enemies or competitors. It makes them responsible brothers in Christ.

Nor was the confrontation a territorial dispute. The division of labor, Peter preaching to the circumcision, and Paul to the Gentiles, was a general sphere of activity, not a hard rule. Peter opened the door to the Gentiles and actively witnessed to Gentiles in Antioch. He wasn't shy about sharing his faith with anyone. Paul, the Apostle to the Gentiles, always went to the Jew first and then to the Greek.

Why did Peter say he was in *Babylon*? First, as a sheep among wolves, he is following the Lord's admonition to be shrewd as a serpent by protecting the Christians there. He knew they were already being accused of disloyalty to Rome. He uses the name without clarification, just as John does in Revelation 14 and 17, indicating that Christians were familiar with this metaphor.

Second, I think the allusion to Babylon would encourage his savvy readers. They were now under the last of the four Gentile kingdoms that were prophesied by Daniel (Daniel 2). What comes next is the kingdom cut out without hands that will crush the kingdoms of men and will, itself, endure forever. This is the millennial kingdom that Jesus will institute when He returns. Daniel prophesied from Babylon, the idolatrous capitol of the first kingdom, and now Peter writes from Rome, the idolatrous capitol of the fourth kingdom.

In II Corinthians 4:17f, Paul takes that same encouragement even further:

momentary, light affliction is producing for us an eternal weight of glory far beyond all comparison, while we look not at the things which are seen, but at the things which are not seen; for the things which are seen are temporal, but the things which are not seen are eternal.

In the midst of our trials, we should never lose that perspective.

This letter was probably written around July, AD 64. That was when the insane Emperor Nero ordered his agents to set fire to Rome while he was in another city establishing an alibi. He wanted to re-build Rome according to his own plans and for his own glory. So he ordered the fire in order to make room for the new construction. The fire was intended mostly for the tenement buildings that housed the lower classes. And newly homeless people were hot about their loss. Suspicion naturally fell on Nero, and Romans turned up the heat on him. He couldn't shake the political fallout with the usual political tricks, so he shifted blame to the Christians. They were already under suspicion in that city because they refused to join in the dissipation and to sacrifice to the emperor. This was blatant hate-mongering and blame-shifting on Nero's part, but it coincided with the Romans' religious bigotry, so they bought it.

Severe persecution followed. Nero even invited friends to his gardens to see Christians burned on stakes while he dressed like a buffoon. That was a little much, even for the pagans. But when Peter referred to the fiery ordeal he wasn't exaggerating. It's almost certain that Peter came to the death Jesus predicted during this persecution (c. 67).

Peter's first epistle may have been written before this persecution began since there is no mention of deaths. But he mentions testing by fire in 1:7 and the fiery ordeal in 4:12, so he may have written after the Rome fire but before the persecution spread full force to the provinces. Persecution usually doesn't strike out of nowhere. It starts small and tentative, and as the persecutors suffer no repercussions, they grow bolder, and increase the scope and intensity of their persecution. We see many warning signs and even the initial, tentative persecutions in our country today. That's why I think we are well-advised to prepare ourselves spiritually.

Purpose and Theme

The propositional question for the whole letter is "How should Christians deal with suffering?" Short answer: focus on Jesus Christ and what He has done for us and submit to God.

Unofficial persecution may come from society in general or from other religions (including evolutionism and atheism). It may take the form of marginalization, slander, ridicule, false accusations, discrimination, and even physical abuse and inquisitions. In our day, many of our fellow believers in other parts of the world are under severe government persecution, adding to the forms just mentioned: confiscation of property, loss of livelihood, imprisonment, confiscation of children, enslavement, deadly work details (Russian Christians were forced to clean up the nuclear disaster at Chernobyl with no protection from the radiation), torture, and even death (currently about 160,000 per year). Our time is the worst period in history for persecution of Christians. The fact that many leaders in America have a strong desire to be like the rest of the world does not bode well for American Christians.

To put the proper perspective on these persecutions, Peter begins his letter with the blessings and privileges we have in Christ. God guarantees that true believers will overcome. God gives us the ability to have a powerful witness and to experience real joy in the midst of these trials.

A careful study of this epistle will enable us to discern the author's outline. The outline of the present text is as follows:

Chosen by God the Father, 1b-2a

Sanctified by the Holy Spirit, 2b

Saved to Obey Jesus, 2c

Chosen According to the Foreknowledge of God the Father, 1b-2a

who are chosen ² according to the foreknowledge of God the Father

Predestination is a doctrine that offends the pride of men and is therefore out of favor with a large segment of declining, humanistic Christendom. If predestination is true, then it removes any basis for boasting, and man's sin nature is a boastful nature. The doctrine of predestination also eliminates the leverage that religious leaders would like to exercise over the people. It removes such clubs as excommunication and the loss of salvation. Nevertheless, predestination is a pervasive and crucial Biblical doctrine. It is essential for a full and correct understanding of the gospel, not to mention the nature of God.

Paul, under the guidance of the Spirit, makes the argument for the doctrine in Romans 9, after asserting in Romans 8:29f:

For whom He foreknew, He also predestined to become conformed to the image of His Son, that He might be the first-born among many brethren; and whom He predestined, these He also called; and whom He called, these He also justified; and whom He justified, these He also glorified.

Note that all who are predestined are glorified. There is no leakage. Paul's argument is an extended categorical syllogism:

All who are predestined are called.

All who are called are justified (saved).

All who are justified are glorified.

Therefore, all who are predestined are glorified.

From pre-appointment before creation to glorification at the consummation, it's all His doing. Jesus taught this repeatedly, just as we read in John 6. Colossians 3:12 says that we are chosen of God. Acts 13:48 says, **as many as had been appointed to eternal life believed.** Ephesians 1:4ff says:

He chose us in Him [Christ] **before the foundation of the world, that we should be holy and blameless before Him. In love He predestined us to adoption as sons through Jesus Christ to Himself, according to the kind intention of His will, to the praise of the glory of His grace, which He freely bestowed on us in the Beloved.**

The basis for God's choice is His love and the kind intention of His will. If God's choice were based upon our merit, or our works, or even our own choice, then it would not be all to the praise of the glory of His grace. It would redound to our glory and give us reason to boast (contrary to I Cor. 1:29; Eph. 2:9; *et al*).

God is sovereign—He **works all things after the counsel of His will**, Ephesians 1:11.

Some, wishing to avoid the doctrine of predestination, say that **foreknowledge** means only that God sees beforehand who will believe and then chooses them on the basis of *their* favorable choice. But Romans 9:16 says, **it *does* not *depend* on the man who wills or the man who runs, but on God who has mercy.**

And the basis for that choice would be foreseen merit. But that contradicts Ephesians 1 which presents a sovereign God who acts according to His *own* will; not a passive God who peeked into the future, and then acts according to someone else's will, claiming credit He doesn't deserve. It contradicts Ephesians 2 which says that people are dead in their trespasses and sins. It contradicts Romans 1-3 which say that no one seeks God. You can't adjust divine doctrine to accommodate human pride without slandering God and filling His word with artificial contradictions.

Peter used the same term for pre-ordaining in Acts 2:23, describing the crucifixion of Christ by the pre-determined plan and foreknowledge of God. It's clear that God didn't just passively foresee the plan of redemption. He pre-ordained it. And in 1 Peter 1:20, God didn't passively foresee that Jesus would be the savior and then acquiesce to the plan, claiming it as His own.

Now, the only basis for choosing some men and not others, if not God's sovereign will, would have to be the foreseen merit of some men over others. (The only other alternative, capriciousness, is not a part of God's character.) Personal merit would give the chosen ones reason to boast. But Ephesians 2:9 says that salvation is **not a result of works, that no one should boast**. Foreseen merit is still merit. And men would still boast. Romans 1-3 is very direct in showing that no man possesses any merit before God.

In Matthew 5:3 Jesus said, **"Blessed are the poor in spirit, for theirs is the kingdom of heaven."** The term *poor* means having absolutely nothing and no means to get anything. One who is poor in spirit knows that he is in total, abject poverty as concerns any merit before God. He can't make a deal with God, because he has nothing to deal with. So the first condition for salvation, according to the Savior, is to know (to admit to oneself) that salvation can only be by God's grace. If it were by man's works, no one could be saved. Works/merit and grace are mutually exclusive. If works or merit are involved at all in gaining our salvation, then our salvation is not by grace (Rom. 11:6).

II Timothy 1:8f asserts that **God has saved us, and called us with a holy calling, not according to our works, but according to His own purpose and grace which was granted us in Christ Jesus from all eternity**. So *foreknowledge* must mean pre-ordained by a sovereign God. The doctrine of predestination is presented as a tremendous comfort to those who face the uncertainties of persecution. Otherwise they might worry that their inadequate response could cost them their eternal destiny. Persecution cannot change what God has predestined. The doctrine of election is crucial to Peter's argument, and he will develop it in the body of his epistle. But even in his salutation, he encourages his readers with this comforting truth.

Sanctified by the Spirit, 2b

by the sanctifying work of the Spirit

The salvation that was pre-ordained by the Father and provided by the Son is applied to the chosen ones by the sanctifying work of the Holy Spirit, for the purpose of glorifying God. The term *sanctified* is the verb form of *hagios*, the Greek word for holy. It's the word used in the name Holy Spirit (*pneumatos hagios*).

What actually causes Christ's finished work of salvation to be applied to a repentant sinner is that the *hagios* Spirit comes into that sinner and *hagios*-izes him. He imputes Christ's perfect righteousness to him. From that point on, he is no longer a sinner in God's eyes (who never again refers to him as a sinner), but is a saint (a *hagios* one) and a beloved son. This is the argument of Romans 6.

Salvation, then, is the work of all three members of the Trinity. It's the Father's choice and plan. In eternity past He chose by sovereign decree those who would be pulled from the population of unbelieving rebels to be saved. Jesus executed the plan by becoming a man and living a perfectly spotless life. Then, as the spotless Lamb of God, He took our sin upon Himself, died in our place, and rose from the dead. And the Holy Spirit applies Christ's work to those who are chosen and called by the Father. It's all to the praise of the glory of His grace.

There is a critical moment of sanctification—that is the point in time when salvation and regeneration actually take place, when the Spirit gives us the gift of saving faith (Ephesians 2:8f). The Holy Spirit makes us holy by setting us apart *from* unbelief and sin *to* faith and righteousness.

Judicially, it starts with justification—the Spirit graciously imputes Christ's righteousness to the repentant sinner's account and declares him just before God. So the Christian is **found in Christ, not having a righteousness of his own derived from the Law, but that which is through faith in Christ, the righteousness which comes from God on the basis of faith**, Phil. 3:9.

This is the instantaneous aspect of sanctification, when the chosen sinner is called out of darkness and placed into God's marvelous light. His old sin nature is crucified with Christ and buried. He is raised up with Christ with a new nature. (Rom. 6.) The old nature stays dead and buried.

There is also a continuing *process* of sanctification, which begins at conversion, continues throughout our Christian life, and is finished when we see Jesus. At that point we receive the final sanctification, called glorification, which is the completion of our salvation when we are made like Christ. Anytime the Bible speaks of some aspect of our salvation as a future thing, something yet to be received, as in Peter's next paragraph, it is this completion of our sanctification that is in view. I John 3:2 refers to the believer's final sanctification: **Beloved, now we are children of God, and it has not appeared as yet what we shall be. We know that, when He appears, we shall be like Him, because we shall see Him just as He is.**

So this continuing sanctification will be completed when we see Jesus face to face. That is a certainty, guaranteed by the Holy Spirit who is given to us as a pledge. **The gifts and the calling of God are irrevocable,** Rom. 11:29. But the path which that life-long process of sanctification takes and the rate at which it happens, depend to a considerable degree upon our faithful obedience to God's word, either running well or else allowing ourselves to be hindered and entangled by sin. So I John 3:3 continues, **And everyone who has this hope fixed on Him purifies himself, just as He is pure.** With that obedience in mind, Peter continues in his salutation to the second Person of the Trinity, saying that we are …

Saved to Obey Jesus, 2c

that you may obey Jesus Christ and be sprinkled with His blood: May grace and peace be yours in fullest measure.

The place of obedience in salvation has been hotly debated since the first century: How is obedience related to our salvation, if at all? This debate is perpetuated only because of the weak form of Christianity that has been propagated by churches that are more concerned with attracting people than they are with God's truth and holy living. Galatians and James, taken together, as they should be, settled this issue in the first century. The whole Bible is consistent with this answer:

Obedience is not the cause of salvation, but it is the purpose and result of salvation. Disobedient people don't get into the kingdom of God. We've seen that salvation comes to us by grace, according to God's sovereign choice, not according to works. But if our faith is the genuine faith that God gives, then it produces not only salvation, but also obedience. This has been the plan all along. **The scepter shall not depart from Judah, nor the ruler's staff from between his feet, until Shiloh comes, and to him shall be the obedience of the peoples,** Genesis 49:10. See also Deuteronomy 30.

We can represent the three views of the place of obedience as formulas, using the > sign to mean *produces*:

Faith + Works > Salvation (the legalistic view; refuted by Galatians)

Faith > Salvation (works not involved at all; the licentious view, refuted by James)

Faith > Salvation, and Salvation > Works (the universal biblical teaching)

Of the three elements, faith, works, and salvation, only works can be seen by men. So that visible element eventually got moved, in keeping with human nature, from the effect side of the equation to the cause side. People desperately want something they can see on the cause side of the equation so they can know that they've done what is necessary in order to cause their salvation. They trust themselves more than they trust God. We have a saying for it, "If you want something done right, you have to do it yourself."

Taking matters into our own hands is what caused the whole sin problem to begin with. If we understand the problem of sin, then it is clear that doing the same thing again will not fix the problem. The Bible says that the righteous man walks by faith, not by sight (Gal. 3:11).

The purpose of salvation is the obedience of faith. This purpose is clearly expressed in Ephesians 2:8-10:

For by grace you have been saved through faith; and that not of yourselves, it is the gift of God; not as a result of works, that no one should boast. For we are His workmanship, created in Christ Jesus for good works,

which God prepared beforehand, that we should walk in them.

We are saved *by* grace, *through* the faith that God gives us, *for* good works. Good works are not the cause of salvation; they are the result of salvation. A changed life is one of the evidences that one is truly regenerated. A good tree brings forth good fruit.

Disobedience is due to disbelief, and that is the very sin problem that the plan of salvation addresses. The solution must fix the problem, or it's not a solution. In Luke 6:46, Jesus asks, **why do you call Me, 'Lord, Lord,' and do not do what I say?** And in John 14:21 He says, **He who has My commandments and keeps them, he it is who loves Me; and he who loves Me shall be loved by My Father, and I will love him, and will disclose Myself to him.**

In Romans 15:18 Paul writes, **I will not presume to speak of anything except what Christ has accomplished through me, resulting in the obedience of the Gentiles by word and deed.** Paul argued extensively in Romans that Law keeping did not work to change the sinner's nature or to produce obedience, but the gospel of salvation by grace through faith does work.

In Psalm 81:15 we read, **Those who hate the LORD would pretend obedience to Him; and their time of punishment would be forever.** Sinners are people who hate God. (The Hebrew term *hate* always means neglect. It may or may not include feelings of animosity.) Some of those will *pretend* to obey God, as the Pharisees did. Genuine salvation does not produce hypocrisy in the person who is saved. Genuine salvation is all about confronting reality.

Peter very pointedly says that those who are chosen are sprinkled with His blood. It's the substitutionary blood of Jesus, shed for us on the cross, that saved us and that continually cleanses us from our sins. (See Hebrews 9.) Peter connects that truth with the sprinkling written of in Exodus 24:7f:

Then [Moses] took the book of the covenant and read it in the hearing of the people; and they said, "All that the LORD has spoken we will do, and we will be obedient!" So

Moses took the blood and sprinkled it on the people, and said, "Behold the blood of the covenant, which the LORD has made with you in accordance with all these words."

And then Peter couples that with Exodus 29:21, the only other time in the Old Testament that men were sprinkled with blood:

Then you shall take some of the blood that is on the altar and some of the anointing oil, and sprinkle it on Aaron and on his garments, and on his sons and on his sons' garments with him; so he and his garments shall be consecrated, as well as his sons and his sons' garments with him.

So the sprinkling Peter mentions (of which the sprinkling in Exodus was a type--a prophetic illustration) sets believers apart to be both God's people and God's priesthood. Peter makes the point in 2:9f that the church has taken over this role for the present age:

But you are A CHOSEN RACE, A royal PRIESTHOOD, A HOLY NATION, A PEOPLE FOR God's OWN POSSESSION, that you may proclaim the excellencies of Him who has called you out of darkness into His marvelous light; for you once were NOT A PEOPLE, but now you are THE PEOPLE OF GOD; you had NOT RECEIVED MERCY, but now you have RECEIVED MERCY.

Peter's point about the sprinkling of blood is this: salvation is a covenant between God and His chosen ones. The chosen ones promise to love and obey God, and God promises to love them and to forgive them on those occasions when they fail to obey.

God makes no covenant with people who make no commitment to obey Him. To them He promises eternal judgment. To them Jesus says, **Depart from Me, I never knew you, you who practice lawlessness** (Mt. 7:23).

The Christian's commitment to that covenant obligation might be tested at any time, even by fire. So we need to stand firm and stick to our promise to obey. With this in mind Peter prays that God's grace and peace will be theirs in fullest measure. Grace reminds them that God will supply all their needs should they face persecution, and His peace will steady and calm their hearts. Peter will say more about that later.

Jesus promised His disciples, **"Peace I leave with you; My peace I give to you; not as the world gives, do I give to you. Let not your heart be troubled, nor let it be fearful,"** John14:27. The Lord's grace and peace have always enabled His children to suffer persecution with courage and resolve. And when they do, it has always been a powerful witness to onlookers.

With storm clouds of persecution gathering on the horizon, Peter writes this survival guide: *How to Suffer Successfully for the Name of Christ*. Peter is not concerned merely with the survival of first century Christians; he is concerned with the survival of the gospel and its credibility among those in succeeding centuries who are chosen but who are still in darkness and who will be watching to see if Christianity is real (see Heb. 11).

Preachers will occasionally warn that Christianity is always one generation from extinction. That doesn't take into account God's sovereignty or the fact that His word abides forever, but the point is well-taken. The world has sunk back into long periods of darkness more than once since Peter wrote this letter.

His salutation introduces the themes of his letter—the blessedness and certainty of salvation, and the obligations that go with that salvation.

Chapter 2

1:3-5, The Security of Our Inheritance

³ Blessed be the God and Father of our Lord Jesus Christ, who according to His great mercy has caused us to be born again to a living hope through the resurrection of Jesus Christ from the dead,
⁴ to *obtain* an inheritance *which is* imperishable and undefiled and will not fade away, reserved in heaven for you,
⁵ who are protected by the power of God through faith for a salvation ready to be revealed in the last time.

In a dangerous and uncertain world, we need a firm and secure place to stand. And we want it to be a good place, a place that events won't turn into a bad place. Many people have taken stands in a place where they should not be. I think of Custer's last stand, as one example. Pride goes before a fall, and it often causes self-willed people to take a stand where they have no business being. Then all they *can* do is fall. By the way, Custer's two brothers, a cousin, and a brother-in-law died with him at the Little Big Horn. Apparently, there is a down side to nepotism. One brother, Tom, had been awarded two Medals of Honor in the Civil War. So we want to be sure we are standing in the right place.

Uncertainty makes courage difficult, to say the least. Boldness and steadfastness depend upon certainty (or else ignorant bull-headedness, which is hardly a suitable substitute). And they require something *worth* suffering for, should suffering come into the picture. When pressure is applied to remove me from my position, I have to know that I *am* where I *ought* to be, and that it's important that I stay there. And if God guarantees ultimate victory, then I am indeed in a strong position and will be sufficiently motivated to stay put. Peter tells us, at the end of this letter, where we should stake our stand: **"this is the true grace of God. Stand firm in it!"**

In this doxology of praise to God, Peter tells his readers about the certainty and importance of their position in Christ, and that they can't lose. So he points out:

The Nature of Our Salvation, 3

The Nature of Our Inheritance, 4

The Nature of Our Security, 5.

The Nature of Our Salvation, 3

[3] Blessed be the God and Father of our Lord Jesus Christ, who according to His great mercy has caused us to be born again to a living hope through the resurrection of Jesus Christ from the dead,

The word **Blessed** is the Greek term *eulogeo*, which means to speak well of, to praise, or to celebrate with praises. This is not the same word for blessed used in the beatitudes, *makarios*, which means happy. *Makarios* is often used in the New Testament to speak of those who follow God, but *eulogeo* is used only of God. It acknowledges God's absolute goodness and manifests a desire for His glory. God doesn't save people because *they* are good; He saves them because *He* is good. That fact elicits praise from the saved for God's goodness and mercy. And it is an essential point to the understanding of Peter's epistle. It is, in fact, one of the over-arching themes of the Bible. It is a prime truth upon which many other truths are based.

This passage assures its readers of the believer's eternal security. Our salvation is eternally secure because it's based upon God's goodness, rather than our own. Whenever we discuss salvation with some unbeliever, we must make it clear that becoming good is a purpose of salvation, but not the cause of salvation. And we must speak well of God and of how He provides salvation, just as Peter does here. In other words, we must glorify God, so the unbeliever will think more highly of God and be more willing to repent of his disbelief and rebellion and trust what God has done for his salvation. We do this by our words, of course, but also by the good works that God produces in His obedient children.

By our faithfulness **we adorn the doctrine of God our Savior,** Titus 2:10. The term *adorn*, by the way, doesn't mean that we make the doctrine of God nicer. It's already perfect and attractive in every way, objectively. But rebels don't see it that way. So our faithfulness helps the rebels see how good God's truth is as they see what it does in us.

The phrase, **the God and Father of our Lord Jesus Christ,** is a compact confession of everything the Bible says about Jesus. It is reminiscent of Peter's divinely-inspired confession in Matthew 16. Jesus is the incarnate God-man, the mediator between God and man who died on the cross and rose again for our salvation, and ascended into heaven to prepare a place for us. God is the Father of our Lord, meaning that they are one essence; everything that the Father is, Jesus is. Paul dealt with that great truth in Colossians. And Hebrews 1:3 says that Jesus is **the radiance of His glory and the exact representation of His nature.** Jesus is co-equal with the Father in every way. Jesus told Philip, **he who has seen Me has seen the Father,** John 14:9.

Colossians 2:9 says, **in Him all the fullness of Deity dwells in bodily form.** No one can be saved who does not believe this. Whatever faith he has, it's not the saving faith that God gives. The whole Bible says that those who would come to God (Yahweh, the real God) must come on God's terms. But man insists that God must meet man on man's terms, saying, in effect, "God must save me, not *from* my sins, but *in* my sins, leaving me to live as I see fit." That will never happen. There will be no rebels in heaven.

Jesus is Lord, meaning that He is the sovereign ruler of all. **The Father loves the Son, and has given all things into His hand,** John 3:35. Jesus is the **Christ,** the anointed Messiah, the Expected One, the glorious King so fully described in Old Testament prophecy and type, who gives the chosen ones their inheritance.

And we should not overlook the personal pronoun there. Jesus is the Lord of all, but more specifically here, He is **our** Lord. The promises and principles Peter discusses in this epistle apply to every true believer. So all that Peter says about our salvation, our inheritance, and our security applies to all believers. This personal pronoun also suggests the personal nature of our relationship to our Lord. It isn't distant or impersonal.

God has caused us to be born again. Peter is determined to make us understand that the entire *cause* of our salvation is in God Himself. If we don't have a good grasp of that fact, then we are not in a solid position to face hard times. We would see persecution as a threat to our salvation because it might scare us into abandoning God. Peter wants his readers to know that persecution is not a threat to genuine salvation. (However, it will reveal those who are faking it.)

The standard that God used to determine whom to save is expressed in the words, **"According to His great mercy."** **According** is *kata,* in the Greek; a preposition that introduces a standard by which something is done. The basis for our being chosen was God's great mercy toward our hopeless, miserable condition. The first human step toward salvation is to recognize our hopeless, miserable condition. That's what Jesus said in Matthew 5:3, **"Blessed are the poor in spirit, for theirs is the kingdom of God."**

Ephesians 2:4-7says:

But God, being rich in mercy, because of His great love with which He loved us, even when we were dead in our transgressions, made us alive together with Christ (by grace you have been saved), and raised us up with Him, and seated us with Him in the heavenly places, in Christ Jesus, in order that in the ages to come He might show the surpassing riches of His grace in kindness toward us in Christ Jesus.

When Paul writes that God **raised us and seated us,** he uses the past tense, the Greek aorist tense, even though he speaks of a future event. When Greek writers used the aorist tense to speak of a future event, they meant that the event was so certain to happen that it was as good as done. We do that when we say, "God saved me from my sins." The transaction and justification are in the past, we are presently being saved from the practice of sin, and in the future we will be saved from the presence of sin. We quite properly include all of this when we use the past tense to say, "God saved me."

Who will receive that mercy is a matter of God's sovereign choice. **He said to Moses, "I WILL HAVE MERCY ON WHOM I HAVE MERCY, AND I WILL HAVE COMPASSION ON WHOM I HAVE COMPASSION,"** Romans 9:15. Since all men are rebels against God and are spiritually dead and non-responsive, if God didn't sovereignly intervene in the lives of some, no one would be saved. See John 3:16-20.

None of this means that the chosen one is passive. The condition for forgiveness is repentance. And we must respond in faith (even though that faith is a gift of God, Eph. 2:8f)). See Acts 17:30f. Repentance and faith are not saving works. Did the paralytic work to heal himself by rising when Jesus told him to (Mk. 2:10-12)? Repentance is the age-old condition for forgiveness. That stands to reason since salvation is God's solution to man's rebellion problem. Faith is how God connects us to Himself. That also stands to reason since not trusting God is what led to the rebellion.

As to the effect of that mercy, Peter writes that we are born again to a living hope. Hope is very important to us. Job 8:13 says, **the hope of the godless will perish.** Whatever kind of faith the godless have, it's a rebellious faith and it won't work with God. Their hope, having no basis in fact, will come to nothing. But according to Romans 5:5, the Christian's **hope does not disappoint, because the love of God has been poured out within our hearts through the Holy Spirit who was given to us.** And Hebrews 6:19 says, **This hope we have as an anchor of the soul, a hope both sure and steadfast.** This is a hope based upon the work, promises, and character of God. Therefore, it isn't called hope because it's uncertain (it isn't), but because it is still in the future.

That our salvation is an accomplished fact is borne out by how and when it was accomplished. It was accomplished,

Peter says, **through the resurrection of Jesus Christ from the dead** (cf. Romans 6). It's an accomplished fact, since that resurrection took place nearly 2,000 years ago.

Or do you not know that all of us who have been baptized into Christ Jesus have been baptized into His death? Therefore we have been buried with Him through baptism into death, in order that as Christ was raised from the dead through the glory of the Father, so we too might walk in newness of life. For if we have become united with Him in the likeness of His death, certainly we shall be also in the likeness of His resurrection, Romans 6:3-5.

Jesus said, **because I live, you shall live also**, John 14:16. Colossians 3:1-3 says,

If then you have been raised up with Christ, keep seeking the things above, where Christ is, seated at the right hand of God. Set your mind on the things above, not on the things that are on earth. For you have died and your life is hidden with Christ in God.

The whole of Christianity stands or falls with the resurrection of our Lord Jesus Christ (see I Corinthians 15).

What then is the nature of our salvation? It is entirely a divine decree that was accomplished entirely by the work of God. We are the happy recipients of the grace of God.

The Nature of Our Inheritance, 4

[4] **to *obtain* an inheritance *which is* imperishable and undefiled and will not fade away, reserved in heaven for you,**

Our inheritance is, by its nature, permanent and guaranteed, since it is based on the nature of God who is perfect in faithfulness. The **living hope**, for which we were saved, is this inheritance. **Living hope** and **inheritance** refer to the same thing. God caused us to be born again to obtain an inheritance that is reserved in heaven for us.

Because it is reserved in heaven, we can't lose it. Paul was pretty adamant about this in Romans 8:35-39:

Who shall separate us from the love of Christ? Shall tribulation, or distress, or persecution, or famine, or nakedness, or peril, or sword? Just as it is written, "FOR THY SAKE WE ARE BEING PUT TO DEATH ALL DAY LONG; WE WERE CONSIDERED AS SHEEP TO BE SLAUGHTERED." But in all these things we overwhelmingly conquer through Him who loved us. [That is our guarantee of victory.] **For I am convinced that neither death, nor life, nor angels, nor principalities, nor things present, nor things to come, nor powers, nor height, nor depth, nor any other created thing, shall be able to separate us from the love of God, which is in Christ Jesus our Lord.**

If you read this passage to someone who teaches that a Christian can lose his salvation, he will respond with something like, "Yes, but you can separate yourself." How could we do that? If we are one of those created things, if all our sins are paid for already on the cross, if God chose us before the foundation of the world (and He doesn't make mistakes), if our salvation is entirely His work, and nothing surprises the omniscient God, then how could we do that?

If we got our salvation by our works in any way, then it stands to reason that we could lose it. But if salvation is by the sovereign decree of God, as He says, then we can't lose it. God is not in our hands that we might drop Him because of our weakness. We are in His hands that we might be preserved by His omnipotence. The nature of our salvation determines the nature of our inheritance. Both are based on the character and work of God.

Why would God reserve something in heaven for us if we might not get there? (That doesn't seem very omniscient.) Why does He say that we *have* eternal life if we only have the *chance* of eternal life? (That doesn't seem very honest.) Is it one of those, "You may already be a winner!" kind of come-ons? You cannot alter divine doctrine to accommodate human pride without slandering God. Peter began this doxology by saying that we should speak well of God. It doesn't speak well of God to say that He might go back on His word or fail in His intent. **God is not a man, that He should lie, nor a son of man, that He should repent; has He said, and will He not do it? Or has He spoken, and will He not make it good,** Numbers 23:19. Is God sovereign or not? Revelation, empirical evidence, and reason say that He is.

Peter lists three things that our inheritance is *not*: By its nature, our inheritance is *not* perishable, *not* defilable, and *not* fadable. I say it that way because that's how the original Greek looks. Part of Peter's rhythmic style of writing is to accumulate synonyms.

We live on a perishing planet, in a perishing tent (body), enjoying perishing things for a perishing amount of time. You can't escape the law of entropy on this earth; everything is moving toward disorder. Whatever doesn't rot, rust, or run down, dissipates in some other way. But that doesn't apply in heaven, where our inheritance is being kept for us. It is **imperishable,** like everything else in heaven.

It is also **undefiled**. Whatever sin touches, it defiles. If we received our inheritance before we saw Christ face to face and were made like Him, we would defile it, and the world would defile it. See Haggai 2:11-13. So it's being kept for us where there is no sin. That requires some patience on our part to endure the delayed gratification, but consider the alternative. Do you want to make do with a dirty, old defiled inheritance for all of eternity?

It **will not fade away**. The flower fades; our own beauty (if we ever had any) fades. Colors and aromas fade. On earth, everything fades. In heaven everything stays brilliant and glorious and fresh forever. Our inheritance will be as new and exciting and vibrant and lovely to us in 10 million years as it is the first day we see it. In heaven, the bloom never goes off the rose.

So what is this marvelous, incorruptible inheritance? I can't even begin to describe it adequately. But for starters imagine this life with only one change – no sin or effects of sin anywhere. No sinners to spoil our good time. Wouldn't that be something! But wait; there's more.

It is everything that a good and loving God wants to give His children. The hardest thing for God to do is to bless His people the way He would like to bless us. The difficulty isn't with God, of course; it's with us. Too much blessing tends to ruin us; we forget God and worship the blessing. But when we are perfected, we will have the capacity for being blessed without being ruined. Then God will pour it on.

It will be everything that is holy and just and good and right and lovely, and nothing that is not. It will be perfect fellowship with God, the angels, and all our brothers and sisters. It will be perfect in peace, happiness, and prosperity. We will have perfect jobs with perfect hours, and plenty of vacation time (as if we would want to use it). **In His temple, everything says "Glory,"** Ps. 29:9.

Our bodies will be perfect, without the limitations we now endure. It will be fun without end. It will be more thrilling, gratifying, and meaningful than we could endure in our present state. In God's eternal kingdom there is no law of diminishing returns. We'll continually be in awe of God, in His very presence. It will make all the trouble we ever faced on earth seem like nothing.

Our inheritance is completed salvation and the full possession of all that is promised to believers. It will be undiminished, undefiled, unfading fullness of joy forever.

When we are in heaven with the Lord, we will be rejoicing and thanking God forever that when we were on earth He put us where we ought to have been and that He kept us there when things got rough.

We'll be glad that we believed Jesus when He told us:

Do not lay up for yourselves treasures upon earth, where moth and rust destroy, and where thieves break in and steal. But lay up for yourselves treasures in heaven, where neither moth nor rust destroys, and where thieves do not break in or steal; for where your treasure is, there will your heart be also, Matthew 6:19ff.

We are joint heirs with Jesus. Whatever He gets, we get. If there were a possibility that we could lose that, the

Christian's life would be lived in paralyzing fear. God doesn't want that, so His plan of salvation makes us eternally security:

The Nature of Our Security, 5

[5] who are protected by the power of God through faith for a salvation ready to be revealed in the last time.

Like our inheritance, the nature of our security derives in part from the nature of our salvation (which itself derives from the nature of God). Those who think a Christian can lose his salvation don't understand the nature of our salvation or how we got it. If we somehow took part in earning our salvation, then perhaps we could lose it. Every doctrinal system that teaches salvation by works, to be consistent, must also include the possibility of losing salvation. So if you're looking for a firm place to stand in an uncertain world, a salvation based upon works is not it.

But if salvation is purely the gift of God, based upon His divine nature and His sovereign decree in eternity past, and accomplished by His work in our lives, then it cannot be lost. God is omniscient and knew everything about our entire lives before He chose us. He will never say, "Well, if I had known you were going to be this much trouble, I never would have called you." Those who say we can lose our salvation slander God's omniscience, His omnipotence, His faithfulness, and His love.

Moses understood that the completion of our salvation depends upon God's all-sufficient power. In Numbers 14, the Israelites wanted to return to Egypt instead of attacking the Canaanites. So God offered to destroy the Israelites and make a better nation from Moses' descendants. Moses responded to his duty as mediator by seeing God's words as an invitation to intercede for his people. His intercession was based on God's reputation:

Then the Egyptians will hear of it, for by Thy strength Thou didst bring up this people from their midst, and they will tell it to the inhabitants of this land. They have heard that

Thou, O LORD, art in the midst of this people ... Now if Thou dost slay this people as one man, then the nations who have heard of Thy fame will say, "Because the LORD could not bring this people into the land which He promised them by oath, therefore He slaughtered them in the wilderness." But now, I pray, let the power of the Lord be great, just as Thou hast declared, Numbers 14:13-17.

Telling of this in Deuteronomy 9:28, Moses added that God's love would be called into question.

Our security depends upon God's ability to accomplish what He promises. **Faithful is He who calls you; He will also bring it to pass,** I Thessalonians 5:24. Jesus gave us a promise in John 10:27-30:

My sheep hear My voice, and I know them, and they follow Me; and I give eternal life to them, and they shall never perish; and no one shall snatch them out of My hand. My Father, who has given them to Me, is greater than all; and no one is able to snatch them out of the Father's hand. I and the Father are one.

And so Peter says, we **are protected by the power of God**. This doesn't mean that persecution can't touch us. It means that it can't ruin us. God has several, very good reasons for allowing our persecution including our sanctification, the credibility and power of our witness, our joy (which is a soldier's joy), and the glory that goes to God when His people value Him so much that they will endure for His sake.

Being **protected by the power of God** means that we are shielded whenever we have to endure those persecutions, so that we can always overcome them in victory, even if that involves our untimely death, or as I like to call it, our early retirement.

But doesn't our faith have anything to do with persevering? Yes, it certainly does. It is the means by which God protects us. The preposition **through** is the Greek preposition *dia.* When used with a noun in the accusative case *dia* means because of, on account of. But when *dia* is used with the genitive case, as it is here, it means *through* or *by,* speaking of the agency or instrument that God uses to preserve us.

So Peter is not saying that our faith is the reason for our protection, as in "God will protect us if we keep the faith." He is saying that faith is the means that God uses to preserve us. The faith that comes from God is a durable faith. Ephesians 6 refers to "the shield of faith." The saving faith that God gives is a forever faith. It is more than a glue that God might have used to bind us permanently to Himself. We are actually *in* Christ, not just attached to Him, and are sealed in Him by the Holy Spirit (Ephesians 1).

This eternally-saving faith is the very hand of God wrapped around us in an omnipotent, unfailing grip of love. Years ago, whenever my little sons were with me in a dangerous area, like near the edge of a cliff or at a street corner, I held their hands. Their safety didn't depend on the strength of their grip on me. It was my grip on them that kept them safe. **No one is able to snatch us out of the Father's hand,** John 10:29.

So Peter's statement does not even allow that the faith that God gives us *might* be lost. That would be no protection at all. That would be like saying, "You are protected for as long as you protect yourself." That would be like a warranty that says, "This product is unconditionally guaranteed until it breaks." That would mean that whenever our faith is attacked, our protection vanishes. We aren't preserved by our faith. We **are protected by the power of God**. God's "grip" on us is the faith that He gives us. We **are protected by the power of God through faith.**

There are three ways people customarily refer to the protection Peter speaks of. Revelation 14:12 refers to 'the perseverance of the saints' – that's how it looks on the human side. True saints persevere. Peter and Jude refer to 'the preservation of the saints' – that's the divine action that actually does the protecting and causes the saints to persevere. 'Eternal security' is the bottom-line result. I like them all. But the one Peter selects is the heart of the issue – we **are preserved by the power of God.**

God protects us for **a salvation ready to be revealed in the last time**. Jesus told His disciples, **"I go to prepare a place for you,"** John 14:2. This is another way of referring to the
38

inheritance that is reserved in heaven for us. We know that what we are experiencing now on earth is not all there is to being saved.

We are still plagued by sin – our own and everyone else's. We are still liable to persecutions, grief, losses, failures, disappointments, weakness, sickness, temporal death, etc. The limitations of our earthly bodies still hold us down. Sin and it's effects are no part of our eternal state in heaven. In God's perfect wisdom, the temporary suffering comes first, then the eternal glory. Proverbs 15:33 tells us, **The fear of the LORD is the instruction for wisdom, And before honor *comes* humility.**

The nature of our salvation determines the nature of our inheritance and the nature of our security. Because our salvation is entirely the work of God, it is not a mistake, it is not probationary, and is not subject to being revoked. **It does not depend upon the man who wills or the man who runs, but on God who has mercy,** Romans 9:16. Since it doesn't depend on man, man can't mess it up. Of all those whom the Father gives to the Son, He loses none, John 6:39.

And since our salvation is certain, so is our inheritance – the completion phase of that salvation. Because God saved us, God preserves us. He doesn't waste His efforts by saving some people and then letting them slip away. "Oops" is not in God's vocabulary. **Faithful is He who calls you, He will also bring it to pass,** I Thessalonians 5:24.

Does this not give us good reason to celebrate with praises the lovingkindness and power of God? Let us lose no opportunity to speak well of the God and Father of our Lord Jesus Christ.

Chapter 3

1:6-9, The Proof of Your Faith

⁶ In this you greatly rejoice, even though now for a little while, if necessary, you have been distressed by various trials,
⁷ that the proof of your faith, *being* more precious than gold which is perishable, even though tested by fire, may be found to result in praise and glory and honor at the revelation of Jesus Christ;
⁸ and though you have not seen Him, you love Him, and though you do not see Him now, but believe in Him, you greatly rejoice with joy inexpressible and full of glory,
⁹ obtaining as the outcome of your faith the salvation of your souls.

I Peter has two connected themes: rejoicing in our eternal salvation, and successfully enduring our temporary trials. These are intertwined throughout the epistle; Peter's point being that since it has a heavenly basis, our rejoicing far outweighs earthly persecution. Rejoicing in the midst of trials is a win-win-win situation:

1. God is glorified,

2. Believers are sanctified,

3. Unbelievers are mystified, which induces some of them to re-examine their disbelief and consider the claims of Christ (2:12).

The question before us is this: Will our great joy be broken when we encounter various trials? If joy happens for us only when things are going our way, how is that any different, or any better, than the world's joy? Well, okay, it's still a lot better, but not as much as God means it to be.

Unassailable joy comes from the assurance that we have an imperishable inheritance protected by the power of God through an unbreakable faith. Unbreakable joy, then, comes through unbreakable faith.

For this reason God proves our faith – He proves it to us, and He proves it to the world. By getting us through our persecutions victoriously, God proves two things. He proves that our faith is the genuine saving faith that comes from Him. And He proves the value of that faith to the world.

So Peter says that Christians should rejoice in…

The Source of Our Faith, 6a,

The Proof of Our Faith, 6b-7a, and in

The Results of Our Faith, 7b-9.

Rejoicing in the Source of Our Faith, 6a

6a In this you greatly rejoice,

"**In this**" refers directly to verses 3-5. But then verses 3-5 refer to verses 1 and 2. So "**in this**" refers to everything Peter has said so far. We are chosen by the Father before the foundation of the world, sanctified (made holy) by the Holy Spirit, and by the sprinkling of the blood of Jesus, commissioned to a life of obedient service as God's own people.

Salvation is a big deal. Having it as opposed to needing it is a big deal. It is far bigger than persecution's worst-case scenario. The consummation of our salvation, when we receive everything God has promised, is a big deal. When we're heading for that, it doesn't matter what we have to march through to get there. It is the pearl of great price.

We don't find that great, continual rejoicing in those churches that are trying to fit in with their worldly, materialistic society. Nor do we see the resolve to obey God rather than men. Perhaps they don't understand the greatness of the inheritance. Perhaps the worries of the world and the deceitfulness of riches are choking out the word. Or perhaps the threat of persecutions, light as they are, so far in America, causes them to fall away. One of God's purposes for persecution is to clear up the confusion concerning who speaks for God and who doesn't.

"**In this**" refers to the living hope of our full inheritance, given by our heavenly Father, through the resurrection of the Son, preserved by the power of God, and ready to be revealed. I Corinthians 1:30 says, **by His doing you are in Christ Jesus**. If it's by God's doing, then it won't be ruined by the true believer's failures. Living in this hope makes a big difference in how we face adversity, either as certain winners or as possible losers.

Our inheritance is huge, if you don't mind an understatement. It is worth more than the whole world. In Mark 8:36f Jesus asked a question that no one should ignore, **"what does it profit a man to gain the whole world, and forfeit his soul? For what shall a man give in exchange for his soul?"**

If our salvation rested upon our own works, trials would be a cause of great anxiety. We would run like scared rabbits from anything that might threaten our faith, lest we succumb to the pressure and lose our salvation. So we would be living like losers at the bottom of the food chain. And anything we read in the Bible suggesting that we are free would seem like a mockery. We would be slaves to fear, not servants of God. Being the appointed servants of the most-high God produces courage.

If our salvation were in constant jeopardy, our focus would be on ourselves, and not on glorifying God or advancing His purposes. Fear is a very self-centered emotion that causes us to shrink back and retreat. We would live our Christian life like an athletic team cautiously playing so as not to lose, rather than playing to win (a strategy that often results in losing). But I Corinthians 9:24 tells us that we should, **Run in such a way that you may win**, not, 'Run in such a way that you may not lose.' There's a big difference. Christians are called to advance, not to shrink back. The times we need to fall back into a defensive posture should be rare.

If trials posed a threat to our salvation, we certainly could not rejoice when facing trials. But since our saving faith rests upon the foreknowledge and power of God, who gave that faith to us, we greatly rejoice, knowing that nothing shall separate us from the love of God, or deprive us of that inheritance reserved in heaven for us. We would rejoice because trials are an opportunity for great gain.

God is sovereign, and He loves His children. So great rejoicing is the only reasonable and appropriate state of mind for those who belong to Him. We can easily see the state of mind of those who are in rebellion against Him. So be reasonable – grin through it all, with a grin that comes from a heart set free from sin, the grin of an overcomer (which is what God calls us in the book of Revelation).

Jesus said, **'He who believes in Me, as the Scripture said, "From his innermost being shall flow rivers of living water."' But this He spoke of the Spirit,** John 7:38. Given what we have to rejoice about, it should take a lot to overshadow our joy. It should take more than the world has. But whatever we allow to obscure our joy; that, in our own minds, is greater than God, the source of that joy. It is your duty to see things as they really are; to see the big picture, as God sees it. If you do, the witness of your great rejoicing will be a powerful witness. It says to the world that the real God is much bigger than any suffering. Many people are unwilling to come to Christ for salvation because they are afraid of what the world will do to them.

Rejoicing in the Proof of Our Faith, 6b-7a

6b even though now for a little while, if necessary, you have been distressed by various trials, 7a that the proof of your faith, *being* more precious than gold which is perishable,

Peter says several things about trials that those who face them ought to know. They happen in this life and for a little while only. They are not permanent. They are momentary, light afflictions, compared to the eternal weight of glory (II Corinthians 4:17). (Paul also spoke from long experience – this isn't just theory.)

Trials are sometimes necessary. They are necessary because of our situation. We are aliens to those who don't know Jesus (verse 1). And some of them want to remove all reminders of a righteous Creator who will judge them. The thought of being judged for their sins takes the fun out of sinning. So they sometimes swat at us. Trials are an expected part of the war we are fighting. Paul encouraged Timothy, **Suffer hardship with me, as a good soldier of Christ Jesus**, II Timothy 2:3. A part of knowing God's will for our lives is that we don't insist upon a path that avoids the chance of suffering.

Trials are necessary because they make us more like Christ. This process is called sanctification (the progressive kind). We need to be sanctified. Suffering of all kinds, including persecution by God-haters, is part of our refining process. It makes us more useful to God, more confident in His ability. The first time I ever flew in an airplane, I was the one flying the plane. It was an introductory flight lesson. When I took off from the airport and banked to the left, I got the uneasy feeling that I might bank the airplane too far and upset it, like a tractor or a load of hay (my frame of reference at the time). A few years later, I had the opportunity to do some stunt flying with a pilot friend. He rolled the plane all the way around, looped it, snap-rolled it, spun it, and by the time we were done, I had no fear that an airplane might upset.

The experience of trials gives us more confidence in God. They strengthen our faith because we get to know Him better, and we get to know reality better. We fear a lot of things that aren't real.

Trials are necessary because the world needs proof that our faith is real and efficacious. Objectively, the content of our faith is real. Therefore it works. Subjectively, the trust that genuine Christians put in God's truth is also real. It forms a real bond between us and God and takes us ever closer to Him. Fair weather obedience doesn't impress anyone, but durable obedience proves the genuineness of our faith. It gives non-believers reason to trust what this Christian says. They can see the difference between suffering Christians and part-time Christians. The former are real; the latter are fake.

Trials are distressing and can be painful. Peter makes no attempt to hide that fact. He, like Paul, speaks from experience. When Paul and Silas were thrown in jail in Philippi for preaching the gospel, they sang praises to God. When God threw the prison doors open and unfastened everyone's chains, the rest of the prisoners didn't fly like birds. They hung around to see what Paul's God would do. The jailer and his family believed in Christ and were saved. I wonder if any of the other prisoners were also saved. Peter, too, had been imprisoned, beaten, sentenced to death.

Distress does not contradict faith, unless our faith includes the false belief that Christians will never be persecuted. True faith is known by the obedience it produces, and we can obey even under duress. Faith doesn't keep pain from hurting, or insults from stinging, or takeaways from feeling unfair. But God always gives us what we need at the time we need it. His grace is always sufficient for the moment. And God never made a bad deal for His children. Whatever we temporarily lose, we get back much more forever. Jesus said,

"Truly I say to you, there is no one who has left house or brothers or sisters or mother or father or children or farms, for My sake and for the gospel's sake, [30] but that he shall receive a hundred times as much now in the present age, houses and brothers and sisters and mothers and children and farms, along with persecutions; and in the age to come, eternal life," Mk. 10:29f.

These trials come in **various** forms. The term for **various** is *poikilois,* which means multi-colored. Some trials are a light yellow kind of trial; some are red; some are dark gray. Our Father puts His different children through different types of trials. The kind and severity of the trial depends upon what He wants to accomplish with that child's witness. It depends upon what His child needs in the way of sanctification. And it depends upon how mature and durable that child is. But He always provides a grace that exactly matches the trial.

I Peter 4:10 speaks of **the manifold grace of God**. The term *manifold* is that same word *poikilois,* multi-colored. If our trial is a green kind of trial, then God gives us a green kind of grace. If it is red, so is the grace. If it is a very dark blue, so is the grace. As the trial, so is the grace. The grace is always matched to the trial, color for color, and the grace is always sufficient (II Cor. 12:9). So we all experience different kinds of trials and different kinds of grace from God. Every trial God allows is to accomplish His good purposes. We all have our own custom regimen of trials. Call them unique opportunities. Those who experience greater trials also get to experience greater grace.

The result of these trials is **the proof of our faith**. Peter compares our faith to a substance of lesser value, gold. Both faith and gold are refined by fire. And once they are refined, it is fire again that tests, or assays, the purity of both, a practice Paul alluded to in I Corinthians 3:11ff:

For no man can lay a foundation other than the one which is laid, which is Jesus Christ. Now if any man builds upon the foundation with gold, silver, precious stones, wood, hay, straw, each man's work will become evident; for the day will show it, because it is to be revealed with fire; and the fire itself will test the quality of each man's work.

The term *proof* in I Peter 1:7, is the same as the word *test* in I Corinthians 3:12. It is a metallurgical term that means tested and approved.

Testing by fire seems kind of severe, but the need determines the means. Christians have put their faith in Jesus Christ, for the most part. We are partly refined and look like gold, but still have pockets of impurities trapped in various places in our lives, which sometimes cause us to put our faith in our own ways. If we find ourselves looking for loopholes in the Bible, we can tell that we still have those impurities trapped inside.

Those impurities in our faith are hard to get rid of, like the inclusions bonded within the partly refined gold. In the refining process the gold with its remaining inclusions is heated in the fire. This process burns those impurities to ash and moves them to the surface so they can be skimmed off, leaving gold that is more pure and valuable. Then, just as the gold is feeling pretty good about itself, the refiner drops some flux into the crucible with the molten gold (cf. Isa. 1:25). This causes a violent flair-up of smoke and fire and releases the last stubborn bits of slag to float to the surface where they can be skimmed off. The purer we are, the more Christ shines in us and the more valuable we are in His service.

Goldsmiths put a proof-mark on the item they've made, certifying it as, say, 99% fine. Anytime God wants to prove the quality of our faith, He might use the fire assay method to demonstrate the purity of our faith. So our response to trials are the proof-mark of the genuineness and purity of our faith. In Galatians 6:17 Paul says as much, **I bear on my body the brand-marks of Jesus.** These proofs are important to the salvation of people who are called but not yet saved, because they need to know that the faith God gives is real and really works.

Paul spoke of this in Colossians 1:24, **Now I rejoice in my sufferings for your sake, and in my flesh I do my share on behalf of His body (which is the church) in filling up that which is lacking in Christ's afflictions.** We suffer, not as a substitutionary atonement (only the spotless Lamb of God could do that), but as a demonstration of the power of saving faith. What's **lacking in Christ's afflictions** (meaning the afflictions God's enemies lay on believers) is the proof to present-day sinners that faith in the completed work of Jesus Christ really does save. God uses our suffering to help bring other people to salvation. Are you willing for God to use you that way? Our forefathers in the faith were.

You can't buy salvation, not for yourself or for anyone else, no matter how much gold you have. So the saving faith that God gives is **more precious than gold which is perishable.** It is precious, in part, because of its basis (see verses 18-19).

In these uncertain times, people are buying up gold as fast as they can. But in uncertain times, like any other times, it is saving faith that has the permanent and supreme value. How sad, then, that so many are neglecting their eternity to go after that which perishes. **What shall it profit a man to gain the whole *world* and sacrifice his soul?** But like Esau, they are trading away a precious inheritance to get a bowl of bean soup.

Rejoicing in the Results of Our Faith, 7b-9

7 that the proof of your faith, *being* more precious than gold which is perishable, even though tested by fire, may be found to result in praise and glory and honor at the revelation of Jesus Christ;
8 and though you have not seen Him, you love Him, and though you do not see Him now, but believe in Him, you greatly rejoice with joy inexpressible and full of glory,
9 obtaining as the outcome of your faith the salvation of your souls.

The proof of our faith produces present results, here and now, and also future results, at the second coming of Christ. Peter arranges the results in a 'then, now, now, then' order:

<u>Then</u>, because we keep the faith, even through persecutions and trials, we will receive praise, glory, and honor when Jesus returns for us.

<u>Now</u>, we experience a deeper love relationship with our Savior, who suffered for us, because we suffer for Him.

<u>Now</u>, also, we rejoice with joy inexpressible and full of glory.

<u>Then</u>, we will obtain the end of our faith: complete perfection and fulfillment of all the promises of salvation.

Let's look at these one at a time. We will receive praise, glory, and honor when Jesus returns. At the end of the Bible, Jesus said, **Behold, I am coming quickly, and My reward is with Me,** Revelation 22:12.

In Matthew 25, Jesus told the parable of the talents. A master gave three servants money to invest while he went on a trip. The two faithful slaves took risks in order to produce a good return for their master's investment, trusting his assessment of their abilities. And no doubt they were very excited and gratified, when their master returned, to present him with the principle plus the gain their faithful efforts had earned. And for this, their master praised and rewarded them. But the fearful slave who avoided risk, suffered rebuke and loss because he produced no return on his master's investment. He had less ability than the other two, but he had enough ability to make use of the one talent, had he chosen to try. Only the faithful slaves entered into the joy of their master. (A talent, if our resources are correct, was 75 pounds of gold or silver.)

God ordained that salvation would depend upon His work, not ours, freeing us from that worry so we are in a position to take the risks associated with serving Him. We can run to win (as the faithful slaves did), not just to avoid losing (as the wicked slave did). What kind of a return are you producing on your Master's investment? (It's good to evaluate your portfolio from time to time.)

These rewards for faithfulness will be ours forever in the millennial kingdom and in the perfect, eternal state that follows. Our faithfulness on earth will be rewarded by our eternal stature in Heaven. That's why Paul says that our momentary, light afflictions are producing for us an eternal weight of glory. Apparently, then, we will have a station in heaven, just as we have a station in life.

Our station in life, whether rich or poor, influential or obscure, carefree or troubled, lasts only for a few years. But our station in heaven lasts forever. That station in heaven is not determined by our station in this life, but by how faithful we are in this life to obey the Lord. The guy who is poor and humble but a faithful steward on earth may be your boss in heaven.

And though you have not seen Him, you love him. There is nothing like suffering with someone in a common cause to build a love relationship. Soldiers from WW II are still holding reunions because of the bond they developed over 70 years ago. When we suffer for Christ and for His cause, we learn some things about His suffering for us. That deepens our love for Him, even though we've never seen Him. Christians who have been through trials on behalf of Jesus share a history and a love with Jesus that the non-risk-takers don't know. If you really want to know Jesus, you have to follow Him into the battles.

King David said, **I will not offer burnt offerings to the LORD my God which cost me nothing,** II Samuel 24:24.

And though you do not see Him now, but believe in Him, you greatly rejoice with joy inexpressible and full of glory. Jesus said to Thomas, **Because you have seen Me, have you believed? Blessed are they who did not see, and yet believed,** John 20:29. Why is it more blessed to believe in Jesus when we *haven't* seen Him than it would be to believe in Him because we *had* seen Him? Answer: Because it is God who decides how much to bless, and He rewards faith. He wants us to walk by faith, not by sight.

Eve walked by sight when tempted by Satan. So she believed the father of lies, rather than the God of truth. In God's economy, the greater the faith, the greater the reward. Consider also Gehazi's view by sight compared to Elisha's view by faith in II Kings 6:14-17.

We who have not seen Jesus must depend upon the word of God to learn about Him. It pleases God when we trust what He tells us about anything, but most especially what He tells us about His Son. The world fell into sin because Adam and Eve did not believe what God told them.

This faith that needs no sight produces a joy that exceeds what the mouth can express. It is full of the rich glory of God. In fact it glorifies God. It says to the whole world, "you can trust whatever God says." If you want a really joyful life, don't doubt God. Don't doubt anything He says in the Bible.

Obtaining as the outcome of your faith the salvation of your souls, verse 9. At first glance this verse might seem to be saying that our salvation is the outcome of our faith. And no doubt many use it as a proof text to say that a Christian can lose his salvation, missing everything Peter has said so far about how we get our salvation. But the word **outcome** is *telos*, a word which means the end, the termination or limit of an act or state; here referring to our faith.

Romans 8:24 says, **in hope we have been saved, but hope that is seen is not hope; for why does one also hope for what he sees?** When we actually see all that has been promised, when we actually have all that was reserved in heaven for us, then faith ends and sight begins. So this verse speaks of the terminus of our faith, which is the time when our faith is made sight; when we see Jesus as He is and are made like Him. So it's the future aspect of salvation in view here: the completion of our salvation, which is our perfection and glorification.

Obtaining is the present ongoing aspect of salvation, the process of sanctification. That process, which involves these trials, has an end point, which is spoken of in I John 3:2, **We know that, when He appears, we shall be like Him, because we shall see Him just as He is.** Seeing Jesus face to face will complete our sanctification and commence our glorification.

The sanctification process, with its various trials, is the realm where our own, subjective faith plays its largest role. (By subjective faith I don't mean the content of our faith, which must be objective, if our subjective faith is to have any value. Subjective faith is the credence we put in that objective body of truth.) We believe God; so we trust and obey Him, not shrinking back from persecutions. Doing that makes us more and more like Jesus.

The saving faith that God gives us doesn't just sit there passively. Faith is an enervating life force, spiritually speaking. It energizes us to action. The Spirit breathes His life into us, and we live for God.

Verse 9, then, refers to the same time frame as verse 5. It speaks of the salvation ready to be revealed in the last time. Christians are often accused of being too "pie in the sky" in their focus. This is a bogus criticism that often comes from people who care only about enjoying this life. I hope we are focused on the future, because there is such a pie in the sky, a pie we can't even begin to imagine. If we know about our inheritance, we can face anything on earth with unbroken rejoicing.

So the source, the proof, and the results of our salvation cause us to rejoice with joy inexpressible and full of glory, even if we have to endure various trials occasionally. The living hope of a glorious inheritance laid up for us furnishes us with motivation that is adequate for any challenge. Subjectively, our confidence comes from knowing that our faith is the real faith that God gives, and not some assumption of our own. So God proves to us, and to the rest of the world, that our faith is the real thing by exposing it to fiery trials. Those whose faith rests on assumptions or self-delusions (now called "personal truth") won't pass the test. Those who pass the test come through it with a greater love for Jesus, a greater confidence in serving Him, and a higher station in the eternal life to come.

Chapter 4
1:10-12, The Predicted Plan Fulfilled

**¹⁰ As to this salvation, the prophets who prophesied of the grace that *would come* to you made careful search and inquiry,
¹¹ seeking to know what person or time the Spirit of Christ within them was indicating as He predicted the sufferings of Christ and the glories to follow.
¹² It was revealed to them that they were not serving themselves, but you, in these things which now have been announced to you through those who preached the gospel to you by the Holy Spirit sent from heaven-- things into which angels long to look.**

Knowing that his readers are facing persecution for the cause of Christ, Peter has one over-riding concern for them. They must be certain of their ultimate salvation. Paul referred to **the helmet of salvation,** Ephesians 6:17, because the certainty of salvation is what protects our head. It's what keeps our thinking right. If salvation isn't a certain thing, then this life is all a person can be sure of. People can see the problems with risking all they have in this life in exchange for an uncertain afterlife.

Any uncertainty concerning our salvation will make it difficult to be courageous. So Peter has reminded them of the security of their inheritance (verses 3-5) and the proof of their faith (verses 6-9). Now, he writes that the gospel in which they trust was predicted by the Spirit of Christ (the Holy Spirit) to the prophets of old. Thus Peter assures his readers that the gospel is not a novelty. Nor is it a departure from God's plan. It has been God's plan from the beginning.

So he writes that the pre-ordained plan of salvation was predicted by the prophets and preached to us. It was revealed by the Holy Spirit through both the prophets and the preachers. This is Peter's outline for our text:

Proper Timing, 10-11a

Predicting a Mystery, 10-11

Preaching a Marvel, 12

Proper Timing, 10-11a

¹⁰ As to this salvation, the prophets who prophesied of the grace that *would come* to you made careful search and inquiry,
^{11a} seeking to know what… time

The world had been in existence for about 4,000 years when Peter's audience received this epistle. (They would have known that from the genealogies in Genesis 5 and 11.) Now, after all that time and in the midst of all kinds of religions based on works and merit, this gospel comes along presenting a means of salvation that is fundamentally different from any other in the world.

It's a latecomer to the religious scene, why should anyone believe it? And why didn't it come until now? If it's new, it can't be true. These are the challenges Christianity's detractors might have used against the believers, trying to get them to recant.

God's timing has always been something of a mystery and a concern to mankind, especially with regard to His prophetic promises. This confusion about timing began with Adam and Eve. In Genesis 3:15 God predicted a Savior. Eve thought this prediction was fulfilled in her first-born son. At Cain's birth she said, "I have gotten a man, the Lord." She was very bright – she understood that the Savior would be the Lord, but she made an incorrect assumption about the timing.

Peter is focused on timing issues in this first chapter. I count 16 direct or indirect references to time in 25 verses. In Matthew 24:3, the Olivet Discourse was our Lord's answer to the disciples' question, **"Tell us, when will these things be, and what will be the sign of Your coming, and of the end of**

54

the age?" Just before Jesus ascended back into heaven, they asked Him:

"Lord, is it at this time You are restoring the kingdom to Israel?" He said to them, "It is not for you to know times or epochs which the Father has fixed by His own authority; but you shall receive power when the Holy Spirit has come upon you; and you shall be My witnesses," Acts 1:6-8.

In God's wisdom He does not tell us when Jesus will return or when Israel's fortunes will be restored. Instead, He gives His soldiers their marching orders. And He tells us:

"Take heed, keep on the alert; for you do not know when the appointed time is. Therefore, be on the alert-- for you do not know when the master of the house is coming, whether in the evening, at midnight, at cockcrowing, or in the morning-- lest he come suddenly and find you asleep. And what I say to you I say to all, 'Be on the alert,'" Mk. 13:33ff.

David asks, **How long, O LORD? Wilt Thou forget me forever? How long wilt Thou hide Thy face from me? How long shall I take counsel in my soul, having sorrow in my heart all the day? How long will my enemy be exalted over me?** Ps. 13:1f.

In Psalm 90:13, Moses prayed, **Do return, O LORD; how long will it be? And be sorry for Thy servants.** Psalm 94:3 asks, **How long shall the wicked, O LORD, how long shall the wicked exult?**

In Revelation 6, even **the souls of those who had been slain because of the word of God** [during the Tribulation], **and because of the testimony which they had maintained; cried out with a loud voice, saying, "How long, O Lord, holy and true, wilt Thou refrain from judging and avenging our blood on those who dwell on the earth?"**

"How long?" is the concern of all those who suffer for the sake of the gospel and are determined not to shrink away. Peter can certainly anticipate that his readers will have the same question. How long until we receive our inheritance? How long will God's enemies have things their way on earth? How long will the suffering last before we get our glorification?

Peter doesn't know how long. No one on earth is given that information. That schedule stays in heaven. Even when the Son of Man was on earth, in His humanity He somehow was denied that information. That timing issue was a problem for the prophets, as Peter relates in verses 10f.

Predicting a Mystery, 10-11

¹⁰ As to this salvation, the prophets who prophesied of the grace that *would come* to you made careful search and inquiry,
¹¹ seeking to know what person or time the Spirit of Christ within them was indicating as He predicted the sufferings of Christ and the glories to follow.

Peter doesn't actually use the term *mystery*, as Paul does, but he describes it. A mystery is a future event or era (such as the church age) that is not revealed in the Old Testament. It can't be known by any means other than divine revelation.

This salvation follows from verse 9 and refers, as verse 9 does, to the final aspect of salvation: the consummation, the glorification of Christ and His saints, when we, as joint heirs with Christ, receive all that was promised, when the hard times are over for good.

The Old Testament prophets received extensive revelation about the completion of salvation and the glories ahead, but not much about the *timing* of it. That was a mystery.

They all knew, for example, that salvation would be by grace, not by works. That's what the Law-giver Moses taught, according to Romans 10:4-8:

For Christ is the end [goal] of the law for righteousness to everyone who believes. For Moses writes that the man who practices the righteousness which is based on law shall live by that righteousness. But the righteousness based on faith

56

speaks thus, "DO NOT SAY IN YOUR HEART, 'WHO WILL ASCEND INTO HEAVEN?' (that is, to bring Christ down), or 'WHO WILL DESCEND INTO THE ABYSS?' (that is, to bring Christ up from the dead)." But what does it say? "THE WORD IS NEAR YOU, IN YOUR MOUTH AND IN YOUR HEART"-- that is, the word of faith which we are preaching.

In this Romans passage Paul forms a deductive argument to prove beyond rebuttal, that Moses taught salvation by grace through faith, not works, because he is quoting Moses. So the gospel of grace is not a latecomer after all.

They knew that the Messiah would have to suffer before He would be glorified. Check out Isaiah 53, Psalm 22, and Zechariah 13. They knew from Zechariah 12:10 that the Messiah would suffer and be rejected:

And I will pour out on the house of David and on the inhabitants of Jerusalem, the Spirit of grace and of supplication, so that they will look on Me whom they have pierced; and they will mourn for Him, as one mourns for an only son, and they will weep bitterly over Him, like the bitter weeping over a first-born.

They knew He would be a conquering King. Psalm 2, for example, says:

But as for Me, I have installed My King upon Zion, My holy mountain. I will surely tell of the decree of the LORD: He said to Me, 'Thou art My Son, today I have begotten Thee. Ask of Me, and I will surely give the nations as Thine inheritance, and the very ends of the earth as Thy possession. Thou shalt break them with a rod of iron, Thou shalt shatter them like earthenware.'

So they knew about both the suffering and the glory of the Messiah. But they had trouble reconciling the two descriptions. God didn't specify the timing of end time events partly because He was allowing for the Israelites to meet the Messiah's condition of repentance, in which case the kingdom would be set up almost immediately. (Jesus began His ministry saying, "Repent, for the kingdom of God is at hand.") They wouldn't repent, and God knew they wouldn't, but His offer was genuine all the same. So in prophetic revelation, God left room for it by leaving the date line blank. Keep in mind, however, that God is omniscient and has always known the precise time of the second coming.

From Daniel 9, they even knew when the Messiah should come and that He would be cut off and have nothing for some (unspecified) period of time. But they didn't know exactly when these things would take place, especially the glory at the end of the age. God withheld that information:

[1] "Now at that time Michael, the great prince who stands *guard* over the sons of your people, will arise. And there will be a time of distress such as never occurred since there was a nation until that time; and at that time your people, everyone who is found written in the book, will be rescued. [2] "And many of those who sleep in the dust of the ground will awake, these to everlasting life, but the others to disgrace *and* everlasting contempt. [3] "And those who have insight will shine brightly like the brightness of the expanse of heaven, and those who lead the many to righteousness, like the stars forever and ever. [4] "But as for you, Daniel, conceal these words and seal up the book until the end of time; many will go back and forth, and knowledge will increase." [5] Then I, Daniel, looked and behold, two others were standing, one on this bank of the river, and the other on that bank of the river. [6] And one said to the man dressed in linen, who was above the waters of the river, " How long *will it be* until the end of *these* wonders?" [7] And I heard the man dressed in linen, who was above the waters of the river, as he raised his right hand and his left toward heaven, and swore by Him who lives forever that it would be for a time, times, and half *a time;* and as soon as they finish shattering the power of the holy people, all these *events* will be completed. [8] As for me, I heard but could not understand; so I said, "My lord, what *will be* the outcome of these *events?"* [9] And he said, "Go *your way,* Daniel, for *these* words are concealed and sealed up until the end time, Daniel 12:1-9.

Some end-time prophecies are like that to us – they are mostly for the believers who are alive during those hard times and who will be able to connect the prophecies with the people and times as they see the predicted events unfold. Therefore, they will know that God is in control of the events and be encouraged. That will be one way that God gives particular grace to meet the particular need.

The prophets knew that salvation would be extended to the Gentiles, though they never saw it happen on any large scale. See Isaiah 45:22; 49:6; 52:10. They themselves received this gracious salvation, but they knew less about it than we do, because Jesus had not yet lived and died and been raised from the dead. We understand from history and the New Testament that Jesus came the first time as suffering servant, ascended back to heaven, and will return a second time as conquering king. And we know why those two advents are widely separated to include the church age, about which the prophets had no substantial information. Only some of salvation's events are still future to us; most of it was future to them.

All the prophets spoke of and had a deep interest in God's gracious salvation. In Matthew 13:17, Jesus said, **For truly I say to you, that many prophets and righteous men desired to see what you see, and did not see it; and to hear what you hear, and did not hear it.** So the prophets made a careful and extensive study of it in their own writings.

We get some insight here into how prophecy was received. The Holy Spirit's role on earth has always been to make Christ known. The prophets got their revelations from the Spirit of Christ who was working within them. But they didn't always understand what they wrote about. So they got out their exegetical shovels and delved into their own writings to try to figure out **who or what sort of time the Spirit was indicating**.

By the way, modern students of end time prophecy have the same questions. We want to know the identities of the 10 horns (nations), the Antichrist, the false prophet and other key people, and exactly when these things will take place. Some information would be a stumbling block to Christians or to unbelievers, so God withholds it.

Peter tells us more about the prophetic process in II Peter 1:16-21:

16 For we did not follow cleverly devised tales when we made known to you the power and coming of our Lord Jesus Christ, but we were eyewitnesses of His majesty.
17 For when He received honor and glory from God the Father, such an utterance as this was made to Him by the Majestic Glory, "This is My beloved Son with whom I am well-pleased"-- 18 and we ourselves heard this utterance made from heaven when we were with Him on the holy mountain.
19 And *so* we have the prophetic word *made* more sure, to which you do well to pay attention as to a lamp shining in a dark place, until the day dawns and the morning star arises in your hearts.
20 But know this first of all, that no prophecy of Scripture is *a matter* of one's own interpretation,
21 for no prophecy was ever made by an act of human will, but men moved by the Holy Spirit spoke from God.

Here Peter does what he did in his first epistle; he bases what he knows on what the prophets have said. Even though he was an eye witness on the Mount of Transfiguration, he has a higher regard for the "more sure prophetic word." The italicized words *so* and *made* in verse 19 are not in the original. They were supplied by the translators. The verse actually reads, **And we have the prophetic word, more sure, ...** We, like Peter, should put more confidence in God's word than we do in what we see. (Politicians and other illusionists make a living by confusing people's perception.) Peter believed God's word above all. Consequently, in his first sermon in Acts 2, even though he was an eye-witness, he drew his support from the prophets repeatedly, quoting from Joel, David, Samuel, and I Kings.

No prophecy was ever made because some guy had nothing in particular to do one day and decided it might be a nice to write some prophecy. Prophecy was never an act of human will or human creativity. And neither was it a record of some man's interpretation of social, historical, or theological issues. Prophecy is not exalted human insight.

The prophets were moved, literally *borne along*, by the Holy Spirit, as a cork might be borne along in a stream. The Spirit took them where He wanted them to go. And they didn't understand everything they wrote about. But they knew they were the instruments of divine revelation, writing God's inerrant word. So they would receive the words from the Spirit, and then sometimes they had to do intensive Bible study on what they and their colleagues had written to see if they could figure it out.

We see an example of this in Daniel 9:2:

in the first year of his reign I, Daniel, observed in the books the number of the years which was revealed as the word of the LORD to Jeremiah the prophet for the completion of the desolations of Jerusalem, namely, seventy years.

II Peter goes on to warn about false prophets. They did prophesy by an act of their own will, they did deliver their own interpretations, and they had nothing to do with the Holy Spirit. And false teachers follow in their footsteps.

People wonder why God doesn't stop these false prophets and teachers. Why doesn't He give us divine protection? We might as well ask why He doesn't give us divine protection from lions or skunks. God wants us to be diligent students of His word. If we are, we *have* our protection (Eph. 6:10-18). God's word with its truth and its warnings is our divine protection. But if we aren't students of the Bible, then we are in danger. People are more alert, wiser, more prudent, more eager to be informed, and more humble when lions are about. That's why God made lions. When there is no longer any need to teach men to fear dangers, lions will go back to eating grass.

Peter makes one more point here: Jesus Himself had to suffer first, and *then* receive the glory. This is a consistent Biblical principle. We like the 'buy now, pay later' plan, because we figure there's always a chance that we won't have to pay later. But we esteem lightly what we achieve too easily. And God has many purposes for the hard times He puts us through. The glory is greater if the going is tougher.

¹² It was revealed to them that they were not serving themselves, but you, in these things which now have been announced to you through those who preached the gospel to you by the Holy Spirit sent from heaven-- things into which angels long to look.

As any serious Bible student will do, these prophets were asking God for insight into the Scriptures as they studied. What a privilege it is to have the Author present with you as you study His word. He doesn't just hand us the answers, because answers aren't necessarily understanding. But He works to illumine us to the extent that we are diligent to study.

All Bible study should be attentive fellowship with God. That makes it exciting, productive, and life-changing. It also seems to make us more certain when we arrive at the correct interpretation. Many times I have the sense that I am on the right track but haven't yet figured a passage out totally. As I continue working to understand, researching, meditating (thinking deeply about the passage and how it all fits together), reading the passage and its context over and over again, making more observations, and praying, I eventually come to the interpretation that satisfies my theological mind. Or sometimes I just have to leave it to work on later.

The Spirit often helps us notice things in the passage that we would otherwise overlook. He points out arguments against bad interpretations and for the right interpretation, brings parallel passages to mind, gives us illustrations and applications. He really does guide us; He is the Spirit of truth.

But beware: it is not legitimate to say that God has given us the "inspired interpretation." The Spirit inspired the original authors; we have God's word on that. But we have no similar promise of inspired interpretation. Interpretation is the work of the fallible believer. How well we do that work depends upon many factors, including our skill and training, how much we already know, our spiritual gifts, our maturity in Christ, our sensitivity to the Spirit's leading, our diligence, our discernment, our experience, our honesty as we approach the

Word of God, our ability to exclude the errant philosophies of men, and our willingness to obey what we learn. Paul exhorted Timothy, **Be diligent to present yourself approved to God as a workman who does not need to be ashamed, handling accurately the word of truth**, II Timothy 2:15. Peter warns against distorting the Scriptures in II Peter 3:16.

These prophets had the Holy Spirit actually *revealing* things to *them*. And one of the things He revealed was that they were not receiving certain prophetic utterances for their own benefit, but for the benefit of those who would come later, just as we read in Daniel 12. What the inspired prophets and Apostles delivered, for other people's benefit, we should study, not just for our own benefit, but also for the benefit of others. We should learn well enough that we can teach. And then we should pass on what we learn.

The term **predicted** in verse 11 is a word that means 'pre-witnessed.' The prophets were pre-witnesses. Characteristically they witnessed future events by means of visions. (Prophets were originally called seers.) Then they revealed God's word to others. They told us what would happen before it happened. We are post-witnesses; we study and teach the word that they delivered. We should be intense students of the word because it is *God's* word. It is of supreme importance. It transforms us into the likeness of Christ. We should study the word so we can answer life's questions. The Bible has far more answers to life's questions than most believers realize. If they studied it more they would know more answers.

We are talking here about the priesthood of the believer, which Peter addresses in the next chapter. Most Christians leave Bible study and teaching to the pastors, the "pros." That is an abdication of our God-given duty and privilege as priests **to proclaim the excellencies of Him who has called us out of darkness into His marvelous light,** I Peter 2:9. That attitude goes back to the early years of the Roman Catholic Church, which came to see the Church as consisting of the clergy, with the congregation being there only to pay the bills. They didn't trust the laymen to interpret God's word the way the Church wanted, so didn't even allow them to see a Bible. They were to leave Bible study to the pros. The stained glass windows were designed to teach simple theology to the ignorant masses, sort of a comic book version of Bible stories.

Martin Luther earned his doctorate in theology before he ever saw a Bible. That attitude left the congregation very vulnerable, of course, and history records how devastating that was. They filled the revelational void with superstition, human philosophy, views taken from other religions, doctrines of their own devising, and guesswork.

We see in American Christianity a falling away from the Bible. Consequently, we see a societal decrease in literacy in general and a corruption of our language (making clear communication difficult) and of logic, not to mention widespread ignorance of the Bible and of sound theology. Soon, communicating God's word with any degree of clarity or certainty will be all but impossible. That is Satan's hope, of course, and the reason he promotes the dumbing down of America. We need to be teachers of God's word while there are still people who can understand.

But to get back to Peter's main point here, salvation is a big deal. We speak of the seven wonders of the ancient world and the wonders of the modern world. But you could put all the wonders of the world together in one pile, and they could not compare to the marvel of salvation. It was predicted by the prophets of old and now is announced to everyone in the church age.

Side note: It seems to me that once we accept Genesis 1:1, nothing else in the Bible is surprising--it all follows logically from the fact that **in the beginning God created the heavens and earth**. I don't mean that it's not magnificent, because it certainly is. But it all follows from the fact that God exists and created the universe and everything in it. Revelation is to be expected. Warnings against disobedience, the Mosaic Law, the prophets with the foreknowledge they revealed, judgment, even the resurrection of Jesus Christ all follow logically from the fact that in the beginning God created the heavens and the earth.

It all makes perfect sense, except for one thing. There is no way that the incarnation would have been expected logically.

No one could have reasoned his way to the incarnation. (Some pagan religions and myths have some corrupted form of incarnation by some sort of incredible means. But this was a distortion of what God had already revealed, perverted by Satan to confuse people about the real incarnation.)

People had reason to expect the incarnation only because of other revelations that followed Genesis 1:1 (starting with Genesis 3:16). The incarnation is a marvel--that God would become one of us, be absolutely sin free, and take on our sin and die in our place. That is such a marvel that it would be incredible if not for overwhelming evidence. Perhaps that's why God spent so much time and effort to prepare us to accept the fact.

Why did God allow Satan's false religions to teach some sort of incarnation? What Satan intends for evil, God uses for good. He used the pagan mystery religions in several ways to introduce certain theological concepts to the Gentiles who had no divine revelation to prepare them to understand the gospel. Stories of incarnations that didn't make sense prepared them to understand and accept the one that did.

This announcement was delivered through **those who preached the gospel to you by the Holy Spirit sent from heaven,** verse 12. This is a reference to Pentecost when the Holy Spirit was sent from heaven to indwell every believer. That was a big deal, too, and gave everyone to know that God was announcing His gospel, and doing so through the Apostles.

Peter says all this to make his readers more certain about this salvation in which they hope. Their faith will be challenged when trials come. Peter wants to strengthen and solidify their faith. So he tells them again, by way of reminder, that their faith rests upon the revealed word of God. This faith was **sent from heaven**. It's a sure thing.

Furthermore, **angels** have an intense interest in this salvation. Angels have no experience of salvation. The angels that rebelled with Satan had no remedy. Hebrews 2:16 says, **For assuredly He does not give help to angels, but He gives help to the descendant of Abraham.** Salvation depends upon the solidarity of the human race, the fact that we are all one blood. God decreed that fact to be the operating principle so that by the same principle, the one death of our Savior, the Son of man, can count for all of us (see Rom. 5). But angels are not a race, they were created individually, so they don't have any racial solidarity. And Jesus is not of the same essence as angels, as He is with us since His incarnation. Not being one of them, He could not die for them. Hebrews 2:17 says, **Therefore, He had to be made like His brethren in all things, that He might become a merciful and faithful high priest in things pertaining to God, to make propitiation for the sins of the people.** So the second person of the Trinity, who was and still is 100% God, became also 100% human. He didn't alter His immutable divine nature. He took on human nature (but without sin).

And those angels who fell from heaven had full knowledge of the God Whom they were rejecting. So there is nothing to bring them to repentance; no new information. Incidentally, Peter's readers might pick up on the fact that they who have experienced the salvation of God are more favored than the angels.

The angels were involved in the giving of the law, according to Acts 7:53 and Galatians 3:19. Hebrews 2:2f says, **For if the word spoken through angels proved unalterable, and every transgression and disobedience received a just recompense, how shall we escape if we neglect so great a salvation?**

God wants the angels to know about the salvation He provides by grace. They're all about praising God, and a salvation provided by God on the basis of grace is a marvel that stirs praise to God. They've been involved in God's redemptive work from the start. That includes the giving the Mosaic Law which condemns men in order to lead them to Christ. They were involved in God's judgments which proved man's need for salvation. So it's only right that they should get to see it through. Ephesians 3:10 says, **in order that the manifold wisdom of God might now be made known through the church to the rulers and the authorities in the heavenly places.** Angels in heaven have a lot to marvel about, so it's telling that they marvel at our salvation.

Hebrews 1:14 says that angels **are ministering spirits, sent out to render service for the sake of those who will inherit salvation.** The angels in heaven are scandalized by the rebellion of men. Apparently, the rebellion of the fallen angels in heaven was dealt with immediately, since God had no intention of laying out a plan of salvation for them. The holy angles can't stand to see God not receiving the glory and obedience He deserves from all His creation. That may be the point Paul is making in I Corinthians 11:10, **Therefore the woman ought to have a symbol of authority on her head, because of the angels.** The context speaks of women who were cutting off their hair as an expression of their rebellion, as some are doing in our day. This rebelliousness upsets God's holy angels. This makes sense, because their whole focus is the glory of God.

Believers have every reason to be certain about our eternal salvation and the glorious inheritance that is reserved in heaven for us. That salvation is based upon the foreknowledge and sovereign choice of God and applied to us by the Holy Spirit. The resurrection of Jesus Christ is our guarantee of our own resurrection.

We are protected by the power of God, which is greater than any earthly power that would presume to separate us from the love of God. Our faith is proven to be the genuine article by the trials that we go through. So we shouldn't shy away from them. (If your faith isn't genuine, you would want to know that while there is time to do something about it, right?)

Salvation is not a new thing. It was God's plan from before the foundation of the world. It was predicted by God's prophets. And it was announced by the Holy Spirit through the Lord's Apostles.

We are safe from all harm when we are in the arms of God. His love and power will get us through any trials that may come our way. What a marvelous thing this salvation is!

Chapter 5

1:13-17, That You May Obey

¹³ Therefore, gird your minds for action, keep sober *in spirit,* fix your hope completely on the grace to be brought to you at the revelation of Jesus Christ.
¹⁴ As obedient children, do not be conformed to the former lusts *which were yours* in your ignorance,
¹⁵ but like the Holy One who called you, be holy yourselves also in all *your* behavior;
¹⁶ because it is written, " YOU SHALL BE HOLY, FOR I AM HOLY."
¹⁷ And if you address as Father the One who impartially judges according to each man's work, conduct yourselves in fear during the time of your stay *upon earth*;

God created mankind so He could enjoy His loving, obedient children. Mankind's fall into sin ruined that relationship and turned men into rebels who want to be their own gods and who are not fit to be in God's presence.

God knew that would happen and had His plan ready. He created man good, but not confirmed in good, because love is a choice. Creating man in His image, God gave us a will and made us self-determining. To love God freely man must choose to be holy. In Ecclesiastes 7:29 we read, **God made men upright, but they have sought out many devices.**

It was the same with the angels. They were created good but had to confirm their own choice of good. The occasion for that happened when Lucifer led a revolt against God. (The Bible doesn't tell us when that took place.) In that rebellion two-thirds of the angels remained obedient to God and were confirmed in good, while the other third followed Satan and were confirmed in evil (see Revelation 12:4). The book of Hebrews tells us that God provided no remedy for the angels who sinned (see the previous chapter).

God's plan for man gave the human race the initial opportunity to be confirmed in good or to rebel and turn to evil. In the Garden of Eden, God placed two special trees: the tree of life and the tree of the knowledge of good and evil. Adam and Eve disobeyed God and chose the latter, even though they were forbidden to eat of it and were warned what would happen if they did. God knew that they would. But, for mankind, God provided a remedy. Ever since Adam, all his descendants are born in sin, but not confirmed (locked into) in sin. We are each given plenty of opportunity to leave sin and be confirmed in good by obeying the gospel of Jesus Christ and becoming God's loving and obedient children.

How can those who are spiritually dead (Ephesians 2:1) respond to God who is spirit (John 4:24)? And what would cause a rebel who is dedicated to following his sin nature to turn to God? Can the leopard change his spots (Jeremiah 13:23)? This is where God's sovereignty and the biblical doctrine of predestination come to the rescue:

Blessed *be* the God and Father of our Lord Jesus Christ, who has blessed us with every spiritual blessing in the heavenly *places* in Christ, just as He chose us in Him before the foundation of the world, that we should be holy and blameless before Him. In love He predestined us to adoption as sons through Jesus Christ to Himself, according to the kind intention of His will, Ephesians 1:3-5.

In Romans 8:29 Paul wrote: **For whom He foreknew, He also predestined to become conformed to the image of His Son, that He might be the first-born among many brethren.** And Hebrews 3:1 says, **therefore, holy brethren, partakers of a heavenly calling, consider Jesus, the Apostle and High Priest of our confession.**

God's plan of redemption, being the perfect plan of a holy, omniscient, and omnipotent God, is a marvelous plan that solves every problem that sin created, confirms believers in good forever, and fully satisfies God's desire for holy, loving, obedient children. All this was accomplished in a way that conforms perfectly to God's nature and attributes.

Peter, under the inspiration of the Holy Spirit, has laid out a long list of reasons to support the commands he is about to give his readers. The reasons are in verses 1-12:

1. We are chosen by God according to His foreknowledge, His pre-determined plan.

2. We are sanctified by the Holy Spirit.

3. We are sprinkled by the blood of Jesus Christ for covenant faithfulness and priestly service.

4. Grace and peace are ours in fullest measure.

5. The Father caused us to be born again to a living hope.

6. Our inheritance is already laid up for us in heaven, imperishable, undefiled, and unfading.

7. We are protected by the power of God.

8. Trials prove the genuineness of our faith.

9. Trials result in our praise, glory, and honor when Jesus is revealed.

10. We love Him and believe in Him.

11. The faith was foretold by the Holy Spirit through the prophets.

12. This faith was announced by the Holy Spirit through the apostles.

That's a hefty set of reasons. It qualifies us to be heavy lifters whenever persecution confronts us.

The commands to follow are the Christian's logical response in light of the marvelous grace in which we stand. This is how we can endure trials in a manner worthy of our calling. It's what Paul meant in Romans 12:1, **I urge you therefore, brethren, by the mercies of God, to present your bodies a living and holy sacrifice, acceptable to God, which is your logical service of worship.** (Your version, like mine, may translate the word as *spiritual*, but the word is *logiken*, from *logos*, meaning logical or reasonable.)

That logical response is indicated by the term **therefore** and by the three finite, imperative verbs that we find in these verses. After listing these 12 reasons, Peter says **therefore** and

70

issues the reasonable commands in verses 13-17. These three commands form Peter's outline. We are to be:

Steadfast in Hope, 13;

Consistent in Holiness, 14-16; and

Fearful in Obedience, 17.

The verb tense in each of these is the aorist imperative, which sent me back to my Greek grammar books. The aorist tense views an action simply as occurring, without reference to its progress. It presents the action as attained, without regard for the time taken in its accomplishment. The imperative mood is the command form, of course. When you put the two together you get the aorist imperative, a command viewed in its entirety as something attained. Its force is best expressed in the words, "Get it done!" And the emphasis is on *done*.

Be Steadfast in Hope, 13

13 Therefore, gird[ing] your minds for action, keep[ing] sober *in spirit*, fix your hope completely on the grace to be brought to you at the revelation of Jesus Christ.

Attached to the finite command, **hope completely**, are two participles, **girding** and **keeping sober**, which get their imperative force from the finite verb and explain *how* to get our minds under control, so that we can be steadfast in hope.

Have you ever met someone who lets his mind just flop in the breeze? We are told to **gird our minds for action**, and **keep sober.** Putting those two together, I get a picture of a sailing ship with its sails flapping in the wind like so many white flags instead of driving the ship forward. When someone is completely under the influence of alcohol, people might say that he is "three sheets to the wind." Sheets on a sailing ship are not what the sailors sleep on or what the sails are made of. They are the adjustable lines (ropes) fastened to the loose corners of the sails and used to tighten down and adjust the sails to catch the power of the wind for best effect.

Imagine a warship lying dead in the water, with the sails and sheets on all three masts just flapping and whipping around in the wind because no one has brought them under control. Maybe the ship has a drunken crew. Imagine, then, that an enemy warship attacks the undisciplined ship. The outcome would be quick and predictable.

Peter urges us to not let that condition describe our minds. In a time of persecution, that would be disastrous. **Girding** referred to pulling the loose skirts of one's long, middle-eastern robe up and tucking them into his belt in preparation for action, so he wouldn't trip over them. The word **mind**, here, speaks of our understanding. It's what was **darkened** in Ephesians 4:18 and **hostile** toward God in Colossians 1:21. It's what the Son of God has given us in order that we might know Him who is true, I John 5:20.

If we neglect to discipline our understanding, if there are a bunch of loose ends, then whenever we go into battle our mind won't function as it should and we will trip over its flapping ends, with predictable results. Ephesians 4:14 says, **we are no longer to be children, tossed here and there by waves, and carried about by every wind of doctrine, by the trickery of men, by craftiness in deceitful scheming**.

Sober is a picturesque metaphor referring to moral alertness; being calm, sober, and circumspect (which is to say, considering our proposed action from all angles), having our wits about us. Moral attacks have been very successful in American churches, just as they have been everywhere else. Soberness is whatever one gives up by becoming physically drunk: self-restraint, a sense of propriety, discretion, wisdom, mental acuity, balance, co-ordination, and whatever is the opposite of dissipation.

What makes a mind taut and disciplined and able to stand firm under pressure? It's what we know and understand. You've heard of tough love. This is tough faith. And tough faith depends upon our certainty about what God's word says. Ephesians 6:14, **Stand firm therefore, HAVING GIRDED**

YOUR LOINS WITH TRUTH. Whenever you add to your understanding of God's truth, you are strengthening your fortress. You are girding your mind for action.

The main command in verse 13 is **hope completely** or perfectly. That hope is to be fixed solely upon **the grace to be brought to you at the revelation of Jesus Christ,** in other words, upon our ultimate, completed salvation (I John 3:2). This is the fourth time Peter has referred to Christ's return and the consummation of our salvation (verses 5, 7, 9). This confidence in our ultimate salvation and glory is our driving force, our mindset and motivation. And it's a very powerful motivation, more powerful than fear of our adversaries. We are to fix our hope completely on this one thing.

What else might a Christian be tempted to hope in? I can think of several possibilities:

Christians might follow the world's example by hoping in wealth. Paul told a young pastor, **Instruct those who are rich in this present world not to be conceited or to fix their hope on the uncertainty of riches, but on God, who richly supplies us with all things to enjoy,** I Timothy 6:17. Psalm 52:6f cautions against trusting in riches, **the righteous will see and fear, and will laugh at him, saying, "Behold, the man who would not make God his refuge, but trusted in the abundance of his riches, and was strong in his evil desire."**

Psalm 33:16-20 warns against several false hopes and then tells where our real hope lies:

The king is not saved by a mighty army; A warrior is not delivered by great strength.
A horse is a false hope for victory; Nor does it deliver anyone by its great strength.
Behold, the eye of the LORD is on those who fear Him, On those who hope for His lovingkindness, To deliver their soul from death, And to keep them alive in famine.
Our soul waits for the LORD; He is our help and our shield.

We can place our hope in men. Galatians 1:10, **Am I now seeking the favor of men, or of God? Or am I striving to please men? If I were still trying to please men, I would not be a bond-servant of Christ.**

Self-sufficiency is a false hope. Jeremiah 46:11 says, **In vain have you multiplied remedies.**

Knowledge/science is a false hope. I Tim. 6:20f says, **O Timothy, guard what has been entrusted to you, avoiding worldly and empty chatter and the opposing arguments of what is falsely called "knowledge"** [*science* is the Latin equivalent]**--which some have professed and thus gone astray from the faith.**

A common false hope is alliances formed with unbelievers or false gods. Hosea 8: 10f says,

Even though they hire allies among the nations, now I will gather them up; and they will begin to diminish because of the burden of the king of princes. Since Ephraim has multiplied altars for sin, they have become altars of sinning for him.

Desire is a false hope. Psalm 9:10 says, **the wicked boasts of his heart's desire.** But Psalm 112:10 says, **the desire of the wicked will perish.**

Many put their hope in government. God has demonstrated that all human governments are inadequate. Politicians like to present themselves as the country's savior. But far more politicians follow Machiavelli's principles than follow Christ's.

There are a lot of alternatives to fixing your hope on the return of Jesus Christ. But no alternatives work in the final analysis. Diluting your faith by adding any of these false hopes would put you in a weakened, diseased condition. We need to fix our eyes on Jesus, the author and perfecter of our faith.

This is one part of how you **walk in a manner worthy of the God who calls you into His own kingdom and glory,** as I Thessalonians 2:12 puts it. Another part is…

Be Consistent in Holiness, 14-16

14 As obedient children, do not be conformed to the former lusts *which were yours* **in your ignorance,**
15 but like the Holy One who called you, be holy yourselves

also in all *your* behavior;
[16] because it is written, " YOU SHALL BE HOLY, FOR I AM HOLY."

In the phrase, **children of obedience,** the term **obedience** is a part of Greek grammar called the genitive of quality. It doesn't mean that we were born of obedience (genitive of source) or are owned by obedience (genitive of possession). It expresses our nature, like the phrase, "He's a man of steel." Obedience expresses the new nature of a born-again Christian.

Before salvation, we were sons of disobedience (Ephesians 2:2; 5:6). That was our old nature. Now we are children of obedience as Romans 6:17f indicates:

But thanks be to God that though you were slaves of sin, you became obedient from the heart to that form of teaching to which you were committed, and having been freed from sin, you became slaves of righteousness.

As children characterized by obedience, we have nothing to do with our old manner of life. That old way of life was encouraged by ignorance or denial of its consequences and characterized by its offensiveness to God. So we should no longer conform ourselves to it. Since we still live in the world, we always feel the pressure to conform to the world as we used to. Refusing to conform ourselves to the world's sins may provoke some of the persecution we face. Don't worry about it. 2 Timothy 3:12 says, **all who desire to live godly in Christ Jesus will be persecuted.**

In Colossians 3:4-10 Paul wrote:

When Christ, who is our life, is revealed, then you also will be revealed with Him in glory. Therefore consider the members of your earthly body as dead to immorality, impurity, passion, evil desire, and greed, which amounts to idolatry. For it is on account of these things that the wrath of God will come, and in them you also once walked, when you were living in them. But now you also put them all aside: anger, wrath, malice, slander, and abusive speech

from your mouth. Do not lie to one another, since you laid aside the old self with its evil practices, and have put on the new self who is being renewed to a true knowledge according to the image of the One who created him.

Facing the wrath of the world is nothing compared to facing the wrath of God. God's requirement for His children has always been, **"YOU SHALL BE HOLY, FOR I AM HOLY."** Cf. Leviticus 11:45, *et al.* Hebrews 12:14 says that we are to **Pursue ... the sanctification without which no one will see the Lord.** *Holy* means set apart from what is common, profane, unclean, or sinful.

If we are not holy, then obviously God keeps Himself apart from us, because He is holy. But the Holy One has called us to Himself. He sees us as holy in His Son because the Holy Spirit has given believers the righteousness of Christ. As Peter said in verse 2, we are sanctified by the work of the Spirit. Christianity, approached as a mere religion, does not produce this change in us.

Hebrews 10:14-22 describes how God qualified us:

For by one offering He has perfected for all time those who are sanctified. And the Holy Spirit also bears witness to us; for after saying, "THIS IS THE COVENANT THAT I WILL MAKE WITH THEM AFTER THOSE DAYS, SAYS THE LORD: I WILL PUT MY LAWS UPON THEIR HEART, AND UPON THEIR MIND I WILL WRITE THEM," He then says, "AND THEIR SINS AND THEIR LAWLESS DEEDS I WILL REMEMBER NO MORE." Now where there is forgiveness of these things, there is no longer any offering for sin. Since therefore, brethren, we have confidence to enter the holy place by the blood of Jesus, by a new and living way which He inaugurated for us through the veil, that is, His flesh, and since we have a great priest over the house of God, let us draw near with a sincere heart in full assurance of faith, having our hearts sprinkled clean from an evil conscience and our bodies washed with pure water.

We have this imputed holiness because we **have died and our life is hidden with Christ in God**, Colossians 3:3.

Romans 6 explains it more fully. But our daily walk must conform to that holiness, rather than to our former lusts. Zacharias, John the Baptist's father, spoke of the oath God swore to Abraham, **to grant us that we, being delivered from the hand of our enemies, might serve Him without fear, in holiness and righteousness before Him all our days.** Later in this epistle, Peter will show that holiness is an indispensable asset when it comes to persecution.

Be Fearful in Conduct, 17

[17] And if you address as Father the One who impartially judges according to each man's work, conduct yourselves in fear during the time of your stay *upon earth*;

When Peter writes **conduct yourselves in fear,** the word **fear** is *phobos*, from which we get the word phobia. Nowadays, in clinical psychology, a phobia is an anxiety disorder in which the phobic person tries like crazy to avoid the cause of his extreme and irrational fear, or, if he can't avoid it, lives in marked distress. That is not at all what Peter means here. He is talking about how we relate to our Father.

Our Father will judge each believer's *work*, and that believer will be rewarded or suffer loss. I Corinthians 3:10-15 describes this judgment:

According to the grace of God which was given to me, as a wise master builder I laid a foundation, and another is building upon it. But let each man be careful how he builds upon it. For no man can lay a foundation other than the one which is laid, which is Jesus Christ. Now if any man builds upon the foundation with gold, silver, precious stones, wood, hay, straw, each man's work will become evident; for the day will show it, because it is to be revealed with fire; and the fire itself will test the quality of each man's work. If any man's work which he has built upon it remains, he shall receive a reward. If any man's work is burned up, he shall suffer loss; but he himself shall be saved, yet so as through fire.

Some of what we do during our life on earth will be useful to God and will be eternally rewarded, and some will be useless and will be burned up. **For we must all appear before the judgment seat of Christ, that each one may be recompensed for his deeds in the body, according to what he has done, whether good or bad** [meaning, not evil, but worthless], II Corinthians 5:10. The reward for our useful work will be eternal and will far exceed what it cost us. Our useless work will turn out to be a complete waste of time. So in that regard we should conduct ourselves in fear.

But this concept of fear deserves a more thorough examination. We are told to work out our salvation **with fear and trembling** in Philippians 2:12. We are told to fear, and we are told not to fear (I John 4:18, the same word, *phobos*). This isn't a contradiction, the meaning is shown by the context. (In interpreting languages, word meaning is important, but context is determinative. For example, if one should say, "He's hot," one of several meanings for hot might be intended--he's good-looking; he's angry; he's overheated; he's enjoying a string of successes. Or consider how many meanings we find in the dictionary for the word *run*.) So there are some things that believers should fear, and some things that believers should not fear. Or to put it differently, we fear some things in one way, and other things in another way.

If we trust God we don't fear eternal judgment, for example, and we don't fear men. Many of the synonyms and causes for fear do not apply because of our relationship with our loving Father: anxiety, cowardice, punishment, wrath, nervousness, misgivings, pre-emptive outbreaks of violence, retribution, worry, suspicion, abhorrence, angst, despair, and foreboding, for example. These are the fears of which John writes in I John 4:18, **There is no fear in love; but perfect love casts out fear, because fear involves punishment, and the one who fears is not perfected in love.** So any fear of punishment is not a part of the believer's fear of God. These are the kinds of fear that cause a person to run away from God.

The fear of God causes the believer to run to God and to cling to Him. The fear that love casts out is a self-centered fear. The fear of the Lord is a God-centered fear.

So what is the fear of God? Fear is closely related 1)to faith--what we believe, 2) to respect--what we regard as powerful, and 3) to obedience--what we see as our obligation, especially when we are talking about the fear of God. The fear of God has positive and negative aspects.

On the negative side, we should fear the bad consequences of bad choices. These consequences might affect ourselves or those we love. There is a fear of disappointing or failing someone, or of doing something that will reflect poorly on someone we love. We should have a fear of dishonoring God, or of displeasing Him who loves us so much and deserves our unfailing love.

On the positive side, fear of God is an awe-filled respect that is commensurate with our view of God (which should be very high). It causes us to obey God, owing to our great respect for Him and for His acknowledged superiority. Our fear is based upon faith – what we believe about God and about what He rightly deserves.

The fear of God is more than reverential awe, although that is certainly a part of it. To fear God means to commit oneself to obeying Him because we believe everything He has revealed of Himself.

The fear of God is, in fact, a descriptive term for salvation in the Old Testament. It is an awe-filled attitude of receptivity manifested in belief, love, worship, and obedience to the living God who created us and then redeemed us instead of abandoning us to the fate we deserved.

According to Proverbs, this fear of God is the beginning of knowledge and wisdom. It is a fountain of life, that one may avoid the snares of death. The fear of God is to hate evil, pride, arrogance, and the evil way. It prolongs life. The reward of humility and the fear of the Lord are riches, honor, and life. In the fear of the Lord there is strong confidence.

So the fear of the Lord is not a bad thing; it's a very good thing, deserving more extended study than we can give it now. Psalm 112, for example, begins, **How blessed is the man who fears the Lord**, and then develops that theme. Our definition of the fear of the Lord must take into account the fact that God's every intention and action toward His children is good.

The fear of God causes us to avoid all that is contrary to God's character: lying, cheating, stealing, fraud, trying to be like the world, and everything else that is designated as a sin. It gives us a tender conscience (an eagerness to respond to God) and a great desire to please God.

Unbelievers deny the truth about God and therefore do not fear God in the same way the holy angels and saints do, so they have to fear God like the demons do. It is about unbelievers that God warns, **It is a terrifying thing to fall into the hands of the living God,** Hebrews 10:31. They are the ones who have **a certain terrifying expectation of judgment, and THE FURY OF A FIRE WHICH WILL CONSUME THE ADVERSARIES,** Hebrews 10:27. Believers joyfully fear God. Unbelievers are scared of God.

So one way or another, everyone will respect God. The godless ones who persecute God's believers do so because they are scared to death. They have reason to be. But we, who are persecuted for our faith, have no reason to fear men. They can do nothing to us that God hasn't chosen to allow for His good reasons.

An ounce of temporary persecution produces a pound of rewards in eternity, one could say. But we don't, for that reason, seek out persecution. That sounds stupid, I know, but some have done that. To cause our own persecution would be to ruin its effects, I Pet. 4:15. God alone knows how to use persecution successfully. It's a powerful tool. We should leave it in His hands.

The eighteenth century Irish/British statesman, Edmund Burke observed, "No passion so effectually robs the mind of all its powers of acting and reasoning as fear." That describes those sinners who are terrified of God's punishment, even if they won't admit it. He also said, in line with our present study, "He who fears God fears nothing else."

God has a great salvation in store for us. Our appropriate response is to fix our hope fully and exclusively on the salvation that is to be revealed, to be holy as He is holy, and

80

to conduct ourselves in the fear of the Lord. This is the appropriate and victorious way to face any trials we might encounter. Being rightly related to the King of Kings carries with it some obligations. *Noblesse oblige*: nobility has its obligations.

Chapter 6

1:18-25, That You May Love

[18] knowing that you were not redeemed with perishable things like silver or gold from your futile way of life inherited from your forefathers,
[19] but with precious blood, as of a lamb unblemished and spotless, *the blood* of Christ.
[20] For He was foreknown before the foundation of the world, but has appeared in these last times for the sake of you
[21] who through Him are believers in God, who raised Him from the dead and gave Him glory, so that your faith and hope are in God.
[22] Since you have in obedience to the truth purified your souls for a sincere love of the brethren, fervently love one another from the heart,
[23] for you have been born again not of seed which is perishable but imperishable, *that is,* through the living and abiding word of God.
[24] For, " ALL FLESH IS LIKE GRASS, AND ALL ITS GLORY LIKE THE FLOWER OF GRASS. THE GRASS WITHERS, AND THE FLOWER FALLS OFF,
[25] BUT THE WORD OF THE LORD ABIDES FOREVER." And this is the word which was preached to you.

God created mankind so He could enjoy loving, obedient children. In the previous verses Peter showed that salvation produces obedient children. In the current text he shows that salvation produces loving children. Peter moves seamlessly from verses 12-17 to verses 18-25, so smoothly, in fact, that verse 17 applies to both, providing the transition between the two.

These two logical and fitting responses to our imperishable hope – holy fear (obedience) and love for the brethren – are central in two of the three Great C's that form the outline for the church's ministry: the Great Confession (Mt. 16:16), and the Great Commandment (Jn. 13:34). And they are a prime motivation for the third, the Great Commission (Mt. 18:18-20).

Because we are saved by Jesus Christ, the Son of the living God, because the Holy Spirit has given us the righteousness of Christ (which is the only valid "ticket" to heaven) and because God is our perfect provider in all things, we have everything we need in Christ. So we are freed from self-concern and can love the other children of our God. We can also love those who aren't children of God yet, but might become His children if they could get a good look at God's love working in us. One way that our love for God is expressed on earth is our love for God's other children.

Here is Peter's outline:

Imperishable Redemption, 17-21

Fervent Love, 22

Imperishable Seed, 23-25

Imperishable Redemption, 17-21

[17] And if you address as Father the One who impartially judges according to each man's work, conduct yourselves in fear during the time of your stay *upon earth*;
[18] knowing that you were not redeemed with perishable things like silver or gold from your futile way of life inherited from your forefathers,
[19] but with precious blood, as of a lamb unblemished and spotless, *the blood* of Christ.
[20] For He was foreknown before the foundation of the world, but has appeared in these last times for the sake of you
[21] who through Him are believers in God, who raised Him from the dead and gave Him glory, so that your faith and hope are in God.

Peter returns to a word he used in verses 4 and 7, again contrasting our permanent redemption with perishable things like silver or gold. It is characteristic of Peter's style to contrast the negative with the positive. (By the way, I see that style also in the book of Hebrews. This, taken with the common subjects in I Peter and Hebrews, makes me wonder if the apostle to the circumcision had some part in writing that book. I also see many elements of Paul's style. Did Peter and Paul collaborate in the writing of Hebrews? They were both in Rome around A.D. 60-62. And there were good reasons to keep their names out of the book, in part so readers wouldn't reject it *a priori*. It's an interesting question.)

It is Paul's style in his letters to present first the theological basis, and then the practical applications. Peter does that, too. But he also weaves practical applications in with the doctrinal basis in the early part of his letter. Our eternal salvation is woven in with our temporary trials; our great redemption is woven in with our obligations while on this earth; the reasons for our certainty are woven in with our duty to act like people who are certain.

Paul, the tent maker, cuts out all of his material accurately and then sews it all together. Peter, the fisherman, weaves his net. Whatever the servant of God does, if it has value in God's kingdom, is actually done by the Holy Spirit working in us. Yet the Spirit allows His children's hearts and personalities to show through in God's work (like a dad allowing his children to put their hand prints in the wet concrete).

Peter is addressing his readers' hearts now as he directs their minds to the cost of their redemption. It wasn't cheap. Salvation is free to us, but not cheap. It's free to us because the price was too high for us to pay. So God paid it. In Isaiah 52:3, God told Jerusalem, **"You were sold for nothing and you will be redeemed without money."** The Bible frequently mentions our inability to redeem ourselves. **No man can by any means redeem his brother, or give to God a ransom for him – for the redemption of his soul is costly, and he should cease trying forever – that he should live on eternally,** Psalm 49:7ff.

The sign of the Abrahamic covenant was circumcision (Genesis 17:11). It was an early indication that, **"It is the Spirit who gives life; the flesh profits nothing; the words that I have spoken to you are spirit and are life,"** John 6:63. The new covenant, by the way, is the fulfillment of the Abrahamic covenant. So the New Covenant is older than the Old Covenant (the Mosaic covenant). See Galatians 3.

The sign of the Mosaic covenant was the Sabbath. **For six days work may be done, but on the seventh day there is a sabbath of complete rest, holy to the LORD; whoever does any work on the sabbath day shall surely be put to death,** Exodus 31:15. Its purpose in the midst of the Mosaic law was to be a weekly reminder that salvation was not by works but by resting in what God would do to accomplish salvation. **"And also I gave them My sabbaths to be a sign between Me and them, that they might know that I am the LORD who sanctifies them,"** Ezekiel 20:12.

The Day of Atonement was a yearly reminder that salvation was not by works:

"And *this* shall be a permanent statute for you: in the seventh month, on the tenth day of the month, you shall humble your souls, and not do any work, whether the native, or the alien who sojourns among you; for it is on this day that atonement shall be made for you to cleanse you; you shall be clean from all your sins before the LORD. "It is to be a sabbath of solemn rest for you, that you may humble your souls; it is a permanent statute, Leviticus 16:29-31.

Note that this passage says twice that they must humble themselves. Salvation by works appeals to man's pride. But salvation by grace through faith gives man no basis for boasting.

Hebrews 4:1-11 connects that Sabbath rest with God's salvation:

[1] Therefore, let us fear lest, while a promise remains of entering His rest, any one of you should seem to have come short of it.
[2] For indeed we have had good news preached to us, just as

they also; but the word they heard did not profit them, because it was not united by faith in those who heard.
³ For we who have believed enter that rest, just as He has said, " AS I SWORE IN MY WRATH, THEY SHALL NOT ENTER MY REST," although His works were finished from the foundation of the world.
⁴ For He has thus said somewhere concerning the seventh *day*, " AND GOD RESTED ON THE SEVENTH DAY FROM ALL HIS WORKS";
⁵ and again in this *passage*, " THEY SHALL NOT ENTER MY REST."
⁶ Since therefore it remains for some to enter it, and those who formerly had good news preached to them failed to enter because of disobedience,
⁷ He again fixes a certain day, "Today," saying through David after so long a time just as has been said before, " TODAY IF YOU HEAR HIS VOICE, DO NOT HARDEN YOUR HEARTS." ⁸ For if Joshua had given them rest, He would not have spoken of another day after that.
⁹ There remains therefore a Sabbath rest for the people of God.
¹⁰ For the one who has entered His rest has himself also rested from his works, as God did from His.
¹¹ Let us therefore be diligent to enter that rest, lest anyone fall through *following* the same example of disobedience.

It seems as if it would have been easier for God to create fresh, new people than to redeem the fallen ones. But God's love is great for the people He created, and His plan was flawless from the beginning. Working His plan, He produces people who are confirmed in goodness and confirmed in His love. As verse 21 puts it, **so that your faith and hope are in God.**

A redemption bought with perishable things would suggest a perishable redemption. That is Peter's point. And his intent throughout his letter is to argue for the imperishable nature of our salvation and our living hope.

From what were we redeemed? Not from Satan. Even if one should "sell his soul to the Devil," Satan doesn't own that person. All souls belong to God (Ezek. 18:4). Verse 18b says that the sinner's way of life is **futile**, vain, useless, just like every other sinner's way of life, since time began. Don't say that the old days were better (logicians call this the fallacy of antiquity). Don't say, "It's always been done this way," and expect that to be of any value to God. Nothing, perhaps, is as much of a stumbling block as religious tradition, which gives man false comfort and blinds him to his need for Christ. Peter has fought against this way of thinking for his entire ministry (except for that one time in Antioch when he yielded to intimidation).

We can point to great accomplishments natural men have achieved through the centuries, but none have gotten men any closer to God. The book of Ecclesiastes nailed that lid down 3,000 years ago, **"Vanity of vanities, all is vanity."** As I Corinthians 1:21 says, **the world in its wisdom did not come to know God.** Mankind is in bondage to sin and to the wrath of God. What can a pyramid or the Great Wall of China do about that? We were conformed to our former lusts in our ignorance, verse 14 says.

Paul spoke of this bondage to sin in Titus 3:3ff:

... we also once were foolish ourselves, disobedient, deceived, enslaved to various lusts and pleasures, spending our life in malice and envy, hateful, hating one another. But when the kindness of God our Savior and His love for mankind appeared, He saved us, not on the basis of deeds which we have done in righteousness, but according to His mercy, by the washing of regeneration and renewing by the Holy Spirit, whom He poured out upon us richly through Jesus Christ our Savior, that being justified by His grace we might be made heirs according to the hope of eternal life.

Romans 5:8-9 tells us what we were redeemed from:

But God demonstrates His own love toward us, in that while we were yet sinners, Christ died for us. Much more then, having now been justified by His blood, we shall be saved from the wrath of God through Him.

God made all the gold and silver. So how could we buy anything from God for gold or silver? In the first place, He has no need for gold or silver, nor is He dazzled by it. In the second place, if He *wanted* some, He could simply take what's already His, since He already owns everything, or else He could make some more. In the third place, God is not the least bit impressed by anyone's gold or silver, that He should corrupt His perfect justice for a bribe. Nor is His holiness so lightly offended, or His wrath against sin so mild, that silver and gold could satisfy it. James 5:3 advises, **Your gold and your silver have rusted; and their rust will be a witness against you and will consume your flesh like fire. It is in the last days that you have stored up your treasure!**

Peter told Simon Magus, **"May your silver perish with you, because you thought you could obtain the gift of God with money,"** Acts 8:20. The richest man in the world can't buy anything from God. God's perfect righteousness can be satisfied only by perfect justice. So Peter writes, **you were not redeemed with perishable things like silver or gold**, verse 18.

We were redeemed

with precious blood, as of a lamb unblemished and spotless, *the blood* of Christ. For He was foreknown before the foundation of the world, but has appeared in these last times for the sake of you who through Him are believers in God, who raised Him from the dead and gave Him glory, so that your faith and hope are in God, verses 19-21.

All our sins were imputed to His account and then He was put to death to pay for those sins (Isaiah 53; Romans 6; Colossians 2). The fact that God then raised Him from the dead proves that the sacrifice was accepted by God as payment in full (Romans 4:25).

Certainly Peter had in mind the first Passover in Egypt and its association with the one Passover that was burned indelibly into his heart. Peter watched Jesus pay for our redemption from sin. You can be sure that Peter never took sin lightly after seeing the precious blood of his Lord dripping into the dirt as payment for his sin.

The blood of Jesus is precious because it was the lifeblood of God's own Son. It was precious because Jesus had no sin of His own to die for, so our sins could be imputed to Him and He could die for our sins. The perfectly righteous life of Christ was the only life that could impute righteousness to us. It was precious because that death bought salvation for everyone in the world who would repent and believe. No other sacrifice would be acceptable to God.

Imagine finding yourself locked in an inescapable, steel room with one opening. That door is tightly bolted shut, with actual bolts. Never mind how you got there; maybe you're James Bond--he always gets in situations like that. Your air supply is running out. In such a situation, which would be more precious to you, a ton of gold or a wrench that fit those bolts? Our sin is like that steel box. We're trapped and we can't get out. Our time is running out. The blood of Christ is precious because it is the only way to get out of our sin condition. His sacrificial (bloody) death is the only substitute God will accept as atonement for our sins.

The atonement was sufficient for the sins of all mankind, according to I John 2:2, **He Himself is the propitiation for our sins; and not for ours only, but also for those of the whole world.** But that propitiation is applied only to those **who through Him are believers in God,** as Peter says in verse 21.

In fact, I John 2:3-6 goes on to say the same thing:

And by this we know that we have come to know Him, if we keep His commandments. The one who says, "I have come to know Him," and does not keep His commandments, is a liar, and the truth is not in him; but whoever keeps His word, in him the love of God has truly been perfected. By this we know that we are in Him: the one who says he abides in Him ought himself to walk in the same manner as He walked.

Christians sometimes speak of the blood of Christ in terms of pagan superstition, as if the mention of it had magical power. The blood of Christ refers to His death, a particular kind of death--a bloody, sacrificial death, as pictured by the Old Testament sacrifices. To underscore that point, God made sure that the crucifixion took place at Jerusalem and during Passover. The parallel construction of verses 8-10 in Romans 5 shows that references to the blood of Christ are speaking of His sacrificial, atoning death:

But God demonstrates His own love toward us, in that while we were yet sinners, Christ died for us. Much more then, having now been justified by His blood, we shall be saved from the wrath of God through Him. For if while we were enemies, we were reconciled to God through the death of His Son, much more, having been reconciled, we shall be saved by His life.

This method of salvation was God's plan even before the foundation of the world was laid, according to verse 20. Those who think that *foreknowledge* means nothing more than *foreseen ahead of time* will have a hard time with this verse.

In Peter's first sermon, he said that Jesus was **delivered up by the predetermined plan and foreknowledge of God,** Acts 2;23. So *foreknowledge* means pre-ordained. God is not a passive observer in our salvation; He is the sovereign provider. He didn't react; He initiated. Given that God did all this for us, that is, for all of His chosen ones, it is to be expected that those of us who share in this great salvation and who thereby share in the love of our heavenly Father, should love one another. And that is Peter's second point in verse 22.

Fervent Love, 22

[22] Since you have in obedience to the truth purified your souls for a sincere love of the brethren, fervently love one another from the heart,

Ezekiel 36:25-27 tells how God accomplished this purification:

I will sprinkle clean water on you, and you will be clean; I will cleanse you from all your filthiness and from all your idols. Moreover, I will give you a new heart and put a new spirit within you; and I will remove the heart of stone from your flesh and give you a heart of flesh, and I will put My Spirit within you and cause you to walk in My statutes, and you will be careful to observe My ordinances.

90

So purification is the work of the Holy Spirit, as Peter already said in verse 2. But Peter, I think, is considering this work of God from the human standpoint, referring to our obedience to the truth. That's what it looks like from our side – we obeyed the gospel and came over to its truth. God's saving action is the cause; the saved one's obedience to the truth is one of the results.

Another result of God's saving action is this purifying of the soul. And a third result, made possible by the purifying of the soul, is a sincere love for the brethren. In his first epistle, John had two concerns, truth and love (in that order, as they *must* be). In I John 2:9-11 he wrote:

The one who says he is in the light and yet hates his brother is in the darkness until now. The one who loves his brother abides in the light and there is no cause for stumbling in him. But the one who hates his brother is in the darkness and walks in the darkness, and does not know where he is going because the darkness has blinded his eyes.

Love requires a purified heart:

Do not love the world, nor the things in the world. If anyone loves the world, the love of the Father is not in him. For all that is in the world, the lust of the flesh and the lust of the eyes and the boastful pride of life, is not from the Father, but is from the world. And the world is passing away, and also its lusts; but the one who does the will of God abides forever. If you know that He is righteous, you know that everyone also who practices righteousness is born of Him, I John 2:15-17, 29.

All these impurities, being self-serving, prevent sincere love. **For this is the message which you have heard from the beginning, that we should love one another; not as Cain, who was of the evil one, and slew his brother. And for what reason did he slay him? Because his deeds were evil,** I John 3:11f.

Once we are pure, then we can love others. I John 4:7-9 says:

Beloved, let us love one another, for love is from God; and everyone who loves is born of God and knows God. The one who does not love does not know God, for God is love. By this the love of God was manifested in us, that God has sent His only begotten Son into the world so that we might live through Him.

John wrote about *agape* love, the unconditional commitment of the will to put other's interests ahead of one's own. The only source of *agape* is God, making it a vibrant witness to the saving and transforming power of the gospel. Loving the brethren with this genuine *agape* love is one of the distinguishing marks of a true believer.

To be **sincere** (the word means unhypocritical) requires an adjustment to our souls. Before we were saved, our souls were only self-seeking and self-serving. That's half the reason why non-Christians can't love with this *agape* love. The other half of the reason is that *agape* does not exist in the sinful human heart; it comes only from God. In fact, the Greek language had no word for this kind of unconditional love. So Jesus took an obscure Greek word, *agape*, and gave it a biblical definition to describe God's kind of love.

Imagine our capacity for love as a large hose through which would pass God's *agape* love for other people. Before salvation, that hose was plugged up with all the sticky sludge of self-interest. After salvation, the pipe is cleaned out so God's love can flow through it. But we can still choose to be like the Corinthian believers who, because of self-interest, were restrained in their own affections (I Corinthians 6:12). We can kink the hose, trying to keep God's love to ourselves. But that doesn't work very well, and it damages the hose. Think of doing that to a garden hose: the pressure builds up, the hose gets no new water, and stagnation eventually replaces freshness.

So we need to open up and be **fervent** in our love for one another. The word *fervent* means stretched out, and speaks of a love that causes us to exert ourselves on behalf of others. Love is an act of the will, our will. It is a choice that we make to do good to others. If we make that choice, then the loving providence of God flows through us, as through an open hose, to meet other people's needs. If we do that, then God's love is always flowing in us, fresh and abundant.

I John 3:16-19 says:

We know love by this, that He laid down His life for us; and we ought to lay down our lives for the brethren. But whoever has the world's goods, and beholds his brother in need and closes his heart against him, how does the love of God abide in him? Little children, let us not love with word or with tongue, but in deed and truth. We shall know by this that we are of the truth, and shall assure our heart before Him.

Peter exhorts his readers to love because love is crucial to the survival and cohesiveness of a church that is going through trials. Speaking on Mt. Olivet about judgment day, Jesus said:

"Then the King will say to those on His right, 'Come, you who are blessed of My Father, inherit the kingdom prepared for you from the foundation of the world. 'For I was hungry, and you gave Me something to eat; I was thirsty, and you gave Me drink; I was a stranger, and you invited Me in; naked, and you clothed Me; I was sick, and you visited Me; I was in prison, and you came to Me.' "Then the righteous will answer Him, saying, 'Lord, when did we [do all these things] to You?' "And the King will answer and say to them, 'Truly I say to you, to the extent that you did it to one of these brothers of Mine, even the least of them, you did it to Me,' Matthew 25:34-40.

This exhortation is not about evangelistic prison ministries. Prison ministries are good, but they don't get their mandate here. The Great Commission is their mandate. Jesus is referring here to **these brothers of Mine**, not to convicts incarcerated for *actual* crimes. This is about the rough times tribulation saints will endure in the last days, including being jailed for their faith, and about other Christians coming alongside to help in their distress, even at the risk of putting themselves in danger. Paul's companions who ministered to him while he was in prison were obeying this instruction. So if a brother or sister is arrested or put through some other trial for the cause of Christ, we don't shrink away and say, "Better you than me." We don't leave him to endure the trial on his own; we go and take care of him.

Paul was often in need of such visits. In II Tim. 4:10 he wrote, **Demas, having loved this present world, has deserted me and gone to Thessalonica.** And in verse 16, **At my first defense no one supported me, but all deserted me; may it not be counted against them.** He did go on to say:

But the Lord stood with me, and strengthened me, in order that through me the proclamation might be fully accomplished, and that all the Gentiles might hear; and I was delivered out of the lion's mouth. The Lord will deliver me from every evil deed, and will bring me safely to His heavenly kingdom; to Him be the glory forever and ever, II Timothy 4:17f.

Not long after that, Paul was executed in Nero's persecutions. In the meantime, what a comfort it was that Luke was with him and that Timothy and Mark were coming.

Hebrews 13:3 commands, **Remember the prisoners, as though in prison with them, and those who are ill-treated, since you yourselves also are in the body.** So this is about fellow believers. I Corinthians 12:26 points out that **if one member** [of the body] **suffers, all the members suffer with it.** We're all in this together, so we need to stick together. The divide and conquer strategy should not work on Christians, because we shouldn't allow ourselves to be divided.

Now, I mentioned that Peter weaves doctrine together with application. Here he weaves love for one another in between the doctrines of redemption and new birth. I hope now you can see his logic.

Imperishable Seed, 23-25

23 for you have been born again not of seed which is perishable but imperishable, *that is,* **through the living and abiding word of God.**
24 For, " ALL FLESH IS LIKE GRASS, AND ALL ITS GLORY LIKE THE FLOWER OF GRASS. THE GRASS

**WITHERS, AND THE FLOWER FALLS OFF,
²⁵ BUT THE WORD OF THE LORD ABIDES
FOREVER." And this is the word which was preached to
you.**

Peter has laid great stress on the difference between
perishable and **imperishable**. (Maybe it's because he dealt
with fish for so long. Fish go bad in a hurry.) He is developing
the idea that Paul touched on in II Corinthians 4:17, **For
momentary, light affliction is producing for us an eternal
weight of glory far beyond all comparison**. As Peter
describes our living hope in this first chapter, his every
emphasis is on its permanence and certainty. God has put us in
a situation as Christians where we cannot lose eternally, no
matter what we have to go through temporarily. In fact, the
more we have to go through, the greater the glory.

Our spiritual birth is irrevocable because God gave it to
us through the living and abiding word of God. **THE WORD
OF THE LORD ABIDES FOREVER**. James 1:18 says, **In
the exercise of His will He brought us forth by the word of
truth.** God doesn't lie and He never goes back on His word.

Concerning God's word Isaiah said:

**as the rain and the snow come down from heaven, and do
not return there without watering the earth, and making it
bear and sprout, and furnishing seed to the sower and
bread to the eater; so shall My word be which goes forth
from My mouth; it shall not return to Me empty, without
accomplishing what I desire, and without succeeding in the
matter for which I sent it,** Isaiah 55:10f.

Jesus said, **"Heaven and earth will pass away, but My
words will not pass away,"** Luke 21:33.

In verses 23 and 25, Peter uses two synonyms to speak
of the word of God: *logos* and *rhema*. In verse 23 the term is
logos, which, especially in contrast to *rhema*, emphasizes the
meaning conveyed by the words, what logicians call the
proposition. And in verse 25 the term is *rhema*, which refers to

the actual words used, the manner in which the propositional truth is expressed.

Some think that the main thoughts (which would correspond to *logos*) in the Bible are inspired by God, but not the particular words (*rhema*). But God's word, itself, says that both the *logos* and the *rhema* are inspired and permanent. Both the forest and the trees, even to the smallest branches and twigs, are all inspired by God and will never pass away. Jesus said that the smallest letter and even the smallest part of a letter are inspired by God and will not fail (Mt. 5:18).

Someone might ask, "How do you know what, exactly, it takes to be saved? And how do you know you have what it takes? It seems quite arrogant to think you can be sure!" Our answer is: "I have God's word on it. And it is not arrogant to believe God. Nor is it risky." If you ever get such a challenge, take the skeptic to I Peter, chapter 1.

We are permanent sons of God, and permanent brothers and sisters to Christ and to each other. We are, in fact, blood brothers, by the most precious blood of Jesus Christ. We who have the right to address God as our Father are one family, united in His love.

The world likes to speak of the family of man and the brotherhood of man. And that was God's intent, and it is God's current and ultimate plan for those who are willing to be separated from their sin and to put their trust in His Son. But in the world of sinners, those ties are remote at best, and are often superseded by religious, political, and ethnic differences, not to mention conflicting self-wills.

And the great divide is Jesus Christ. Those who hate Him will hate us. A slave is not greater than his master.

Whoever believes that Jesus is the Christ is born of God; and whoever loves the Father loves the child born of Him, I John 5:1.

We were not redeemed by perishable things, so our redemption is not perishable. We were not born of perishable seed, so our regeneration is not perishable. It is irrevocable, and our new life will not wither. Everything God does in order to save a people for His Son is permanent. **The gifts and the calling of God are irrevocable,** Romans 11:29. As Jesus said in John 6:39, **this is the will of Him who sent Me, that of all that He has given Me I lose nothing, but raise it up on the last day.**

And because all our needs are met in God, who preserves us by His power, we are free from self-concern and self-preservation so we can love one another.

Blessed be the God and Father of our Lord Jesus Christ.

Chapter 7

2:1-5, That You May Grow

[1] Therefore, putting aside all malice and all guile and hypocrisy and envy and all slander,
[2] like newborn babes, long for the pure milk of the word, that by it you may grow in respect to salvation,
[3] if you have tasted the kindness of the Lord.
[4] And coming to Him as to a living stone, rejected by men, but choice and precious in the sight of God,
[5] you also, as living stones, are being built up as a spiritual house for a holy priesthood, to offer up spiritual sacrifices acceptable to God through Jesus Christ.

God wants loving and obedient children. And it should go without saying that He wants those children to grow and become fruitful. Why do some Christians grow strong while others struggle to survive? Why do some produce fruit a hundredfold, while others are hard-pressed to produce thirty fold (Matthew 13:8)?

How do we go from being a weak babe in Christ to being a strong soldier for Christ? We know that it somehow involves being students of the word of God. But sometimes even when we are diligent to study the Bible for ourselves, and even when we pay close attention when others teach us, we still don't see the personal, spiritual growth we expect.

Our text employs an agricultural metaphor. So we might ask, how is it that some farmers who apply nutrients to their fields see a substantial increase in their yields, while other farmers apply the same fertilizer at the same rate, but see little or no increase in yields? The answer: plants require more than nutrients to grow at a good rate. So do Christians. All Christians, at least in America, have access to the word of God, even if most do not study it. Some Christians who are well-fed don't grow because they can't take up and use those nutrients.

Having told his readers that they were saved in order to obey God and to love their brothers in Christ, Peter now tells his readers how to grow into mature, fruitful plants. Tender, young plants will not fair well when hard times come. There is no advantage to staying young in this case. God wants His children to harden up in their faith.

We understand that people are different, with different backgrounds and personalities, different starting points, different gifts, different manifestations of those gifts, and so forth. So we don't all develop at the same rate or in the same ways. But we all should grow at a healthy rate and become strong and fruitful.

Growing into mature, fruitful plants involves three factors. Those three factors form the outline for Peter's text. For proper growth, plants require:

The Proper Environment, 1

The Proper Nutrition, 2 and

Water and Light, 4-5 (which work together).

If any of these three factors are lacking, then growth is retarded. If they are present, then growth happens.

Proper Environment, 1

[1] Therefore, putting aside all malice and all guile and hypocrisy and envy and all slander,

If the soil in a farmer's field is too acidic or too alkaline, then applying more nutrients in the form of fertilizer is a waste of time and money. This is because the nutrients in the soil can't be taken up and utilized by the plants. The nutrients are not available to the plant, even though they are present in the soil.

So any farmer worthy of that exalted title tests the soil's pH. Based on test results, he adds lime to the soil to raise the pH, making it less acidic, or else sulfur to lower it, making it less alkaline. The parable of the four soils should come to mind, as well. You can't grow corn very well in rocky or shallow soil, and you can't let the weeds and briers grow with the corn, competing for the necessities of plant life.

Finally, you can't grow every plant in every temperature zone. You can't grow cotton in Canada or bananas in Buffalo. The environment has to be right in terms of temperature, length of growing season, soil conditions, and amount of rainfall.

In short, you have to provide the plant with the proper environment. Now in terms of spiritual growth, the proper environment for a Christian is a sin-free environment. The more sin a Christian permits in his life, the less favorable the conditions are for spiritual growth.

According to I Peter 1:23, we were born of imperishable seed, **the living and abiding word of God**. So the seed is good, even if it doesn't sprout and bear fruit in certain soils. The environment is the issue, and that is our concern. Believers must approach God's word with a clean heart.

Job 17:9 says, **Nevertheless the righteous shall hold to his way, and he who has clean hands shall grow stronger and stronger.** Psalm 119: 9ff asks, **How can a young man keep his way pure? By keeping it according to Thy word. With all my heart I have sought Thee; do not let me wander from Thy commandments. Thy word I have treasured in my heart, that I may not sin against Thee.**

And Psalm 92:12ff promise that:

the righteous man will flourish like the palm tree, he will grow like a cedar in Lebanon. Planted in the house of the LORD, they will flourish in the courts of our God. They will still yield fruit in old age; they shall be full of sap and very green.

Psalm 1:1ff address the proper environment and proper nutrition and then the result:

How blessed is the man who does not walk in the counsel of the wicked, nor stand in the path of sinners, nor sit in the seat of scoffers! But his delight is in the law of the LORD,

100

and in His law he meditates day and night. And he will be like a tree firmly planted by streams of water, which yields its fruit in its season, and its leaf does not wither; and in whatever he does, he prospers.

If a Christian wants the blessed, fruitful, and successful part, he has to study and delight in (gladly heed) God's word. So Peter starts this section with the word **therefore**. We have our spiritual life and the great inheritance that goes with it because of the word of God that we heard and received. Therefore, if you want to grow, the word of God that gave you life is the word that will cause you to grow.

But sin is the spoiler. It doesn't matter how much you study God's word, if you harbor sin. That sin blocks the uptake of those rich nutrients, just like too much acid in the soil. Psalm 66:18 says, **If I regard wickedness in my heart, The Lord will not hear**.

So Peter tells us that growth requires that we put aside sin – that we reject it and put it away from ourselves, just as David said in Psalm 1. If we do, then we are in the right environment to grow.

Peter mentions five specific sins in verse 1. It's easy to deny that sin is an issue in your life when it's spoken of in general terms, but it's harder when the one confronting you gets specific. That's perhaps what Jesus was doing when He stooped down to write in the dirt when the Jews brought the woman taken in sin, and Jesus said, **"Let him who is without sin cast the first stone,"** John 8:7. I think Jesus was writing specific sins of the accusers. One by one, as they saw their sins written in the dirt, they walked away.

Here, too, Peter lists a few, specific sins in order to forestall denial. He is not saying that these are the only sins that retard your growth, while other sins are okay. I Corinthians, for example, lists other sins that inhibited the Corinthians' growth.

In fact, the first sin Peter mentions really covers a whole range of sins. **Malice** is badness in quality; wickedness, depravity, malignity. It is used of whatever is morally or ethically evil, injurious, or destructive. Three times Peter uses the term **all**, meaning every kind or variety. He is saying,

"Reject this category of behavior in its entirety; have no part in any of this."

Guile is craftiness or deceit. Homer used the term of bait or a snare. Verse 22 says there was no deceit in Jesus at all. That should be true of His followers as well. It was true of Nathanael (John 1:47).

Hypocrisy refers to play-acting and pretense. We all know what hypocrisy is because we see so much of it in others. God takes a dim view of hypocrisy. Ananias and Sapphira were judged by God when they threatened to infect the infant church with their hypocrisy (Acts 5). The hypocrite is, in reality, lying to the Holy Spirit. And that is an insult to God, as if He were stupid instead of omniscient.

Envy is the feeling of displeasure that a self-serving person gets from learning of someone else's prosperity or advantage. It is one of the deeds of the flesh listed in Galatians 5:21.

Slander means to speak evil of someone or to rail at someone. It's putting someone down, verbally. It has the idea of backbiting and defamation of character.

Other passages also teach the principle that growth requires the proper environment. For example, Colossians 3:4ff says:

Consider the members of your earthly body as dead to immorality, impurity, passion, evil desire, and greed, which amounts to idolatry ... put aside anger, wrath, malice, slander, and abusive speech from your mouth. Do not lie to one another, since you laid aside the old self with its evil practices, and have put on the new self who is being renewed to a true knowledge according to the image of the One who created him.

James 1:18ff says, **putting aside all filthiness and all that remains of wickedness, in humility receive the word implanted, which is able to save your souls.**

Titus 3:1ff is another parallel passage:

Remind them to be subject to rulers, to authorities, to be obedient, to be ready for every good deed, to malign no one,

102

to be uncontentious, gentle, showing every consideration for all men. For we also once were foolish ourselves, disobedient, deceived, enslaved to various lusts and pleasures, spending our life in malice and envy, hateful, hating one another.

You can do whatever else you want for a plant: speak lovingly to it, hold its hand, give it some mulch, or whatever, but if you don't put it in the proper environment, you won't see much in the way of growth. As you might imagine, God is not inclined to bless His people if they stay committed to their sin. Jeremiah 5:25ff warns that sin blocks growth and fruitfulness:

Hear this, O foolish and senseless people, who have eyes, but see not; who have ears, but hear not. 'Do you not fear Me?' declares the LORD. 'Do you not tremble in My presence? …They do not say in their heart, "Let us now fear the LORD our God, Who gives rain in its season, both the autumn rain and the spring rain, Who keeps for us the appointed weeks of the harvest." 'Your iniquities have turned these away, and your sins have withheld good from you.

Isaiah 59:1ff says that sin is a block between us and God:

Behold, the LORD'S hand is not so short that it cannot save; neither is His ear so dull that it cannot hear. But your iniquities have made a separation between you and your God, and your sins have hidden His face from you, so that He does not hear.

It is essential to provide the right environment for growth. Our growth is a growing away from sinfulness. We can't grow closer to Christ without growing away from sin. If we want to hang on to sin, we can't grow. But if the environment is good, then the proper nutrition can do its thing.

Proper Nutrition, 2

2 like newborn babes, long for the pure milk of the word, that by it you may grow in respect to salvation,

The phrase **like newborn babes** does not mean that they *were* immature babes in Christ (most of them weren't). It speaks of the manner in which they are to long for the word of God – namely, the same way a newborn baby longs for milk. (**Newborn** refers to a baby of the age to be on a two-hour feeding schedule. So this is saying that we need regular feeding times.) And the term **milk**, as used here, does not refer necessarily to the elementary principles of the faith (as it does in Hebrews 5:12f). The basics are basic, and it's to our detriment if we ever depart from them. But the Jewish rabbis referred to God's law as milk. And I think here Peter means the whole word of God – whether basic doctrine, or intermediate, or advanced.

Milk is the dominant desire of newborn infants. It is the essential input for their health and growth. God built the desire for that essential nutrient into their systems to keep them from starving, since they aren't yet in the habit of eating. When we're speaking of Christians and the word of God, that input which is so essential for the Christian's infancy, is also the essential input for the rest of his life.

Unless the baby is sick, it will desire milk on a regular basis. So will a Christian if he is not sick due to sin in his life. If the baby has no desire for milk, or the Christian has no desire for the word of God, then something is wrong and it's time for quick, corrective action before malnutrition takes its toll. If a baby stopped being hungry when he should be, no good mother would say, "Oh well, he'll eventually start eating again." She would take him to the doctor and get him fixed.

If we don't have time in our day to study God's word, I think we would be well-advised to skip a meal to make time. We'll miss the physical nutrition less than we'll miss the spiritual nutrition.

The term **long for** speaks of an intense, recurring, insatiable desire. Job 23:12 quotes Job: **I have not departed from the command of His lips; I have treasured the words of His mouth more than my necessary food.** David expresses this desire in Psalm 119: 40, **Behold, I long for Thy precepts; revive me through Thy righteousness.** And in verse 131, **I opened my mouth wide and panted, for I longed for Thy**

commandments. In Jeremiah 15:16 the prophet said, **Thy words were found and I ate them, And Thy words became for me a joy and the delight of my heart; For I have been called by Thy name, O LORD God of hosts.**

The Bible says we should read the Word, study it, meditate upon it, teach it, preach it, search it, memorize it, and obey it. But here Peter is encouraging the affinity most fundamental – we must *long* for the word. It is this insatiable desire that drives us to do those other things.

We are to **long for the *pure* milk of the word**. The nutrition by which we grow must be pure and unadulterated; otherwise our food becomes a poison. Psalm 19:8f says:

The precepts of the LORD are right, rejoicing the heart; the commandment of the LORD is pure, enlightening the eyes. The fear of the LORD is clean, enduring forever; the judgments of the LORD are true; they are righteous altogether.

We've seen what happens when tainted foods get out on the market. We know how discomforting, and, in some cases, deadly, tainted foods can be. Imagine how dangerous it is to mix human ideas or the doctrines of false religions in with God's word, tainting it. Or instead of imagining, just look at the current state of much of Christendom, compromised until it is indistinguishable from human ideology.

There is a place, certainly, for books written by mature, godly, knowledgeable believers. You're reading one now. They can encourage our growth by helping us to a better understanding of God's word. But we must look with a critical eye at any work of men. It is only in God's inerrant word that we can rest with assured confidence.

The moment you find a human author's doctrine taking a dangerous direction, drop his book and spit out whatever you were about to swallow. Test his life and his words against the standard of God's revealed truth. Don't expect absolute perfection from men, but if you find significant error, leave that author in the dust. If you read the word regularly, any error you hear from teachers should send up a caution flag. Don't ignore it. In our day we see many well-regarded Bible teachers

compromising with **what is falsely called "knowledge,"** I
Timothy 6:20. Satan's most successful deceptions (apart from
those that justify sins) involve sneaking lies in alongside the
truth in the hope that the undiscerning will accept both. Satan
loves to slip us a "Mickey," poisoning our milk.

In the computer age we have an axiom, "garbage in,
garbage out." What kind of influences do you admit into your
thinking? If it isn't good input, don't put it in. I do my best
thinking when God's word is my dominant input. And all the
other books I read, I always test against God's word.

It is by the word of God that we **grow in respect to
salvation**. As usual, Peter is referring to the final
consummation of our salvation. Our life-long sanctification is
what he has in view, and he always seems to extend that view
to our final glorification. The word for **grow** is the normal word
for plant growth. The nutrient we need for growth is the word
of God. So a plant must have the proper environment and the
proper nutrients, but those are of no use without the actual
mechanism of growth. That mechanism requires...

Water and Light, 3-5

³ if you have tasted the kindness of the Lord.
**⁴ And coming to Him as to a living stone, rejected by men,
but choice and precious in the sight of God,**
**⁵ you also, as living stones, are being built up as a spiritual
house for a holy priesthood, to offer up spiritual sacrifices
acceptable to God through Jesus Christ.**

Those of us who paid attention in biology class know
that water is what draws the nutrients out of the soil and
transports them up through the roots and stems into the leaves
where photosynthesis takes place, and then transports the sugar
to wherever it's needed. But did you know that water is also
needed for the chemical process of photosynthesis?

Photosynthesis, of course, is the solar-powered process
that converts mineral nutrients into the glucose that feeds the
plant (and provides us with maple syrup). Light energy splits

106

the water into hydrogen ions, oxygen, and electrons that are essential to the actual process of photosynthesis. It's a fascinating process which I would be happy to explain, if I had the time… and the comprehension. But the bottom line is that chemical reactions powered by the sun take six molecules of H_2O and six molecules of CO_2 and produce one molecule of sugar and six molecules of O_2. (We should not get too excited about carbon sequestration--if we eliminate all the carbon, we will eliminate all organic life, and that includes ourselves.)

So the third factor in growth is the actual mechanism by which growth takes place. We don't have to understand it any more than the plant has to understand the process of changing light energy into chemical energy. God is the one who makes it happen. And it happens very well, if the other factors are in place. Jesus told Nicodemus, **The wind blows where it wishes and you hear the sound of it, but do not know where it comes from and where it is going; so is everyone who is born of the Spirit,** John 3:8.

Jesus is **the light of the world**, John 8:12, so we have all the light we need. And in John 7:37f we read:

Now on the last day, the great day of the feast, Jesus stood and cried out, saying, "If any man is thirsty, let him come to Me and drink. He who believes in Me, as the Scripture said, 'From his innermost being shall flow rivers of living water.'" But this He spoke of the Spirit.

So we have all the water we need. At least they are abundantly available to us. We still must choose to walk in the light (see Ps. 56:13; 89:15; Jn. 8:12; Eph. 5:8; I Jn. 1:7). and we still have to come to Jesus to drink (Jn. 4:10; I Cor. 10:4).

You can take a dead stick, put it in the soil, give it the right environment, plenty of nutrients, and lots of light and water, but it will not grow. I know, because I've tried. All this information about growth pre-supposes that the plant is alive to begin with. Everything said in Peter's first chapter is true of Peter's audience. So they are alive and ready to grow.

They have already **tasted of the kindness of the Lord**. The **if** is a fulfilled condition, meaning "if, as is the case." It's used to suggest a logical argument: "If you have tasted the kindness of the Lord, and you have, then you will know that you should be longing for the pure milk of the word." So they know what they are getting into, and it's good! Christianity actually works in real life.

Perfect likeness to Christ is our goal. We know that we won't reach that goal until we see Christ face to face and are made like Him (I John 3:2). So if it's going to happen anyway, and if we will not reach that goal during our lifetime, why concern ourselves with it now? Because what we do determines how close we get to Christ-likeness now. The closer we get to perfect Christ-likeness, the better our lives will be in every way. We'll get better at representing Christ to a lost world. We'll be more fruitful. We'll be stronger and healthier. We'll enjoy a closer relationship with Him. We'll earn a greater position and reward in eternity. We'll be freer from sin's nastiness. The more we become like Jesus the more benefits will accrue to us (and to those around us) in this life and in the age to come. And that is without even mentioning the greater glory and joy we'll bring to our heavenly Father.

On the other hand, if we resist what God is doing to sanctify us, then God will use harsher methods to accomplish His purpose. He *will* sanctify the genuine believer. That's a given. God's love can be tough and even rough, because our sanctification is essential. Resistance is brutal.

Our greatest good in life is to be with Jesus and to be like Him (see Phil. 3:20-21; Ps. 73:28). We start our Christian life not very much like Jesus, and not really sure how to walk with Him. That changes as we habitually come near to Jesus, verse 4. (**Coming** is in the present tense, speaking of a continual action.) Drawing near to God was a privilege granted to the priests. Deuteronomy 21:5 says, **Then the priests, the sons of Levi, shall come near, for the LORD your God has chosen them to serve Him and to bless in the name of the LORD.** Even that was subject to limitations. Hebrews 9:6ff says:

the priests are continually entering the outer tabernacle, performing the divine worship, but into the second only the high priest enters, once a year, not without taking blood, which he offers for himself and for the sins of the people

committed in ignorance. The Holy Spirit is signifying this, that the way into the holy place has not yet been disclosed, while the outer tabernacle is still standing.

Even the high priest didn't have much access to God. But Hebrews goes on to say, **[Christ], having offered one sacrifice for sins for all time, SAT DOWN AT THE RIGHT HAND OF GOD**, 10:11f. And verses 19-22 tell what that means to us:

Since therefore, brethren, we have confidence to enter the holy place by the blood of Jesus, by a new and living way which He inaugurated for us through the veil, that is, His flesh, and since we have a great priest over the house of God, let us draw near with a sincere heart in full assurance of faith, having our hearts sprinkled clean from an evil conscience and our bodies washed with pure water.

So the believer has continual, full, and intimate access to God. This is the prize of the ages. It is the pearl of great price. Can you imagine, then, that some would reject Jesus? We will put that topic off until next the next chapter when we can give it due consideration.

We know how to come to Jesus for initial salvation. But how do you come to Jesus in the close, habitual approach that Peter prescribes? I can give you 10 quick ideas to get you started:

1. Colossians 2:6, **As you therefore have received Christ Jesus the Lord, so walk in Him** (we were saved by grace through faith, Ephesians 2:8-9, so we walk by grace through faith also). Gal. 3:2-3 asks the pertinent question:

   This is the only thing I want to find out from you: did you receive the Spirit by the works of the Law, or by hearing with faith? Are you so foolish? Having begun by the Spirit, are you now being perfected by the flesh?

   God began your spiritual life by causing you to be born again. He will also cause you to grow, just as He causes the lilies of the field to grow. Paul said, **"I planted,**

Apollos watered, but God was causing the growth," I Corinthians 3:6. **Faithful is He who calls you; He will also bring it to pass,** I Thessalonians 5:24.

2. Forsake sin. We already covered that. But be hard on yourself in your striving against sin, even to the point of shedding blood (I Cor. 9:27; Hebrews 12:4). Sin blocks the growth process, but God blesses our determination to resist sin.

3. Meet with the Lord in regular, intimate communication, praying and studying the Bible together, in a back and forth dialog with the Lord. This is what Moses did, and Joshua followed his example. Exodus 33 tells how:

   the LORD used to speak to Moses face to face, just as a man speaks to his friend. When Moses returned to the camp, his servant Joshua, the son of Nun, a young man, would not depart from the tent.

   The phrase **coming to Him** is in the present tense, indicating a close, habitual approach. Moses provides a good example as he habitually went out to the tent of meeting. II Cor. 3:18 applies Moses' example to us

4. Apply what you learn, because Jesus goes with you when you obey and coaches you along the way. Educators have said that we remember 10% of what we read, 50% of what we see, and 90% of what we practice. At least, I think that's what I read.

5. Do things together. Whatever you do during the day, do it with Jesus (one way that we **pray without ceasing**). And do you save time and energy for doing what Jesus wants to do? We have to involve ourselves in His work.

6. Share Jesus with others. When we enter into discussions with others about Jesus Christ, then Jesus is there with us, just as He promised in the Great Commission (Matthew 18:18-20). If people should ask us questions that we can't answer, great! That motivates us to go back and learn more about Jesus. It also increases our credibility if we tell someone, "That's a good question. I don't know the answer to that, but I think I can find out.

I'll get back to you." It shows that we aren't just making all this stuff up as we go. When you do get back to the person, he is eager to hear what you say. We are Jesus' disciples, His learners.

7. Love others in Jesus' name. Ephesians 4:15 says, **speaking the truth in love, we are to grow up in all aspects into Him, who is the head, even Christ.**

8. Continually thank God (I Thes. 5:18). Nothing endears a relationship like gratitude expressed, or spoils one like ingratitude.

9. Suffer with Him. Paul certainly knew Jesus well, and he speaks of knowing **the fellowship of His sufferings,** Philippians 3:10. You grow closer to people when you suffer with them.

10. Be real. God is all about reality and doesn't suffer hypocrisy. If you've got something amiss, don't try to hide it from Jesus; bring it out where He can cure it. People in a healthy, intimate relationship don't hide things from each other (except just before Christmas).

Given the right nutrients and the right environment, God then causes the growth, verse 5. His Holy Spirit works in us in ways that are further beyond our understanding than photosynthesis is. You've noticed that Peter shifts metaphors from an infant to a growing plant to a house being built up of **living stones**. We often say the church is not a building, but it is; just not a regular stick and brick building. It's a building made up of **living stones**, holding on to one another like bricks laid up in a running bond.

Here, we should look at Ephesians 4 again:

speaking the truth in love, we are to grow up in all aspects into Him, who is the head, even Christ, from whom the whole body, being fitted and held together by that which every joint supplies, according to the proper working of each individual part, causes the growth of the body for the building up of itself in love.

So we should add this to our list of 10 ideas: we grow a lot by helping others grow.

Whether we are talking about a newborn babe, a plant, or living stones, the same principles apply. We need the right environment and the right nutrients. Then light and water, which Jesus supplies in copious amounts, will cause the growth.

Growth requires an investment on our part: in time, resources, and effort. It would be unwise, knowing what we now know, to try to economize by investing *some* of what is required for growth but not *all* that is required. The right environment by itself won't cause growth, nor will the right nutrition by itself.

Both together won't cause growth if there is no spiritual life to begin with. If you are a dead stick, obviously you can't grow. But all is not lost – yet. If God can cause Aaron's stick to sprout blossoms (Hebrews 9:4) and if He can revive Israel's dry bones (Ezekiel 37:4), then He can give you new life. You have to be born again by the living and abiding word of God. You need to go back to Peter's first chapter and start there.

God designed plants and Christians to grow and to reproduce themselves – to bear fruit. If you aren't bearing much in the way of fruit, probably you should give more attention to your growth: either your environment or your nutritional intake, or both. Or maybe you don't concern yourself to walk closely with Jesus. If so, don't expect growth.

We'll let the words of Jesus close our discussion:

[You] **Abide in Me, and I in you. As the branch cannot bear fruit of itself, unless it abides in the vine, so neither can you, unless you abide in Me. I am the vine, you are the branches; he who abides in Me, and I in him, he bears much fruit; for apart from Me you can do nothing,** John 15:4-5.

Chapter 8

2:5, 9-10, That You May Be a Royal Priesthood

⁵ you also, as living stones, are being built up as a spiritual house for a holy priesthood, to offer up spiritual sacrifices acceptable to God through Jesus Christ.

⁹ But you are A CHOSEN RACE, A royal PRIESTHOOD, A HOLY NATION, A PEOPLE FOR *God's* OWN POSSESSION, that you may proclaim the excellencies of Him who has called you out of darkness into His marvelous light;
¹⁰ for you once were NOT A PEOPLE, but now you are THE PEOPLE OF GOD; you had NOT RECEIVED MERCY, but now you have RECEIVED MERCY.

On the next page I have diagrammed I Peter 2: 5, 9-10, with modifiers centered under the word they modify; equal parts of speech and conjunctions are flush left with each other. We will refer to this diagram repeatedly as we study the text.

Verse 5

You are being built up
> **also,**
> **as living stones,**
>> **as a house**
>>> **spiritual**
>>> **for a holy priesthood,**
>>> **to offer up sacrifices**
>>>> **spiritual**
>>>> **acceptable**
>>>>> **to God**
>>>>> **through Jesus Christ.**

Verses 9-10

> **You are**
>>> **a chosen race,**
>>> **a royal priesthood,**
>>> **a holy nation,**
>>> **a people for God's own possession,**
>>> **that**
>>> **you may proclaim the excellencies**
>>>>> **of Him**
>>>>>> **who called you**
>>>>>>> **out of darkness**
>>>>>>> **into His marvelous light;**
>>>>>>> **for**
>>>>>>> **once you were not a people,**
>>>>>>> **but**
>>>>>>> **now you are the people of God;**
>>>>>>> **you had not received mercy,**
>>>>>>> **but**
>>>>>>> **now you have received mercy.**

We have been taking an unconventional approach to the first part of chapter 2, analyzing it from several, different angles rather than following Peter's order. It's not that I know better than Peter and the Holy Spirit how to present these concepts, but because, as one who is called upon to explain God's word and not just to read it, it seemed good to me not to pass too quickly over principles that are so fundamental to our walk and too heavy to treat lightly. Peter is talking about foundation stones. The worst way to economize on a building is to lay a shallow foundation.

Verses 1-5 tell us that all the blessings described in the first chapter of this epistle were given to us that we may grow into something that we weren't before we met Christ. Verses 6-8, which we'll pull out for more extensive treatment in the next chapter, remind us that we are following One who has been rejected by men. We need to get a good grasp on that fact and know why it is the case. Jesus never understated the fact that following Him involved some danger and sacrifice. Christianity, lived right, is an adventure.

Now in verses 5, 9, and 10 Peter says that we are being built into a royal priesthood. Priests were go-betweens, concerned with representing the people before God and with representing God before the people. And those two duties will form our outline.

I have included my diagram of these verses above because we'll need to refer to them as this chapter progresses. Unless the sentence is a simple one, and sometimes even if it is, it is often very helpful when interpreting a passage, to diagram the sentences. The Bible is very precise. Diagramming helps us to be precise with our interpretations. This might be a new tool for you to put in your Bible study methods toolbox.

Diagramming is a great way to make observations from the word of God that you might otherwise miss. You'll find relationships, lists, contrasts, parallels, logical connections, and, not incidentally, the author's outline. Diagramming forces you to decide why each word is in the sentence, what noun or verb each modifier is addressing and what it is saying about it. It is the best way I know for figuring out what the sentence is actually saying grammatically and to get a visual understanding.

There is no need, usually, to know all the parts of speech, although that helps. I just put the core sentence on one line: subject, verb (which might be a form of *to be* under which I would place the predicate nominative(s)), and direct object if there is one. Then I put (most) modifiers/modifying phrases under the middle of the word or phrase it modifies. Adjectives, adverbs, prepositional phrases, and subordinate clauses are all modifiers. Equal parts of speech, such as the four predicate nominatives in verse 9, are aligned directly below one another. I don't concern myself to make a complete diagram. For example, I don't separate out every modifier, necessarily. I only do enough to figure out the sentence.

Look at the diagram and you'll see what I mean. This diagram reveals the outline of the passage and sets out words and concepts that call for further investigation. If you examine the diagram you will see that the priesthood was responsible for two things, mainly: offering sacrifices (verse 5) and telling people about God (verses 9-10). So the believer is chosen by God and built up…

To Offer Spiritual Sacrifices, 5

To Proclaim His Excellencies, 9-10

We are a spiritual house for a holy priesthood in order...

To Offer Spiritual Sacrifices, 5

5 you also, as living stones, are being built up as a spiritual house for a holy priesthood, to offer up spiritual sacrifices acceptable to God through Jesus Christ.

We'll start with the subject of the sentence, **you**, speaking of regular Christians. All Christians form the priesthood, not just some who are designated pastors. Martin Luther, during the Reformation, came to realize from his study
116

of this passage that every Christian is designated a priest, so he began to teach concept of the priesthood of the believer. Good for him. But in trying to implement this doctrine in the churches, he found that the ordinary Christian was making a mess of it, so he abandoned a sound doctrine. You can't expect one man to accomplish everything in so large an undertaking as the Reformation.

But there were two problems that could have been corrected had time permitted: 1) Luther had some wrong ideas, carried over from his Roman Catholic days, about what the priests should be doing, and 2) he was dealing with a woefully untaught bunch of believers, since the Roman Catholic Church prohibited laymen from having Bibles.

Initial failure in application does not make a good doctrine into a bad doctrine. We should persist in sound doctrine if we want success (Josh. 1:8).

Looking at the diagram, the modifiers under **you** are **also** and **as living stones.** The word **also** refers back to verse 4 where Jesus is called a living stone and where Peter points out two important facts about Jesus—He was **rejected by men**, and He is **choice and precious in the sight of God**.

Those two distinctions are applied to those who follow Jesus by the word **also** in verse 5. We **also** are **rejected by men**, because of our relationship to the rejected Messiah. But we **also** are **choice and precious in the sight of God,** for the same reason. If I am choice and precious in the sight of God, then rejection by men is not a great worry.

We are also living stones—living building blocks—that the Master Builder will put together into a living temple, a spiritual house. And that is the predicate part of the sentence— we **are being built up.** This is a passive verb—it's something that is being done to us. It is also a present tense verb—we are an ongoing construction site. Pardon our dust.

The Holy Spirit is the Master Builder, the on-sight Architect. He directs the process, dresses the building stones so they all fit, and ensures the successful completion of the building according to God's blueprint. Here's an interesting question: If the Spirit is the Master Builder and we are the construction site, who are the construction workers employed by the Spirit? We could name and describe a few of them: Bible Study (has a scholarly but playful look), Prayer (always looks serene), Hard Times (has a nasty disposition but does good work), Perseverance (has a gritty look but a pleasant demeanor).

Besides these, other Christians are also construction workers, according to Ephesians 4:11-16. The construction workers have to be recruited and trained; this is the job of the evangelists and the pastors and teachers. Then the trained construction workers build up the body of Christ, if they have a will to work according to God's orders. I say that because some neglect the work, and some workers, with a distorted view of things, see their job as demolition workers. The Master Builder deals with them in verses 17-32. (You should read those verses if you favor that kind of work.)

The church grows in two ways—inner growth (edification) and outer growth (evangelism). If neither is happening, the church will die a quick death. If only one is happening, it will die a slow death. If only inner edification is happening, the members will eventually get old and die off or else get bored and leave, with no one coming in to replace them. If only evangelism is happening, there will be no depth, no protection from disease or doctrinal attacks, no cohesiveness, and the church will eventually break up. If both are happening, the church will be strong and healthy, fruitful, and disease resistant.

Looking at the diagram, two phrases modify the predicate, which is to say, they put limits on what the verb means. Modifiers always limit the meaning of the word they modify. They make the meaning more specific (for example, "red, two-story house with a porch" is more specific than "house").

We are being built up **as a house.** What kind of house? The first modifier says that it's a **spiritual** house; a temple. You **know that your body is a temple of the Holy Spirit who is in you,** I Cor. 6:19. But we form a larger, more imposing edifice when we join together, as we are commanded to do. We are being built up as a spiritual house. We form a composite unity,
118

made up of living stones of all shapes and sizes and functions, held together by the Holy Spirit.

If we change metaphors for a minute and think of the body, all the cells in the body have certain essential needs, characteristics, and functions in common. They all have the same DNA, for example. They all have cell walls and nuclei. But cells differentiate to perform all the various duties the body needs to grow and stay healthy and functional. Heart cells cannot do what liver cells do, and vice versa. Both are necessary to the body, as are bone cells and brain cells. I have occasionally been called a bone head, sometimes even by other people, but bone cells don't function well as brain cells, at least in my experience.

If we forsake the assembling of ourselves together, as is the habit of some (Hebrews 10:25), then we function like a bunch of building blocks just scattered around on the ground, in actual effect being more like stumbling blocks than anything else.

Some people like to argue that a person can be a Christian without being a member of a church. Maybe so, if a single cell can continue to live on its own without being a member of the body. But Proverbs 18:1 says, **He who separates himself seeks *his own* desire, He quarrels against all sound wisdom**. The church is a redemptive agency, designed by God to make us more like Christ. Those who don't want to be a vital part of this redemptive agency reject God's purpose for themselves so they can continue to be their own gods with no one bothering them about it. This runs contrary to sound wisdom. Such people should take a good look to see if they really are true believers. II Corinthians 13:5 warns, **Test yourselves *to see* if you are in the faith; examine yourselves! Or do you not recognize this about yourselves, that Jesus Christ is in you-- unless indeed you fail the test?** According to I John, one of the distinguishing marks of a true believer is love for the brethren.

Except for extenuating circumstances, one cannot be an obedient Christian, or a growing Christian, or a construction worker Christian according to Ephesians 4, without functioning as an integral member of a local church. One living stone does not make a house. It just makes a stumbling block. And anyone who thinks he can walk with Christ on his own is betraying this fact: he is not coming to Christ in the close, habitual approach that verse 4 demands. If he were, verse 5 would be working in him, and he wouldn't be a loner.

The house that God is building up is **for a priesthood**, not for a single priest. What kind of priesthood? As the diagram reveals, the priesthood is a **holy** one, one that can offer **acceptable sacrifices**. Holiness in the priesthood is a non-negotiable with God. The acceptability of the gift is determined by the acceptability of the giver. **The sacrifice of the wicked is an abomination to the LORD**, Proverbs 15:8.

The priesthood represents God. Priests stand in God's place before the people. People judge God by what they see in His priests. The priests had better be holy! They had better be in a position of moral authority so they can demand holiness from God's people. Otherwise, they grossly misrepresent God. An unholy priesthood would be a lie, a blasphemy.

One specific caveat I should mention: God has zero tolerance for priests who also serve other gods. I would direct you to Jeremiah 44, Ezekiel 20, and the book of Hosea.

The diagram shows that the term **priesthood** is also modified by the purpose phrase, **to offer up sacrifices**. Now we get to the gist of the first sentence, why is God doing all of this? Offering sacrifices is the priest's duty toward God. The sacrifices we are to offer are spiritual sacrifices, as opposed to bulls and goats. What are spiritual sacrifices? Here is a partial list (called out by my underlines):

- **The sacrifices of God are <u>a broken spirit</u>; A broken and a contrite heart**, [when we have sinned], Psalm 51:17.

- **Offer to God a sacrifice of <u>thanksgiving</u>**, Psalm 50:14, This sacrifice is mentioned repeatedly throughout the Bible. And it's in contrast to those who suppress the knowledge of God and refuse to give thanks (Romans 1).

120

- **To do <u>righteousness</u> and <u>justice</u> is desired by the LORD rather than sacrifice,** Proverbs 21:3.

- **I delight in <u>loyalty</u> rather than sacrifice, and in <u>the knowledge of God</u> rather than burnt offerings,** Hosea 6:6.

- **I DESIRE <u>COMPASSION</u>, AND NOT SACRIFICE,** Matthew 9:13.

- **I urge you therefore, brethren, by the mercies of God, to present <u>your bodies</u> a living and holy sacrifice, acceptable to God, which is your** [logical] **service of worship,** Romans 12:1.

- **Walk in <u>love</u>, just as Christ also loved you, and gave Himself up for us, an offering and a sacrifice to God as a fragrant aroma,** Ephesians 5:2. **AND <u>TO LOVE HIM</u> WITH ALL THE HEART AND WITH ALL THE UNDERSTANDING AND WITH ALL THE STRENGTH, AND <u>TO LOVE ONE'S NEIGHBOR</u> AS HIMSELF, is much more than all burnt offerings and sacrifices,** Mark 12:33.

- **Even if I am being poured out as a drink offering upon the <u>sacrifice and service of your faith</u>, I rejoice and share my joy with you all,** Philippians 2:17.

- **I have received everything in full, and have an abundance; I am amply supplied, having received from Epaphroditus what you have sent, a fragrant aroma, an acceptable sacrifice, well-pleasing to God,** Philippians 4:18. This refers to the <u>financial support</u> for God's work, sent by the financially-challenged church in Philippi.

- **Through Him then, let us continually offer up a sacrifice of <u>praise</u> to God, that is, the fruit of lips that <u>give thanks to His name</u>,** Hebrews 13:15.

- **Do not neglect <u>doing good</u> and <u>sharing</u>; for with such sacrifices God is pleased,** Hebrews 13:16

- **Ministering as a priest the gospel of God, that my offering of the Gentiles might become acceptable,**

sanctified by the Holy Spirit, Romans 15:16. This refers to making new disciples.

All these constitute sacrifices acceptable to God if they are done through Jesus Christ by a holy priesthood. Only those who are in Christ are acceptable to God and can therefore offer sacrifices that are acceptable. Offering spiritual sacrifices is the duty of a priest toward God. Now we move on to the duty of the priest toward men.

To Proclaim His Excellencies, 9-10

9 But you are A CHOSEN RACE, A royal PRIESTHOOD, A HOLY NATION, A PEOPLE FOR *God's* OWN POSSESSION, that you may proclaim the excellencies of Him who has called you out of darkness into His marvelous light;
10 for you once were NOT A PEOPLE, but now you are THE PEOPLE OF GOD; you had NOT RECEIVED MERCY, but now you have RECEIVED MERCY.

Referring again to our diagram, verses 9-10 contain four Old Testament allusions, all of which carry significant meaning. The phrase **a chosen race** refers us back to I Peter 1:1-2, **we are chosen according to the foreknowledge of God the Father**. Israel was God's chosen people long before the church was, but was set aside for the duration of the church age. The phrase comes from Deuteronomy 7:6-9:

"For you are a holy people to the LORD your God; the LORD your God has chosen you to be a people for His own possession out of all the peoples who are on the face of the earth. The LORD did not set His love on you nor choose you because you were more in number than any of the peoples, for you were the fewest of all peoples, but because the LORD loved you and kept the oath which He swore to your forefathers, the LORD brought you out by a mighty hand, and redeemed you from the house of slavery, from the hand of Pharaoh king of Egypt. Know therefore that the LORD your God, He is God, the faithful God, who keeps

His covenant and His lovingkindness to a thousandth generation with those who love Him and keep His commandments.

Then Peter uses a curious phrase. He says that we are a **royal priesthood.** Those two words normally weren't used together. The Aaronic priests were not royalty. They came from the tribe of Levi, whereas David's line of kings came from the tribe of Judah. The Mosaic Law kept the priesthood separate from the government and vice versa (although the government was *not* to be separate from faithful obedience to God). To understand this combination, we have to go back before the Aaronic priesthood to the patriarchs.

The patriarchs were rulers who served as priests before the Mosaic covenant was received (c. BC 1445). These included Abraham, Isaac, and Jacob, Job, Jethro, Moses, and, of course, Melchizedek, the king-priest of Salem. We are saved according to the covenant made with Abraham and fulfilled by Christ, not according to the Mosaic covenant (Galatians 3). So our priesthood also harkens back to a time before the Mosaic covenant.

We don't have to be from Aaron's lineage to be a priest. We do have to be born into God's family through Jesus Christ. Revelation 5:9f says, **for Thou wast slain, and didst purchase for God with Thy blood men from every tribe and tongue and people and nation. And Thou hast made them to be a kingdom and priests to our God; and they will reign upon the earth.** Jesus is **a high priest forever according to the order of Melchizedek** (Hebrews 6:20), because He was not from Aaron's line. So we who are in Christ would be priests of that same order. And, like Melchizedek and Jesus, we abide as priests perpetually.

Peter then says that we are **a holy nation.** He gets this from Exodus 19:5-6:

"'Now then, if you will indeed obey My voice and keep My covenant, then you shall be My own possession among all the peoples, for all the earth is Mine; and you shall be to Me a kingdom of priests and a holy nation.' These are the words that you shall speak to the sons of Israel."

Israel was set aside because of their apostasy; they refused to be holy, even when their long-expected Messiah appeared calling for their repentance. Because they would not be holy (they thought they already were, but they weren't), they failed to produce the fruit God expected of them. So as Jesus said in Matthew 21:43, **"Therefore I say to you, the kingdom of God will be taken away from you, and be given to a nation producing the fruit of it."** The church is that holy nation during the church age. (Nevertheless, the promises made to Israel will be fulfilled to Israel. The Bible is very insistent on that point. After the church is raptured, the last seven years of Israel's time will resume, Dan. 9.)

Peter says that we are **a people for God's own possession.** This also came from Exodus 19:5. **The Word became flesh and dwelt among** us, John 1:14. **He came to His own** [the Jews]**, and His own did not receive Him**, John 1:11. So God gave another chosen people to His Son for His own possession. In fact, that choice was made sometime in eternity past (Ephesians 1). In John 6:36f Jesus said, **But I said to you, that you have seen Me, and yet do not believe. All that the Father gives Me shall come to Me, and the one who comes to Me I will certainly not cast out.** And in John 10:16 He said, **I have other sheep, which are not of this fold** [i.e., not of Israel]**; I must bring them also, and they shall hear My voice; and they shall become one flock with one shepherd.** The gospel broke down the barrier of the dividing wall so that Jews and Gentiles were together in the body of Christ.

In our diagram, the word **that** in verse 9 introduces a purpose clause. Why has God done all these things for us? Here we come to the gist of verses 9-10. Our purpose, that for which we were chosen and blessed by God, is **that we may proclaim the excellencies of Him who has called us**.

One of the profound questions of life is this: Why am I here; what is my purpose on this earth? Failure to find a satisfactory answer to that question has caused many people to follow vain pursuits in search of meaning and eventually to give up all hope for meaning. (See Ecclesiastes.) Others abandon themselves to the despair of meaninglessness. Many end their own lives as a result. Some of those, lashing out in anger at the cruel world, take others with them in mass-murder suicides. The Bible provides a rich, multi-faceted answer to the question. One facet of that purpose is to proclaim the excellencies of God. That is a great and worthy purpose. **Proclaim** is a unique word that speaks of publishing or advertising something otherwise unknown.

What are these **excellencies** that we are to proclaim? The word speaks primarily of God's great deeds, particularly His great work of redemption. This is an expansion, by the way, of what Peter said in 1:3, **Blessed be the God and Father of our Lord Jesus Christ.** To bless God means to speak well of Him. We speak well of Him by proclaiming His excellencies.

I Peter 1:3 mentions one of the excellencies, **His great mercy**. With that wondrous trait priming our pump, we would also proclaim His attributes that drive His actions: His love, His grace, His truthfulness, His sovereignty over the universe He created, and His unfathomable wisdom.

In fact, every attribute of God, every character trait, and, in particular, every action of God make up the body of what Peter calls His **excellencies**. So we proclaim His omniscience, omnipotence, omnipresence, and immutability, His holiness, righteousness, absolute perfection in every way, goodness, kindness, longsuffering love, and justice. The Psalms are continually extolling God's nature and character, and His mighty deeds. You can get a big list from Psalms.

The priest is to speak well of God. He presents God in His glory to the people. This is essential for bringing people to Christ, telling them all about God's great deeds and all His perfections. Many people neglect Christ because they don't think highly enough of God. We are in a particularly strong position to tell people about the great things God can do for them, because He has done those things for us.

If we consult our diagram again for the last part of verse 9 and verse 10, we will see three contrasts (these didn't reveal themselves to me as such until I diagrammed the sentence). Three negatives are contrasted with three positives concerning how we were before we met Christ and what He has now done for us.

On the negative side, we used to be in **darkness** (we didn't really know anything, spiritually speaking), we were once **not a people** (we didn't really belong anywhere), and we had **not received mercy** (we didn't really have any hope).

On the positive side, now we are in **His marvelous light** (we are a royal priesthood, so we are light-bearers), **we are the people of God** (a holy nation and a people for His own possession), and **we have received mercy** (a chosen race with a great eternal destiny).

Blessed be the God and Father of our Lord Jesus Christ! Our very existence, in our present condition as opposed to our former condition, is a trophy of God's triumphant grace.

This is why God chose us and called us. This is why He builds us up. We are a priesthood formed to offer up spiritual sacrifices to God and to proclaim the excellencies of God. If you want to know God's will for your life, there it is. Everything else is just details. But if you ignore your main purpose, the details seem overwhelming and undirected.

What applications can we draw from this passage?

1. Our first objective should be to come to Christ in that close, habitual approach that verse 4 commands and that is so beautifully exemplified in Exodus 33 by Moses and Joshua going regularly outside the camp to the tent of meeting to interact with God face to face. All the rest of what they did, and their amazing successes, came from those meetings with God.

2. As living stones, we have our place and function in the spiritual house. We have other living stones surrounding us and holding us in place, and we help hold them in place.

3. We are to be a holy priesthood. God has always demanded, **"You shall be holy for I am holy."** Nothing you do for God is acceptable to God unless you are holy. Only our unity with Jesus makes us holy.

4. You have an identity as a member of God's chosen race.

5. You are royalty; your destiny is to reign with Christ forever.

6. You have sacred duties as a priest. You must concern yourself with faithful attendance to those duties.

7. You are owned by God; He bought you with a price. He will not let you go. This is the basis for both our service and our security.

8. You have a message worth publishing abroad. Other people are still in darkness and need to hear it, and some want to know if there is a God who can really accomplish their redemption.

9. Humility does not mean that we ought to feel small and unimportant. Humility means that we live in obedience to God. The arrogance of man says, "I know better than God; I'll do what I want." Humility says, "God knows best; I'll do what He wants." The fact of the matter is that we are very important, not only to the God who made us and redeemed us and gave us important work to do, but also to the fellow Christians whom we are building up, and to people who are also called but who haven't yet come to Christ for salvation.

It is very important how we live—what we are, what we do, and what we say. So Peter addresses our lifestyle in the rest of his letter.

Chapter 9
2:6-8, Rejected by Men
or
What Were They Thinking?

⁶ For *this* is contained in Scripture: "BEHOLD I LAY IN ZION A CHOICE STONE, A PRECIOUS CORNER *stone*, AND HE WHO BELIEVES IN HIM SHALL NOT BE DISAPPOINTED."

⁷ This precious value, then, is for you who believe. But for those who disbelieve, "THE STONE WHICH THE BUILDERS REJECTED, THIS BECAME THE VERY CORNER *stone*,"

⁸ and, "A STONE OF STUMBLING AND A ROCK OF OFFENSE"; for they stumble because they are disobedient to the word, and to this *doom* they were also appointed.

Why was Jesus, the long-expected Messiah, rejected by the people He came to save? This is a vitally important question. A wrong answer here will give us the wrong answer to the *most* important questions of life: Who is Jesus Christ, and what am I going to do about Him?

So we must ask, was the rejection of Jesus based on sound wisdom, or was it incredibly foolish? Was it based upon truth or upon falsehoods? Does rejecting Jesus protect us from an evil man, or does it subject us to the judgment of God? If Jesus was rejected by His own people, as John 1:11 admits, why should anyone else believe in Him? It's an important question, because if the Jewish leaders of Jesus' day were right to reject Jesus, then people are right to reject Him today.

It is important to us, personally, because we have put our faith in Jesus alone for our eternal salvation, and as Paul pointed out, **if Christ has not been raised, your faith is worthless; you are still in your sins. If we have hoped in**

Christ in this life only, we are of all men most to be pitied, I
Cor. 15:17, 19. Peter's original audience was feeling the
rejection of those who rejected Jesus. In other words, they were
rejected by their peers. That was a disconcerting state of affairs.
They needed to know that they made the right choice.

It is important to us, personally, because a lot of people
we care about are rejecting Jesus right now, either actively or
by their indifference. If we can understand why the majority of
Jesus' contemporaries rejected Him we might be able to
address those reasons as we urge people to trust Christ today.
So what were they thinking?

In this chapter we will look at the precious cornerstone
to see what kind of a person it is that people are rejecting. Then
we will look at the rejection itself, to see if we can figure out
what they were thinking. Peter's outline is:

The Precious Cornerstone, 4-7a

Rejected by Men, 7b-8

The Precious Cornerstone, 4-7a

**⁶ For *this* is contained in Scripture: " BEHOLD I LAY IN
ZION A CHOICE STONE, A PRECIOUS CORNER *stone*,
AND HE WHO BELIEVES IN HIM SHALL NOT BE
DISAPPOINTED."**

⁷ This precious value, then, is for you who believe.

Who is this Jesus who claims to be the Christ, the
Anointed One, appointed by God to be the savior and the judge
of the world? This list could go on for many pages but we'll
limit it to these 12:

1. He is the light of the world, John 1:4f; 9:5.

2. He is the anointed one, Luke 4:18f; John 3:34; Psalm 2.

3. He is the good shepherd, John 10:14.

4. He is the bread of life, John 6:35, 51.

5. He is the healer and forgiver, Luke 5:22-25; Mark 2:5-11.

6. He is the way, the truth, and the life, John 10:9; 14:6.

7. He is the resurrection and the life, John 11:25f.

8. He holds the keys of death, Revelation 1:17f.

9. He is the Prince of Peace, Isaiah 9:6.

10. He is the power and wisdom of God, I Corinthians 1:24; Colossians 2:2f.

11. He is the only begotten Son of God, John 3:16.

12. He is the exact representation of God's nature, Hebrews 1:3.

Consider the nature of the one rejected by men but choice and precious in the sight of God. Jesus was the most attractive person who ever lived on earth (Isaiah 53:2). Yet He had no stately form or majesty or astounding good looks, that people should be drawn to Him on that account. Yet they *were* drawn to Him, in droves. How many truth-tellers in our day could draw an all-day audience of over 10,000 without trying? His attractiveness was in who He was and how He was in His personal and public life. It was in His interactions with people and in the truth and grace of His teaching.

He was humble and gentle. He had a loving sense of humor, calling James and John "sons of thunder," and talking about camels going through the eyes of needles. He loved people. Children crowded around Him; everyone did. He was affectionate and compassionate. He was an encourager. He was not judgmental, but was a forgiver. He was full of grace and truth.

He never wronged anyone, never lied, never did any of those things that rightly incur resentment. He didn't have a selfish bone in His body. He never tricked anyone into anything; never exploited or took unfair advantage of anyone. He was never rude, even to those who were rude to Him.

He wasn't a grasping individual, but would take the servant's role, even when no one else would. But that doesn't mean that He was weak, for He was not. He deferred to no man.

He was courageous, and steady as a rock; perfect in obeying God. But He had no need to throw his weight around. He was without reproach in His use of authority.

He did all things well. His mind was quick and precise, deep and insightful. He was a thinker's thinker and a man of action's man of action. He was in favor with God and with men. He was incredibly wise and yet He could teach so that anyone with ears to hear could understand. He was the embodiment of wholesomeness and truth and righteousness. Jesus was exactly the kind of man you would want for a king.

He was in fact, the man of God's own choosing to be the Messiah of Israel, the Savior of the world, and the King of Kings. Verse 4 says that Jesus was precious in the sight of God. That means that He was prized, honored, costly, in fact unequalled in value, irreplaceable. No one else could have done what Jesus did.

Those who say that Jesus is just one of many ways to God do not understand the problem Jesus had to solve, what He had to do to be the way, the truth, and the life, and what He had to be in order to do what He had to do. In fact, it could be said that such people don't understand anything at all about the real God or the nature of their sin problem.

He is a living stone, and in fact a living stone that gives life to other stones—us who believe in Him. Verse 6 is a quotation of Isaiah 28:16: **Therefore thus says the Lord GOD, "Behold, I am laying in Zion a stone, a tested stone, a costly cornerstone for the foundation, firmly placed. He who believes in it will not be disturbed."** Here God says that Jesus is a tested stone, fit to establish the character of the whole building.

It's enlightening to study megalithic construction practices from ancient times, how they constructed large buildings using stones that weighed up to 80 tons. (Semi trucks normally are limited to carrying 40 tons.) They were very precise in laying out their building, in quarrying the huge stones and getting the sizes and angles perfect, within a small fraction of a degree. They could do things 4,000 years ago that we can't do now. We can build a skyscraper over 800 meters high in

Dubai, but we can't build a pyramid to equal the ones at Giza in Egypt. They could shape their stones off site, to the specifications they received for each stone, haul them to the building site, and lift them into place.

We read in I Kings 6:1 about the construction of Solomon's Temple: **And the house, while it was being built, was built of stone prepared at the quarry, and there was neither hammer nor axe nor any iron tool heard in the house while it was being built.** These great stones were transported by various means to the building site. Then they would lift them up and put them in place with a perfect fit. In many (perhaps all) cases, each stone was cut to fit in one, specific place. Many of the stones had interlocking notches so they wouldn't be dislodged by temperature changes and earthquakes.

I Kings 7:9ff tell of the stones used to build Solomon's Temple:

All these were of costly stones, of stone cut according to measure, sawed with saws, inside and outside; even from the foundation to the coping, and so on the outside to the great court. And the foundation was of costly stones, even large stones, stones of ten cubits and stones of eight cubits. And above were costly stones, stone cut according to measure, and cedar.

This work required a large work force. II Chronicles 2:17f tell about it:

Solomon numbered all the aliens who were in the land of Israel, following the census which his father David had taken; and 153,600 were found. And he appointed 70,000 of them to carry loads, and 80,000 to quarry stones in the mountains, and 3,600 supervisors to make the people work.

Given the difficulty in moving and raising the stone, you can bet that they tested every stone before it left the quarry to be absolutely certain that it matched the specifications. The specifications that Jesus had to meet had been spelled out by God in the hundreds of Old Testament prophecies that identified the Messiah and described what He would do. He was a tested stone.

He was not just any stone, at that; He was the costly cornerstone. This isn't the *ceremonial* cornerstone we can see above ground in more recent public buildings—the one inscribed with the date and names of dignitaries. The cornerstone that Peter has in mind was the first stone set when the foundation was laid. It was a big deal, accompanied by great ceremony. Often in pagan cultures, animal or human sacrifices were buried under the cornerstone.

The cornerstone determined the location and orientation of the entire building. It was the determining factor. If the cornerstone was not right, the building would not be right, and the builder would be ridiculed; and good luck finding another job.

I don't know if they actually did this, but one could cut the cornerstone to the exact, scaled proportions of the planned building and place the stone very precisely. Then the builders could sight along the corners of the stone to lay out the corners of the building and step off the dimensions of the cornerstone to get the lengths and height of the walls.

The cornerstone was firmly fixed so it could not be moved during the laying of the rest of the foundation stones and the other stones forming the building. When God lays His cornerstone, do you think that He will change it just because some disagreeable men find it not to their liking? Whenever a builder does his work, idlers gather to offer their advice, but no one listens to them.

God's cornerstone comes with a guarantee. I Peter 2:6 promises, **those who believe in Jesus will not be disappointed**, or as Isaiah put it, *disturbed*. If the cornerstone is firmly placed so it will not shift, then those who trust in Him and build their lives on Him will not be disturbed either. We won't have our hopes disappointed, as will **those who have bartered for another god,** Psalm 16:4.

Remember what Jesus said at the conclusion of His sermon on the mount:

Therefore everyone who hears these words of Mine, and acts upon them, may be compared to a wise man, who built his house upon the rock. And the rain descended, and the

floods came, and the winds blew, and burst against that house; and yet it did not fall, for it had been founded upon the rock. And everyone who hears these words of Mine, and does not act upon them, will be like a foolish man, who built his house upon the sand. And the rain descended, and the floods came, and the winds blew, and burst against that house; and it fell, and great was its fall.

Jesus is a precious value to us who believe in Him and build our lives upon Him. When I built my house in 1998, I laid the foundation footer under my house. No one ever sees it; I can't see it. But I value it more than any other part of the house.

The most important word in these verses is the giant word, "I", as in **"I lay in Zion a choice stone."** Man's rejection of the cornerstone does not change God's choice.

Psalm 2 should be very disturbing to any rebel who reads it:

The kings of the earth take their stand, and the rulers take counsel together against the LORD and against His Anointed: "Let us tear their fetters apart, and cast away their cords from us!" He who sits in the heavens laughs, the Lord scoffs at them. Then He will speak to them in His anger and terrify them in His fury: "But as for Me, I have installed My King upon Zion, My holy mountain."

Why would anyone think that he can nullify God's choice, or get around it somehow? God's sovereign choice is not subject to veto or amendment by anyone. Man doesn't get to choose who will be the Messiah, or what qualifications He must meet, how He will rule, what He will do, or when He does it. Man does not get to decide anything in that regard except whether he will go with God's choice or be shattered, like earthenware shattered by a rod of iron.

Now therefore, O kings, show discernment; take warning, O judges of the earth. Worship the LORD with reverence, and rejoice with trembling. Do homage to the Son, lest He become angry, and you perish in the way, for His wrath may soon be kindled. How blessed are all who take refuge in Him, Psalm 2:10-12.

How could anyone reject Jesus when He was precisely the Savior and Messiah God ordained and exactly what our sins required? But He was, indeed, rejected by men. On what possible basis, then? What were they thinking when they decided that they would not have the Son of God to rule over them?

Rejected by Men, 7b-8

7bBut for those who disbelieve, "THE STONE WHICH THE BUILDERS REJECTED, THIS BECAME THE VERY CORNER *stone*,"

8 and, "A STONE OF STUMBLING AND A ROCK OF OFFENSE"; for they stumble because they are disobedient to the word, and to this *doom* they were also appointed.

The builders were the political and religious leaders of the Jews, the ones who were so anxious to kill Jesus. So the question is: were they right, or were they wrong? Should others accept their verdict, or was their decision based upon the wrong kind of evaluation? It's critical that we ask this question. Many people trust their religious leaders to make the religious decisions for them, figuring that if the decision is wrong, the religious leaders will be held guilty and those who trusted them will be excused because they didn't know any better.

To put it simply, that is the stupidest thing I've ever heard. Each individual will be judged for his own choices. See, for example, Ezekiel 33:1-6. God doesn't let sinners shift their responsibility onto someone else. On judgment day, He will remove all sin and all who refuse to be separated from their sin from the earth forever. It won't matter what their religion was or who made their choices for them.

The term **disbelieve** does not mean unable to believe; it means unwilling to believe. Belief is a choice. And that choice is not always based upon sound logic or the relevant facts as it should be. An honest man will say, "I can't believe that," if he sees that the conclusion is not supported by facts and sound logic. But an honest man will change his mind if the facts and the reasoning support the conclusion.

But here's the problem: man's mind does not always work in an honest way. You've been in enough arguments to know that. The mind has three parts: intellect, will, and emotions. Neither the will nor the emotions are inclined or equipped to work rationally. They can't evaluate truth claims, consult history, analyze arguments, reason, or predict the consequences of choices. God designed the intellect to do those things and to decide what to believe and what to choose. Sinful men often operate according to their will and emotions rather than their intellect. Genesis 3 shows the result when desire usurps the place of the intellect. If the will has its own agenda, then it will reject any contrary facts and arguments, no matter how compelling, and no matter how intellectually astute the person is otherwise.

The disobedient will compels the intellect to reject truth and to accept falsehoods as if they were true. Eventually the abused intellect can't tell the difference between real truth and "expedient truth." This "personal truth," as it's also called, is nothing but the old self-delusion. Disobedience causes disbelief, and disbelief causes disobedience. If they were planets, disbelief and disobedience would be orbiting each other.

People have a facility for refusing to believe anything that gets in the way of their own desires. It's very common, when the authors of the Scriptures are speaking about disbelief, to skip the cause (leaving the reader to infer disbelief) and go straight to the result, which is disobedience. That's how inseparably disbelief and disobedience are connected. On the other hand, belief and obedience are also intertwined. Obedience implies belief, and belief implies obedience.

So, it seems to me that in trying to explain why anyone would reject Jesus, the answer will involve man's desire to do his own thing rather than obey his Creator. Independent desire was the root of the Fall of man, and it is the root of continued disobedience.

136

To disobey God, one has to do something about his knowledge of the righteous Judge. He has to somehow deny it or suppress it – keep it out of sight and out of mind. That's why Adam and Eve hid from God after they ate the forbidden fruit. Everyone knows that there is a God who created everything and to whom they are accountable. Romans 1 says, **that which is known about God is evident within them; for God made it evident to them.** I believe that. I remember things that happened when I was two years old. But I don't remember a time in my life when I did not know that there is a God who is in charge of everything. There was never a time when my mind realized, "What?! There's a God! I had no idea!"

Knowledge of God's existence is one of life's givens. It's hard-wired into our brains before we were born. It's suppressed by many, but it's there, all the same. In urgent times of great fear or tragedy, when our conscious mind is too absorbed with the immediate concern to keep the knowledge of God suppressed, out it pops. That innate knowledge of God is jarred out by extreme circumstances when "personal truth" isn't working. That's why they say there are no atheists in foxholes.

Those who hate God should explain to us why they harbor such bitter animosity toward someone they say doesn't even exist. I have no hatred whatsoever for trolls or goblins or fairies or flying, purple people-eaters (and not just because I am not purple). I have no hatred for Molech, or Isis, or Ba'al, or any other false god; they don't really exist. They are non-entities. Why would you waste your time hating a god that doesn't exist?

So what about the people who say God doesn't exist? All we *can* say is that there is a disconnection between what they know, deep down inside, and what they *think* they believe. Romans 1 says that they suppress the truth about God.

On one level, we could call it the operational level, they don't believe that God exists and so don't believe His word. This way of thinking permits the sinner to operate according to his own will without being scared to death of God. So it is his chosen way of thinking. It doesn't exactly match what he knows, but how many of us live in a way that is perfectly consistent with what we know?

Sinful people learn to live with their inconsistencies and eventually even deny that truth needs to be consistent. That's why eastern religions don't care about absolute truth. I've noticed that the further one gets from God the more comfortable he is with inconsistencies. But truth is consistent, so such people are not living in truth.

The leaders of the Jews could not deny that Jesus did miracles as the Old Testament predicted, demonstrating His divine identity and authority. Or that He healed like the Messiah was supposed to do. Or that He had no sin. Or that He taught like the Messiah was supposed to do. Or that He fulfilled Messianic prophecies. Jesus had all the credentials. No one could deny it.

The problem was that Jesus was a threat to their vested interests. If He was in, they were out. They hoped for a Messiah who would meet their demands and make none of His own. They wanted a Messiah who wouldn't mess with their profits. They weren't willing to lose the power, privilege, and prestige of their office. The unacceptable (to them) consequence of making the right choice compelled them to make the wrong choice. Their self-serving disobedience compelled their disbelief. They put all their eggs in a fallacious *ad consequentium* argument (appeal to consequences). "We don't like the consequences of this being true, therefore, it isn't true." One should be suspicious of such reasoning.

And they were greatly mistaken, thinking that they were in charge and that their decision actually determined who could be the Messiah. They tested Jesus (*rejected* has the same root word used twice in 1:7, *proof* and *tested*) and found Him not to be what they were looking for in a Messiah.

Talk about blowing a test! They thought they were testing Jesus, but Jesus *is* the test! God's test question is, "What are you going to do about My Son Jesus Christ?" How could they have been so wrong? They ignored God's standards, and graded Jesus against their own standards. A bad test question will give you bad results. Jesus had all the right answers, but they were asking the wrong questions and had the wrong grading sheet.

They wanted a Messiah who would do things their way, meet their conditions, and in their time frame. They picked the Old Testament prophecies that they liked for the Messiah, and ignored the rest. And they refused to meet the conditions the Old Testament said would have to be met before the kingdom would be restored.

So, they gave Jesus a failing grade instead of the perfect score He deserved. They tested Jesus, and *they* failed the test, because God gave Jesus a perfect score.

If we consider the reasoning process that resulted in the rejection of the Messiah, we see that their intent was dishonorable, their data was irrelevant, their process was illogical, their parameters were wrong, they improperly excluded critical data, their analysis was faulty, and their whole process was smeared with bias. It would be absurd to expect that such thorough blundering could produce a correct answer!

And yet many people since that time have rejected the Messiah without even conducting any test or examining any data for themselves. Instead, they just rubber-stamp other people's blundering and biased evaluations without question. That's a foolish and deadly mistake. But it's as common as intellectual and spiritual laziness; which is to say, very common. I wonder how many billions of people will suffer in hell forever, blaming someone else's bad choice? Believing someone else's bad choice was their own bad choice, and they are accountable for it. Bad choices produce bad consequences, no matter who makes the choice for you.

Jesus was rejected by men, but is choice and precious in God's sight. Choose carefully who you side with. Don't trust other people's bad choices; trust the proven word of God. The problem with living in denial is that you eventually slam into reality.

Picture a guy walking through the darkness, telling himself there is no danger ahead, even though many people have warned him about the big stone at the edge of a cliff. He is in charge of his own life. And it's more convenient to his purposes to deny the existence of the stone and the cliff. The stone, however, will not undo its existence, nor step aside, to please the man. So the man stumbles over the stone, falls over the cliff, and gets mangled. And then he curses the stone for being in his way.

People today have a great saying, "It is what it is." This is a simple statement of one of the fundamental presuppositions of logic. But they don't apply it very consistently.

Some take the phrase **and to this also they were appointed** as proof of the doctrine of double predestination. Some do this because they want to disprove the Biblical doctrine of predestination, others because they want to prove the unbiblical doctrine of double predestination. They interpret this phrase to mean that God predestines some to mercy, while the rest are divinely closed off from salvation, being predestined by God to eternal punishment.

But that doctrine would contradict all the "whosoever will may come" passages, such as John 3:16. It would make a mockery of Biblical statements like Acts 17:30f:

"Therefore having overlooked the times of ignorance, God is now declaring to men that all everywhere should repent, because He has fixed a day in which He will judge the world in righteousness through a Man whom He has appointed, having furnished proof to all men by raising Him from the dead."

How can God declare in good faith that all men everywhere should repent if He has previously decreed that most men are denied repentance by God's decree and doomed to hell? God never contradicts Himself or acts against His own will.

So the phrase has to be taken in its context to mean that God has appointed all those who are disobedient to the word to stumble over Jesus, just as the Jewish leaders did. In other words, God has no other plan for their salvation. And that interpretation has full, biblical support with no contradiction. We saw it in Psalm 2, for example. John 3:18 says, **He who believes in Him is not judged; he who does not believe has been judged already** [because Adam's sin is imputed to all men, Rom. 5; all men are born under the death penalty], **because he has not believed in the name of the only begotten**

Son of God [by which belief Christ's righteousness would have been imputed to him]. And John 3:36 says, **He who believes in the Son has eternal life; but he who does not obey the Son shall not see life, but the wrath of God abides on him.**

Why do people reject Jesus when the vast weight of evidence makes it unreasonable to reject Him? Jesus answers that question in John 3: 19f, **this is the judgment, that the light is come into the world, and men loved the darkness rather than the light; for their deeds were evil. For everyone who does evil hates the light, and does not come to the light, lest his deeds should be exposed.**

Disobedience compels disbelief. The desire to continue in one's sin requires the sinner to reject Jesus Christ, despite overwhelming evidence that Jesus is, indeed, the Son of God, the Savior of the world. The rejection of the Son of God certainly was not a good choice in Peter's day, and it is not a good choice now. The rejection of Jesus Christ was the cause of incredible loss for the Jews, a loss they are still suffering 2,000 years later.

All who reject Jesus will, in fact, suffer incredible loss for all of eternity. Eternal condemnation (where absolutely nothing goes the sinner's way) is a high price to pay for 70 years of vainly trying to have things his way. Those who reject Jesus in order to serve themselves do themselves the ultimate disservice.

The rejection of God's precious cornerstone was a terrible choice, made for all the wrong reasons and in spite of all the right reasons for accepting the One who was choice and precious in the sight of God.

The rejection of Jesus was not based on sound wisdom. It was incredibly foolish. It was not based upon the facts of the case. It was based upon falsehoods contrived to justify disobedience rather than an honest dealing with the word of God.

So, no one should concur with the decision of those who crucified the Son of God. The one who comes to Jesus **will not be disappointed**.

Chapter 10

2:11-12, The Witness of Excellent Behavior

**¹¹ Beloved, I urge you as aliens and strangers to abstain from fleshly lusts, which wage war against the soul.
¹² Keep your behavior excellent among the Gentiles, so that in the thing in which they slander you as evildoers, they may on account of your good deeds, as they observe *them,* glorify God in the day of visitation.**

Peter's first letter divides into two sections. The first part was 1:3—2:10: Salvation Is Secured to You by the Work of God. We now take up the second part, 2:11—5:14: Salvation Is Spread to Others by Your Excellent Behavior.

Some Christians try to excuse themselves from the duty of evangelism by saying, "I witness with my life." That's good, if they really do. This second part of I Peter is all about what it means to witness with our lives. And we will discover that witnessing with our lives includes witnessing with our mouths.

In fact, a credible and convincing witness requires both excellent behavior and the ready ability to explain the hope that is in us. People are motivated to consider Christ by watching Christians who are doing it the right way. But no one is saved apart from hearing and trusting the gospel (Romans 10:14).

Our text introduces Peter's second section, which teaches us about excellent behavior in the various areas of our lives. Peter knows where he's going with this letter before he starts it. So he has already shown the connection between salvation and behavior. Holy behavior is the logical (Rom. 12:1f) and inevitable (Jn. 7:38f) response to genuine salvation, 1:14-19. So Peter develops his first section in such a way as to "set up his shot" for the second section. To put it in more biblical terms, he first gives us the basis for action and then tells us what actions are fitting in that light.

There is an inner and an outer dimension to holiness. First there must be a compelling commitment to moral holiness in our inner life. This develops as a result of our personal, active commitment to obey our Lord and to let the Holy Spirit do His work. This is the subject of verse 11.

And then there is a consistent Christ-like behavior that grows from that inner root and shows outwardly in how we live our lives. Jesus spoke of this in John 7:38f:

"He who believes in Me, as the Scripture said, 'From his innermost being shall flow rivers of living water.'" But this He spoke of the Spirit, whom those who believed in Him were to receive; for the Spirit was not yet given, because Jesus was not yet glorified.

That is the subject of verse 12.

God does this sanctifying work on the inside; as He said in Jeremiah 31:33: **"I will put My law within them, and on their heart I will write it; and I will be their God, and they shall be My people."** Trying to appear holy on the outside while refusing God's sanctifying work inside is what causes hypocrisy and ruins our credibility. In such cases one's good deeds look like what they are: fake fruit put up for show on the branches of some nondescript bush. Jesus said that we know the tree by its fruit; a good tree produces good fruit and a bad tree produces bad fruit.

So Peter encourages first inner and then outward holiness, which will show in consistent, excellent behavior. If we want a successful witness, this is where we focus. His outline is simple:

Win the War Inside, 11

Keep Your Behavior Excellent, 12

Win the War Inside, 11

¹¹ Beloved, I urge you as aliens and strangers to abstain from fleshly lusts, which wage war against the soul.

A great way for one country to gain military advantage over another nation is to secretly infiltrate that nation with a flood of its own operatives ahead of time. And then when war happens, the infiltrated nation finds itself fighting the enemy within. An example of this is what Islam has been doing with the western nations the last couple of decades. Communists did it to America in the mid-1900's.

Like our Lord, we are the aggressors in the great battle to call sinners out of darkness into Christ's marvelous light. We are the "church militant," meaning that we are not to be passive in our evangelism. Every individual in the church is a soldier for Christ. And Christ infiltrates the world with His operatives. The difference is that we aren't to "fit in" by living like the world. We are to let our light shine for all to see. There's nothing sneaky or tricky about how we go about infiltrating our world. God wants the world to see us and to know what we're doing.

We have an enemy – our flesh, which wages war against the spirit. We were saved to be the aggressor (God told Adam to rule and subdue), but we were born infiltrated by sin. According to Romans 7 & 8 and Galatians 5, I am my own worst enemy. Consider who it is that gives you the most trouble in your walk with the Lord.

If we want to have individual victory outside, we first have to win the war inside against strong fleshly desires. In point of fact, we have three enemies: the flesh, Satan, and the evil world system all wage war against our soul, trying to turn us to their advantage, or at least to neutralize us in the battle so that our behavior is too inconsistent to be convincing. These fleshly lusts include sexual immorality, but almost every evil of humanity's sinful nature can still infect our flesh even though we no longer have a sin nature.

But it turns out that if we win the inner war against the flesh, we pretty much block the world and Satan in the bargain, as far as our own usefulness is concerned, because they make their appeal to the flesh.

Now the deeds of the flesh are evident, which are: immorality, impurity, sensuality, idolatry, sorcery, enmities,

strife, jealousy, outbursts of anger, disputes, dissensions, factions, envying, drunkenness, carousing, and things like these, of which I forewarn you just as I have forewarned you that those who practice such things shall not inherit the kingdom of God, Galatians 5: 19-21.

Do you not know that the unrighteous shall not inherit the kingdom of God? Do not be deceived; neither fornicators, nor idolaters, nor adulterers, nor effeminate, nor homosexuals, nor thieves, nor the covetous, nor drunkards, nor revilers, nor swindlers, shall inherit the kingdom of God. And such were some of you; but you were washed, but you were sanctified, but you were justified in the name of the Lord Jesus Christ, and in the Spirit of our God, I Corinthians 6:9-11.

These are some of the lusts that wage war against our souls. This war is a relentless, malicious aggression, and it rages within us. That makes it a civil war, which is the most *un*civil kind of war. So don't expect victory to come easily. And don't expect victory to bring a lasting peace! Paul, using another analogy, says:

Everyone who competes in the games exercises self-control in all things. They then do it to receive a perishable wreath, but we an imperishable. Therefore I run in such a way, as not without aim; I box in such a way, as not beating the air; but I buffet my body and make it my slave, lest possibly, after I have preached to others, I myself should be disqualified, I Corinthians 9:25ff.

Paul described this battle within when he wrote Romans 7:14-23. Hebrews 12 tells us to lay aside every encumbrance and the sin which so easily entangles us. It reminds us that Jesus endured the cross instead of (Greek *anti*) the joy set before Him, referring to His place in heaven that He left to come to earth. So we really fall short of His example if we have not yet resisted to the point of shedding blood in our striving against sin. A civil war is an unpleasant and bloody war.

We find in Hebrews 12 that the key to winning the inner war is to fix our eyes on Jesus, as our pattern and especially as our goal, but also as the author and perfecter of our faith. Your leader is Jesus Christ. Follow your leader and you will win the war.

Peter addresses his readers as **beloved**. We are the beloved of God. Being loved puts us under obligation. It does so even in human relationships, but all the more when the one who loves us is Jesus Christ. We must always keep in mind the extent of His love, how much it cost Him, and how much we have benefited from it. Such determined love, even being unconditional, calls for determined reciprocation. **"We love because He first loved us."**

This is before we even consider His lordship and providence in our lives. If Jesus commands us to continually abstain, then He also enables us to obey His command. He gave us a new nature and the Holy Spirit, so we can abstain from fleshly lusts even when the natives around us are promoting sensuality, immorality, and moral relativism.

How do you **abstain from fleshly lusts**? Lust is any strong desire, but usually has a negative connotation in the New Testament. You can't "just say *no*" to sin and expect the temptation to go away. If you just say *no* but continue to hang around the temptation, then you are giving yourself the opportunity to reconsider your choice. You have to make *no* your final answer and then get away from the enticement, otherwise *no* isn't really your final answer. You have to flee the temptation, not indulge in it. Nature abhors a vacuum; so does desire. You have to replace the bad desire with a good one.

Besides that, we have some other tips for victory over the fleshly lusts. Galatians 5:16 tells us, **Walk by the Spirit, and you will not carry out the desire of the flesh.** Do you walk each day in conscious reliance upon the Holy Spirit?

Romans 13:14 says, **Put on the Lord Jesus Christ, and make no provision for the flesh in regard to its lusts.** To indulge fleshly lusts, you have to step away from your Master. When you are presented with that choice, stay with Jesus. A good way to abstain from fleshly lusts is to build a stronger desire for what is good and right and honorable. "Clothes make the man." I don't put on good clothes to work under the truck. Put on the Lord Jesus Christ, whatever you are doing. If you have to step away from the Lord (put Him out of your mind) to do something, you shouldn't be doing that thing.

Galatians 5:13 says, **You were called to freedom, brethren; only do not turn your freedom into an opportunity for the flesh, but through love serve one another.** If we love others and focus on their needs, we will have less time and inclination to indulge ourselves. Don't pamper yourself by self-indulgence.

Ephesians 2:3 recalls: **Among them we too all formerly lived in the lusts of our flesh, indulging the desires of the flesh and of the mind, and were by nature children of wrath, even as the rest.** Self-indulgence defines our past, and it's hard to leave it behind.

It may help to remember Galatians 6:8: **For the one who sows to his own flesh shall from the flesh reap corruption, but the one who sows to the Spirit shall from the Spirit reap eternal life.** Our loving God warns us away from sins because they are by nature damaging, corrupting, and harmful.

In Proverbs 2 Solomon gave some very good advice that he wasn't wise enough to follow during part of his life:

Make your ear attentive to wisdom, incline your heart to understanding. Then you will discern the fear of the LORD, and discover the knowledge of God. Then you will discern righteousness and justice and equity and every good course. For wisdom will enter your heart, and knowledge will be pleasant to your soul; discretion will guard you, understanding will watch over you, to deliver you from the way of evil.

A *caveat* is in order: Don't take all this as if sanctification were a do-it-yourself project. You cannot sanctify yourself by fleshly effort. Remember Philippians 3:3: **we are the true circumcision, who worship in the Spirit of God and glory in Christ Jesus and put no confidence in the flesh.** And Galatians 3:3: **having begun by the Spirit, are you now being perfected by the flesh?** The Holy Spirit sanctifies us as we obey God. Fleshly efforts do not give us victory over fleshly lusts. That would be a conflict of interests, and it wouldn't work in our favor.

These fleshly lusts wage war against your soul. Fight them. Fight them like David fought Goliath – kill them all the way dead. After he dropped Goliath by slapping a stone deep into the giant's brain, David ran up and cut off his head, in case Goliath was playing possum. What a disaster that David didn't fight and win the war within when it came to Bathsheba. If you want to win the external battles, you first have to win the war inside.

Keep Your Behavior Excellent, 12

12 Keep your behavior excellent among the Gentiles, so that in the thing in which they slander you as evildoers, they may on account of your good deeds, as they observe *them*, glorify God in the day of visitation.

In verse 11 Peter called his readers **aliens and strangers**. *Alien* (sojourner) is a compound word that means to dwell beside. *Stranger* (pilgrim) is a synonym that means to travel through a strange place, away from one's own people, perhaps residing there for a short time. His point is that we are different than the natives here; we are foreigners. So we start off in a hole when it comes to changing the minds of those who are of the world.

Our world-view, our motives, our ethics, our ways, even our language are all different. So the natives will naturally be wary of us and perhaps biased against us, depending upon how excellent our behavior is and how rebellious they are toward God. They won't be swayed toward a godly world-view by the occasional good deed. They've seen that before, and even do good deeds themselves if it doesn't cost too much or interfere too much with their plans, or if it's for a friend, or if something is to be gained by it. They have their world-view; we have ours. The only way they will see the Biblical world-view as superior to theirs is if we who claim to follow the Bible are consistent in excellent behavior.

So, Peter puts the command **abstain** in verse 11 in the present tense, instructing us to abstain as a continual practice. We must be consistent. He emphasizes consistency again in verse 12 when he says, **Keep your behavior excellent.**

Consider what it means to keep something that others want to take away: how diligent you must be to guard it, how hard you must work and even fight to keep it, how you would avoid situations that would make it easier to lose what you want to keep. Do you remember the animated *Ice Age* movies, with the mammoth and the sloth? Think of that scrawny, little pre-historic squirrel trying to keep his one and only acorn. That's how we should struggle to keep our behavior excellent among the Gentiles.

Among the Gentiles is a phrase that referred to unsaved people. We are to keep our behavior excellent on a field that is slanted steeply toward immoral behavior. So we have to be all the more cautious, and we must not depend upon the cheers of a friendly crowd. Sin runs downhill; Christians have to run up hill.

We are playing an away game. It's their turf, and they play by their rules, and try to convince us that we have to play by their rules, too. But we don't. We aren't trying to win a game – Christ has already won it. We're trying to win them. We cannot win them to Christ playing by their rules. So we don't want to. And this world doesn't really belong to them or to Satan, anyway. It really belongs to our God. So we don't have to play by their rules.

The world in which we sojourn …

pursues a course of sensuality, lusts, drunkenness, carousals, drinking parties, and abominable idolatries. And in all this, they are surprised that we don't run with them into the same excess of dissipation, and they malign us, I Peter 4:3f.

These evil-doers slander Christians as the evil ones. If they think that what's twisted is straight, then what really *is* straight will look twisted to them. They're like the kid hanging upside-down by his knees on the swing-set, saying, "Hey, why is everyone upside-down?!"

Even now, true Christians are being classed with terrorist bombers as dangerous fundamentalists, even though it's been longer than I can remember since a fundamentalist Christian pastor called for jihad. This is nothing new. It's been the shape of the game from the beginning, when God created man as His agent to rule and subdue the earth. Satan is the accuser of the brethren, and his children follow suit. One of the best ways for a dangerous person to hide his dangerous intentions is to accuse his opponents of being the dangerous one.

If our ways are consistently better than the ways of non-believers, then some of them will be unable to avoid the conclusion that our Biblical world-view is better than theirs, because one's world-view is the ground out of which his actions grow. Once people start doubting their own world-view and begin to see the superiority of the Biblical world-view, then we have the opportunity to explain the reason for the hope that is in us.

Our excellent behavior will have built for us the podium from which we can proclaim the gospel effectively. So witnessing with our lives is essential. And to be effective, it must by consistent.

Whenever a politician is caught in some disqualifying sin, his own party rallies behind him to say that we must consider the whole body of his work and not hold this indiscretion against him in the coming election. They don't give Christians the same free pass. Whenever a Christian in public falls, worldlings gleefully exult, "How the 'mighty' have fallen! He's no better than the rest of us, so obviously his beliefs are no better than ours!" It's not a level playing field. So we have to be consistent.

It isn't our excellent behavior that saves us, of course. But our behavior is directly involved in the salvation of others because if affects the credibility of our gospel. If we do fail, the only remedy is genuine, heartfelt confession and repentance. And if the sin is public, then the confession and repentance must also be public so people don't blame God. And then it will take a considerable time of consistent excellent behavior to rebuild our credibility.

I built my own house and I can tell you that it takes much skill, effort, and expense to build a house. But we all know that one fool with a match can undo all that work in a few minutes. Every sin in our life is a fool with a match, ready to destroy the excellent reputation we've worked so hard to build.

All the members of a local church share a joint burden to keep all of our behaviors excellent. If we are watchful as we should be and see one of our fellow believers falling behind, we need to go get him before he falls into sin. To switch metaphors (and metaphors are made for switching), we must not let anyone in the herd straggle behind to face the hungry wolves alone.

If, in spite of our efforts, or due to our lack of effort, someone falls into sin, the others must rush to bring the errant believer back into obedience to God. And if they can't, because the one taken in sin refuses to repent, then the church needs to obey the Lord's discipline procedure for the sake of that person and for the sake of the church's witness.

I have been in churches long enough to have seen the biblical discipline procedure carried out several times according to the directions in Galatians 6:1, Matthew 18, Titus 3:10, and related passages. And I have seen believers who were taken in sin repent and return to following the Lord because that procedure was followed as far as necessary. I have also seen how sober the church got about avoiding sin when one of their members refused to repent after all four steps in Matthew 18 were applied and the rebellious person was put out of fellowship. How can the world take the church seriously if the church doesn't take sin seriously? If sin is a mere trifle, then the gospel is much adieu about nothing. And the church is irrelevant.

Now, concerning the **slander** – you should expect it, especially if you have the good witness of consistent excellent behavior. There will always be those who love their sin so much that they hate God with an active hatred. And they will hate everyone who makes God seem legitimate. So they eagerly join in Satan's efforts to ruin that Christian's witness. That's why **all who desire to live godly in Christ Jesus will be persecuted,** II Timothy 3:12. If they have no real accusations to bring against your character, they will make up false accusations. Don't worry about that. They did the same to Jesus. They also do it to each other around election time.

The readers of this letter were accused of rebelling against Rome, of cannibalism, of incest, of subversive activities against Rome's economy and social progress. They were accused of atheism for refusing to worship the emperor and the Roman gods. There is only one effective rebuttal to such false accusations, and that is the irrefutable witness of a consistently pure and benevolent life. Peter returns to this situation at the end of chapter 4. But here he says that people will observe your good deeds and respond positively when God visits them with the opportunity for salvation.

They will **glorify God in the day of visitation**. The day of visitation was an Old Testament concept that referred to occasions when God visited mankind for either judgment or blessing. Those who reject the blessing of God get the judgment of God.

In the New Testament the day of visitation usually indicates blessing and redemption, as Zacharias used it in Luke 1:68, for example: **"Blessed be the Lord God of Israel, for He has visited us and accomplished redemption for His people."**

The result of this day of visitation will be that those who are visited will glorify God, which most naturally would be the result of their experience of salvation, especially since Peter uses the words **so they may** (subjunctive mood). In other words they will glorify God voluntarily. The day of visitation, then, refers to the day the Holy Spirit brings that person to an understanding of his need for salvation and softens his heart to give up his sin and to respond in trusting obedience to the gospel.

Some of the people who slander us now will eventually join us in the kingdom of God. So our excellent behavior is a contributing factor in bringing them to saving faith.

Faithfulness in keeping our behavior excellent involves not only what we abstain from, but also the good things that we do. The term *excellent* (*kalos*) means beautiful of outward form.

152

In fact, it takes several words to convey the full meaning: lovely, winsome, gracious, fair to look at, noble. It describes the appearance of the outward behavior of those who are winning the inner war. Those who are excellent on the inside show up as excellent on the outside.

In fact there's another Greek term used in the Bible for inner goodness, *agathos*. This term describes that which, being good in its character or constitution, is beneficial in its effect. In other words, if your inner character is *agathos* then your outward behavior will be *kalos*. So Peter charges his readers not only to abstain from fleshly lusts, but also to do consistently the good deeds that reveal good character. He will return to this positive aspect of our behavior again when he exhorts us to fervently love one another.

It's obvious that the message of Christendom to the unsaved world is confused, to say the least. To an alarming extent, many church people have given themselves over to every one of the sins of the unsaved and see no problem with that behavior. Those who consider themselves to be Christians have denied much of God's word and many have denied that any of the Bible is God's word, in any real sense. If one denies the word of God, and lives like a non-Christian, then he is a non-Christian, no matter he thinks he is. If he walks like he's lost, and wanders around like he's lost, and talks like he's lost, then he must still be lost. God demanded, through John the Baptist, **"Bring forth fruits in keeping with your repentance."** Is it any wonder that unbelievers are confused?

Those who are God's genuine believers must be different. We must keep our behavior excellent in this world. It's important. Our behavior grows out of what's inside the person. In Mark 7:21ff, Jesus said,

"For from within, out of the heart of men, proceed the evil thoughts, fornications, thefts, murders, adulteries, deeds of coveting and wickedness, as well as deceit, sensuality, envy, slander, pride and foolishness. All these evil things proceed from within and defile the man."

But in Matthew 5:8 He said, **"Blessed are the pure in heart, for they shall see God."** And in Luke.6:45, **"The good**

man out of the good treasure of his heart brings forth what is good; and the evil man out of the evil treasure brings forth what is evil; for his mouth speaks from that which fills his heart."

In the parable of the soils Jesus described the ones who truly received the gospel:

"And the seed in the good soil, these are the ones who have heard the word in an honest and good heart, and hold it fast, and bear fruit with perseverance. Now no one after lighting a lamp covers it over with a container, or puts it under a bed; but he puts it on a lampstand, in order that those who come in may see the light," Luke 8:15f.

That fruit of which Jesus speaks is, in large part, the fruit of a life that has been changed from the inside out, a life that is different from what it was before, different from the world, a life that looks saved and regenerated, a life that is excellent in behavior. Such a life will be a contributing cause in the salvation of those who observe your good deeds.

Good deeds are a beacon of hope in a darkening world. Don't underestimate their importance!

Chapter 11
2:13-17, Excellent Citizens

13 Submit yourselves for the Lord's sake to every human institution, whether to a king as the one in authority,
14 or to governors as sent by him for the punishment of evildoers and the praise of those who do right.
15 For such is the will of God that by doing right you may silence the ignorance of foolish men. 16 *Act* as free men, and do not use your freedom as a covering for evil, but *use it* as bondslaves of God.
17 Honor all men; love the brotherhood, fear God, honor the king.

Peter has just written that we are aliens on this planet and even in our native country. So our behavior must be consistently excellent as we represent our Lord. Philippians 3:17-20 stresses the importance of behavior:

Brethren, join in following my example, and observe those who walk according to the pattern you have in us. For many walk, of whom I often told you, and now tell you even weeping, that they are enemies of the cross of Christ, whose end is destruction, whose god is their appetite, and whose glory is in their shame, who set their minds on earthly things. For our citizenship is in heaven, from which also we eagerly wait for a Savior, the Lord Jesus Christ.

So we do not set our minds on earthly things. Our primary goal is **the prize of the upward call of God in Christ Jesus,** Philippians 3:14. Our secondary goal is to take as many people with us as will respond to our gospel. Our excellent behavior has a direct influence on how the unbelieving citizens of earth respond to the gospel.

Having established that overall principle, Peter now moves to three specific areas of life in which our behavior exerts its strongest influence on the watching world: our behavior as citizens, our behavior in the workplace, and our behavior in the family.

He starts with how to have a good witness as excellent citizens in our native land. Although we are in fact citizens of the kingdom of God; legally speaking, we are still citizens of our country. We can't control the attitude our government has toward Christianity in general and Christians in particular. **We know that we are of God, and the whole world lies in the evil one,** I John 5:19.

But we can exert either a positive or a negative influence, both on government and on our fellow citizens. A prominent question in the minds of everyone will be, "Does becoming a follower of Jesus Christ make someone a good citizen or a trouble-maker?" A study of the book of Acts shows that this was a prominent issue with the authorities and the populations of the places where the gospel was carried.

We will consider three aspects of excellent citizenship in the same order that Peter presents them:

The Principle, 13-15

The Approach, 16

The Practice, 17

The Principle, 13-15

[13] **Submit yourselves for the Lord's sake to every human institution, whether to a king as the one in authority,** [14] **or to governors as sent by him for the punishment of evildoers and the praise of those who do right.** [15] **For such is the will of God that by doing right you may silence the ignorance of foolish men.**

Submitting to Human Government Is Submitting to God.

God commands us to submit to the human authorities that He has ordained. This is such an important principle that

156

Peter and Paul both taught it in their letters and by their example. It is why the church did not attack the institution of slavery nor call for the replacement of the evil and deranged emperor Nero. It's why they didn't organize demonstrations. They did nothing to undermine the governing authorities, even when they disagreed and even suffered under the government's policies. They endured the confiscation of their property, persecutions, and even death.

Jesus didn't argue with Pilates' authority to put Him to death. Paul told the Roman Governor Felix:

"I am standing before Caesar's tribunal, where I ought to be tried. I have done no wrong to the Jews, as you also very well know. If then I am a wrongdoer, and have committed anything worthy of death, I do not refuse to die; but if none of those things is true of which these men accuse me, no one can hand me over to them. I appeal to Caesar," Ac. 24:10f.

So Paul submitted to trial as a Roman citizen and acknowledged Rome's authority to put him to death if he was an evil-doer. But he also insisted upon his citizenship rights. We can't claim government's protection while rejecting government's authority.

The principle is this: human government is ordained by God, and He orders all men, including His own people, to obey it. The alternative is anarchy and chaos. In Judges 21:25, the concluding remark is: **In those days there was no king in Israel; everyone did what was right in his own eyes.** The result was wide-spread evil. **God is not a God of confusion but of peace,** I Corinthians 14:33.

So after God gave men just enough experience of anarchy to see the need for order, He instituted human government. He knows that humans are flawed, and that any government run by humans will be flawed also. But given the fallen nature of mankind, government is necessary in spite of its flaws and inherent evils. In due time we will have a perfect government ruled by a perfect King.

Paul discusses the purpose and source of human governmental authority in Romans 13. **There is no authority except from God, and those which exist are established by**

God, Romans 13:1. This means that our current president was put in power by God. Abraham Lincoln was put in power by God. And so was Hitler. God puts each and every leader into power according to God's purpose for that nation, whether to bless the nation or to punish it, or to do both at the same time.

Rom. 13:3f say:

For rulers are not a cause of fear for good behavior, but for evil. Do you want to have no fear of authority? Do what is good, and you will have praise from the same; for it is a minister of God to you for good. But if you do what is evil, be afraid; for it does not bear the sword for nothing; for it is a minister of God, an avenger who brings wrath upon the one who practices evil.

Nations, like individuals, choose to walk either in God's good ways or in their own evil ways (which they mistakenly consider to be better than God's ways). God installs good, wise, and just rulers to bless nations and individuals who follow His ways. If a society rejects God's ways, then He installs evil, unjust, and foolish rulers. **Therefore he who resists authority has opposed the ordinance of God; and they who have opposed will receive condemnation upon themselves,** Romans 13:2.

If people won't submit willingly to the benevolent authority of the good God who made them, then God will subject them to harsh, human oppressors who will teach them to submit. This is just what He did when He repeatedly sent godless armies to plunder stiff-necked Israel and finally subjugated Israel to the Assyrians and Judah to the Babylonians. We can learn the easy way, or we can learn the hard way. Either way, we are going to learn that we can't be our own gods.

God punishes evil people by sending attackers who, oftentimes, are more evil than the nation God is rebuking. When the New York City Trade Towers were destroyed on 9/11/2001, some preachers pointed out that this was God's judgment. They were immediately condemned by Americans who had less understanding of God's ways, and who were in denial about the sins of our country that call for God's judgment. Consequently that judgment has continued at the hands of terrorists for over 15 years.

As America has rejected God and chosen evil ways, God has chosen our rulers for the purpose of judgment. They don't know they were put in office to judge, usually. In fact, they often see themselves as the nation's savior. But their bad decisions accomplish God's judgment. Nations get the rulers they deserve. And a nation's judgment grows more severe in accord with the severity of its rebellion, just as God warned in Deuteronomy 28 and demonstrated in the rest of the Old Testament.

I would urge you to make yourself very familiar with Deuteronomy 28. Although it was written to the Hebrew nation, the principles involved will enable you to answer many of the questions that come up about what God is doing with America when some calamity strikes.

We can easily trace America's gradual transition from an obedient nation, enjoying God's blessing, to a rebellious nation, suffering God's judgment. It goes back at least as far as the Civil War, but its roots go much further back. Abraham Lincoln evaluated the Civil War in his second inaugural address:

"Yet, if God wills that it [slavery] continue until all the wealth piled by the bondsman's two hundred and fifty years of unrequited toil shall be sunk, and until every drop of blood drawn with the lash shall be paid by another drawn with the sword, as was said three thousand years ago, so still it must be said 'the judgments of the Lord are true and righteous altogether.'"

But the tipping point, as near as I can tell, was the 1960's. From that point on, America has officially rejected God and His ways, with all three branches of government ruling against God's ways.

Israel was the nation chosen by God to demonstrate that principle; and we lose for not learning from their history. A nation's government has God's authority, but it had better be sure that it uses that authority for good and not evil, or else God will judge it.

So, individuals are required by God to obey civil government. If that government needs correction, God will do the correcting. The two main purposes of government are to punish evil-doers and encourage good behavior, as I Peter 2:14 says. If it does the opposite, God will soon replace it.

Therefore he who resists authority has opposed the ordinance of God; and they who have opposed will receive condemnation upon themselves, Romans 13:2. When Peter drew his sword to attack the posse sent out to arrest Jesus in the garden, Jesus told him,

"Put your sword back into its place; for all those who take up the sword shall perish by the sword. Or do you think that I cannot appeal to My Father, and He will at once put at My disposal more than twelve legions of angels," Matthew 26:52.

Jesus is calling upon two principles: 1) those who oppose government will be punished by government, and 2) government cannot do anything that the sovereign God does not allow.

Jesus had told His disciples earlier in the evening, **let him who has no sword sell his robe and buy one,** Luke 22:36. This is not a contradiction. He said they should arm themselves in the interest of self defense, since He was sending them out as sheep in the midst of wolves. It was for defense against evil individuals, not for the purpose of civil disobedience.

When Herod arrested Peter to kill him, as he had killed his brother James, Peter did not resist arrest. But God prevented the intended execution. We have to trust the sovereignty of God. If God decides that I should die, then I should die. The wait for heaven's rewards will be over! Or if He decides that I should live, then I will live. It's my duty to live, unless God says otherwise. But that choice is God's. And if that's true of life, then it is true of lesser issues like freedom and property rights also.

If a nation is getting too materialistic for its own good, then God will send rulers to attack those property rights, often by excessive taxation. If a nation uses its health care system to murder 60 million babies, then God will send rulers to attack the health care system. God always does what is right and fitting. His judgments always point to the nature of our sin, if we are smart enough to notice.

The framers of our Constitution based their thinking largely on the Bible, so they included in that foundation for all American law, the fact that God does not give human governments the right to deprive people of life, liberty, or property without just, legal procedure.

Government does not own its citizens, or their property, or their minds or bodies, or their children. God does. As our nation's population has rejected the Bible, they are losing those basic, God-given rights. This is how God's judgment works in a nation.

I've spent some time on this because these are the issues that cause Christians to seek ways to avoid this principle of submission to governing authorities. Christians have always experienced this tension between obeying God and obeying a godless government. The answer is to do what God says and trust Him with the consequences (I Pet. 4:19).

The word **submit** means "to arrange in military array under." God has established a chain of command for the sake of order. The law of entropy, it turns out, also applies to human behavior – all individuals tend toward anarchy. That may be one reason why all governments tend toward totalitarianism.

So, we are to submit **to every human institution**. The term **institution** is the regular New Testament word for *creation*. They aren't called human because they were created by humans but because that is the sphere in which they operate. God created the institutions of human society – family, work, and government. These are all redemptive agencies used by God to teach us to submit to Him. It turns out that one of the main ways to deal with persecution or hard times in general is to be submissive to God.

We are to submit **for the Lord's sake**, according to verse 13. Obeying earthly rulers is, in reality, honoring God's sovereignty, just as Jesus did. Jesus would denounce the sins of rulers, but He never sought to overturn their authority. He never led or encouraged demonstrations against the institutions of government. We shouldn't, either.

Submitting to human government demonstrates godly character in a genuine concern for society and good order. It seeks peace and seeks to prevent trouble and crime. Rulers watch to see, "What kind of people are these followers of Jesus? Should we encourage citizens to follow Jesus Christ or forbid it?" Those who slander Christians will give one answer. Our behavior had better give a different, and more convincing, answer. How we respond to the civil authorities redounds either to the Lord's credit or to His dishonor. God's glory bears directly upon His purpose to save people. So we submit for the Lord's sake. We submit to human government for the sake of the kingdom of God.

If we live our lives as good citizens, then we will **silence the ignorance of foolish men**, verse 15. **Silence** means to restrain, to muzzle, to make speechless. Our good citizenship will put an effective gag order on our critics. Or God might simply marginalize those critics, destroying the credibility of their accusations. **When a man's ways are pleasing to the LORD, He makes even his enemies to be at peace with him**, Prov. 16:7. For a case study, see Acts 18:9-16.

The term for **ignorance** used here doesn't mean lack of knowledge (there's a related word for that). It means willful, hostile rejection of the truth. It is a settled lack of perception which is further described as **foolish**, meaning senseless, without reason, and may even imply lack of mental sanity. It's the willful and illogical ignorance of foolish men that makes them hate God and slander God's representatives.

We see the idea in Titus 3:1-3:

Remind them to be subject to rulers, to authorities, to be obedient, to be ready for every good deed, to malign no one, to be uncontentious, gentle, showing every consideration for all men. For we also once were foolish ourselves, disobedient, deceived, enslaved to various lusts and pleasures, spending our life in malice and envy, hateful, hating one another.

The principle, then, is to submit to human government at every level: king, governor, or mayor, and to do so even if the government is not doing what Christians think it should be doing. Behind it all, our God rules. Never forget that. God is sovereign. It would be unwise to expect God to protect us while we rebel against our government.

The Roman Empire in which those first century Christians lived was decadent and evil, openly immoral, with homosexuality, infanticide, government corruption at all levels, abuse of women, immorality, and violence. But neither Peter nor Paul offered any exemption from the duty to submit for the Lord's sake. Even in cases where Christians must obey God rather than men, they are still obligated to respect the government and submit to the consequences. (More about that shortly.)

To God, and to those who are watching and judging Christianity, it matters, not only what we do, but also the frame of mind in which we do it. So Peter addresses our approach to submission in verse 16.

The Approach, 16

[16] *Act* as free men, and do not use your freedom as a covering for evil, but *use it* as bondslaves of God.

Act As Free Men.

The tyranny that matters the most in the long run is the tyranny of sin. Even for Christians, the main reason we chafe at authority is that it hinders the free expression of our self-will. But if we give free expression to our self-will, we become slaves to sin. Slaves to sin have a hard time submitting to someone else's will. People who are free from self-will's tyranny can submit to government.

So a free man can be a slave in all practicality, and a slave can be a free man, even while a slave. Many of Peter's readers actually were slaves, owned by other men, but free in Christ. It all depends upon whose will you have decided to follow. If you are committed to following your own will, then you are in reality a slave to the flesh, even if you are a king. If you are committed to following God's will, then you are free indeed, no matter what your station in life.

Jesus said, **"Truly, truly, I say to you, everyone who commits sin is the slave of sin. And the slave does not remain in the house forever; the son does remain forever. If therefore the Son shall make you free, you shall be free indeed,"** John 8:34ff.

In Galatians 5:13 Paul wrote, **For you were called to freedom, brethren; only do not turn your freedom into an opportunity for the flesh, but through love serve one another.**

So Jesus did not make us free to sin. That would be to make us slaves again. He set us free indeed. Submission to human government does not negate our liberty in Christ. But Peter is writing so believers won't think: "I'm free in Christ, so I don't have to obey the government."

Think how severely our freedoms would be curtailed if there were no government to compel men's obedience. We wouldn't be free to own property, because someone else who also has no government to obey would come and steal it. We wouldn't be free to leave our house, because someone with no laws to obey would attack us for fun or profit. On the other hand, we wouldn't be free to stay in our house, either, because some lawless arson might come by at any moment to set it on fire.

Do you get the idea? It's only by living in an ordered society under the rule of law that we have any freedoms. It isn't anarchy that makes us free; it's law. Government doesn't prevent us from acting like free men. Government is what makes it possible to act like free men. That's why God gave us human government. He is interested in freedom without disorder. Freedom cannot exist unless men are willing to submit to an authority that restricts their baser natures.

Consider what would happen if anarchy reigned. No one would be safe from anyone else. The bigger, meaner people would exploit and oppress the weaker people. So the weaker people would band together as a tribe to defend themselves from the oppressor. The oppressor types would then band together to counter the defender types. Tribes can't exist without submission to the rules of the tribe. So anarchy can't exist for long. No one would abide it. Government is a necessity, whether it's righteous or evil.

It's been said, "That government is best that governs least." But it's also true, "Those citizens are best that require the least government."

We should just be glad that God oversees governments. If we are obedient to God as a people, then God sees to it that submitting to our government is not an odious burden. If a people refuse to submit to God, then He teaches them to submit by giving them an oppressive government that will force them to submit.

For this reason we are not to use our freedom as a covering for evil. It is true that we answer to a higher authority than human government and that we are citizens of a heavenly city. But we are also ambassadors for Christ, and no responsible ambassador would defame his home country by hiding behind diplomatic immunity to commit crimes in his host country. So God doesn't give His people diplomatic immunity. Rather He says, **he who does wrong will receive the consequences of the wrong which he has done, and that without partiality,** Colossians 3:25.

It isn't our station in life that determines our degree of freedom, it is our relationship with Jesus Christ and our behavior as citizens. It's hard for a government to condemn Christians as evil-doers and send us to prison if we always conduct ourselves as excellent citizens. More to the point, it's harder for them to put the bad-mouth on God if His people are the best citizens in the country.

That's not to say that it won't happen, because it does, as we will see in chapter 4, because humans are in rebellion against God and don't want to be reminded that God is the ultimate judge. But it shouldn't happen because Christians are acting in ways that dishonor God.

We are to use our freedom as bondslaves of God. God uses His people to change unjust governments, as He did by causing the church and barbaric nations, assisted by Rome's own moral weakness, to overcome the Roman Empire. So we must be the Lord's bondslaves and let Him use us as He wills. Many Christians were killed by Nero and a few of the other Roman emperors in the 300 years before the Roman emperor Constantine made Christianity the legal "religion" of the empire. But that removal of persecution made way for greater impurity in the church. Persecution has a valuable purifying effect. The legalization of Christianity was the beginning of a 1200-year decline.

You may be wondering how some of the Apostles who were placed in a position where they had to obey God rather than men were being obedient to this principle of submitting to human government. Acts 4 is one example.

First, their refusal to obey the governing authorities was not based on their own preferences. They did so only when the authorities required them to stop doing what God had commanded them to do. Others disobeyed when told to do something that God expressly forbade. These are the only Biblical reasons to disobey one's government – when a government commands what God forbids, or forbids what God commands, and no reconciliation is possible.

A third reason, acknowledged by governments themselves, would be when the letter of the law violates the spirit of the law or a higher duty. For example, it is against the law to break into someone's house, and for good reason. But if someone comes upon a house-fire and has reason to think that people are trapped in the house, then he is legally justified to break into that house to save the people. And no one would cite you for ignoring the "Keep off the grass" sign on the statehouse lawn to rescue a child who was being attacked by a mad dog.

But even in cases where we have to obey God rather than men, we still have to honor the government and submit to the consequences. If God wants to prohibit the consequences,

He is able to do so and will not be found asleep at His post. We will not suffer government penalties for obeying God unless God wills it so. We see plenty of examples of how this works in the book of Acts.

Only God's bondslaves are truly free men. Our approach to submitting ourselves to human authority is to behave as men who are free from self-will, which is sin.

The Practice, 17

17 Honor all men; love the brotherhood, fear God, honor the king.

Honor Everyone

The word **honor** is primarily a valuing. So we are to see the value in all men. God does. They are valuable because they are created in the image of God. They are in that way, if in no other, connected to their Creator. Therefore, every person is due some degree of respect and consideration. God owns every human being. We need to respect His property.

Furthermore, Jesus died for every person. Even if that person never responds to the opportunity to be saved, God gives him that opportunity and **declares to men that all everywhere should repent,** Acts 17:30. All men are potential brothers in Christ. Disrespect will not draw them to the Savior.

In the first century most people viewed slaves as non-people with no rights. But Colossians 3:1 says, **Masters, grant to your slaves justice and fairness, knowing that you too have a Master in heaven.** And the Biblical principle of the value of every person is found in Galatians 3:2: **There is neither Jew nor Greek, there is neither slave nor free man, there is neither male nor female; for you are all one in Christ Jesus.** This doesn't mean that we honor their godless beliefs or affirm their godless choices. But God's people are not to discriminate against any class of people for ethnic reasons or because of economic status. Society unravels wherever men do not honor the rights and value of their fellows. So Romans 12:17 says, **Respect what is right in the sight of all men.**

Love the Brotherhood

We might honor everyone else and treat them with respect, but treat our own family harshly, perhaps presuming upon their grace or desire to preserve the family's good name. Citizenship starts with family relationships, and society cannot survive without them. The Soviet Russians tried to dismantle the family in order to further their goals of communism. But they found that as the family structure was dismantled, society broke down. So they had to restore the importance of the family.

Even those who slandered the first century Christians were forced to acknowledge how the Christians loved one another. In a dog-eat-dog world where everyone looks out for himself, this makes a big impact on how people view Christians.

On the other hand, if Christians behave the way the world does, serving self instead of one another, then we destroy the seeker's tentative hope that there might be something to the Biblical world-view. Love is the very heart of citizenship. Serving others for the common good, instead of abusing others for selfish gain is what holds a society together more than any other factor. And this guiding light of society ought to shine brightest in the body of Christ.

Fear God

The fear of God doesn't mean being scared of God. It means placing a higher value on God and His purpose than we do on anything or anyone else. The fear of the Lord is the appropriate respect, honor, and obedience due to the awesome God of the universe. It is a descriptive term for salvation. **Behold, the fear of the Lord, that is wisdom; and to depart from evil is understanding,** Job 28:28. **The fear of the LORD is the beginning of wisdom,** Psalm 111:10. **The fear of the LORD is the beginning of knowledge,** Proverbs 1:7.

Proverbs 2:5 and 9:10 equate the fear of the LORD with the knowledge of God. Proverbs 8:13 says, **The fear of the**

LORD is to hate evil. Proverbs 10:27 promises, **The fear of the LORD prolongs life.** Proverbs goes on and on with the fear of the Lord: **In the fear of the LORD there is strong confidence,** 14:26; **The fear of the LORD is a fountain of life, that one may avoid the snares of death;** 14:27; **by the fear of the LORD one keeps away from evil;** 16:6; **The fear of the LORD leads to life, so that one may sleep satisfied, untouched by evil;** 19:23. Isaiah says the fear of the Lord is a delight and a treasure.

If these words describe the Christian citizen, how can Christians fail to impress their government and their fellow citizens? Following God is obviously something to be encouraged by any government that means to punish evil-doers and praise those who do right.

Every problem in the world and in government is due to one fact, men don't fear God. Believers must show the world that the fear of God is a great thing.

Honor the King

A government doesn't have to be a constitutional republic to please God or be useful to Him. God can use a monarchy, an oligarchy, a dictatorship, a democracy, or even a socialist state (I suppose) to bless those who do right and to punish those who do evil. Some governments are inherently better than others, but God is sovereign over all forms of government.

What is required of Christians is that we honor those who rule over us – that we value them as ministers of God who were put in office for our good.

Christians can have a say in how their government behaves. In I Timothy 2:1ff we have this command:

First of all, then, I urge that entreaties and prayers, petitions and thanksgivings, be made on behalf of all men, for kings and all who are in authority, in order that we may lead a tranquil and quiet life in all godliness and dignity. This is good and acceptable in the sight of God our Savior,

who desires all men to be saved and to come to the knowledge of the truth.

In addition to providing order and freedom in society, governments are instruments of God's redemptive work among men. Don't get in God's way by rebelling against those whom God has put in authority for His own good reasons. We can't know all of those reasons, so we can't know what we might be messing up.

God uses governments to teach people to submit to Him. II Chronicles 12:8 says, **"But they will become his slaves so that they may learn *the difference between* My service and the service of the kingdoms of the countries."** Here God is telling Judah why He will send Shishak of Egypt against them. They were stiff-necked enough that they required this treatment several times, finally being deported to Babylon.

The principle, then, is that God has established every human institution: government, work, and family. All government authority is given by God for man's good. And we are commanded by God to submit to these authorities. God's redemptive plan and mankind's survival depends upon it, so He will see that we submit, one way or another.

God's command to submit is perhaps the biggest "yes-but" principle in the Bible. We can't argue against the principle or the logic behind it, nor refute the Biblical support for it. We have to agree with the principle. So we say, "Yes, but…" and try to argue with its applications. "Yes, it's good in theory, but…" Some will remind us that in theory, theory and practice are the same; in practice they are not. We all understand those hesitations. But God doesn't have theories. Theories are for people who are trying to discover the truth. God already knows all truth.

We must approach this principle, not as self-willed slaves to sin who know better than God knows, but as free men. Our freedom is in Christ, and that freedom is not subject to the whims of human government. They didn't grant us that freedom, and they can't take it away. They are under God's sovereign control. Our freedom comes from being God's bondslave. That includes trusting His principles.

The way to practice this excellent citizenship is to honor all men and to honor the ordinances of God. We must respect the value people have by virtue of being created in the image of God. (Those who deny God's creation do not elevate themselves. They lower themselves. Our history since Darwin's folly proves that.)

Our citizenship has to be guided by God's unconditional love. We have to live it on a higher level than those who are mere earthlings. Our membership in the body of Christ and how we love the brethren develops the kind of citizens we will be in our community, our state, and our nation.

Our submission to government is based upon our fear of God – we put a higher value on God and His purposes than we do on ourselves and our purpose and convenience. Rulers are sent by God for the good of the human race. We need to honor our rulers if we want to honor the God who put those rulers into power. This is the question you have to settle in your mind: Does God know His business?

Our subject is the witness of excellent citizenship. We either enhance our witness or discredit our witness, based upon what kind of citizens we are. We must be excellent citizens for the sake of God.

Chapter 12

2:18-25, Excellent Servants

**18 Servants, be submissive to your masters with all respect, not only to those who are good and gentle, but also to those who are unreasonable.
19 For this *finds* favor, if for the sake of conscience toward God a man bears up under sorrows when suffering unjustly.
20 For what credit is there if, when you sin and are harshly treated, you endure it with patience? But if when you do what is right and suffer *for it* you patiently endure it, this *finds* favor with God.
21 For you have been called for this purpose, since Christ also suffered for you, leaving you an example for you to follow in His steps,
22 WHO COMMITTED NO SIN, NOR WAS ANY DECEIT FOUND IN HIS MOUTH;
23 and while being reviled, He did not revile in return; while suffering, He uttered no threats, but kept entrusting *Himself* to Him who judges righteously;
24 and He Himself bore our sins in His body on the cross, that we might die to sin and live to righteousness; for by His wounds you were healed.
25 For you were continually straying like sheep, but now you have returned to the Shepherd and Guardian of your souls.**

What is it that human beings least like to do? Go to war? Go to the dentist? Eat Brussels's sprouts? Pay a fine? Pick up a snake?

I think what human beings least like to do is to submit to someone else's will. When Adam and Eve rebelled against God, they made their own self-will supreme over God's will, and that has stuck with their race ever since. So we have the hardest time submitting our will to someone else's will.

Children have a hard time learning to submit to their parents. Soldiers have a hard time learning to submit to their sergeants. Politicians have a hard time submitting to the Constitution. Scientists have a hard time submitting to empirical evidence if it goes against their self-will. Sin, itself, is an unwillingness to submit to God.

This problem we have with submission has caused a lot of trouble. I think we could make a strong case for blaming all the world's troubles on self-will. Undoing the problem of independent desire is a major part of God's redemptive program.

Peter teaches two principles in his first epistle: 1) salvation is secured to us by the work of God, and 2) salvation is spread to others by our excellent behavior.

Having stated the second principle in verses 11-12 of chapter 2, he applies it by saying we must submit to governing authorities in verses 13-17, and in our present text, verses 18-25, we must submit to our masters, which in our day refers to our bosses. Peter will go on in chapter 3 to apply it to our family relationships and to relationships in general.

The biggest difficulty in evangelism is to convince self-willed sinners that submitting to God is a beneficial thing. Only the Holy Spirit can convict the world concerning sin, righteousness, and judgment (John 16:8). It goes against their grain, just as it went against ours when we were unsaved. But if it still goes against our grain, then the world has good reason to question our sincerity when we tell them that submitting to God is the key to life and eternity.

So, Peter began this series of exhortations with verses 11-12. First win the war inside, and then keep your behavior excellent. We must submit, but we must submit with the right attitude.

A big part of that attitude is the belief that our own will is not supreme. Man's unwillingness to submit to the God who made him is at the heart of our fallen nature and is the root of our sin. God intends to live with His redeemed children forever, but that requires that we be holy in every way, entirely separated from our sin. So our sanctification is essential.

Hebrews 12:14 says, **Pursue ... the sanctification without which no one will see the Lord.** And Romans 6:22, **But now having been freed from sin and enslaved to God, you derive your benefit, resulting in sanctification, and the outcome, eternal life.**

So God *will* sanctify His children. And we must cooperate with that plan. Resistance is brutal. That is the point of Hebrews 12:4-11:

⁴You have not yet resisted to the point of shedding blood in your striving against sin;
⁵ and you have forgotten the exhortation which is addressed to you as sons, " MY SON, DO NOT REGARD LIGHTLY THE DISCIPLINE OF THE LORD, NOR FAINT WHEN YOU ARE REPROVED BY HIM;
⁶ FOR THOSE WHOM THE LORD LOVES HE DISCIPLINES, AND HE SCOURGES EVERY SON WHOM HE RECEIVES."
⁷ It is for discipline that you endure; God deals with you as with sons; for what son is there whom *his* father does not discipline?
⁸ But if you are without discipline, of which all have become partakers, then you are illegitimate children and not sons.
⁹ Furthermore, we had earthly fathers to discipline us, and we respected them; shall we not much rather be subject to the Father of spirits, and live?
¹⁰ For they disciplined us for a short time as seemed best to them, but He *disciplines us* for *our* good, that we may share His holiness.
¹¹ All discipline for the moment seems not to be joyful, but sorrowful; yet to those who have been trained by it, afterwards it yields the peaceful fruit of righteousness.

We can be sanctified the easy way or the hard way, at least in those cases where it depends upon us. My experience has shown me that it's smarter to learn my lessons the first time. We can't, by our good choices, eliminate *all* suffering, because **All who desire to live godly in Christ Jesus will be persecuted**, II Tim. 3:12. People who hate Jesus will hate His followers according to John 15:18-21:

18 " If the world hates you, you know that it has hated Me before *it hated* you.

19 "If you were of the world, the world would love its own; but because you are not of the world, but I chose you out of the world, therefore the world hates you.

20 "Remember the word that I said to you, ' A slave is not greater than his master.' If they persecuted Me, they will also persecute you; if they kept My word, they will keep yours also.

21 "But all these things they will do to you for My name's sake, because they do not know the One who sent Me.

Many try to follow Jesus at a distance, hoping to avoid this "guilt" by association. Psalm 73:27-28 serves to correct this way of thinking:

For, behold, those who are far from Thee will perish; Thou hast destroyed all those who are unfaithful to Thee. 28 But as for me, the nearness of God is my good; I have made the Lord GOD my refuge, That I may tell of all Thy works.

Since the refusal to submit ourselves to God is the major problem, God has designed some human institutions to teach us to submit to others. If we can learn to submit to others who are not perfect, then we should be able to submit to God who is. Theologians refer to these human institutions as redemptive agencies. Peter employs three of them here in reverse order of their creation and primacy: government, work, and family. There is another redemptive agency, the church, but is it not included here because it's actually a divine-human institution.

Government sits on (is based upon) work, and work sits on family. Family is the foundation of society. If it crumbles everything else falls apart. Works sits on family because people work to support their families. And government sits on work because people who have no work with its income are very hard to govern. They tend to riot in the streets. As to motives, government depends upon force, work depends upon necessity, and the family depends upon love.

Peter's outline here can be expressed in the three parts of one propositional statement:

We Must Submit with All Respect, 18-20,

Following Christ's Example, 21-23,

In Order to Accomplish God's Redemptive Purpose, 24-25.

Submit with All Respect, 18-20

[18] **Servants, be submissive to your masters with all respect, not only to those who are good and gentle, but also to those who are unreasonable.** [19] **For this *finds* favor, if for the sake of conscience toward God a man bears up under sorrows when suffering unjustly.** [20] **For what credit is there if, when you sin and are harshly treated, you endure it with patience? But if when you do what is right and suffer *for it* you patiently endure it, this *finds* favor with God.**

To really understand a Biblical passage it helps a lot to know the situation of the original recipients, the problems the author was addressing. Many of Peter's readers, perhaps even a majority, would have been slaves. All his readers had first-hand knowledge of slavery. As the gospel spread through the Greco-Roman empire, a high percentage of converts were slaves.

Consequently, much of the New Testament instructs slaves. Let me give you some pertinent examples:

Let each man remain in that condition in which he was called. Were you called while a slave? Do not worry about it; but if you are able also to become free, rather do that. For he who was called in the Lord while a slave is the Lord's freedman; likewise he who was called while free, is Christ's slave. You were bought with a price; do not become slaves of men, I Corinthians 7:20ff.

Slaves, be obedient to those who are your masters according to the flesh, with fear and trembling, in the sincerity of your heart, as to Christ; not by way of eye service, as men-pleasers, but as slaves of Christ, doing the will of God from the heart. With good will render service, as to the Lord, and not to men, knowing that whatever good thing each one does, this he will receive back from the Lord, whether slave

or free. And, masters, do the same things to them, and give up threatening, knowing that both their Master and yours is in heaven, and there is no partiality with Him, Ephesians 6:5ff.

Let all who are under the yoke as slaves regard their own masters as worthy of all honor so that the name of God and our doctrine may not be spoken against. And let those who have believers as their masters not be disrespectful to them because they are brethren, but let them serve them all the more, because those who partake of the benefit are believers and beloved. Teach and preach these principles, I Timothy 6:1f.

Urge bondslaves to be subject to their own masters in everything, to be well-pleasing, not argumentative, not pilfering, but showing all good faith that they may adorn the doctrine of God our Savior in every respect. For the grace of God has appeared, bringing salvation to all men, instructing us to deny ungodliness and worldly desires and to live sensibly, righteously and godly in the present age, looking for the blessed hope and the appearing of the glory of our great God and Savior, Christ Jesus; who gave Himself for us, that He might redeem us from every lawless deed and purify for Himself a people for His own possession, zealous for good deeds. These things speak and exhort and reprove with all authority. Let no one disregard you, Titus 2:9ff.

Paul returned Onesimus, an escaped slave who found Christ when in Rome, to Philemon, Paul's friend and brother in Christ. Along with the returning slave, Paul sent a letter urging Philemon to receive him back as a brother in Christ and not to punish him.

One of the many slanders spoken against Christians was that they were trying to overthrow the institution of slavery. It wasn't true, although Christians certainly were against the practice. Meetings of believers might have seemed to some like a gathering of slaves. And why would slaves gather except to plan an uprising? Slave holders tend to be fearful people.

Inciting a slave rebellion would be both futile and fatal. It would be a violation of the Biblical principle of submission to governing authorities that Peter just commanded in the previous verses. And the Roman economy was based upon the institution of slavery. Their wars were funded by the sale of slaves that they captured in those wars. Two-thirds of Rome's population was in bondage, so Rome was in constant fear of slave revolts.

An assault of any kind on slavery would have provoked the government to put an end to Christianity, but would have done nothing to end slavery. Consider how great a civil war we fought in this country to end slavery, even when most people did not own slaves. (About 10% of the American population were slaves at the time of the Civil War.)

Biblically, slavery is an undesirable condition, of course. God never tells His people to right the wrongs of a pagan society, as if it were in their power to do so. Society's faults demonstrate the sinfulness of sin. The church is called to be merciful, but insurrection is forbidden. So put away your Don Quixote outfit.

This doesn't mean that Christianity can do nothing to change its society. If Christians live according to God's ways, then society can see convincing evidence that God's ways are superior to man's ways. And then it has the option of changing how it does business.

Christians are not to attack their society. We are to win society, if it will be won, by living and presenting God's truth. And if we want our witness to have any credibility, we must demonstrate a full commitment to that truth ourselves. Historically, wherever real Christianity took root, the ills of that society faded away. And when succeeding generations thought that Christianity was no longer needed, those ills returned.

In the Old Testament, God told the Israelites that if they kept the covenant faithfully, they wouldn't have any poor. But He knew they wouldn't be faithful and therefore would have poor people. So in cases of personal economic destitution, God permitted Israelites to sell themselves for a limited period of time as slaves. It would be more accurate to think of them as

indentured servants. God protected their rights in the Mosaic
Law. The bondage was to end at the prescribed time, and the
master was not to send his slave away empty handed when his
time of servitude ended. He was to stake him for a new start in
life.

This was a humane and dignified way to deal with the
harsh realities of life. It set a person back on his feet after he
fell into poverty, whether by misfortune or his own bad choices.
He got food, clothing, and shelter, had the opportunity to learn
some life lessons by working for a successful man, gained some
motivation to better his station in life, and got a second chance
at success. All done without cost to the taxpayers. That was a
better solution than the welfare system we have now, which has
proven to be no solution at all. The current welfare system has
no real time limit, and in fact tends to rob indigent people of
their drive and dignity and make them a life-long slave to sloth
and dependency. God knows better than man how to recover
those who are down-trodden.

Roman law, on the other hand, gave slaves no legal
rights or protection. Aristotle wrote, "A slave is a living tool,
and a tool is an inanimate slave." The Roman nobleman Varro
asserted that the only difference between a slave and a beast or
a cart was that the slave could talk. So slaves were considered
property and had no more rights than a shovel. There were no
slave unions to negotiate for better conditions, no government
intervention (since slaves had no vote and were a source of
income), no civil law suits for redress of grievances.

Slaves could be subjected to unjust and brutal
punishments, inadequate food, long hours of strenuous work.
Or they might serve as teachers or family doctors, depending
upon their ability and training. And, of course, their working
conditions depended mostly upon their master's temperament.
Some masters were good and kind and loved their slaves like
members of the family. In fact, some were adopted as sons.
Under some masters, slavery was little different than regular
employment, as far as working conditions were concerned.
Other masters were crooked and perverse.

Many of these slaves came to Christ. No one
understands slavery as well as a slave, so the gospel would

strike a cord with them when it gave them the opportunity to be free from their slavery to sin.

These believing slaves filled the churches and, as they grew in spiritual maturity, might become leaders and teachers. It might happen that a slave would serve as an elder, and his master, as a regular member of the church, would be under his spiritual oversight. And Paul wrote in Galatians 3:28, **There is neither Jew nor Greek, there is neither slave nor free man, there is neither male nor female; for you are all one in Christ Jesus.**

So was the slave still required to be submissive in the workplace? Or is he due some elevation in society because of his spiritual gifts and leadership in the church? How does this new-found equality work out?

These were very real issues. And the answer was difficult to accept, for the very reason that it went against self-will. So we see Peter working hard in this passage to show how important it is to God's redemptive program for slaves to submit to their masters with the proper attitude. Paul wrote in Colossians 3:22f:

Slaves, in all things obey those who are your masters on earth, not with external service, as those who merely please men, but with sincerity of heart, fearing the Lord. Whatever you do, do your work heartily, as for the Lord rather than for men.

Attitude is crucial to the success of God's purpose. The key phrase in I Peter 2:18 is **with all respect**. The word translated **respect** is *phobos*, the word for fear, as in **fear God**, in verse. 17. Fear is a genuine, personal commitment to obey. It is the willing submission of our own will to God's rightful authority, which here tells us to be submissive to our masters, just as verse 13 told us to be submissive to our government and I Peter 3 tells wives to be submissive to their husbands.

Verse 16 says we are **bondslaves of God**. A slave master could rent his slaves out to someone else. And then the slave had to serve that master also. That's what God has done, not to get some extra income, but to accomplish His redemptive purposes.

Government, work, and marriage are all redemptive agencies. They are institutions that God created to teach us how to submit so we would learn to be submissive to His authority. Life experiences are redemptive agencies. Some redemptive agencies are powered by force of law, others by love. But they all are created by God to sift out and discard our commitment to self-will. What Adam and Eve put into the human race in one fell swoop, God has to undo one person at a time.

So we each have a custom-made set of redemptive agencies working under God's direction to transform us from self-willed rebels into submissive servants of God. This process is called sanctification.

Some of us can respond to gentle means; some of us need more severe treatments. We all have different starting points. Some of us are tougher nuts to crack. Some of us don't pay particularly close attention, or don't remember what we've been taught, or aren't very diligent to apply it. So in the workplace, some masters are good and kind, some are perverted and mean-spirited. My guess is that Christians who are less willing to give up self-will, and those who are called to tougher or more exalted roles in the body of Christ, get the rougher treatment, generally speaking.

The bottom line is that is that when we submit to our government and our masters, or wives to their husbands, or children to their parents, we are in fact submitting to God. So Paul wrote in Ephesians 6:5:

Slaves, be obedient to those who are your masters according to the flesh, with fear and trembling, in the sincerity of your heart, as to Christ; not by way of eye service, as men-pleasers, but as slaves of Christ, doing the will of God from the heart.

Our attitude, then, is that we need what God is doing in our lives, whether that is some pleasant service or a tough row to hoe. It all makes us more like Christ, and that is our greatest good and is worth whatever it costs us. God doesn't treat us all equally because we don't have equal needs, we don't respond equally, and He doesn't have equal jobs for us.

Favor, verse 19 and again in verse 20, is the word *charis*, grace. Grace is not something we can earn – if we earned it, it wouldn't be grace. So this means that God gives grace to those who need it for the obedient course they have chosen to walk. **This finds favor with God** could be translated *this is the grace of God*. In other words, if we respond in the way Peter says, then we are experiencing the grace of God. That grace includes a closer, more intimate walk with the Lord, because, as verse 21 says, we are walking in His steps. Serving difficult masters is one of those multi-colored trials for which God gives a matching color grace (1:6 cf. 4:10, *poikilois*).

That grace is not given where it is not needed, nor is it given before it is needed. If we had a pre-existent grace for dealing with trouble, for instance, we would be inclined to look for trouble, human nature being what it is. So don't wait for a feeling of God's grace before you submit to your master. Submit to your master and the grace will be there, whether you feel it or not, as soon as you need it and for as long as you need it.

I don't particularly enjoy roller coasters. But I've been stunt-flying in an airplane, with a friend at the controls, and I'd rather be in the airplane. But I learned something that applies to both. When you are at the top of that first climb on a roller coaster, about to be cast over the top to an uncertain fate, or if you nose into a dive to gain momentum for an aerobatic maneuver, and you know that you aren't in control of what happens next, you can lean back, as if to delay the unpleasant sensation of having your world drop out from under you. But if you do, you get a very uncomfortable feeling. But I found that if, instead of leaning away from the experience, I lean into it, I don't get that sick feeling and fear is replaced by interest.

What Peter is saying here about our attitude toward serving someone else's will is, "This is God's will; lean into it." Don't try to go and not go at the same time. I don't think that would work very well. I say that because I once had a car that would get stuck between Drive and Park. Ironically, I had named that car Fearless.

When you are in a master-servant relationship, whether pleasant or not, keep in mind that it is the Lord Jesus Christ whom you are serving, and act accordingly.

In verse 13 Peter wrote that we should submit **for the Lord's sake.** Now in verse 19 he says that we should bear up under sorrows, **for the sake of conscience toward God.** The word **conscience** means a general awareness of God's presence. It is God-consciousness. If you're conscious of your earthly master only, you will have a hard time with God's command to submit in the workplace with a good attitude. Being God-conscious and knowing what Jesus did for our sake puts us in a better frame of mind should we be mistreated for His sake.

Suffering unjustly is another, very important aspect to a redemptive agency. It not only makes us more redeemed from our former manner of life, it also demonstrates to the unsaved what it means to be redeemed. They can look at how we live our lives and learn what they can expect should they become Christians.

Mistreatment by an employer is an especially powerful opportunity to glorify our Lord. True character shows in extreme situations. Everyone knows that and pays attention to how we behave *in extremis.* If we are trusting and serving God, then we will respond with equanimity, acceptance, and willing obedience, even going beyond the minimum requirement because we want our employer to be successful. If we are self-willed, then we will respond with anger, grudging obedience, and resentment, probably bad-mouthing our employer and wishing or even conspiring for his failure.

Submission without the **all fear** (meaning willing and respectful obedience) does not produce a good witness, because whatever we are doing on the outside, we are still disobedient on the inside. And people who are seriously interested in the gospel are intent to find out what Christians are on the inside.

It seems obvious to us that easy times are good times and hard times are bad times. And they are if we are mainly concerned with our own will and convenience. But it's just the opposite for the sake of the gospel. That's one of the reasons God permits difficulties from time to time. He doesn't permit difficulties all the time. He doesn't leave His soldiers in battle continually – that would be poor generalship. Such a general would run out of soldiers before he ran out of war. And being a good general, God always sees to it that His troops are supplied with all they need, including R&R when they need it.

So, take your over-arching concern for God's glory with you into the workplace. It isn't too hard to understand the point Peter is making; the hard part is living it out should we find ourselves working for a despot. That's when our self-will is really confronted. If you're the boss, and take all this as approval for being a despot boss, then remember that God judges despots.

So, Peter appeals to the example Christ left for us when He did the work that gave us our eternal lives.

Following Christ's Example, 21-23

21 For you have been called for this purpose, since Christ also suffered for you, leaving you an example for you to follow in His steps,
22 WHO COMMITTED NO SIN, NOR WAS ANY DECEIT FOUND IN HIS MOUTH;
23 and while being reviled, He did not revile in return; while suffering, He uttered no threats, but kept entrusting *Himself* to Him who judges righteously;

We were called to receive the redemption that Jesus provided for us and also to be involved in passing that redemption on to others (II Cor. 5:18), even if that involves hardship. If Jesus suffered for us, it is hardly a fitting or grateful response to refuse to suffer for His sake.

Paul wrote, **Now I rejoice in my sufferings for your sake, and in my flesh I do my share on behalf of His body (which is the church) in filling up that which is lacking in Christ's afflictions**, Colossians 1:24. Passing on the gospel often involves some suffering. It isn't a vicarious suffering that provides atonement for sin; only Jesus Christ could do that. But those who would persecute Jesus will also persecute His followers. **"A slave is not greater than his Master,"** John 15:20. One of the greatest acts of love we can do for a non-believer is to tell him how to find eternal life in Christ. But some people take that as being judgmental and respond with irritation.

If Jesus suffered so much to buy other people's salvation, can we not suffer a little to tell them about it? Philippians 1:29 tells us, **For to you it has been granted for Christ's sake, not only to believe in Him, but also to suffer for His sake.**

Jesus left us a pattern to copy. Have you ever seen a horn book? In the old days they took the outer layer of a cow's horn, boiled it, straightened it out, polished it to make it transparent, and nailed it onto a board, covering a paper on which the teacher had printed the alphabet. Then students could trace over those letters and wipe them off as many times as necessary to learn how to write the alphabet. That's what Jesus left for us. A pattern that we could trace over with our own steps, following the example He set.

Look at those steps:

- He **committed no sin**, no independent desire! This is why He was the perfect and acceptable sacrifice. The world's greatest and purest benefactor was given the treatment reserved for the worst malefactors. And He took it in order to accomplish the Father's plan for our redemption.

- **Nor was any deceit found in His mouth**. Deceit is a general term for sinful corruption, which always seems to find verbal expression sooner or later.

- **While being reviled, He did not revile in return**. To revile is to heap abusive, vile language on someone. How hard it is to hold your tongue when you are suffering this kind of harsh and unjust verbal abuse. Our resistant and aggravated spirit makes us want to fight back verbally, if that's all we can do. Through all that, Jesus was resolute and peaceful.

- **While suffering, He uttered no threats**. Think of the powerful and legitimate threats Jesus could have made. His mouth spoke the universe into existence. His tongue will slay the wicked in due time. But now He was not judging sinners; He was saving those who had been chosen before the foundation of the world.

- **He kept entrusting Himself to Him who judges righteously**. He repeatedly turned Himself over to the Father, trusting in the absolute equity of God's judgment.

- **He Himself bore our sins in His body on the cross, that we might die to sin and live to righteousness;** This we cannot copy. We can only learn how to live for others.

- **by His wounds you were healed.** He suffered for the sake of others' spiritual benefit.

Through all this, Jesus was content to let the Father reconcile all the accounts in due time. Notice that Peter draws heavily from Isaiah 53. Jesus was *the* suffering servant. Jesus is our great pattern.

But He isn't the only one who has suffered unjustly. Think of David's abuse at the hands of King Saul. Think of Daniel in the lion's den, and his three friends in the fiery furnace. Think of Jeremiah, who suffered so much but said in Lamentations 3:39, **Why should any living mortal, or any man, offer complaint in view of his sins?**

All of these believers gained the courage and patience they needed under adversity because they depended upon the sovereignty of God. A sovereign ruler isn't necessarily wise or good. But when God's sovereignty is flanked on one side by His love and on the other side by His wisdom, then the sovereignty of God is the greatest and most effective encouragement I know of.

In Order to Accomplish God's Redemptive Purpose, 24-25

24 and He Himself bore our sins in His body on the cross, that we might die to sin and live to righteousness; for by His wounds you were healed.
25 For you were continually straying like sheep, but now you have returned to the Shepherd and Guardian of your souls.

If God did not want to involve us in saving others, He would perhaps just grab each person He wants and take him straight to heaven, and then go after the next guy in sort of a rolling rapture.

But God has chosen to use believers to introduce non-believers to the Savior. That is part of our **participation in the gospel,** Philippians 1:5. And our involvement is another one of those redemptive agencies that make us more like Jesus. We can suffer for the sake of bringing others to the Savior, even though we can't suffer vicariously in the place of others. Our suffering cannot atone for sin. We are not qualified to be an unblemished offering for sin, and we aren't chosen by God to be a substitutionary sacrifice. His plan of salvation requires and permits only one Redeemer.

In verse 24, Peter is careful to point out that only Jesus Himself can do the work of redemption by bearing our sins in His body on the cross. We are totally unqualified to participate in the accomplishing of redemption, our own or anyone else's.

Peter is pouring on the motivation in order to convince his readers to submit to someone else's will instead of following self-will. If we submit, we walk in God's grace. Jesus left us a pattern to follow, as He suffered for our sake. The righteous Judge will judge righteously.

And now he reminds them that Jesus died for us so we could die to sin, that is, to self-will and all the trouble it causes. Jesus did not save us so we could keep on sinning without fear of judgment. He saved us so we could die to sin and live to righteousness, according to verse 24.

Sadly this fact is going out of favor in the church at large. But the church does not have authority to change God's word. No one does. The church is the pillar and support of the truth, not the editor. We are to hold forth the word of truth, not alter it so sinners might like it better.

God sternly warns against adding to or subtracting from His word or twisting it to fit man's sinful desires (Deut 4:2; 12:32; Prov 30:6; Rev 22:18f). I Peter 4:17 says, **it is time for judgment to begin with the household of God; and if it begins with us first, what will be the outcome for those who do not obey the gospel of God?**

The end of verse 24 has been ripped out of context for years. When people interpret a text in a way that is inconsistent with its context they cause two problems: they make the Bible say something that it doesn't say, and they miss what it does say. Peter is still drawing from Isaiah 53. Both Isaiah and Peter define the nature of that healing for us. It is not physical healing, at least not in this life, otherwise Christians would never die. But it's obvious that we do die, including those who say that this statement is a promise of physical health.

Verse 25 starts with the word **for**, which introduces an explanation of what we were healed from. We were continually straying like sheep. That was our sickness: sin. And the phrase **by His wounds you were healed** is also begun with the word **for**, explaining the previous phrase, **that we might die to sin and live to righteousness.**

So, the context of that healing is iron-clad, front to back, it's about healing us from our disease of sin. You will find the same thing in Isaiah 53:5f:

But He was pierced through for our transgressions, He was crushed for our iniquities; the chastening for our well-being fell upon Him, and by His scourging we are healed. All of us like sheep have gone astray, each of us has turned to his own way; but the LORD has caused the iniquity of us all to fall on Him.

Peter's point is that we were taken away from the life of self-will and self-serving, in other words **that we might die to sin,** when Jesus saved us from our sin and iniquity. And Peter reinforces his statement that Jesus **bore our sins...that we might die to sin and live to righteousness** when he writes in verse 25, **you have returned to the Shepherd and Guardian of your souls**. This is repentance, the *sine qua non* of salvation. There is no salvation without repentance from sin. So as hard as it is to submit to a perverted government or to a perverse slave master, Christians have that obligation before God. We turn away from self-will to obey God's will, even if we don't have the wisdom or insight to agree with it.

The difficulty we have with the whole issue of submission, including our submission to God (which is the main problem), calls for the difficult extraction of self-will. This is a difficult extraction because self-will has metastasized throughout our being. Removing it isn't a quick operation, nor is it painless (being so deeply ingrained and so firmly attached). But God will perform that operation if it takes your whole, earthly life, because it is what fits us for heaven. And if the operation calls for a sledge hammer, so be it. God's mercy is severe where severity is required.

But redemptive agencies can also be sweet and pleasant. We will get to that in the next chapter, when Peter applies the principle of submission to the family.

This has been a heavy discussion: the subject of keeping our behavior excellent among the Gentiles in the spheres of governing authorities and workplace authority. These demands root out the very core of our sin nature, our independent desire. They get right at the heart of our greatest need in the sanctification process. This is the heavy lifting part of our Christian lives, and it causes us to do some deep soul searching. God will not allow us to neglect the heavy lifting. So we must not shy away from it. Submission is the gateway to all of God's greatest and deepest blessings.

Peter went the extra mile in giving us the motivations we need to submit to these demands. The purpose of God in His redemptive plan and the pattern Jesus left for us are heavy-duty motivations. So is the fact that non-believers are watching how you, personally, trust God and submit to His commands. Your attitudes, choices, and perseverance under unpleasant circumstances form the answer to the non-believer's question,

"Is that person's God real?" That's a heavy responsibility, Christian, and it's yours, like it or not. It is for this purpose that you were called.

Now I won't leave you with a heavy burden without reminding you of the power you have to cope with it.

II Corinthians. 3:5f give us some relief:

Not that we are adequate in ourselves to consider anything as coming from ourselves, but our adequacy is from God, who also made us adequate as servants of a new covenant, not of the letter, but of the Spirit; for the letter kills, but the Spirit gives life.

Do you know what impresses me the most about myself? (I don't think you'll accuse me of bragging when I say this.) It is the depth and breadth of my inadequacy. I'm a versatile guy – I can be inadequate in many fields of endeavor. But that doesn't excuse me from serving God, because His Spirit in me makes me adequate. In fact, we have to say with Paul, that in our weakness, God's strength is made manifest. Unbelievers watch believers, not to see how strong we are, but to see how strong our God is.

II Corinthians 12:9 is also a comfort: **And He has said to me, "My grace is sufficient for you, for power is perfected in weakness." Most gladly, therefore, I will rather boast about my weaknesses, that the power of Christ may dwell in me.** Whose power does an unbeliever really need to see—ours or Christ's?

Romans 6:19 says, **For just as you presented your members as slaves to impurity and to lawlessness, resulting in further lawlessness, so now present your members as slaves to righteousness, resulting in sanctification.** Can you do that? Yes, you can. Will you?

Chapter 13

3:1-7, Excellent Marriages

[1] In the same way, you wives, be submissive to your own husbands so that even if any *of them* are disobedient to the word, they may be won without a word by the behavior of their wives,

[2] as they observe your chaste and respectful behavior.

[3] And let not your adornment be *merely* external-- braiding the hair, and wearing gold jewelry, or putting on dresses;

[4] but *let it be* the hidden person of the heart, with the imperishable quality of a gentle and quiet spirit, which is precious in the sight of God.

[5] For in this way in former times the holy women also, who hoped in God, used to adorn themselves, being submissive to their own husbands.

[6] Thus Sarah obeyed Abraham, calling him lord, and you have become her children if you do what is right without being frightened by any fear.

[7] You husbands likewise, live with *your wives* in an understanding way, as with a weaker vessel, since she is a woman; and grant her honor as a fellow heir of the grace of life, so that your prayers may not be hindered.

The Apostle Peter has been saying that we are to keep our behavior excellent among the Gentiles. This is because we are to be holy as our God is holy. And it is also for the purpose of leading unbelievers to the saving knowledge of Jesus Christ (2:12).

Peter started with the over-arching principle that Christians are to submit to the human institutions that God created. God created these institutions for the sake of the His redemptive purpose and also for the sake of maintaining order in society. Peter has been applying that principle to how we relate to governing authorities and to authority in the workplace.

Now, in 3:1-7, he applies the principle to the institution of marriage. Marriage is the prime social institution and the prime redemptive agency.

In The Heritage Foundation's Backgrounder # 1026, *The Real Root Cause of Violent Crime: The Breakdown of Marriage, Family, and Community,* 3/17/1995, author Patrick F. Fagan, Ph.D., began with this introduction:

A review of the empirical evidence in the professional literature of the social sciences gives policymakers an insight into the root causes of crime. Consider, for instance:

- Over the past thirty years, the rise in violent crime parallels the rise in families abandoned by fathers.

- High-crime neighborhoods are characterized by high concentrations of families abandoned by fathers.

- State-by-state analysis by Heritage scholars indicates that a 10 percent increase in the percentage of children living in single-parent homes leads typically to a 17 percent increase in juvenile crime.

- The rate of violent teenage crime corresponds with the number of families abandoned by fathers.

- The type of aggression and hostility demonstrated by a future criminal often is foreshadowed in unusual aggressiveness as early as age five or six.

- The future criminal tends to be an individual rejected by other children as early as the first grade who goes on to form his own group of friends, often the future delinquent gang. But on the other hand:

- Neighborhoods with a high degree of religious practice are not high-crime neighborhoods.

- Even in high-crime inner-city neighborhoods, well over 90 percent of children from safe, stable homes do not become delinquents. By contrast only 10 percent of children from unsafe, unstable homes in these neighborhoods avoid crime.

- Criminals capable of sustaining marriage gradually move away from a life of crime after they get married.

- The mother's strong affectionate attachment to her child is the child's best buffer against a life of crime.

- The father's authority and involvement in raising his children are also a great buffer against a life of crime.

The article goes on to document how the disintegration of the institution of marriage is a direct cause of the disintegration of society. This should come as no surprise to those who study God's word.

When God created mankind, the first and most important relationship He set up was between mankind and Himself, of course. But the first on the horizontal level was the marriage relationship between the husband and wife, starting with Adam and Eve. So when man's relationship with God broke down, marriage became the prime institution for maintaining order in a fallen society and for encouraging people to give up independent desire. But that institution itself did not escape damage from the Fall.

Peter's outline is obvious:

The Importance of Marriage in God's Plan,

The Winning Wife, 1-6, and

The Understanding Husband, 7.

The Importance of Marriage in God's Plan

Marriage is the first and most basic social institution. It is both the foundation upon which society is built and the adhesive force that holds society together. It is also the primary educational institution. Ask any educator how well students learn if their home is dysfunctional. Destroying the foundation of a building will quickly bring down the whole building. Just so, destroying the fundamental institution of marriage will quickly cause society to fall apart.

Marriage was created by God before government, before work, and before any religious organization. And it outranks them in importance and influence. Only marriage and the family make law, government, labor, and any other social relationship important enough to an individual that he will subjugate his own wishes to the needs of society.

Marriage is a redemptive agency in that it gives married people reason and motivation to think of others before they consider their own wishes. And it's a redemptive agency in that a godly marriage is a convincing witness to the goodness of obeying God. It helps to redeem the society as well as the individual.

The family is where we live. It is the main source of our personal identity and security, our sense of belonging and hence of community, our love, our provision, our sense of value. Family is the main socializing influence in a child's life.

According to professional literature, the absence of the father is the single most important cause of poverty. The father's absence is a major factor in delinquency and criminal behavior of the children, lower intellectual development, higher levels of illegitimate parenting in the teenage years, and higher levels of welfare dependency.

Broken homes are much more likely to raise psychopaths, because the child, having a more emotionally distant relationship with his over-worked and over-stressed single mother, never learns empathy for others. It is of supreme importance that single mothers raise their children in the nurture of a caring and godly church. This extended family can supply some of what would otherwise be lacking in the child's upbringing.

The only remedy for fractured families is to get right with God. Right doctrine, rightly applied, by people rightly related to God, is the solution to mankind's problems. It was rebellion against God's word and God's ways that caused all the problems in the first place, and continued rebellion continues to cause all the problems.

The only place to get right doctrine, by which we can make right choices, is from God's infallible word. No other source has worked. Alternative sources just make the problems worse. God's word is the only source of sound doctrine. If we dismiss God's word as the source of answers, all we have left is the pursuit of the best wrong answers.

Refusing to listen to God's word has led to role reversals in the marriage, where the wife is the head, and the husband, if he hasn't bailed out, is the submissive one. Because of this battle between the sexes (predicted in Genesis 3), with the resultant high divorce rate, and people's desire to live for themselves, many are now delaying marriage or avoiding the marriage commitment altogether. In other words, self-will and role reversal have led to role refusal. This is a tragic mistake. Having no societal foundation to begin with is as bad as a destroyed foundation.

In point of fact, we see all three of the redemptive agencies Peter addresses being increasingly rejected by the younger segment of our society. Lawlessness is increasing. Commitment to employers is fading as some of our young people have adopted the practice of getting a job, earning enough to live on for awhile, then quitting so they can live as they like. When their money runs out they get another job.

Many young people are putting off marriage in order to pursue their own desires. Others live together in an intimate, non-committal relationship as long as both find it convenient. They are unwilling to submit themselves to any authority.

The Christian wife must consider her responsibility to her Lord.

The Winning Wife, 1-6

[1] In the same way, you wives, be submissive to your own husbands so that even if any *of them* are disobedient to the word, they may be won without a word by the behavior of their wives,
[2] as they observe your chaste and respectful behavior.
[3] And let not your adornment be *merely* external-- braiding the hair, and wearing gold jewelry, or putting on dresses;
[4] but *let it be* the hidden person of the heart, with the imperishable quality of a gentle and quiet spirit, which is precious in the sight of God.
[5] For in this way in former times the holy women also, who hoped in God, used to adorn themselves, being submissive to their own husbands.

**[6] Thus Sarah obeyed Abraham, calling him lord, and you
have become her children if you do what is right without
being frightened by any fear.**

Submitting with Respect

Long, long ago in a land far, far away, a young wife in
the church I was pastoring came to me for counseling. She told
me, "I don't respect my husband." My counsel to her was that
she needed to repent, because the Bible commands wives to
respect their husbands. Her husband, by the way, was a very
respectable man who loved his wife. But I suspect that she
didn't feel that love and so had responded by withholding the
respect he needed. I wasn't smart enough at the time to pursue
that possibility.

Longer ago, in a land farther away, God set up the chain
of command. He did so when He created Adam first and then
Eve. And to underscore the man's authority over the wife, God
then had Adam name the wife, showing both of them that He
was giving the husband authority over the wife. (See the entry
Names in a good Bible dictionary.)

In Genesis 3:16f, after this chain of command had been
violated, to the world's great loss, God told Adam and Eve the
consequences of their rebellion:

**To the woman He said, "I will greatly multiply your pain in
childbirth, in pain you shall bring forth children; yet your
desire shall be for your husband** [not in a romantic sense, but
to usurp control over him], **and he shall rule over you** [in a
harsh, dominating way]**." Then to Adam He said, "Because
you have listened to the voice of your wife** [the
leader/submitter roles were established *before* the Fall and were
reversed in the decision to eat the forbidden fruit—Adam
listened to, which is to say, obeyed, his wife]**, and have eaten
from the tree about which I commanded you, saying, 'You
shall not eat from it'; cursed is the ground because of you;
in toil you shall eat of it all the days of your life.**

The God-ordained chain of command was: the wife
submits to the husband, the husband submits to God. When that

chain of command was not honored, bad results followed. In I Timothy 2:11ff, Paul gave God's instruction for the church:

Let a woman quietly receive instruction with entire submissiveness. But I do not allow a woman to teach or exercise authority over a man, but to remain quiet. For it was Adam who was first created, and then Eve. And it was not Adam who was deceived, but the woman being quite deceived, fell into transgression.

So, the husband/wife roles were not culturally determined, so that we could claim the freedom to follow a different arrangement in our modern culture. They were not determined by eons of conditioning and oppression although, as with everything else God created, sinful man has corrupted what God set up. But the roles go back to original creation, before there was a culture, and before the fall of man into sin.

Paul also mentions the fact that the woman was quite deceived. Men and women were designed by God fill different roles. The obvious used to be obvious, before sinful desire and political correctness blinded people. God created the man with the traits and strengths he needed to fulfill his God-given role. And God made the woman with the traits and strengths she needed to be able to fulfill her role. The man is the fighter--he was told to **rule and subdue**. The wife is the **helper suitable** to him. Every good designer knows that form follows function. Man was designed to lead and to be the contender; the woman was not. She was designed to follow the husband's leadership and to assist him. This isn't politically correct, but it should be evident by now that what is politically correct isn't correct for any other purpose.

Peter is following what Jesus told him in Matthew 16:18f:

"And I also say to you that you are Peter, and upon this rock I will build My church; and the gates of Hades shall not overpower it. I will give you the keys of the kingdom of heaven; and whatever you shall bind on earth shall [have been] bound in heaven, and whatever you shall loose on earth shall [have been] loosed in heaven."

So, operating with his Lord's pre-approval, Peter commands, **In the same way, you wives be submissive to your own husbands.**

In the same way, refers back to the main principle of the passage upon which Peter has been expounding. This whole treatise on submission follows from 2:12. Wives, like everyone else, are to set aside independent desire and submit to the human institutions that God has ordained for the good of society and for the sake of His redemptive plan. Christ is our pattern. In the wife's case, she is to submit to her own husband. She is not told to submit to all men in general – what a nightmare that would be! The wife's chain of command would look like this: God, then her father (before she marries) or her husband (after she marries), then government (which, by the way, recognizes that a wife cannot be forced to testify against her husband), then church elders, and finally the workplace (if applicable).

And she is to submit with **respect**, verse 2. The word here is the same word for fear, *phobos*, that we have seen already in 2:17, referring to a genuine, personal commitment to obey out of due respect for God's authority.

Paul dealt with the subject in detail in Ephesians 5:21ff:

[21] **and be subject to one another in the fear of Christ.** [22] **Wives,** *be subject* **to your own husbands, as to the Lord.**
[23] **For the husband is the head of the wife, as Christ also is the head of the church, He Himself** *being* **the Savior of the body.**
[24] **But as the church is subject to Christ, so also the wives** *ought to be* **to their husbands in everything.**

Ephesians 5:21 states the general principle, **be subject to one another in the fear of Christ.** That principle is followed by the specifics of who submits to whom. This doesn't mean that we all submit to each other. That would be chaotic and meaningless in any practical sense. Some teachers, trying to be politically correct (a bad motive that produces bad results), believe that the submission is to be mutual--the wife submits to the husband, and the husband submits to the wife. Nothing in the Bible supports this absurdity. No Scripture tells us to submit to one another, without also telling who submits to whom, as Ephesians 5 and our present passage do. And mutual submission is an oxymoron. It's a practical impossibility, unless one resorts to equivocation on the meaning of the term *submit*. Every disagreement would end in deadlock.

The self-contradictory idea of mutual submission isn't what the word *hupotasso* means. It means *to arrange in military array under* – in other words, we are to follow God's chain of command. Husbands are never told to submit to their wives. Both Adam and Abraham were rebuked for doing so. No army could function on the basis of mutual submission. That's why the wives get six verses of instruction here, and the husband gets only one. The subject is submission, and the husband isn't told to submit to his wife. His submission has already been covered with regard to government and work.

In verse 22; the wife is told to see past her immediate commander, her husband, to his commander, the Lord. So when she submits to her husband, she is in reality submitting to the Lord, Himself, who set up this chain of command, verse 23. So as verse 24 says, wives are subject to their husbands in everything just as the church is subject to Christ. That doesn't mean that the wife doesn't do anything except what her husband tells her. We don't relate to Christ that way. But she follows his priorities, his ways, his directions when he gives some, his will in general. She helps him to fulfill his role from the Lord. God doesn't micromanage us, and the husband shouldn't try to micromanage his wife. That would be very inefficient. It would sacrifice many of the advantages of being a married couple.

If the divine right of kings is subject to abuse by the kings, so is the divine right of husbands. So Paul checks that potential abuse by including verses 25-33a of Ephesians 5, to which we will refer when we get to the husband's duty to his wife.

Paul concludes with the wife's duty to her husband in Ephesians 5:33, **and let the wife see to it that she respect [fear] her husband.** There is that word, fear, again. Wives, see to it that you maintain that genuine, personal commitment to obey your husband with the respect due to the man whom God has placed over you in the chain of command.

Hopefully, the wife married well, and submission to her husband is a pleasant and secure thing to do. If not, she is still under obligation to obey him with all respect. **You wives, be submissive to your own husbands so that even if any *of them* are disobedient to the word, they may be won without a word by the behavior of their wives.** (The only exception would be if he expressly demands what God forbids or forbids what God demands.)

The wife's duty to obey her husband is not conditioned upon her husband's obedience to God. That would be a loophole she could drive a bus through! Nor is it conditioned upon the wife's agreement with the husband's course of action. Eve disagreed with God's course of action, and look at the result! Remember that marriage is a redemptive agency, designed to teach the wife to give up her independent desire which is fueled by her belief that her ways are best.

Now, back to I Peter 3. Some wives will have a husband who is disobedient to the word of God, as verse 1 says. The chain of command still applies. And it is important for this additional reason – a submissive wife's excellent behavior will put her husband at ease with her Christianity and motivate him to seek the Lord, as 2:12 indicates. It's hard for a husband to resent the gospel when it makes his wife so much better than she used to be.

Peter has more instruction for the wife than he does for the husband. If a husband became a Christian before his wife in that culture, there would not likely be as much problem as there would be if the wife came to Christ before her husband. The unbelieving husband might see his wife's change of religion as an act of defiance and rebellion, not only against him but also against the state. So her attempts to lead her husband to Christ would start off on negative ground.

How does the wife find herself joined to a disobedient husband? It might be by her own bad choice in marrying a non-Christian, contrary to wisdom and the biblical prohibition against being bound together with unbelievers (II Cor. 6:14). Some women, due perhaps to their own pride, want a project husband, someone they can mold and control. It might be because she came to Christ and her husband didn't, or he fooled her into thinking he was a believer when he really wasn't. Or her Christian husband might have gone rogue. Do any of these possibilities justify being disobedient to her husband? Not according to the Bible.

What then are her options for dealing with the situation? Just brainstorming here: murder, divorce, passive resistance, taking charge of the family, submission? The first two were either illegal or inadvisable in her culture. The second two make the family a battleground. Passive resistance is always a popular choice, if not a successful one. Taking charge is what God warned Eve about in Genesis 3. None of these options will adorn the gospel of Jesus Christ. Of all her options, only submission will encourage the disobedient husband to repent and follow Christ. The other options will be stumbling blocks to his repentance.

Peter, like all the Apostles, was a practical theologian. So he tells the believing wife how to win her unbelieving husband. She can do that best by …

Adorning the Gospel

We have two *words* in verse 1; the **word** of the Lord, apart from which no one can be saved, and the wife's **word**s, which might tend to harden the husband against the word of the Lord, because obeying his wife goes against the way God made him.

He can't be saved unless he obeys the gospel, but he won't want to obey the gospel unless he sees that his believing wife is transformed into a better person by her obedience to the gospel. So he will observe his wife. And what will he see? Every guy wants a wife who is attractive, faithful, and easy to live with (i.e., life is a lot better with her than it would be without her). And we all notice early on that when we first see a woman, we have an initial impression of how attractive she is. And then, as we get to know her, she either gets more attractive or less attractive, depending upon her inner character and demeanor. Pretty women can be ugly people. But a plain-looking woman may be fairly worshiped by her adoring husband. Pretty is skin deep; beauty comes from the heart! (Incidentally, this observation works with both genders.)

So will that husband's wife become more attractive to him as her Christian character becomes evident? Or will she become a nag, a complainer, a manipulator, or a judge, or all the above? The real question runs parallel to this one: as he observes his Christian wife's behavior will the gospel become more attractive to him?

Peter has a lot to say about a woman's proper adornment. And it's all relevant to our times. The way a woman dresses says something about her, it makes a statement. It should say, "Here is a woman of quality; spiritual values held supreme."

Some women make a point of looking unattractive. This does not adorn the gospel of God. Others make a point of copying the world's indecent styles and undue attention to outer beauty. This certainly does not adorn the gospel!

The way a woman dresses should not say, "I'm a slob with no self-respect." And it shouldn't say, "Here I am, big boy, come and get me!" Nor should it say, "You can tell by my appearance that I am richer than you, and therefore better than you." Her mode of presenting yourself should not say, "I'm a rebel against God, husband, and decency." Historically, ungodly women have used cosmetology, clothes, and cash in order to conquer men.

A godly woman adorns her native and inner beauty without calling attention to her makeup, jewelry, and clothing, and without attracting unholy attention to her body. Such a woman adorns the gospel of Jesus Christ. She makes her husband glad rather than resentful that she became a Christian. She dresses attractively but not seductively, and not to call undue attention to herself.

The internal graces add to one's beauty and never go out of style, don't fade with age, and are independent of social status. They even add to one's outer beauty. As Abraham Lincoln said, "After 40, you are responsible for your own face."

What is really attractive in a woman is **the imperishable quality of a gentle and quiet spirit**. So let's consider those traits.

Gentle is the word *meek*. It is a temper of spirit in which we accept God's dealings with us as good and therefore not to be disputed or resisted. It means obedient, and is a trait that arises from trusting the sovereignty and goodness of God. It is the opposite of self-assertiveness and self-interest. Jesus used the word to describe Himself in Matthew 11:29.

Quiet means tranquil. We see the word again in I Timothy 2:12, **But I do not allow a woman to teach or exercise authority over a man, but to remain quiet** [tranquil]. Proverbs 14:30 says, **A tranquil heart is life to the body, But passion is rottenness to the bones.**

Put them together and you have a calm and contented acceptance of God's will. From the rest of God's word we find that this should characterize all Christians, not just women. But for wives, this is especially precious in the sight of God because He can use it to lead people to trust the Savior, and especially to lead her husband to Christ.

The church is spoken of as the bride of Christ and Israel is spoken of as God's wife. No doubt the Lord would like to see these two traits in His bride. Unfortunately, the church is becoming more self-assertive and less obedient to God as the years go by. Consequently, the church's witness is becoming more and more counter-productive.

The church and the wife must concern themselves to …

Be Right with God

To make this point, Peter goes back into the Old Testament for examples of adornment that demonstrates submission, citing especially Abraham's wife Sarah, verses 5-6. Sarah was a physically beautiful woman, even as an older lady. The bride of Solomon's song adorned herself. Peter is not saying that dressing nicely or wearing jewelry or makeup is wrong. The wrong is making these things the focus of your appearance or tools for manipulation. It then becomes a literal hypocrisy – a hiding of the real person behind a mask.

Peter is citing women who hoped in God rather than in their womanly wiles. And you know that women can be very wily in getting their own way. Some will even try faking submissiveness to see if they can dominate their husbands that way.

But how did the beautiful Sarah adorn herself? By obeying her husband, (sincerely) calling him **lord**. Sarah obeyed Abraham even when he asked her to say that she was his sister, which he did on two separate occasions because he was afraid the local king would kill him and take his beautiful wife for himself.

Don't Be Afraid to Submit

Sarah was not **frightened by any fear**. She feared her husband in the fear of God, so she did not need to fear any frightening situation that her obedience got her into. She had that meekness and tranquility Peter spoke of in verse 4. And indeed, God prevented anything bad from happening to her in those cases.

If you are right with God and know that you are obeying the sovereign God who is good and attentive to your situation, then there is no need to be frightened, because you have the security of being in God's will. So the godly wife does not need to be afraid that submitting to her husband will go badly for her.

The women's liberation movement has not made women free. It's only made them more enslaved to sin. Only God can set people free. And whenever some group demands equal rights, they may really be going for domination. Historically, genuine Christianity has resulted in the best life women have ever known. A Christian women's lib movement would be an oxymoron, like a Christian abortion clinic or a Christian crime ring. And it would be an affront to the freedom that Christ provides. The women's lib movement is all about liberating women from God's constraints and the constraints of obeying their husbands. Eve tried that and it didn't pan out too well for her or anyone else.

7 You husbands likewise, live with *your wives* in an understanding way, as with a weaker vessel, since she is a woman; and grant her honor as a fellow heir of the grace of life, so that your prayers may not be hindered.

The husband gets just one verse of admonition, with two commands and a warning. Note the word **likewise** again, indicating that the husband is under God's authority and must submit to it. The two commands are: understand her, honor her. This equates to love. A woman's greatest need is love, just as a man's greatest need is respect.

Understand Her as the Weaker Vessel

The literal translation here is *dwell together according to knowledge.* In other words, the husband does not have free reign to rule over his wife harshly. His wife is also a servant of God. She is also a fellow heir in Christ. The standard the husband is obliged to follow is the standard of knowledge. God holds him accountable for that, as the end of the verse indicates.

How can he understand his wife? Comedians all say it can't be done. Merlin told Arthur in the movie *Camelot*, "Don't worry if you don't understand what women are thinking--they don't do it very often."

Women think a lot, I suspect, but they think differently than men think, and with different motives. To understand a woman we have to listen to her. Like the detective on the old *Dragnet* TV series, men want to say, "Just the facts, Ma'am." But to the woman, facts are only part of the story. To her the facts may only be the stimuli for the emotional responses of the people concerned, which is her real story. God made women to be more concerned with relationships and other people's welfare while men are more concerned with solving problems. Together, the man and the woman can make a well-balanced team. If the husband would be more inclined to listen to his wife in the desire to understand her, and the wife would work to understand how her husband listens, then both could make some adjustments and understand each other a lot better.

In what sense is the woman the weaker vessel? Certainly, as genders go, women are on average physically weaker. But how much understanding does it take to realize that? Certainly Peter's readers didn't see that many women on the arm-wrestling circuit. And in some ways women are stronger than men. They are less bothered by temperature extremes, I understand, and generally have a higher pain threshold. So physical strength doesn't seem to be the issue here. Bulk of muscle isn't part of the argument.

I think we have a clue in Paul's statement in I Timothy 2:14, **And it was not Adam who was deceived, but the woman being quite deceived, fell into transgression.** Women are more gullible in spiritual matters. Being relaters more than contenders, they are generally less doctrinally astute, or at least less suspicious and discerning of doctrinal error. And perhaps they're less concerned with doctrinal issues to begin with. They were designed to follow a leader, and in their fallen condition, aren't necessarily the best at discerning whom to follow. They are more trusting perhaps, and therefore less aware when someone is trying to pull the wool over their eyes.

Contrast this to John's evaluation in I John 2:14, **I have written to you, young men, because you are strong, and the word of God abides in you, and you have overcome the evil one.** So Paul says in I Timothy 2:11f, **Let a woman quietly receive instruction with entire submissiveness. But I do not allow a woman to teach or exercise authority over a man, but to remain quiet.** And in I Corinthians 14:34f regarding prophesying in church Paul wrote:

Let the women keep silent in the churches; for they are not permitted to speak, but let them subject themselves, just as the Law also says. And if they desire to learn anything, let them ask their own husbands at home; for it is improper for a woman to speak in church.

In Christ there is **neither male nor female, for you are all one in Christ**, according to Galatians 3:28. But this restoration of equal value in Christ does not erase the original gender characteristics or roles, which God designed into man and woman during Creation. Women were not designed for battle. On the other hand, women are not second class citizens of heaven. Jesus, who submits to the Father, and who, in our text, submitted to the people who put Him on trial and crucified Him, is not in any way second class.

Women found that their place in the church was so much better than it had been in society at large. So judging from issues in the Corinthian church, some of them went too far with their new-found freedom and set aside the roles that God designed for them from Creation. They threw the baby out with the bath water, so to speak. They swung the pendulum too far in the opposite direction. That's understandable, but it called for some correction.

So if doctrinal weakness is the concern, that would explain why women cannot be elders or pastors or in any other way exercise authority over men in the church. They are the weaker vessel in the particular sphere where strength is required. **Weaker** is a comparative form. Men mess up, too. And men are weaker than God. Men are made of clay just as women are. Women are, perhaps, more inclined to let doctrine slide in the interest of empathy or support for a hurting friend. Women don't tend to be doctrinal bulldogs. The man is more inclined to say, hopefully with some empathy, "I know you're having a hard time, but it is always best to obey the word of God. Disobedience is what causes troubles. More disobedience won't fix them."

How does the husband live with his wife **according to knowledge**? He listens to her. He studies his wife. God treats men in an understanding way. He takes into account that we are but dust. And the husband must study the word of God which tells us a lot about how to understand people, including women.

In Philippians 1:9f, Paul writes:

And this I pray, that your love may abound still more and more in real knowledge and all discernment, so that you may approve the things that are excellent, in order to be sincere and blameless until the day of Christ; having been filled with the fruit of righteousness which comes through Jesus Christ, to the glory and praise of God.

Abounding love operates **in real knowledge and all discernment.** Many times, I think, women don't feel loved because they don't recognize their husbands' efforts as acts of love. But that goes the other way as well. Our love must be according to **real knowledge**. This is the term *epignosis*--full and experiential knowledge. That and *agape* **love** are the two marks of spiritual maturity. Abounding love is a thinking love. And thinking takes a lot of time and study, at least the way I do it. Who hasn't been on the receiving end of an attempt at love that wasn't according to knowledge and so was hindered by the attempt instead of helped? Ironically, people respond to such an attempt by saying, "Well, it's the thought that counts." But the attempt failed because of the lack of thought.

The biggest difference Christ makes in a marriage is in the sphere of knowing, discerning, selfless love. Certainly some Gentile husbands loved their wives, but more commonly the wife was just another servant. Biblical doctrine made big changes in Gentile marriages. Ephesians 5:25-33 shows some of those changes.

Christ's sacrificial love for His church is the model for how husbands are to love their wives. This being the case, the husband is to sacrificially sanctify his wife. He is to cleanse her by the washing water of the word of God. He is to be her spiritual leader and teacher, just as Paul wrote in I Corinthians 14 that **if** [wives] **desire to learn anything, let them ask their own husbands at home.**

The husband is the family's primary pastor, their shepherd. Like a shepherd he is to guide, provide for, protect, and heal those under his care. He must be serious about tending his flock. It is his duty to labor in order to present his wife and his children to God **holy and blameless** with **no spot or wrinkle**. God equipped the man to fill this role and holds the husband accountable.

The husband is to love his wife as his own body. The two are, in fact, **one flesh**. So he doesn't just look to his own needs and neglect hers. That would be like nourishing and caring for his right side while neglecting his left side. He is to **nourish and cherish** his wife since he is one flesh with her. Adam said of Eve, **"This is now bone of my bones and flesh of my flesh,"** (Gen. 2:23). How hard would it be for a wife to submit to a husband who does all that for her?

Verse 33 is interesting because I think it indicates that in a marriage, the wife's greatest need is love, and the husband's greatest need is respect. That, I think, is worth contemplating. Put another way, the wife's essential concern is to be respectfully submissive. The husband's essential concern is to love his wife. By original design, the wife already tends to be loving, and the husband already tends to be in charge and to value respect.

But for marriage to be the blessing that God intends, the husband must also honor his wife as **a fellow heir of the grace of life,** I Peter 3:7. The husband is the head, but he is not superior, except in those traits which God designed into him to enable him to be the head and the spiritual warrior. Other than that, headship does not imply superiority, and submission does not imply inferiority. It is simply a godly and necessary chain of command, put in place to secure order in the family.

The wife's major obligation is to serve the Lord. The same is true of the husband. They join together because they can serve God better together than they can separately. The wife's role in the marriage is to help the husband accomplish God's will--to be a helper suitable to him. It is not to be the husband's servant. The man and woman are designed by God to function as a team, each complementing the other, and each working with the other as if they really are one flesh so they can do more together than both could do separately. Think of a sports team that has that "chemistry" and works together as if they shared the same mind.

In the culture of Peter's day, husbands looked down upon their wives and saw them as servants. In fact, the husband may actually have purchased the wife from her father. In the Greco-Roman culture, husbands generally weren't interested in being friends with their wives. But if wives don't have that intimate, understanding companionship with their husbands then they are missing what God intends the marriage relationship to provide. This gives rise to all kinds of sins, aberrations, and uprisings.

Husbands, you serve yourself best when you make sure that your marriage is right with God …

So That Your Prayers May Not Be Hindered

God is sovereign in government and in the workplace. He is also sovereign in the home. He guards those who submit to God-ordained authorities. So if the husband doesn't attend to his duty in a godly way, then God will stop attending to the husband's prayers.

The husband is a vassal king in the home, a viceroy. As such he is subject to the King of Kings, and will give an account for how he ruled his family. If he is rebellious in the home, God can tie a pork chop around his neck and throw him to the dogs. And it's a dog-eat-dog world!

What the word **hinder** really means, though, is *to cut into.* The term was used of impeding people by breaking up the road or by placing an obstacle sharply in the path. Obedient people live in God's grace (2:19f). Disobedient people live in constant danger and impediment. Psalm 68:6 says, **Only the rebellious dwell in a parched land.**

As the poet Ogden Nash put it, reflecting upon a yellow traffic sign, "Cross Children Walk; Cheerful Children Ride."

Marriage is the most basic, most fundamental, and most important social institution. It was ordained by God to under-gird every other institution and to hold society together. When done right, marriage shows the beauty of God's holiness and His ability to come up with a good plan. It demonstrates the love of God. That's why it is the main target of Satan's attacks. Satan works best when chaos, rebellion, and selfishness are the norm.

The glory of God's love is put on display in a marriage. If we obey God and make our marriages excellent, then non-believers will observe and learn that God's ways are best.

Chapter 14
3:8-12, Excellent Relationships

[8] To sum up, let all be harmonious, sympathetic, brotherly, kindhearted, and humble in spirit; [9] not returning evil for evil, or insult for insult, but giving a blessing instead; for you were called for the very purpose that you might inherit a blessing.
[10] For, "LET HIM WHO MEANS TO LOVE LIFE AND SEE GOOD DAYS REFRAIN HIS TONGUE FROM EVIL AND HIS LIPS FROM SPEAKING GUILE.
[11] "AND LET HIM TURN AWAY FROM EVIL AND DO GOOD; LET HIM SEEK PEACE AND PURSUE IT.
[12] "FOR THE EYES OF THE LORD ARE UPON THE RIGHTEOUS, AND HIS EARS ATTEND TO THEIR PRAYER, BUT THE FACE OF THE LORD IS AGAINST THOSE WHO DO EVIL."

How do you warn people you love that hard times are about to get worse? To be forewarned is to be forearmed. But a warning might become a discourage to your friends; you might cause then to recant under pressure, or go into hiding, or stop witnessing. The Christians reading Peter's letter have already suffered some sporadic, unofficial persecution. Peter wrote this letter because he saw official persecution coming over the horizon.

Maybe Peter is seeing with the eye of a prophet, but you don't really need to be a prophet to see the early signs of government-sanctioned attacks on Christianity. We can see those signs in America. An unfriendly government might move from merely overlooking the persecution of Christians to actively promoting it, and then to actually joining in that persecution as official policy. A government doesn't even need to pass laws that specifically name Christianity, it just has to define Christians as enemies of the state. Then it can make policies that can be selectively applied to Christians.

Peter was aware that the Roman Emperor, Nero, was gradually losing his marbles. And he was short on marbles to start with. Peter was writing from Rome in the year AD 64, probably just before or just after Nero hired arsonists to torch Rome so that he could rebuild the capitol city to his glory. After the fire in July of AD 64, suspicion naturally fell upon Nero. Everyone in Rome knew that Nero was *nutso* (Latin term).

Unable to divert suspicion with the usual political tricks, he needed a scapegoat. The Christians were handy and were easy to blame because they refused to join in the pagan debaucheries and would not worship the Emperor or other Roman gods. They also probably suffered some guilt by association because the Jews had lately been troublesome to Rome, and most people still considered Christianity to be a sect of Judaism.

Peter could observe some of this, and the Holy Spirit, of course, knew all about it before it happened. So He directs Peter to teach Christians how to thrive under official persecution. Our text sums up the instruction on excellent behavior that began in 2:11 and begins a seamless transition into handling persecution. Our outline shows the connection between excellent behavior and successfully coping with persecution.

The outline forms our propositional statement:

Excellent Relationships, 8-9,

Afford Us Some Protection from Persecution, 10-11;

God Guards the Righteous, 12.

Remember our overall outline for I Peter:

I. Salvation Is Secured to Us by the Work of God

II. Salvation Is Spread to Others by Our Excellent Behavior

The second part of that outline takes a slight turn starting in chapter 4; not enough, in my opinion, to justify a third outline point, but enough that we should take notice. Chapters 4 and 5 should be distinguished slightly from chapter 3. Chapter 3, verse 8 to the end of the chapter, is the connecting transition between the first half of Point II and the second half.

Excellent Relationships, 8-9

8 To sum up, let all be harmonious, sympathetic, brotherly, kindhearted, and humble in spirit;
9 not returning evil for evil, or insult for insult, but giving a blessing instead; for you were called for the very purpose that you might inherit a blessing.

After promoting excellent behavior in relation to the God-ordained authorities of government, workplace, and marriage, Peter now turns his attention to excellent relationships in general, where submission to authority is not necessarily an issue. Christians are told to give preference to one another in honor (Rom. 12:10). And we are told to honor all men (I Pet. 2:17).

Most of the people we relate to on a daily basis have no authority over us. They are simply fellow citizens, fellow believers, neighbors, co-workers, business associates, and so forth. Even though we are under no obligation to obey them, the way we relate to them not only influences their receptivity to the gospel; it is important in forming the reputation Christians enjoy in their communities. For that reason, it influences how we are treated by others. People tend to respond in kind. If we are good and patient and kind to them, they tend to be good and patient and kind to us. Or at least they try to be, or feel bad if they aren't.

So Peter lays out five traits in verse 8 that will consistently characterize our relationships if we are concerned about the salvation of our fellow man. He is still teaching us how to witness with our lives.

Harmonious

The term harmonious means, literally, of one mind. In Philippians 2:2, Paul wrote, **make my joy complete by being**

of the same mind. Certainly the unity of Christians is crucial to our witness. Disagreements within the body of Christ undercut our witness in the world. That is why we must unite around sound, Biblical doctrine. True unity comes from adhering to true doctrine, not from shedding those doctrines that are deemed "divisive." The only division true doctrine causes is to separate those who do not obey the word of God from those who do.

Christians must not be critical, judgmental, suspicious, or argumentative toward those outside the church. Philippians 4:5 says, **Let your forbearing spirit be known to all men.** Persecution is certainly not a harmonious relationship. So Christians should make sure that for their part, they are doing everything possible to maintain harmony in the community, even if they are being persecuted.

Sympathetic

Sympathy is the trait of being affected by like feelings. Hebrews 10:34 says, **For you showed sympathy to the prisoners.** I take it that this doesn't mean that they held up a sign that said, "I feel your pain," but that they actually risked going to the prisons, and being identified as Christians, in order to minister to their brothers, who were jailed for being Christians.

And have you ever thought of this? Sin hurts! The pleasure that entices one to sin passes quickly, but the hurt remains. That's why God identifies it as sin and warns us against it. Somewhere, beneath the façade of false freedom and enjoyment, the sinner is stung by his sin. The sympathetic Christian is not insensitive or indifferent to the sinner's pain. TV newscasters can contort their faces and their voices to give the appearance of sympathy. But the Christian who wants to win people to Christ scorns empty posturing in favor of sympathetic action.

Brotherly

This word literally means loving like a brother. Romans 12 is a parallel passage to I Peter 3. It says (v. 9f), **Let love be**

214

without hypocrisy... Be devoted to one another in brotherly love; give preference to one another in honor. This brotherly love can be expressed in our actions toward our fellow man, whether he is a Christian or not. It is, in fact, one way in which the unbeliever can taste the kindness of the Lord.

Kindhearted

The term means tender-hearted or compassionate. We have hearts that move us to take action to reduce the sufferings of others. Zechariah 7:9 commands this trait: **Thus has the LORD of hosts said, "Dispense true justice, and practice kindness and compassion each to his brother."** In other words, the difference between cold-heartedness and kindheartedness is action – we practice kindness.

Humble in Spirit

This is the first characteristic of the Christian life (Matthew 5:3) and is the opposite of the self-assertiveness and self-exaltation that we see in our society. Isaiah 57:15 has a great promise for such people:

For thus says the high and exalted One Who lives forever, whose name is Holy, "I dwell on a high and holy place, and also with the contrite and lowly of spirit in order to revive the spirit of the lowly and to revive the heart of the contrite. Proverbs 16:19, says, **It is better to be of a humble spirit with the lowly, than to divide the spoil with the proud.**

I can think of only one Person who had a right to be self-assertive and self-exalting, but He never behaved that way. He described Himself as **gentle and humble in heart**.

Notice that all of these are active traits. They are not simply passive frames of mind or occasional occurrences. They are attitudes that move us to action. Micah 6:8 says, **He has told you, O man, what is good; and what does the LORD require of you but to do justice, to love kindness, and to walk humbly with your God?** All of these traits, if put into action in our neighborhoods, can give unbelievers a taste of the kindness of the Lord. Remember what Jesus taught in the parable of the good Samaritan: "neighbor" is not about where you live; it's about what you are.

And every one of these traits discourages persecution. Unbelievers might be hesitant to go along with the government's persecution of Christians who have been so kind to them. So those Christians would likely find some unexpected allies when the persecution was going on.

The witness that a Christian shows when everything is going well is good and useful to God in bringing others into a saving relationship with Jesus Christ. But our witness in good times could be dismissed as self-serving by skeptical observers. Just as Satan said of Job:

"Does Job fear God for nothing? Hast Thou not made a hedge about him and his house and all that he has, on every side? Thou hast blessed the work of his hands, and his possessions have increased in the land. But put forth Thy hand now and touch all that he has; he will surely curse Thee to Thy face," Job 1:9ff.

No doubt Satan was telling Job's neighbors the same thing in order to nullify Job's excellent witness. So God nullified Satan's accusation. Unbelievers might dismiss our devout lifestyle as nothing more than our way of getting ahead, if everything always goes well with us. Satan still accuses the brethren. So God does not shield us from all trouble. He allows stress and even calamities from time to time in order to make our witness harder to ignore. It is our reaction to abuse that shows our true colors. So verse 9 deals with our response to persecution whenever it does happen.

To have a good witness when people attack us, we must be fully committed to the sovereignty of God in practical terms. And we must be fully committed to what God says about leaving vengeance to Him. For this we return to our parallel passage in Romans 12:17-21:

Never pay back evil for evil to anyone. Respect what is right in the sight of all men. If possible, so far as it depends on you, be at peace with all men. Never take your own revenge, beloved, but leave room for the wrath of God, for it is written, "VENGEANCE IS MINE, I WILL REPAY," says the Lord. "BUT IF YOUR ENEMY IS HUNGRY, FEED HIM, AND IF HE IS THIRSTY, GIVE HIM A DRINK;

FOR IN SO DOING YOU WILL HEAP BURNING COALS UPON HIS HEAD." Do not be overcome by evil, but overcome evil with good.

We are not to **return evil for evil or insult for insult**. We've already seen these words in I Peter. **Evil** is *kakos*: bad, mean, evil, wicked. It's the root of the word *evildoers* in 2:12. Christians are sometimes falsely accused of being evildoers (because in the twisted perspective of real evildoers, who see their own evil actions as good, the good acts of believers are deemed evil). If we do evil to those who do evil to us, we turn the slander into a true accusation. It won't matter that someone else started it. Football referees oftentimes don't see the first act of unsportsmanlike conduct, but they always see the opponent's retaliation and penalize his team. It may not be fair, but it's how things work.

Insult is the word *revile* in I Peter 2:23, where it says that Jesus did not revile in return. It refers to vile and harsh verbal abuse. The mouth that curses men can't very well bless God (Jam. 3:8-12). Instead of these nasty responses, which are not fitting for someone making a claim to godliness, we are to bless instead (Lk. 6:28). We are to speak well of that person and invoke God's blessings upon him.

Any sinner can return evil for evil and curse for curse. But what kind of a person can invoke God's **blessings** on his persecutors?! It would either be an insane person (so try to avoid giving that impression) or else someone who has been genuinely delivered from sinfulness. If you want to mess with a sinner's mind and cause him to examine his unexamined errors, returning good for evil is the way to do it!

This is the Christian's chance to shine with God's glory. As Jesus put it, **let your light shine before men in such a way that they may see your good works, and glorify your Father who is in heaven**, Mt. 5:16. The accusation that Satan spread abroad to undercut Job's witness while he was prospering had no credibility after Job's response to his calamities proved that his devotion was genuine and sincere.

I think nonbelievers who are tiring of their sin are watching for reality and will not make a move toward Jesus Christ unless they see reality in those who follow Him.

For you were called for the very purpose that you might inherit a blessing, verse 9b. If we know the great weight of foul sin that was removed from us and the great blessings we receive in place of the terrible judgment we deserved, it is unthinkable on any moral grounds that we should refuse to forgive those who sin against us. God blesses us in order to bless others.

Jesus told the parable of the unforgiving servant in Matthew 18 and taught us to pray, **forgive us our debts, as we also have forgiven our debtors**, Mt. 6:12. If Christians can forgive those who sin against them, and give a blessing instead of retaliation, then unbelievers have a tangible reason to believe that the Lord who motivates and enables such action is ready to do the same Himself. Sinners need to know that God will forgive them if they repent and trust Him.

Excellent relationships with people both inside and outside the church draw people to Jesus Christ. They also…

Afford Us Some Protection from Persecution, 10-11

[10] For, "LET HIM WHO MEANS TO LOVE LIFE AND SEE GOOD DAYS REFRAIN HIS TONGUE FROM EVIL AND HIS LIPS FROM SPEAKING GUILE.
[11] "AND LET HIM TURN AWAY FROM EVIL AND DO GOOD; LET HIM SEEK PEACE AND PURSUE IT.

Peter was an Apostle. He had all the authority of the Lord Jesus Christ behind him, as we see from Matthew 16:18f and John 16:13ff, *et al*. Yet he doesn't base his teaching on his own authority. Rather, he appeals to the Old Testament scriptures to support his exhortations.

He does so because he also has the Lord's example to guide him. Jesus quoted and referred to the Old Testament constantly. The New Testament directly quotes the Old over 200 times and contains more allusions to the Old Testament

218

than we can count with certainty. To Jesus and therefore to His Apostles also, the Bible was doctrinal boss – they all drew their theological doctrine straight from the Old Testament.

Peter is quoting directly from Psalm 34:12-16, and he takes the words literally. In fact, in every case where one part of the Bible interprets another part of the Bible, it always interprets that passage according to the literal, cultural, historical method of interpretation. Following that consistent example, we do the same, and have no justification for doing otherwise. (Even the one place that uses the term *allegory* (Galatians 4:24) is really using what we would call an analogy, which is a logic term and is part of the literal method.) So we don't guess at how we should interpret Scripture. And we don't get to choose whatever method gives us the interpretation we like best. Scripture itself lays down the hermeneutical rules and principles that we must follow. We don't get to interpret God's word any way we like, because we will be judged according to the literal interpretation.

We also learn from this that the Old Testament is not the Outdated Testament. So let's get to the text. (You might want to compare Psalm 34 to Peter's quotation in our text.) Psalm 34 is all about the Lord's provision and deliverance. It promises, in verse 19, **Many are the afflictions of the righteous; but the LORD delivers him out of them all.** The psalm is addressed to **the man who desires life and loves length of days that he may see good,** 34:12.

Note: Peter was not quoting directly from the Hebrew text. He quoted from the Greek translation of the Old Testament known as the Septuagint (abbreviated LXX, since, according to tradition, 70 men were involved in the translation) as he wrote this letter in Greek. Jesus and the New Testament writers did this often, giving tacit approval to the versions of the Bible that are translated into languages other than the original. Note, however, that the further you depart from a direct translation, as paraphrases and the so-called dynamic equivalent versions do, the less reliable they are. Jesus said that every letter and even the smallest part of a letter are precisely God's word (Mt. 5:18). We lose that precision with paraphrases and "dynamic equivalents."

Peter introduces the Psalm 34 quotation with the word **for** (verse 10), explaining the blessing we were called to inherit (verse 9), which is **to love life and see good days**. This may seem like a strange way to reintroduce the subject of persecution, but Peter's thesis is that we can have joyful and fruitful lives even in the midst of persecutions and difficult times (4:13, 14; cf. James 1:2). Peter draws from Psalm 34 to tell us how to do it.

Let him… refrain his tongue from evil (the word *kakos*, again). Psalm 12:1-4 warns about speaking evil:

Help, LORD, for the godly man ceases to be, for the faithful disappear from among the sons of men. They speak falsehood to one another; with flattering lips and with a double heart they speak. May the LORD cut off all flattering lips, the tongue that speaks great things; who have said, "With our tongue we will prevail; our lips are our own; who is lord over us?"

Evil speaking is consistent with the rebellious, godless lifestyle of sinners, but not with the regenerated lifestyle of those who have been raised to newness of life (Rom. 6) by the God of love. Proverbs 12:19 promises, **Truthful lips will be established forever, but a lying tongue is only for a moment.** And Proverbs 15:4 adds, **A soothing tongue is a tree of life, but perversion in it crushes the spirit.**

The tongue expresses what is in the heart. In Mark 7:21-23 Jesus said:

"For from within, out of the heart of men, proceed the evil thoughts, fornications, thefts, murders, adulteries, deeds of coveting and wickedness, as well as deceit [guile], sensuality, envy, slander, pride and foolishness. All these evil things proceed from within and defile the man."

In I Peter 2:1, Peter told his readers to put away all guile. Guile is using deceit to lay a trap for someone. It's usually translated *deceit* in the New Testament. It's how the Jewish leaders were trying to catch Jesus in order to kill Him. Deceit may be accomplished by words ("lying"), by actions ("deception"; fake right, go left), or by hypocrisy (the "cover-up"). The purpose is always to give false impressions in order to take unrighteous advantage of others. The liar sets up his victim to make a choice that benefits the liar in some way at the expense of the victim (for an example, see Proverbs 23:1-8). It's a form of hatred. Homer used the word of baiting a trap. Satan is the deceiver. Christians should have nothing to do with deceit. That's why Peter says, **AND LET HIM TURN AWAY FROM EVIL AND DO GOOD; LET HIM SEEK PEACE AND PURSUE IT**, verse 11.

These Christians are being slandered. And a bad reputation, even if undeserved, will encourage persecution. So Christians must maintain excellent relationships with those outside the church in order to refute those slanders.

We must **turn away from evil**. This verb describes an intensely strong rejection of whatever is evil. It verges on the violent, as Paul said, **I buffet my body and make it my slave.** Having been saved from the penalty of sin, a Christian might be tempted to get too casual about sin, as if there were no consequences. In fact, there are serious consequences, even if eternal judgment isn't one of them. Colossians 3:25 says, **For he who does wrong will receive the consequences of the wrong which he has done, and that without partiality.** Sin is still harmful to the one who practices it. God never removes the harmfulness of sin. That would be deceitful, causing people to think that there is no harm in sin.

Besides the harm that it does to us and those around us, evildoing also ruins our reputation in the community. A bad reputation ruins our own witness and, by association, the witness of the church, to the gleeful satisfaction of those who want to believe that there is no God and are looking for any excuse to dismiss our gospel. It also seems to justify any persecution aimed at the Christians, at least in the minds of unbelievers.

For these two reasons, Christians must urgently turn away from evil, like we would quickly get away from a coiled rattlesnake. Instead of evil, Christians must do good. We must keep our behavior excellent among the Gentiles. We can still be persecuted for doing good, because righteous lives convict sinners of their evil ways, and they resent that. But no one can honestly justify such persecution, and many unbelievers will take the side of the Christians who are persecuted for their excellent behavior.

We need to understand the nature and the consequences of evil well enough to be repulsed by it. We don't need to experience evil to understand it. God hates evil more than we do, but not because He tried it and didn't like it. It is in God's very nature to hate sin. It should be in our new nature, as well. The more we study God's word and grow by it, the more we will understand and hate evil. If the most intelligent being in the universe hates evil, we should too.

One of the consequences of evil is enmity, lack of peace within the person, lack of peace between people, and lack of peace between nations. (It's why we can't all just get along.) And one of the motivations behind the persecution of Christianity is the Christians' mistaken belief that biblical doctrine calls for antagonism against the social order.

But in Matthew 5:39-47 Jesus said:

"But I say to you, do not resist him who is evil; but whoever slaps you on your right cheek, turn to him the other also. And if anyone wants to sue you, and take your shirt, let him have your coat also. And whoever shall force you to go one mile, go with him two. Give to him who asks of you, and do not turn away from him who wants to borrow from you. You have heard that it was said, 'YOU SHALL LOVE YOUR NEIGHBOR, and hate your enemy.' But I say to you, love your enemies, and pray for those who persecute you in order that you may be sons of your Father who is in heaven; for He causes His sun to rise on the evil and the good, and sends rain on the righteous and the unrighteous. For if you love those who love you, what reward have you? Do not even the tax-gatherers do the same? And if you greet your brothers only, what do you do more than others? Do not even the Gentiles do the same?"

Jesus is directing us to go out of our way to maintain peaceful relationships with everyone. If we do this, we can remove at least some of the motive for persecution. Those who hate God will still take it out on God's people. That's why Romans 12:18 acknowledges the limitation we labor under, **If**

possible, so far as it depends on you, be at peace with all men. Seeing the storm clouds gathering, Peter, like Paul, is aware that it won't always be possible to maintain peace with everyone.

But we can make sure that people have no real reason to hate us if we **seek peace and pursue it.** Both of these terms, **seek** and **pursue,** convey intensity and aggressiveness of action. In other words, we don't just let peace happen if it will, we are to expend no small amount of effort to make peace happen. We can't control what the other guy does, but we can control what we do. Jesus said, **"Blessed are the peacemakers,"** Matthew 5:9.

This is saying that we may be paying a whole lot more to achieve peace than the other guy is willing to pay. He may not be willing to pay anything. So what is our motivation here? Excellent relationships afford us some protection from persecution, plus…

God Guards the Righteous, 12

¹² "FOR THE EYES OF THE LORD ARE UPON THE RIGHTEOUS, AND HIS EARS ATTEND TO THEIR PRAYER, BUT THE FACE OF THE LORD IS AGAINST THOSE WHO DO EVIL."

This is an Old Testament phrase that says God is always looking out for His people. II Chronicles 16:9 says, **For the eyes of the LORD move to and fro throughout the earth that He may strongly support those whose heart is completely His.** Genesis 6:8 provides a good example. The earth was entirely populated by evildoers except for one who did not join in the evil, and God knew him. **Noah found favor in the eyes of the Lord,** and God saved him and his family from the Flood. The righteous Judge of all the earth does not punish the righteous along with the wicked.

Did you ever wonder if you might have to call 911 in a desperate emergency and no one would answer the phone because all the dispatchers were on break? The eyes of the Lord are constantly on the righteous. So your distress call never rings in an empty room. Psalm 50:15 says, **call upon Me in the day of trouble; I shall rescue you, and you will honor Me.**

Psalm 91:14-16 makes a comforting promise:

Because he has loved Me, therefore I will deliver him; I will set him securely on high, because he has known My name. He will call upon Me, and I will answer him; I will be with him in trouble; I will rescue him, and honor him. With a long life I will satisfy him, and let him behold My salvation.

HIS EARS ATTEND TO THEIR PRAYER. Psalm 34:17-19 says:

The righteous cry and the LORD hears, and delivers them out of all their troubles. The LORD is near to the brokenhearted, and saves those who are crushed in spirit. Many are the afflictions of the righteous; but the LORD delivers him out of them all.

One of the most encouraging biblical promises to those who are in some kind of stress is one we see often throughout the Bible, **"I am with you."** Isaiah 41:10 says, **'Do not fear, for I am with you; do not anxiously look about you, for I am your God. I will strengthen you, surely I will help you, surely I will uphold you with My righteous right hand.'**

The Spirit of God told king Asa, **the LORD is with you when you are with Him. And if you seek Him, He will let you find Him; but if you forsake Him, He will forsake you,** II Chronicles 15:2.

God tells us that He is with us to deliver us, to save us, to bless us, to keep us wherever we go, to authorize us and empower us, to make us strong and courageous, and to make us successful in all He commands us to do. I'd rather be in the lions' den with God watching out for me, than to be in my easy chair at home with God ignoring me. More people die in their recliners each year than die in lion's dens.

BUT THE FACE OF THE LORD IS AGAINST THOSE WHO DO EVIL. The face of the Lord can be a great comfort or a great fear, depending upon God's attitude toward the people in question.

224

If God's face is for someone, that is a positive thing; it's a promise to the righteous that we will see all of God's goodness. This is what the priestly blessing of Numbers 6:24-26 says, **The LORD bless you, and keep you; the LORD make His face shine on you, and be gracious to you; the LORD lift up His countenance on you, and give you peace.** David prays in Psalm 27:8, **When Thou didst say, "Seek My face," my heart said to Thee, "Thy face, O LORD, I shall seek."**

However, if God hides His face from a person or people, that is a negative thing; it's a rejection of the unrepentant sinner's distress call. It's what provokes the complaint, "Where was God when I needed Him?" (The answer to that question, by the way, is that God was where He always is, with the righteous. He was leaving the sinner alone, just as the sinner demanded.) Deuteronomy 31:17f warns:

Then My anger will be kindled against them in that day, and I will forsake them and hide My face from them, and they shall be consumed, and many evils and troubles shall come upon them; so that they will say in that day, 'Is it not because our God is not among us that these evils have come upon us?' But I will surely hide My face in that day because of all the evil which they will do, for they will turn to other gods.

And in Jeremiah 18:17 God warns, **I will show them My back and not My face in the day of their calamity.**

But the worst is when God sets His face against a person. That is a very negative thing; it's a promise of judgment. In Jeremiah 21:10, for example, God says, **"For I have set My face against this city for harm and not for good," declares the LORD. "It will be given into the hand of the king of Babylon, and he will burn it with fire."**

God is very much for those who do good, and is very much against those who do evil. This is our motivation for making sure that all our relationships are excellent.

Excellent relationships afford us some protection from persecution. Plus, God guards the righteous. We're not in the same position as the little boy didn't want to behave unless he got paid for it. His mother said to him, "Why can't you be good for nothing, like your father?" We aren't good for nothing. Our pay is great on earth and is a hedge against trouble of all sorts, including persecution. And the eternal rewards are even better.

As persecution against Christianity becomes more severe in our society, and I believe the current trend will continue, the value of excellent behavior and excellent relationships will become all the more evident. Our excellent behavior and our excellent relationships are how we witness with our lives.

And witnessing with our lives is how we earn the credibility to witness effectively with our lips. As the word of God is dismissed by the unbelieving world, we won't necessarily have the Bible as a shared starting point in our evangelism. The moral authority we get from excellent behavior and excellent relationships may be the only authority unbelievers will recognize initially.

Believers have many heavy-duty reasons for keeping our behavior excellent among the Gentiles.

Chapter 15

3:13-16, The Courage of a Clear Conscience

¹³ And who is there to harm you if you prove zealous for what is good?
¹⁴ But even if you should suffer for the sake of righteousness, *you are* blessed. AND DO NOT FEAR THEIR INTIMIDATION, AND DO NOT BE TROUBLED,
¹⁵ but sanctify Christ as Lord in your hearts, always *being* ready to make a defense to everyone who asks you to give an account for the hope that is in you, yet with gentleness and reverence;
¹⁶ and keep a good conscience so that in the thing in which you are slandered, those who revile your good behavior in Christ may be put to shame.

On February 12, in the year 1554, Lady Jane Grey was beheaded in the Tower of London by Queen Mary, partly because of political intrigue and partly because Lady Jane would not deny her Protestant beliefs to accept popish heresies. Mary might have spared Lady Jane's life, but Mary was engaged to the Spanish king, and Spain wanted her to execute the Protestant Lady Jane.

The queen sent her chaplain, John Feckenham, to Jane to try to sway her theology, in view of her pending execution. Lady Jane's father had already been coerced into rejecting his Protestant beliefs to return to Roman Catholic doctrine. His plot to make his daughter queen instead of Mary had led to his daughter's condemnation, although Lady Jane knew nothing of the plot, and had no desire to be queen.

Feckenham began with the statement, "Madam, I lament your heavy case; and yet I doubt not, but that you bear out this sorrow of yours with a constant and patient mind."

Lady Jane replied, "You are welcome unto me sir, if your coming be to give Christian exhortation. And as for my heavy case, I thank God, I do so little lament it, that rather I account it a more manifest declaration of God's favor toward me than ever He showed me at any time before. And therefore, there is no cause why either you, or others who bear me good will, should lament or be grieved with this my case, being a thing so profitable to my soul's health."

Then she responded to Feckenham's attempts to change her thinking, giving a defense for the hope that was in her. She used her ready knowledge of Scripture and sound logic to prove that the communion elements were *not* the literal body and blood of the Lord (the doctrine called "transubstantiation") and that the Roman church did not have authority to contradict the Bible. She stated her case with humility and respect, but with indefatigable commitment to the truth as laid out in God's word, which she rightly took as the only source of doctrine. She knew sound doctrine and how to defend it!

She wrote at least two long letters to her apostate father, stating that she accounted herself most blessed because she had an innocent conscience, and warning him of what Jesus said about putting one's hand to the plow and then looking back. If he had preached to others about courageously obeying the Lord, how could he now deny Christ in order to save his own life?

She left her Greek New Testament to her sister after writing an appeal in the back, urging her to trust Christ.

All of her exhortations showed a wide knowledge of Scripture and a strong confidence in her Lord. She wrote, "Be constant, be constant; fear not for any pain: Christ hath redeemed thee, and heaven is thy gain."

On the scaffold, the executioner knelt down to ask for her forgiveness, which Lady Jane willingly gave. Then she quoted Psalm 51, said, "Lord, into Thy hands I commend my spirit," and placed her neck upon the block.

Lady Jane Grey was 16 years old when she was executed. Her father, the Duke of Suffolk, who tried to save himself by his apostasy, was beheaded 11 days later.

In II Timothy 3:12, Paul warned the churches, **all who desire to live godly in Christ Jesus will be persecuted.** Jesus told His disciples,

If the world hates you, you know that it has hated Me before it hated you. If you were of the world, the world would love its own; but because you are not of the world, but I chose you out of the world, therefore the world hates you. Remember the word that I said to you, 'A slave is not greater than his master.' If they persecuted Me, they will also persecute you; if they kept My word, they will keep yours also. But all these things they will do to you for My name's sake, because they do not know the One who sent Me, John 15:18-21.

Severe persecution has not been the rule during the last 2,000 years. It's been sporadic and usually localized, but it has always been a possibility. And we have seen enough of it in the history of the church to know that it could happen to any Christian at any time in any location. So there is no safe time to be lax in doctrine, commitment, or behavior.

The persecution most American Christians have experienced so far has been subtle rather than severe, taking the form of workplace bias, social snubs, mocking comments, intimidation, and lately the sabotage of the careers of military men who take any stand for Christ. But some Christians have faced the ultimate test. *Foxe's Book of Martyrs*, from which the account of Lady Jane Grey was taken, tells the stories of many of them.

Christians have always known that the world is at enmity with Christ and therefore is not overly enamored with Christians, especially with Christians who are obedient. This began even before Jesus was crucified. John 12:42f informs us that **many even of the rulers believed in Him, but because of the Pharisees they were not confessing Him, lest they should be put out of the synagogue; for they loved the approval of men rather than the approval of God.**

Philippians 1:29f informs us, **to you it has been granted for Christ's sake, not only to believe in Him, but also to suffer for His sake, experiencing the same conflict which you saw in me, and now hear to be in me.** For this reason, God always tells His followers about the spiritual warfare we are engaged in, and calls us to be courageous.

If you must face persecution, you want to come out victorious, right? Our text describes four traits that *cannot* be part a Christian's life if he wants to be victorious:

No Foul, 13

No Fear, 14

No Hesitation, 15

No Shame, 16.

No Foul, No Harm (Usually), 13

And who is there to harm you if you prove zealous for what is good?

We saw in the last chapter that excellent relationships afford us some protection from persecution, and here is the reason for it. People don't usually set out to harm people that they like and admire. If we commit no fouls against governments or fellow citizens, they have no justifiable reason to go out of their way to harm us.

By the way, Christians harm the cause of Christ and promote persecution if they carry out campaigns of aggressive demonstrations and civil disobedience, trying to force their political views on others. The problems America faces are spiritual, not political. So the solutions must be spiritual, not political. Christians are not commissioned to fight all the evils in the world. The evils of the world didn't become institutionalized quickly and they won't be eliminated quickly, if they are eliminated at all. They won't be removed until Jesus returns and makes all things right. He said, **"do not resist him who is evil,"** Matthew 5:39. Romans 12:21 says, **Do not be overcome by evil, but overcome evil with good.** Christians have moral influence but not that much political force. We can speak out and we can vote, but we can't intimidate others to get what we want, and we can't employ civil disobedience.

There is a remnant of the image of God in everyone, so there is a godly dynamic, however weak, still at work in most people; they like good and dislike evil, at least as it is applied to

230

them by others. Most people still admire the Golden Rule and those who live by it. Everyone has been mistreated by others. So we all prefer people who treat us with kindness, thoughtfulness, and respect.

Christians should be zealots for good. Peter had a good friend who, before he came to Christ, had been a member of the radical Jewish political party known as the Zealots. He was one of the Apostles, Simon the Zealot.

The Zealots pledged themselves to rid the Jews of all foreign rule, whatever it took--robbing, lying, assassinations, whatever--even if they lost their own lives in the process. In their view, the end justified the means. They did not succeed, by the way.

To be zealous is to have great ardor and commitment to a specific cause. That's how Christians should be in the cause of Christ. Only we can't do "whatever it takes." We are committed to what is good and right and honorable. We have to be zealous for what is good. If we resort to unrighteous means, we lose automatically. In God's view, a righteous end does not justify unrighteous means.

Titus 2:14 says that Jesus **gave Himself for us, that He might redeem us from every lawless deed and purify for Himself a people for His own possession, zealous for good deeds.** Christians at that time were being slandered as evildoers. The best way to refute such slander is to be zealous for good deeds. Peter listed some specific good deeds in verses 8-9.

Christians today are being slandered as evildoers. Some say we are political radicals, hate mongers, dangerous and regressive extremists who threaten society's progress. They say we are child abusers because we teach children to believe in God instead of evolutionism. They say we are women haters, intolerant bigots, and whatever else they can think of. And they fail to see the irony in their accusations. So Peter's admonition applies to us. We must prove ourselves zealous for what is good in order to show the dishonest and evil intent of our accusers.

How would the people around you finish this sentence, "Those Christians, they're always…" what? What opinion have they formed of Christian character based upon what they observe of the Christians in your area? Does their opinion involve love, grace, and truth or does it involve argumentative and judgmental attitudes?

Do you know what would be really bad? What if they can't even form their own opinion of Christian behavior because Christians are too afraid of ostracism to publicly identify with Jesus? What if unbelievers have no basis for any opinion about Christians except what is slanderously reported about us?

Satan, the accuser of the saints, and his world system will define us as troublemakers and evildoers who ought to be eliminated, if we let them define us (see the book of Acts). So we have to define ourselves by being zealous for what is good.

A second trait has no place in a Christian's life:

No Fear, 14

But even if you should suffer for the sake of righteousness, *you are* blessed. AND DO NOT FEAR THEIR INTIMIDATION, AND DO NOT BE TROUBLED

That first phrase, **"But even if you should suffer…"** is what's called a fourth class condition in the Greek. It indicates a remote possibility. It's possible, but not likely. This echoes what Peter said in verse 10. Proverbs 16:7 says, **When a man's ways are pleasing to Yahweh, He makes even his enemies to be at peace with him.**

But, still those who actively hate God will hate those who, by their words, stance, and lifestyle, remind them of God. This will happen more often in the last days as sinners become bolder in their sins and less tolerant of anyone who reminds them of God's impending judgment (Matthew 24:21). Their ancestors didn't play nicely with the prophets. And we can expect similar treatment because we take up the prophet's mantle to a certain extent simply by refusing to run with them in the same excess of dissipation.

We also suffer from the fact that false believers and frauds have marred the reputation of Christianity, opening the way for persecution. We shouldn't be shy about pointing out to unbelievers that a true Christian is one who actually *follows* Jesus Christ. We can help them to develop some discernment. We can't object to suffering for our own sins, and we can stand momentary, light affliction for the sake of Christ, but we don't want to suffer for the sins of people who claim to be Christians, but aren't.

Jesus said, **when the Son of Man comes, will He find faith on the earth,** Luke 18:8. At this late stage in the Christian era, in America at least (until persecution scares off the false adherents who want to profit by association), much of what goes by the name *Christian* is not. We do ourselves and the cause of the gospel a big favor by letting the world know the difference between true Christians and false. I John will help us in that regard.

Beyond that, God gives us good reason to have no fear of men or governments. Consider II Kings 17:36-39:

But YHWH [Yahweh, God's personal name]**, who brought you up from the land of Egypt with great power and with an outstretched arm, Him you shall fear, and to Him you shall bow yourselves down, and to Him you shall sacrifice. And the statutes and the ordinances and the law and the commandment, which He wrote for you, you shall observe to do forever; and you shall not fear other gods. And the covenant that I have made with you, you shall not forget, nor shall you fear other gods. But YHWH your God you shall fear; and He will deliver you from the hand of all your enemies.**

Proverbs 29:25 advises, **The fear of man brings a snare, but he who trusts in Yahweh will be exalted.** And Proverbs 14:26 promises, **In the fear of Yahweh there is strong confidence.**

In Matthew 10:28-34, Jesus said, **do not fear those who kill the body, but are unable to kill the soul; but rather fear Him who is able to destroy both soul and body in hell.**

Ecclesiastes 10:4 says, **If the ruler's temper rises against you, do not abandon your position, because composure allays great offenses.**

Have you ever thought about how much the world is characterized by fear? Everyone who is "of the world" seems to be fearful—little dogs fear big dogs. Big dogs fear mean cats. Mean cats fear water. Weak men fear strong men; strong men fear weakness; young men fear old age; old men fear death. Most people fear failure. Those who don't fear failure fear work. Everyone fears what other people think of them, even those who are afraid to admit it.

Christians should not be a part of that fear scene. Edmund Burke wrote that those who fear God fear nothing else. Proverbs 28:1 says, **The wicked flee when no one is pursuing, but the righteous are bold as a lion.**

Now, how is it that those who **suffer for the sake of righteousness** are **blessed**? It is an opportunity to receive spiritual blessings, as Jesus pointed out in the Sermon on the Mount, Matthew 5:10-16: the kingdom is ours; our reward in heaven is great; we are in good company, since they also persecuted God's prophets; we are the light of the world. And whenever we suffer for the sake of Christ we experience God's grace in a special way.

James 1:2-4 says,

Consider it all joy, my brethren, when you encounter various trials, knowing that the testing of your faith produces endurance. And let endurance have its perfect result, that you may be perfect and complete, lacking in nothing.

Among my nagging regrets is that after following Christ for over 50 years I am still imperfect and incomplete, lacking in so much. More trials will help fix that imperfection. Another regret is that I am not more effective in evangelism. Persecution adds power to our witness and makes us perfect and complete. So like David, I have to put afflictions on the blessing side of the ledger. In Psalm 119: 67 and 71 he said, **Before I was afflicted I went astray, But now I keep Thy word. [71] It is**

good for me that I was afflicted, That I may learn Thy statutes.

In the same way, Paul wrote in II Corinthians 4:17, **momentary, light affliction is producing for us an eternal weight of glory far beyond all comparison**. That's a blessing!

So what we gain by persecution outweighs and outlasts the cost. Persecution brings spiritual blessings, produces endurance, adds power to our witness, makes us perfect and complete, and gives us a closer, more understanding relationship with Jesus. I think some searching of God's word could add to that list.

Jesus is worthy of whatever price we have to pay to walk with Him. And His purpose is worth any price we have to pay for its accomplishment. Isn't that true?

So **DO NOT FEAR THEIR INTIMIDATION**. Whatever persecutors can't do without risking legal or social repercussions, they try to accomplish by intimidation and fear tactics. Persecutors are all limited in what they can do.

They are limited by God by the various means at His disposal. Judge Morgan, after he sentenced Lady Jane Grey to her death, went mad and in his raving cried out continually to have Lady Jane taken away from him, and so ended his life. Bloody Queen Mary, who despised the break that her father, King Henry VIII, had made with the Roman Church, and who killed hundreds of Protestants, died at age 42 of cancer, after a short reign of five and a half years. She was replaced by the Protestant Queen Elizabeth I, who promptly reversed Mary's attempts to restore England to Roman Catholicism.

Persecutors are limited by their situations, by other authorities or peers, and by their own lack of power. The gates of Hades shall not overpower the church (Matthew 16:18).

Oftentimes they are limited by how long they can keep their opponents ignorant. So like the Wizard of Oz, they rely upon intimidation and dumbing down the population, hoping we are cowards who accept the lie that ignorance is bliss. So there is courage in knowledge.

You've heard the saying, "You can't con an honest man." That's because con men exploit the greed of their victims. Persecutors often have to rely upon character faults in their victims, such as greed, fear, or pride, so they can make their charges stick. So there is courage in a clear conscience, while the guilty are fearful.

But the main problem for persecutors is that they are limited in how much they can do to us. They might take away our earthly freedom, possessions, comfort, and perhaps even our physical lives. But they can't take our souls or our eternity with the Lord. The worst they can do to us is to kill us, which sends us immediately to our eternal reward in heaven. Their worst-case scenario is our best-case scenario!

And as Paul discovered, when one Christian is persecuted, others get braver. He wrote in Philippians 1:12-14:

Now I want you to know, brethren, that my circumstances have turned out for the greater progress of the gospel, so that my imprisonment in the cause of Christ has become well known throughout the whole praetorian guard and to everyone else, and that most of the brethren, trusting in the Lord because of my imprisonment, have far more courage to speak the word of God without fear.

So don't be bothered by intimidation! Don't be troubled or disquieted.

There's a third trait to be avoided:

No Hesitation, 15

but sanctify Christ as Lord in your hearts, always *being* ready to make a defense to everyone who asks you to give an account for the hope that is in you, yet with gentleness and reverence

The only reason (and not a good one) for Christians to be insecure in their beliefs is if they don't know exactly what they believe or why they believe it. And that is a *very* insecure position to put oneself into. It's both dangerous and inexcusable. Isaiah 5:13 says, **Therefore My people go into exile for their lack of knowledge; and their honorable men are famished, and their multitude is parched with thirst.** Hosea 4:6 adds: **My people are destroyed for lack of knowledge.** And Isaiah 27:11 warns: **For they are not a people of discernment, Therefore their Maker will not have compassion on them. And their Creator will not be gracious to them.**

5 But if any of you lacks wisdom, let him ask of God, who gives to all men generously and without reproach, and it will be given to him.
6 But let him ask in faith without any doubting, for the one who doubts is like the surf of the sea driven and tossed by the wind.
7 For let not that man expect that he will receive anything from the Lord,
8 *being* a double-minded man, unstable in all his ways, Jam. 1:5-8.

According to Ephesians 6:16, our faith is our shield by which we are able to extinguish all the flaming missiles of the evil one. *Faith* in this verse is speaking of the objective *content* of our faith. It's the theological content of your faith that protects you, if you adhere to it. Great personal (subjective) faith in falsehood is no protection. The word of God is our sword; better yet, it's also the sword of the Spirit (Eph. 6:17).

Our opponents have weapons and tactics. If they confront us and we don't know what we believe or why we believe it, then we have no shield and no sword, no defense and no offense. I guess that's why so many Christians just go along to get along.

If we want to have no hesitation, then there are a couple of things we need to do.

Set Christ Apart as Lord in Our Hearts

We have many choices when it comes to who calls the shots in our life. We can submit to self-will, or to fearfulness, or to self-gratification, or to materialism and comfort; things like that, as we did before we became Christians. Or we can set Christ apart as the one and only master in our lives. When we gave our lives to Christ, that is what we were doing. We need to follow through on that, for our own sake and for the sake of the gospel. Failure here is failure everywhere, no matter what little temporary success you might fall into.

We might hesitate to make a defense for the hope that is in us because we are too concerned about what others might think of us. Our reputation in that case is more important to us than what people think of our Lord. **The fear of man brings a snare.** Can you be comfortable caring more about what others think about you than you do about people's eternal destiny? One of my seminary professors told us, "We wouldn't worry so much about what others think of us if we realized how seldom they do."

Consider Hebrews 10:32-39 which speaks of the early days of the church in Jerusalem:

But remember the former days, when, after being enlightened, you endured a great conflict of sufferings, partly, by being made a public spectacle through reproaches and tribulations, and partly by becoming sharers with those who were so treated. For you showed sympathy to the prisoners, and accepted joyfully the seizure of your property, knowing that you have for yourselves a better possession and an abiding one. Therefore, do not throw away your confidence, which has a great reward. For you have need of endurance, so that when you have done the will of God, you may receive what was promised. FOR YET IN A VERY LITTLE WHILE, HE WHO IS COMING WILL COME, AND WILL NOT DELAY. BUT MY RIGHTEOUS ONE SHALL LIVE BY FAITH; AND IF HE SHRINKS BACK, MY SOUL HAS NO PLEASURE IN HIM. But we are not of those who shrink back to destruction, but of those who have faith to the preserving of the soul.

If we have set Jesus apart as Lord in our hearts, then all the other issues are settled as they should be, and uncertainty cannot make cowards of us.

Be Ready to Make a Defense

Since God has commissioned us to make disciples, we must prepare ourselves to do just that. So the second thing we must do is to be ready to make a defense to everyone who asks us to give an account for the hope that is in us.

Why does Peter mention hope, specifically? Christians have all three graces, faith, hope, and love. And the greatest of these is love. So why does he single out hope?

Hope is particularly associated with perseverance and is based upon what we know and obey from God's word. And a sure hope is what non-believers don't have. Ephesians 2:12 says they have no hope and are without God in the world (such sad words). So when they see our hope, some will want to know about it. True believers have a true hope. Therefore they persevere through trials. This fact allows the unbelieving world to distinguish true believers from the false believers who abandon Christ when the going gets tough. This is one reason why persecution adds power to our witness. It helps to remove the confusion caused by the bad behavior of false believers.

Ephesians 6:15 says, **Stand firm therefore… having shod YOUR FEET WITH THE PREPARATION OF THE GOSPEL OF PEACE.** If we are prepared then we have our shoes on, ready to go—no need for hesitation. We must be ready with a sound, Biblical and logical defense of what we believe.

You don't have to be a trained theologian to do this. Any Christian who studies his Bible with honesty and diligence knows a lot more than non-believers know. Psalm 119:99 is true: **I have more insight than all my teachers, For Thy testimonies are my meditation.**

People who are right, but don't know it, are easily dislodged from their secure, defensible position. If they take a weak stand, even when occupying a strong position, they will likely lose the day to an opponent who takes a strong stand even when he is in a weak position. People who allow themselves to be intimidated will run away from a battle that they would win if they held their ground. You're going to lose any battle you run away from.

Defense is the word from which we get apologetics, and **account** is the word *logos*, which means a rational expression. Are you able to make a rational argument, a logical defense, in support of the truth of the gospel? We can study how Stephen, Peter, and Paul did it in the book of Acts. They based their arguments on a proper understanding of God's word. You can get that same advantage if you make the study of the Bible a high priority, like they did. And don't forget our overwhelming advantage, we have the Holy Spirit, just as Stephen, Paul, and Peter did.

Then you have to construct some sound arguments. With truth on your side, that isn't too hard, but it takes some thought before the opportunity arises. You should plant your corn before you get hungry. And you should practice with your sword before you need it in a battle. The will to win is pointless without the will to prepare to win. And we need not fear losing an "argument." Failure is not fatal. Success comes when we keep on learning from our failures and trying again. Any biblical truth we can pass on gives the listener the opportunity to advance toward Christ.

We won't take time now to construct arguments. The appendix contains some ideas on that subject. In the mean time, give it some thought. What are the main points of the gospel and how can you support them from the Bible and from reason? What are the most common objections? Consider the basis for those objections and then come up with the answers. It isn't that hard if you work systematically. You'll find most of the objections and their bases in the Bible, along with the answers. A good starting point for your argument is I Corinthians 15.

A word of advice: Never think that your ability to make a good defense determines the outcome when sharing the gospel. If Jesus and Paul didn't depend upon the strength of their arguments to bring people to Christ, why should you (Luke 10:22; I Corinthians 2:1-5)?

You should have a good defense for your hope, and you should be intimately acquainted with it so you are always ready. You would be surprised, I expect, by how many non-believers have no idea how to make a rational defense for their lack of hope. Ask them, "What is the factual/logical basis for
240

your unbelief?" (If they say that their basis is the lack of proof for the gospel, ask them where the proof for the gospel fails. If they don't know the proofs, ask them, gently, if they think ignorance of the proof is a good argument.)

And one last thing before we look at the fourth trait—winning doesn't mean dominating your opponent. In the first place, he isn't your opponent. **Our struggle is not against flesh and blood**, Eph. 6:12. And in the second place, we want to win people to Christ, not destroy them! So we need to be gentle and respectful. **The heart of the wise teaches his mouth, And adds persuasiveness to his lips,** Proverbs 16:23.

There is no place for arrogance in a Christian's life, although we have every right to be confident. Arrogance and confidence are two different things. The difference is the source of our confidence, whether self or Christ. And that difference can be seen in how we respond to being challenged. It is not arrogance to be absolutely certain that the Bible is true and that every contrary proposition must, therefore, be false. The arrogance is to think that one knows better than God. Humility and confidence go very well together if our confidence is in Christ.

The fourth trait to be avoided:

No Shame, 16

and keep a good conscience so that in the thing in which you are slandered, those who revile your good behavior in Christ may be put to shame.

I don't think shame and courage can co-exist; shame and desperation, maybe, shame and bravado certainly, shame and bullying, sure, but not shame and courage. You don't want to go into a trial accusing yourself!

Courage has a moral base. Being a moral attribute it has to have a moral base. The basis for courage, I think, is the certainty that we stand in proper relationship to the truth. (Worth is also a consideration—I am sure that steak is better for me than peanut butter, but I'm not willing to go to war over that issue). I certainly am not willing to take risks for things that are not true. If we get caught off the base of truth, or if we don't stand in right relationship to that truth, we should be scared. A guilty conscience makes us insecure and causes us to shrink back in shame.

Those who oppose God are the ones who should be put to shame. They have reason to be ashamed; we who stand upon the solid Rock do not, because our consciences have been cleansed by the blood of Christ (Hebrews 9:14). Peter will develop that thought in verse 21. Paul wrote, **I am not ashamed of the gospel, for it is the power of God for salvation to everyone who believes**, Romans 1:16. By the time he wrote the Roman epistle, Paul had seen the gospel change even the most vile sinners into saints.

Peter forfeited his clear conscience, and his courage, at his Lord's trial when he denied three times that he was connected to Jesus. He didn't get his courage back until he was put back on track by Jesus (John 21) and filled with the Holy Spirit (Acts 2). From that time on, Peter was a model of courage, except for one instance when he allowed himself to be intimidated away from the truth (Galatians 2:11ff).

When Paul was on trial before Governor Felix, he said, **I also do my best to maintain always a blameless conscience both before God and before men**, Acts 24:16. He instructed Timothy to **fight the good fight, keeping faith and a good conscience, which some have rejected and suffered shipwreck in regard to their faith**, I Tim. 1:19.

This whole passage has been building the principle that courage depends upon a clear conscience and a clearly understood faith (truth and a right relationship to it).

Some people have what seems like a clear conscience only because they don't know any better. They aren't free of sin or its effects; they're just free of any conscious cognizance of sin because they don't pay attention to what they're doing and how it affects others. That is, they are not being circumspect. Or maybe they have suppressed the truth so long that their conscience is seared (I Timothy 4:1-2). This is not a strong position to be in because it's not a clear conscience; it's an empty conscience or a dead conscience.

The word **conscience**, in both Greek and English, conveys the idea of self-judging consciousness. Conscience is the soul reflecting upon itself ("circumspection") and either condemning or affirming one's actions and motives. Every moral choice we make either strengthens or weakens our conscience. Studying God's word informs and strengthens our conscience. In I Timothy 1:5 Paul advised the younger pastor, **the goal of our instruction is love from a pure heart and a good conscience and a sincere faith.**

Verse 16 says that our behavior is **in Christ.** So our behavior had better be good—it reflects directly upon the reputation of our Lord. Our behavior determines how outsiders perceive Jesus Christ. It either speaks well of Him or slanders Him. People who criticize us for following Jesus faithfully should be put to shame when they compare their lives to ours.

Maybe you aren't sure that happens in your case because you have failed to represent Christ with courage and a sound rationale for your belief. Well, so did Peter fail. But that failure didn't define Peter because he didn't quit with that defeat, even though he felt like it. Jesus put him back in the game, and look how he turned out!

One failure doesn't lose the battle. You all know that little poem:

For want of a nail the shoe was lost.
For want of a shoe the horse was lost.
For want of a horse the rider was lost.
For want of a rider the message was lost.
For want of a message the battle was lost.
For want of a battle the kingdom was lost.
And all for the want of a horseshoe nail.

That's a good argument for discouraging sloth in the quartermaster corps, I suppose. And certainly, it's important to be faithful in small things. But God's kingdom does not hang so tenuously upon such a small thing as our occasional failures. God is sovereign and omnipotent.

That little nursery rhyme was an early expression of the chaos theory, which says that tiny, unpredictable events can trigger global catastrophes. That is why some people get so alarmed if the world's average temperature varies by half a degree from what it averaged at some other time in history. They speak of *the butterfly effect* by which a destructive hurricane can supposedly be traced back to whether some butterfly flapped its wings in just the right time and place, or didn't. When people deny the existence of the God of order, chaos theories are about the best they can come up with, I guess.

God's universe does not run by the chaos theory, neither does God's redemptive program. God is sovereign and His hand is always on the throttle.

If you try to make a defense for the hope that is in you and don't do a very good job of it, no harm is done. God can turn mistakes into successes. Learn your trade better and keep trying. You'll get it right. That's what all the Apostles did. Preparation, practice, and perseverance will win in the end.

And in the meantime, whatever rationale you can present in defense of your faith will be way better than the unbeliever's rationale for his disobedience to the gospel. God has put us in the strong position, right? We stand on God's truth. Don't take a weak stand.

So Peter says: Commit no fouls. Have no fear, except the fear of God, which dissolves all other fear. Have no hesitation—be ready always to defend your faith. Have no shame—live your life in such a way that your conscience is clear. Enjoy the courage of a clear conscience and a clear understanding of what you believe.

Chapter 16
3:17-22, Victory in Jesus, Part 1

¹⁷ For it is better, if God should will it so, that you suffer for doing what is right rather than for doing what is wrong.
¹⁸ For Christ also died for sins once for all, *the* just for *the* unjust, in order that He might bring us to God, having been put to death in the flesh, but made alive in the spirit;
¹⁹ in which also He went and made proclamation to the spirits *now* in prison,
²⁰ who once were disobedient, when the patience of God kept waiting in the days of Noah, during the construction of the ark, in which a few, that is, eight persons, were brought safely through *the* water.
²¹ And corresponding to that, baptism now saves you-- not the removal of dirt from the flesh, but an appeal to God for a good conscience-- through the resurrection of Jesus Christ,
²² who is at the right hand of God, having gone into heaven, after angels and authorities and powers had been subjected to Him.

How does this idea of suffering for doing what is right doesn't seem fair. If anyone should suffer in a world that belongs to God, it should be those who hate God, not those who love Him. Our God is a just God. Why should those who love and obey Him be subjected to persecution at the hands of those who don't?"

In today's text Peter addresses that incongruity. Verse 17 re-states verse 14 in order to pick up the subject for further development. Peter mentioned this concept in 2:15, 19-20 and will hit it again in 4:15-16. He knows that suffering for doing right is a difficult concept to accept in principle, and even more difficult to accept in the actual event. So he cites an example to show why it must be this way.

Peter, himself, has done what he is calling his readers to do; he has suffered several times for doing right. And he has experienced God's deliverance each time so far. We can read about some of them in the book of Acts.

But he doesn't point to his own victorious experiences as the example to follow. Peter was humbled by his own failure at Jesus' trial and knows that if left to himself he might fail again and be a bad example. **Let him who thinks he stands take heed lest he fall** (I Cor. 10:12). Instead, Peter points them to the same example he followed, the example that worked for him and is not subject to failure. His readers don't have to be copies of a copy, they can be copies of the original.

Jesus is the ultimate and infallible example. And He can actually enable us to follow His example. Peter can't do that. Galatians 2:20 says, **I have been crucified with Christ; and it is no longer I who live, but Christ lives in me; and the life which I now live in the flesh I live by faith in the Son of God, who loved me, and delivered Himself up for me.**

This is the exchanged life—I am no longer limited by my own capabilities because Jesus lives in me. The same Holy Spirit who commands us also enables us. So when we get the command, we also get the power to obey the command.

In Hebrews 12:1-4 we read:

[1] **Therefore, since we have so great a cloud of witnesses surrounding us, let us also lay aside every encumbrance, and the sin which so easily entangles us, and let us run with endurance the race that is set before us,** [2] **fixing our eyes on Jesus, the author and perfecter of faith, who for** [the Greek term is *anti*, instead of] **the joy set before Him endured the cross, despising the shame, and has sat down at the right hand of the throne of God.** [3] **For consider Him who has endured such hostility by sinners against Himself, so that you may not grow weary and lose heart.** [4] **You have not yet resisted to the point of shedding blood in your striving against sin.**

Peter wants to assure his readers that their suffering has a divine purpose that more than justifies the unpleasantness and inconvenience of suffering. When he exhorts his readers to live

246

for Jesus, he likes to pile on the encouragement. He used the Lord's example in I Peter 2:21-25 as the motive for submitting to authorities. Here he uses the Lord's example to explain why God puts us through experiences of persecution. In both cases he emphasizes that we have already gained far more from Christ's perseverance than any of our own perseverance will cost us.

Hebrews 12 says that Jesus despised the shame. The term despise means to think little of, to count something not worthy of entering into the decision-making process. This take on suffering is reflected in Paul's statement in II Corinthians, 4:17f:

¹⁷ For momentary, light affliction is producing for us an eternal weight of glory far beyond all comparison, ¹⁸ while we look not at the things which are seen, but at the things which are not seen; for the things which are seen are temporal, but the things which are not seen are eternal.

The outline of Peter's argument is straightforward; it follows the verses:

Victory Provided, 18

Victory Proclaimed, 19-20

Victory Imparted, 21

Glorious Victory, 22

Victory Provided, 18

¹⁸ For Christ also died for sins once for all, *the* just for *the* unjust, in order that He might bring us to God, having been put to death in the flesh, but made alive in the spirit;

Jesus furnishes the perfect example of suffering for the sake of righteousness. He had no sins for which He should suffer, yet He suffered for all our sins. His death was the most horrible death imaginable. Yet the most horrible part of the ordeal was His separation from the Father, expressed when Jesus cried out, **"My God, My God, why have You forsaken Me?"** This is when Jesus was dead spiritually—separated from the Father. So Jesus called Him God, not Father. Just before He died, Jesus again addressed God as His Father, saying, **"Father, INTO THY HANDS I COMMIT MY SPIRIT."** (Luke 23:46) Thus Jesus conquered death, which is first and foremost a spiritual condition.

Separation from God is the curse of sin, and if sin isn't dealt with, the ultimate consequence of sin. Every sinner is separated from God, even though in this life everyone enjoys God's good providence—He **sends His rain on the just and the unjust**.

But if a person dies in his sin, he is separated from God, and from everything that is good. This absolute separation will last for all of eternity, without remedy. Such a person will suffer endless physical pain, mental anguish, and spiritual torment. He will have no hope of ever getting out of the fiery pit and no hope of ever again experiencing anything good. The more you read what the Bible says about hell, the less you would want *anyone* to go there.

Why would God allow the just be subjected to any mistreatment from the unjust? One reason is to accomplish God's redemptive purpose. The arrest, mockery, condemnation, and crucifixion of Jesus were unjust from the human point of view. This was the redemptive plan of God, and Jesus executed that plan voluntarily, so it wasn't unjust on God's part. We share the sufferings of Christ for the sake of those who have been called (II Tim. 2:10). Not that we can substitute for someone else; we aren't qualified for that. And there is no need for that, since Jesus has already done it once for all. But through our suffering others can be brought to believe the gospel, repent of their sins, and trust the One who did substitute for them.

If Jesus would die, the just for the unjust, certainly we who have been redeemed by that death can suffer, the just for the unjust. Jesus died for the purpose of bringing us to God. He did the redemptive work. We just need to present the redemptive opportunity to those who need it and urge them to be reconciled to God. And we may be called upon to validate the message of salvation by suffering unjustly.

Jesus died **once for all**, says verse 18. So there is no need for a repeated sacrifice, as in the "sacrifice of the mass," done weekly by some denominations. That, in fact, is a misrepresentation of God's plan of salvation. And Jesus is not still on the cross, as crucifixes depict. When Jesus said on the cross, "It is finished," He meant it. This is a complete contrast to the yearly offerings on the Day of Atonement. Peter chooses the word for sin that was used in the Septuagint--the Greek translation of the Old Testament--for the sin offering on the Day of Atonement.

And atonement is not limited, as 5-point Calvinists insist. The text says, **once for all**. The great theologian John Calvin (1509-1564) did not agree with a doctrine of limited atonement when he wrote his commentary on I John 2:2. That verse says, **and He Himself is the propitiation for our sins; and not for ours only, but also for those of the whole world**. Calvin asserted in his commentary that Jesus died for the sins of the whole world. I don't know whether he argued for limited atonement in some other place; but if he did, he was wrong, even if he was famous. He had to be wrong one way or the other.

All the Bible's universal calls and commands to come to Christ for salvation (like the one we just read in Acts 17) would be a bad-faith invitation and a cruel mockery if Christ died only for some.

The non-elect could indeed accuse God of injustice if limited atonement closed off any opportunity for them to be saved. Paul's argument in Romans 9 makes sense only if two conditions are met: 1) *All* have legitimate opportunity to be saved, and 2) God chose only *some* to be saved. The Bible affirms both.

If *both* of these conditions are met, then it makes sense for Paul to argue as he does. In such a case, the non-elect have no grounds to accuse God of injustice, because Jesus died for the sins of all, giving all a genuine opportunity to be saved. They can repent and believe, if they chose. And the one who comes to Jesus, He will certainly not cast out (Jn. 6:37). God's provision for salvation is always super-abundant, not limited. (See the next chapter for a fuller discussion.)

If not for God's sovereign election, all would be lost, because no one would choose to obey God, according to Romans 3, even though God gives them that opportunity. It's a narrow gate (Mt. 7:13f). Jesus is the only door, (Jn. 10:7). But it's open to anyone who will repent and believe. And all men are dead in their trespasses and therefore unresponsive to God, according to Ephesians 2.

That a sovereign God should choose to over-rule the rebellious choice of some and draw them to Jesus, does no injustice to those whose choices He does not over-rule. The Bible never proclaims or implies double-predestination.

All those who go to hell do so because they reject God's provision of salvation. Now, in saying that, I hope you understand that unlimited atonement does *not* imply universal salvation, as we will see in verse 21. What is made available to all is clearly not accepted by all.

Jesus was **put to death in the flesh, but made alive in the spirit** (verse 18). Some people wish to deny the resurrection of Christ because the resurrection proves that everything Jesus claimed is true. And that in turn proves that the whole Bible is true, because Jesus affirmed every word of it and even the smallest letter and the smallest part of a letter. So to avoid that scary truth, they deny that Jesus really died on the cross.

One of Gary Larson's *Far Side* cartoons showed a bear sitting up in his open casket. All the bears attending the funeral were looking at him in astonishment. The guest of honor said, "For crying out loud, I was hibernating! Don't you guys ever take a pulse?" Jesus was buried by His friends, don't you think they would be sure He was dead before they buried Him? Besides that, the soldiers in the execution detail were responsible to make sure He was dead before they allowed His friends to remove the body from the cross.

The wages of sin is death. Jesus paid the penalty that was to fall upon us. A fake death is a fake payment and therefore would be void in the eyes of a righteous God who saves us according to His righteousness.

"But," some may object, "if Jesus is God, how could He die?" Without giving up His deity (which would be impossible; God is perfect and immutable), Jesus became a man. He took on human flesh and was put to death **in the flesh**, as Peter says here. That is, His human body died. But His spirit could not and did not die. He was still **alive in the spirit.** (This doesn't refer to the Holy Spirit, because there is no article—it isn't "*the* Spirit.")

Jesus died spiritually on the cross when He was separated from the Father. The main meaning of death is separation and the most relevant separation is separation from God. Physical death is the direct, even if delayed, result of spiritual death. So Peter says that Jesus was **made alive in the spirit**. And it's true of every person, by the way, that when he dies his soul and spirit do not cease to function. The soul and its spiritual dimension, the non-material part of a person, are created when that person is conceived. Once brought into existence by God, the soul and spirit never ceases to exist. The soul and spirit, the non-material part of man, goes immediately to be with the Lord, if he is a New Testament believer (if he has been made alive in spirit by the regeneration of the Holy Spirit), and are eventually re-united with his body which will be resurrected in a glorified form suited to eternity with God.

The unbeliever's soul (which never had spiritual life, since all are born spiritually dead) descends immediately to Hades to suffer and await the final judgment of Revelation 20. At that time his body will be raised in a form suited to endure eternal punishment and will be re-united with the soul to stand before the Judge of all men, and then that person will be thrown into the lake of fire because his name was not found in the Lamb's book of life.

But what about the departed Old Testament believers? They had been waiting in Abraham's bosom for the promised atonement to be accomplished so their souls could finally get to heaven. When Jesus accomplished redemption, He didn't forget them.

Victory Proclaimed, 19-20

[20] **who once were disobedient, when the patience of God kept waiting in the days of Noah, during the construction of the ark, in which a few, that is, eight persons, were brought safely through *the* water.**

Ephesians 4:8-10 gives us a great clue to understanding what happened here, quoting Psalm 68:18:

[8] **Therefore it says, " WHEN HE ASCENDED ON HIGH, HE LED CAPTIVE A HOST OF CAPTIVES, AND HE GAVE GIFTS TO MEN." [9] (Now this *expression,* "He ascended," what does it mean except that He also had descended into the lower parts of the earth? [10] He who descended is Himself also He who ascended far above all the heavens, that He might fill all things.)**

The saved souls of Old Testament saints were waiting in Abraham's bosom (also called Paradise) until their promised redemption was actually accomplished so they could escape death. As soon as Jesus paid their ransom, He went down and got them. You remember that He told the repentant thief on the cross, "Today you shall be with Me in Paradise."

So Jesus took these souls who had been held captive by death into His own custody and ascended up to heaven with them. **WHEN HE ASCENDED ON HIGH, HE LED CAPTIVE A HOST OF CAPTIVES.** Imagine if you can what a jubilation day that was for those Old Testament saints! Adam and Eve were there, along with all the other godly people (except Enoch and Elijah, who were already there)--Moses, Joshua, all the true prophets (but none of the false), all the godly priests. Abel was there, and Abraham and Sarah, and all the other Old Testament saints. They had been waiting a long time!

Luke 16:19-31 provides more insight:

[19] **"Now there was a certain rich man, and he habitually dressed in purple and fine linen, gaily living in splendor every day.**

20 "And a certain poor man named Lazarus was laid at his gate, covered with sores,

21 and longing to be fed with the *crumbs* which were falling from the rich man's table; besides, even the dogs were coming and licking his sores.

22 "Now it came about that the poor man died and he was carried away by the angels to Abraham's bosom; and the rich man also died and was buried.

23 "And in Hades he lifted up his eyes, being in torment, and saw Abraham far away, and Lazarus in his bosom.

24 "And he cried out and said, ' Father Abraham, have mercy on me, and send Lazarus, that he may dip the tip of his finger in water and cool off my tongue; for I am in agony in this flame.'

25 "But Abraham said, 'Child, remember that during your life you received your good things, and likewise Lazarus bad things; but now he is being comforted here, and you are in agony.

26 'And besides all this, between us and you there is a great chasm fixed, in order that those who wish to come over from here to you may not be able, and *that* none may cross over from there to us.'

27 "And he said, 'Then I beg you, Father, that you send him to my father's house--

28 for I have five brothers-- that he may warn them, lest they also come to this place of torment.'

29 "But Abraham said, 'They have Moses and the Prophets; let them hear them.'

30 "But he said, 'No, Father Abraham, but if someone goes to them from the dead, they will repent!'

31 "But he said to him, 'If they do not listen to Moses and the Prophets, neither will they be persuaded if someone rises from the dead.'"

So when Jesus led His captives up to heaven, He emptied Abraham's bosom, the Paradise part of Hades, but left the fiery prison part of Hades behind to await final judgment. But when He first got there, He made proclamation to everyone there, some to their great delight, others to their horrible despair.

Imprisoned along with the unbelievers in that prison, were demons who had disobeyed the restrictions God had placed upon their behavior on earth. This word for prison means an actual place, not just a condition. No doubt those demons cherished a forlorn hope that their leader, Satan, would somehow triumph over God and affect their release. Now they know that isn't going to happen. The war is lost.

The word *made proclamation* is the Greek word *kerusso*, to herald a victorious king, not *euangeleo,* to preach good news. Jesus went to the place of the dead to herald His victory, not to offer unbelievers good news of a second chance. **It is appointed for men to die once and after this comes judgment**, Hebrews 9:27. There is no passage in the Bible that even suggests a purgatory for men or demons. (That idea came from the non-biblical *Apocrypha*.)

Jesus made this proclamation **to the spirits in prison**. The term *spirits* always refers to demons unless the term is qualified, as it is in Hebrews 12:23, which refers to "the spirits of righteous men." If Peter were speaking of men he would have used the term *souls* instead of spirits.

Whatever else Jesus said during His time there, He announced to these demons that He had gained the victory over sin, death, Satan, demons, and Hades. Colossians 2:15 says, **When He had disarmed the rulers and authorities, He made a public display of them, having triumphed over them through Him.**

Hebrews 2:14 adds, **Since then the children share in flesh and blood, He Himself likewise also partook of the same, that through death He might render powerless him who had the power of death, that is, the devil.**

I Corinthians 15:54 says, **DEATH IS SWALLOWED UP in victory.**

Demons are generally allowed to roam the earth. So why were some demons kept in prison in Hades? According to verse 20 they **were disobedient, when the patience of God kept waiting in the days of Noah.** Genesis 6:1-4 gives us the history. This is weird:

¹ Now it came about, when men began to multiply on the face of the land, and daughters were born to them, ² that the sons of God saw that the daughters of men were beautiful; and they took wives for themselves, whomever they chose. ³ Then the LORD said, "My Spirit shall not strive with man forever, because he also is flesh; nevertheless his days shall be one hundred and twenty years." ⁴ The Nephilim were on the earth in those days, and also afterward, when the sons of God came in to the daughters of men, and they bore *children* to them. Those were the mighty men who *were* of old, men of renown.

In the days leading up to the Flood, sinful angels (demons) married human women. "Sons of God" in Genesis refers to angels, not to the sons of Seth, as some claim. Old Testament usage tells us that, plus the fact that it would not have taken Seth's sons over a thousand years to notice that girls were pretty. (If it had, Seth wouldn't have had too many sons.) And **the sons of God** are contrasted with **the daughters of men**, not the daughters of Cain. The traditional Jewish view is correct; these were demons.

This was not a case of forced relations; women were actually marrying the demons, who took on the form of men and did human functions, just as the good angels took the form of men when they met Abraham and ate a meal with him before they went on their way to destroy Sodom and Gomorrah. When the two angels appeared in Sodom to retrieve Lot's family, the men of the city lusted to have sexual relations with them.

These unholy unions between demons, taking the form of men (angelic spirits are always spoken of in the masculine gender), and human women produced offspring who were known as the Nephilim, Genesis 6:4. According to verse 5 it was **then** that God saw that the wickedness of men called for destruction. The Nephilim were giants, fierce and deadly warriors, men of power and renown. And they were extremely corrupt and had a very corrupting influence in terms of behavior.

In mythology we read of gods marrying mortals to create mighty men. Whoever started those myths probably got the idea from this actual history, which would have been passed on by Noah's family as a warning to their descendants. It would also be known because of its recurrence after the flood. Some of the prostitution in idol's temples may have been among the remnants of that sordid affair before and after the flood.

Ever since their own fall, Satan and his company of demons have worked to defeat and replace God. In the Garden of Eden, Satan induced Adam and Eve to sin, plunging the whole race into sin because of the principle of the solidarity of the race, described in Romans 5 and Hebrews 7:9.

He tried to eliminate the Jews by genocide in the book of Esther. He tried to destroy the messianic line in II Chronicles 22 and 23. He tried to have Jesus killed while an infant, tempted Jesus to abandon His mission, and finally incited the Jewish leaders to crucify Him, gaining victory at last. Or so he thought.

In I Corinthians 2:7f Paul wrote:

but we speak God's wisdom in a mystery, the hidden wisdom, which God predestined before the ages to our glory; the wisdom which none of the rulers of this age has understood; for if they had understood it, they would not have crucified the Lord of glory.

It was the crucifixion of God's Messiah (which Satan thought was his final victory) that defeated Satan once and for all and sealed his fate. There will be more battles, but the outcome of the war is already determined.

Genesis 6 describes an early attempt to foil God's redemptive plan, this time by corrupting the whole human race, turning it into an unredeemable mongrel race. If the attempt had been ultimately successful, Jesus would not have been able to take on human flesh (as Gen. 3:15 promised) without uniting Himself with unredeemable demons as well. He couldn't be mankind's kinsman redeemer. They would all be related to demons. The redemption of men by the one man, Jesus, depends upon that principle of the solidarity of the human race. Satan would have destroyed that solidarity.

The best interpreter of the Bible is the Bible. So let's trace this out. Peter brings this subject up again in his second epistle, chapter 2, where he is warning about false teachers in the last days and the judgment they will suffer.

[4] For if God did not spare angels when they sinned, but cast them into hell and committed them to pits of darkness, reserved for judgment; [5] and did not spare the ancient world, but preserved Noah, a preacher of righteousness, with seven others, when He brought a flood upon the world of the ungodly; [6] and *if* He condemned the cities of Sodom and Gomorrah to destruction by reducing *them* to ashes, having made them an example to those who would live ungodly thereafter; [7] and *if* He rescued righteous Lot, oppressed by the sensual conduct of unprincipled men [8] (for by what he saw and heard *that* righteous man, while living among them, felt *his* righteous soul tormented day after day with *their* lawless deeds), [9] *then* the Lord knows how to rescue the godly from temptation, and to keep the unrighteous under punishment for the day of judgment, [10] and especially those who indulge the flesh in *its* corrupt desires and despise authority, II Peter 2:4-10a.

The word translated *hell* in v. 4 is the word *Tartarus*, another term from Greek mythology, borrowed to describe Hades. In Greek mythology, it was where the worst sinners were sent. The Bible uses it to describe the punishment side of Hades. Hell and Hades are not the same place. Both are referred to as a pit or an abyss, and both are fiery, but hell is also called Gehenna or the lake of fire. At the final judgment, Hades will be thrown into the lake of fire (Revelation 20).

These demons are reserved in Hades for judgment, meaning they will never be free again. (Revelation 9, says that when the 5th trumpet sounds, some demons will be set loose from the pit, with restrictions, for a certain period of time. Those demons must have been imprisoned for different offenses than the one Genesis 6 describes. If demons don't abide by God's restrictions they get sent down.)

II Peter 2:5 connects this sin of the unholy angels with the destruction of the ancient world in Noah's day, and verse 6 connects it with the destruction of Sodom and Gomorrah. Some other demons made subsequent attempts to restart this mongrel race after the flood. (When God promised not to destroy the earth by water again, apparently the demons thought they had found a loop-hole to exploit.) Genesis 6:4 says, **The Nephilim were on the earth in those days, and also afterward, when the sons of God came in to the daughters of men, and they bore children to them.**

Sodom and Gomorrah were involved in this. You will remember the ugly episode in Genesis 19 when the Sodomites were overwhelmed by lust for the two holy angels who came to rescue Lot before destroying the city.

The point not to be missed in all of these accounts, is that God rescued His righteous ones, Noah's family and Lot's, even as He destroyed the evil ones.

Jude also mentions this episode, verses 5-7:

Now I desire to remind you, though you know all things once for all, that the Lord, after saving a people out of the land of Egypt, subsequently destroyed those who did not believe. And angels who did not keep their own domain, but abandoned their proper abode, He has kept in eternal bonds under darkness for the judgment of the great day. Just as Sodom and Gomorrah and the cities around them, since they in the same way as these indulged in gross immorality and went after strange flesh, are exhibited as an example, in undergoing the punishment of eternal fire.

All these demons who violated God's restrictions in the attempt to defeat God's redemptive program are kept in prison. God enforces His restrictions in order to keep the demons in line. Over 2,400 years later, in Luke 8:31, the demons who possessed the Geresene man still feared that Jesus would command them to depart into the abyss. Had they tried to disobey Him, He would have.

To get back to the Nephilim for a minute: The Nephilim who were born after the flood were also known as the Rephaim, the Emim, the Zamzummim, and the Anakim, after the heads of their families. They lived in the land of Canaan. The 10 spies were afraid of them (Numbers 13:33). All the tribes of the Nephilim were particularly marked out by God for destruction, and the Old Testament traces their destruction particularly.

Knowing their history, we can understand why God ordered the Israelites to kill every man, woman, and child of this unredeemable, mongrel race. God's detractors can call it genocide if they want, but the spread of this unredeemable race had to be stopped if anyone at all was to be saved. Had they been allowed to spread their line, the whole world's population would eventually have become unredeemable. Certainly the Hebrews, from whom Messiah was to come, would have been mongrelized if they married with these Nephilim in Canaan. So God warned the Hebrews sternly not to intermarry with any Canaanites. But they didn't take that warning to heart. Those forbidden intermarriages corrupted Israel, even though the Nephilim were not involved.

Deuteronomy 9:1ff for example, says,

Hear, O Israel! You are crossing over the Jordan today to go in to dispossess nations greater and mightier than you, great cities fortified to heaven, a people great and tall, the sons of the Anakim, whom you know and of whom you have heard it said, 'Who can stand before the sons of Anak?' Know therefore today that it is YHWH your God who is crossing over before you as a consuming fire. He will destroy them and He will subdue them before you, so that you may drive them out and destroy them quickly, just as YHWH has spoken to you.

Joshua 11:21f records:

Then Joshua came at that time and cut off the Anakim from the hill country, from Hebron, from Debir, from Anab and from all the hill country of Judah and from all the hill country of Israel. Joshua utterly destroyed them with their cities. There were no Anakim left in the land of the sons of Israel; only in Gaza, in Gath, and in Ashdod some remained.

Goliath, and other giants from Gath, were later killed by David and others, I Samuel 17:4; I Chronicles 20:5—21:1.

But it was not until the Anakim were destroyed in Israel itself that the land had rest from war (Joshua 11:23 23). (Joshua 14:12-15 says that Caleb killed the last of the Anakim, then the land had rest from war.)

One more point to observe here—the patience of God kept waiting while Noah built the ark. God held off on judgment until He had provided salvation for His righteous ones. In the meantime, the corruption grew in scope and nastiness, and Noah preached warnings to his wicked neighbors who were no doubt mocking his rescue ship. The ratio of bad people to good people in Noah's day was several billion to 8. (Those who do population studies say that somewhere between 2 and 10 billion people perished in the flood.)

Sinners convince themselves that the majority rules, and any gains they make are signs of victory over God. And God's people are always outnumbered. But God always gives the victory to His righteous ones. God chooses to save few, not many.

Chapter 17
3:21-22, Victory in Jesus, Part 2

**[21] And corresponding to that, baptism now saves you-- not the removal of dirt from the flesh, but an appeal to God for a good conscience-- through the resurrection of Jesus Christ,
[22] who is at the right hand of God, having gone into heaven, after angels and authorities and powers had been subjected to Him.**

In the previous chapter we got some idea of the scope of the victory Jesus achieved when we read about Jesus going to the place of the dead, proclaiming His victory over sin and death, and then leading out the Old Testament saints who had been waiting for their promised salvation to be accomplished.

The previous chapter covered the first two points of our outline: Victory Provided, 18; Victory Proclaimed, 19-20. Now in Part 2:

Victory Is Imparted, 21,

The Glory and Certainty of that Victory, 22.

If salvation is provided for all, it does not necessarily follow that it is imparted to all. What is universally provided is not universally received. Given that the debate on the subject of the atonement, whether it is limited or unlimited, has concerned theologians for centuries and is now coming to the forefront again, I think some further comment is useful before we go on to the last two points of Peter's outline.

The debate has been between those who follow John Calvin (AD 1509-1564) and those who follow Jacob Arminius (1560-1609). Romans 5:18 says, **So then as through one transgression there resulted condemnation to all men, even so through one act of righteousness there resulted**

justification of life to all men. Concerning that verse, Calvin wrote:

"He makes this favor common to all, because it is propoundable [put forward for consideration] to all, and not because it is in reality extended to all (i.e. in their experience), for though Christ suffered for the sins of the world, and is offered through God's benignity indiscriminately to all, yet all do not receive Him."

In other words, salvation is provided for all but not imparted to all. Those who continue to reject it don't get it.

From Calvin's *Commentary to the Colossians*, he wrote regarding Colossians 1:14, "This redemption was procured through the blood of Christ, for by the sacrifice of his death, all the sins of the world have been expiated."

Mark 14:24 says, **"This is My blood of the covenant, which is poured out for many."** On this passage Calvin wrote, "By the word 'many' he means not a part of the world only, but the whole human race."

Calvin's commentary on I John 2:2 reads as follows:

"Christ suffered for the sins of the whole world, and in the goodness of God is offered unto all men without distinction, His blood being shed not for a part of the world only, but for the whole human race; for although in the world nothing is found worthy of the favor of God, yet He holds out the propitiation to the whole world, since without exception He summons all to the faith of Christ, which is nothing else than the door unto hope."

It should be noted that Calvin died in 1564 (when Arminius was four years old), and the Synod of Dort (convened to answer Arminianism and against which the "five points" were set forth) didn't happen until 1618 (54 years after Calvin died). Based upon all these considerations, many theologians, the author included, doubt that Calvin can legitimately be considered a five-point Calvinist. The doctrine of limited atonement is a position taken by hyper-Calvinists.

Those five points are Total depravity, Unconditional election, Limited atonement, Irresistible grace, and

Perseverance of the saints. (These have been referred to in the English speaking world since about 1908 by the acronym, TULIP.) Four of those five points are unmistakably Biblical.

The other point, whether the atonement is limited or unlimited, depends upon what you include in your definition of atonement. Atonement is a theological term (one of the few that derive from the Anglo-Saxon). It is not a New Testament term. So the Bible doesn't define it for us. Theologians have to define what they mean by the term.

If their definition of atonement includes not only the provision of salvation but also the application of salvation, then Calvinists and Arminians would both agree that the atonement is limited, because neither side believes in universalism (the unbiblical belief that all will be saved eventually).

If their definition of atonement does not include the application of salvation, then both sides would agree that it is unlimited. They agree that Christ's death is sufficient payment for the sins of the whole world. This, in my opinion, is the definition that best fits the biblical data.

So before you answer someone who asks you whether you are a five-point Calvinist, you must first ask him to define exactly what he means by limited atonement. Does he include salvation (the application of the atonement) in his definition? And you can't let him be slippery with his use of terms, arguing as if for "A," but concluding "B."

We would join Calvin, I think, in being "four-point Calvinists" because it's agreed that the atonement was accomplished by the death of Christ, and the Bible says that Jesus died for the sins of the whole world. Refer to John 1:29 & 3:16f; I Timothy 2:5f & 4:10; Titus 2:11; Hebrews 2:9; II Peter 2:1 & 3:9; and I John 2:2. It's pretty difficult to reconcile these Scriptural statements with the idea of limited atonement.

Both Arminians and Calvinists essentially agree on three facts: 1) Christ's death is sufficient for all, 2) it is applied only to believers, and 3) it does not automatically or eventually save all people, as universalism teaches. Thus, Calvinist and Arminians are more in agreement on limited atonement than they are on the other points.

So how should we define the atonement? Does it imply an individual's salvation or does it just provide all individuals with the opportunity for salvation?

Peter draws upon two Old Testament illustrations—the Day of Atonement (by his choice of terms in verse 18) and Noah's ark (verse 20). As always, we should be guided by the context.

The Day of Atonement is prescribed in Leviticus 16. It served as a reminder that the daily, weekly, and monthly sacrifices were not sufficient to atone for sin. (Meaning that the yearly Day of Atonement wasn't either.) Let's read a few verses to see how the Day of Atonement applied:

And [Aaron] shall make atonement for the holy place, because of the impurities of the sons of Israel, and because of their transgressions, in regard to all their sins; and thus he shall do for the tent of meeting which abides with them in the midst of their impurities. When he goes in to make atonement in the holy place, no one shall be in the tent of meeting until he comes out, that he may make atonement for himself and for his household and for all the assembly of Israel, Leviticus 16: 16f.

Then Aaron shall lay both of his hands on the head of the live goat, and confess over it all the iniquities of the sons of Israel, and all their transgressions in regard to all their sins; and he shall lay them on the head of the goat and send it away into the wilderness by the hand of a man who stands in readiness, Leviticus 16: 21.

He shall also make atonement for the priests and for all the people of the assembly, Leviticus 16: 33.

So this atonement was not limited and did not apply actual salvation to individuals, since it is clear that not everyone in Israel was saved. It would also be out of place to speak of the tent of meeting and the holy place as needing salvation.

The Hebrew word translated *atonement* is the word *kippur*, as in the Jewish holiday *yom kippur*. It means ransom or reconciliation, and involves the substitute death of an innocent life accepted in exchange for the life of the guilty. So we should really translate it the Day of Ransom or the Day of Redemption. It was a temporary and provisional redemption from the *immediate* execution of God's judgment. That's why it applied to all the Hebrews and even to the worship place.

The New Testament uses different terms to add to our understanding of the concept. It is a called a ransom (Mark 10:45; I Timothy 2:6), a propitiation (Hebrews 2:17; I John 2:2), a substitute (Isaiah 53; II Corinthians 5:21; John 11:50), a redemption (Galatians 3:13), and a just satisfaction of God's righteousness (Romans 3:21-26).

Nothing in any of this implies that the work of Christ is automatically applied to anyone, including those who are chosen. None of this actually puts a person *in Christ*. It clears all the obstacles, as far as God is concerned, but it doesn't change the hearts of men. It doesn't remove man's rebellion or impart spiritual life. It clears the way for adoption, but does not complete any adoption. There is nothing in these verses that addresses God's requirements of repentance and trust in Christ. It is universally taught in the Bible that repentance and faith are the requirements for salvation.

What we learn from Noah's ark is consistent with what we learn from the Day of Atonement. The whole time Noah was building the ark, he was warning people of the coming judgment and urging them to repent and get into the ark. As soon as the ark had a door, it stood open to all. And it stayed open to all until the day of judgment. During that whole time the patience of God kept waiting.

But when time was up, God Himself closed that door of salvation, sealing Noah's family in and all the unbelievers out. Up until that day everyone had the opportunity and the provision to be saved. The Ark was plenty large enough to accommodate more than eight people along with all the animal kinds. Each one of those billions of sinners was doomed by his refusal to abandon his wickedness and believe God, not by any lack of patience or provision on God's part. God was perfectly just and very gracious. Judgment is the direct result of spurning God's provision of grace.

So my conclusion is that the theological term *atonement* properly refers to Christ's work that satisfied God's holy justice and provided the means of salvation, but does not include the application of salvation to any individual. That application is a different problem. The provision for salvation was accomplished by Christ. The application of that salvation is accomplished by the Holy Spirit (see Romans 6, for example).

The two-part nature of this solution is seen in I Timothy 4:10, **we have fixed our hope on the living God, who is the Savior of all men, especially of believers.** God is the Savior of all men in that He has made salvation available to all, if they will take it. But He is especially the Savior of the elect because God calls His chosen ones with the effectual and irresistible call spoken of in Romans 8:30: **whom He predestined, these He also called; and whom He called, these He also justified; and whom He justified, these He also glorified.**

Jesus provides the means of salvation; the Holy Spirit imparts it. The Holy Spirit has to make a special effort to apply that salvation to each individual that the Father has chosen. Otherwise, all would continue to reject the opportunity for salvation. (Total depravity means all are absolutely unable and unwilling to change; see Rom. 3.)

Salvation is universally available, because Jesus Christ died once for all. And it's universally encouraged by a loving Creator who is **not wishing for any to perish but for all to come to repentance,** II Peter 3:9. God instructed Ezekiel, **Say to them, 'As I live!' declares the Lord YHWH, 'I take no pleasure in the death of the wicked, but rather that the wicked turn from his way and live. Turn back, turn back from your evil ways,'** Ezekiel 33:11.

The fall of man created three major problems (and some collateral problems) that have to be fixed in order for man to be saved: 1) God's sovereignty was rejected, 2) man is a rebellious sinner with a sin nature, and 3) he is under the penalty of eternal death, meaning separation from God, because his sinfulness comes between him and a holy God.

The atonement satisfied the penalty of eternal death and removed the obstacles to reconciliation. But it didn't reverse man's choice to be his own god--it doesn't address the rejection of God's sovereignty, and it doesn't change man's sin nature.

It doesn't cause repentance. The Holy Spirit does all that work individually in the heart of each person whom God chose from the foundation of the earth to be saved. The Holy Spirit imparts to chosen individuals the salvation that Jesus provided for all. See Romans 6 and John 16:8. Christ procured the victory by His death and resurrection, but how does the Holy Spirit impart salvation to us?

Victory Imparted, 21

And corresponding to that, baptism now saves you-- not the removal of dirt from the flesh, but an appeal to God for a good conscience-- through the resurrection of Jesus Christ,

Now we come to another controversy that has divided theologians and denominations—the question of baptismal regeneration. Is it necessary to be baptized to be saved? We probably all have friends who have been taught that one is not saved until he is baptized in water.

Verse 21 says that **baptism now saves you.** If that was all verse 21 said, it might seem to argue for baptismal regeneration—that is, if we define the term *baptism* the way it's defined by those who believe in baptismal regeneration. Because of centuries of ecclesiastical usage, some define baptism primarily, or even exclusively, as the religious ritual of water baptism and believe that it must have some spiritual efficacy.

The term *sacrament,* which some erroneously apply to the ordinances of baptism and communion, means a visible *form* of an invisible grace (not a symbol or picture, but an actual form of the real thing). Sacraments, according to those churches who put stock in them, actually confer or convey grace. The Roman church, for example, believes that the rite in and of itself has the power to regenerate sinners when performed by the church. The Roman Catholic Church calls this *ex opere operato*—"by the work performed." So when the

Spanish missionaries in the time of Junipero Sera came to the new world, they believed that by sprinkling sacramental water on the natives they automatically became Christian. No need for hearing or understanding the gospel. No need for conviction, repentance, or faith.

Other denominations would not agree with that, but they still think that water baptism is a necessary part of the regeneration of the sinner. In their view, water baptism is a *sine qua non* ('without which, not') of salvation. In other words, they treat baptism as a sacrament.

But Biblically, baptism and communion are symbols of grace, not means, not sacraments. They depict God's grace, they don't bestow it. There are no biblical sacraments. Martin Luther said that the sole value of a so-called sacrament is its witness to the divine promise (which means that it isn't a sacrament at all.)

The confusion is understandable. When you have an important cause-effect relationship and the cause is invisible, people are inclined to turn the visible symbol of the invisible cause into the cause itself. If the effect is important to us, we want to *see* the cause rather than take it by faith. No matter who tells me that the gun is not loaded, I want to check it for myself.

Because of human nature and experience, we tend to walk by sight and not by faith. So the flesh demands that we have some visible token of personal merit to justify our belief that we are saved. For this reason people have held onto the view that baptism provides this merit. So they see baptism as a necessary cause of salvation. And because it is all we can see, it eventually becomes *the* cause of salvation. It gives people who don't know or trust Scripture well enough, reason to say, "I did this ritual; therefore I am saved."

The doctrinal error known as baptismal regeneration came into the church in the second century. To put it into historical context, this was a time of spiritual zeal and doctrinal weakness, because the Bible was not yet widely circulated. Christians were very concerned about their salvation but not sure how to know beyond a doubt that they were saved. When persecutions started, many Christians actually wanted to be martyred, believing that such a death insured their salvation. This is not unlike the Moslems today who are given no certainty about getting into paradise unless they die in *jihad*. So Christians would even jump out of windows when persecutors came, to be sure they died.

In the second and third centuries, the syncretistic religion of Gnosticism almost destroyed Christianity by absorbing it, because of the Christians' doctrinal weakness and lack of discernment. I suppose that while the doctrinal bulldogs of the faith were busy fighting the deadly serious threat of Gnosticism, the doctrine of baptismal regeneration crept in the side door unnoticed.

Gentile believers in the first couple of centuries had a hard time separating their former paganism from Biblical Christianity. They still do, for that matter. Pagan mystery religions all offered mystical, sacramental cleansing from sin. In the religions of Isis and Serapis, that cleansing was by bathing in sacred water. In the cults of the Great Mother and of Mithras, it was by the blood of a bull. These ritual cleansings admitted the person into the cult.

Gentile Christians were influenced by these mystery religions. We can read about it in I Corinthians 12, for example. Furthermore, concern for the destiny of infants who died led the church to accept the efficacy of infant baptism, which, of course, is based upon the belief that baptism conveys saving grace. You can't base theology on desire or pity. A better view of God's sovereignty in election would have provided better understanding about their children's destinies.

So Peter was quick to dismiss any idea of baptismal regeneration. He says, **not the removal of dirt from the flesh**, meaning not water baptism (for so they would take it). Peter writes under the direction of the Holy Spirit, and the Spirit knew that one of the great doctrinal errors in the church would be baptismal regeneration.

Neither author, human or divine, wants to give up the term *baptism*, or the ordinance of water baptism, because it is a very useful term and a very enlightening ritual, but they don't want to be misunderstood, either.

The baptism of which Peter speaks is a baptism that **corresponds** to the salvation accomplished by Noah's ark, verse 20. The word translated "corresponding" is *antitupos* (antitype). A type is a foreshadowing picture of the real thing, given so people will recognize and understand the real thing when it comes later. The Old Testament sacrifices were all types. The antitype is the real thing. The ark was the type, Jesus is the antitype. In other words, the ark was a picture of Christ, a foreshadowing, a visual aid to help us understand what Jesus would do for us.

Noah's family was not baptized in water. The people who were baptized in water in Noah's day (first by sprinkling, then by immersion) were lost forever. It was those who were placed into the ark who were saved, not those who were put in the water. And the water did not symbolize cleansing from sin; it symbolized God's judgment. In fact, it was the actual means of God's judgment. It represents the judgment of death in the ritual of baptism.

Proponents of baptismal regeneration might argue that the baptism of that time did not avail for salvation because it was not united with faith. But if the people of Noah's day had believed God, they would not have been baptized in water! The only ones who were saved were the ones *not* baptized in the water.

Proponents also call upon the Israelites' Red Sea experience as proof of their doctrine, based upon a careless interpretation of I Corinthians 10:2. It was the Egyptian army that was baptized in water at that time. And they were all destroyed, not saved.

What were the Israelites baptized into? I Corinthians 10:2 says that they were **all were baptized into Moses in the cloud and in the sea**. The word *baptize* (Greek, *baptizo*) means to place one thing into another so that the nature and character of that first thing is changed, exactly what Paul described in Romans 6 when the Spirit baptizes us into Christ's death and resurrection. Natural cloth, for example, might be immersed into red dye, baptized in that dye, changing it permanently into red cloth.

The Holy Spirit convicts the world concerning sin, righteousness, and judgment. When God convicts a sinner, grants him repentance, and gives him faith, which Ephesians 2 says is a gift of God, the Holy Spirit places that person into Christ, forever changing that person's nature and character, not to mention his eternal destiny. That is how God imparts to some the victory that Jesus made available to all.

This is the primary meaning of the Greek word baptize. So it is the meaning we should give it in all the New Testament verses that mention baptism, unless we have good, contextual reason to assign it a different meaning.

By the time Paul wrote his epistles, the phrase, *in Christ*, had taken on a specific, theological meaning (not yet developed in the gospels), pointing to the fact that the believer had been placed into Christ and sealed in Christ. And *in Christ* is where all the blessings of salvation are to be found.

A major aspect of baptism, naturally, is identification. The thing baptized takes on the identity of whatever it was baptized in. The symbolic ritual of water baptism is the believer's public act of identification with the Person and work of Jesus Christ. He is publicly professing his unity with Jesus. The New Testament, by the way, never mentions baptism as a means of entering a local church. We aren't baptized into a church; we are baptized into Christ. Isn't that the same thing? No, Romans 6 says that we were baptized into Christ. The Bible is precise, so we should be, too.

So whenever we conduct the ordinance of water baptism, we first determine whether the candidate has repented of his sins and put his trust in Christ alone for salvation. If so, then he is already regenerated. Upon his affirmation that he has indeed been baptized into Christ, he publicly identifies himself with Jesus by demonstrating the manner of his salvation. We "bury" him with Christ in the water, which action pictures his death in Christ. Then we raise him out of the water, out of death, depicting his resurrection in Christ. It's a fantastic, divinely-ordained picture of salvation, not to be discarded. But it's not the means of salvation.

Paul was passionate about people being saved but was not nearly so passionate about water baptism, according to I Corinthians 1:14-17:

I thank God that I baptized none of you except Crispus and Gaius, that no man should say you were baptized in my name. Now I did baptize also the household of Stephanas; beyond that, I do not know whether I baptized any other. For Christ did not send me to baptize, but to preach the gospel.

If water baptism were a requirement for salvation, how could Paul be so careless about it, **beyond that, I do not know whether I baptized any other**? The Holy Spirit, directing Paul's writing, chose not to refresh his memory on this point for the very reason that He didn't want water baptism to be seen as a necessary part of a person's salvation. Or how could Paul, again, under the Holy Spirit's guidance, make such a distinction between the gospel and water baptism, **Christ did not send me to baptize, but to preach the gospel**? He sees the distinction between the real baptism into Christ of Matthew 28:19 that makes a disciple and the water baptism of I Corinthians 1 which identifies him to others as a disciple and illustrates how he became one.

The means by which victory is imparted to someone, viewed from the human side, is a repentant, trusting **appeal to God for a good conscience** (that is, asking for and receiving total and complete forgiveness). Cleansing from sin comes not by water baptism, but by meeting God's conditions of repentance and faith and then simply asking God for forgiveness.

God's salvation is never accomplished by a symbol or type. It is accomplished by the antitype, the real thing, not the picture. There was a guy with mice in his house. He didn't have any cheese to bait a trap, so he found a picture of cheese in a magazine and cut it out to put on the trap. When he checked the trap the next morning he found a picture of a mouse. Pictures don't accomplish the work.

If spiritual victory is not imparted by the ritual of water baptism, then how? Once Peter has qualified what he means by baptism, that he means the real thing, not the picture, he tells us how baptism saves us. It is not by external washing but by **an appeal to God for a good conscience.** And that happens, Peter says, **through the resurrection of Jesus Christ**. Saving work is done on the inside where the sin nature is, not by an external washing.

The word *appeal* was a technical term used in contracts. It referred to agreeing to meet certain divinely-required conditions before God places one into the ark of safety. Anyone who would be saved must come to God with a desire to obtain a good conscience that is, to know that he is forgiven and cleansed on the inside. (His sin nature has to be dealt with). And the sinner must be willing to meet the divine conditions, which are repentance and faith, the same conditions God has always set forth.

When these conditions are met, then the Holy Spirit places that person in Christ, the antitype, the *real* ark of our salvation, and seals him there, just as God closed the door on Noah's ark. That is the baptism of the Holy Spirit, when the Holy Spirit places us into Christ. See Romans 6.

Just as the ark went through divine judgment safely, so did Jesus—He rose from death. And just as all who were in the ark got through God's judgment safely, so do all who are in Christ. So in Romans 6: 3ff, we read:

Do you not know that all of us who have been baptized into Christ Jesus have been baptized into His death? Therefore we have been buried with Him through baptism into death, in order that as Christ was raised from the dead through the glory of the Father, so we too might walk in newness of life. For if we have become united with Him in the likeness of His death, certainly we shall be also in the likeness of His resurrection, knowing this, that our old self was crucified with Him, that our body of sin might be done away with, that we should no longer be slaves to sin; for he who has died is freed from sin. Now if we have died with Christ, we believe that we shall also live with Him.

The vast majority of the people in the world will not agree to God's conditions, even though the Bible warns them of

God's judgment and tells them that trusting in the death and resurrection of Jesus Christ is the only means by which they may be saved. Every religion in the world teaches that men become right with God (however they conceive of divinity) by their own actions and merit. When we go directly against that majority opinion, when we go against every religion in the world, how do we know we are on safe ground? If we are going to trust in something besides our own efforts, how do we know we're on safe ground?

The Glory and Certainty of Victory, 22

who is at the right hand of God, having gone into heaven, after angels and authorities and powers had been subjected to Him.

Jesus is right now seated at the right hand of God the Father. This is the pre-eminent place of honor and prestige, power and authority. If Jesus were an impostor or a fake, or had somehow failed to gain the victory, the Father would not give Him the place of honor and power. Before Jesus ever took on human flesh, He owned that position by right of His deity. Angels worshiped, adored, and obeyed Him.

Then **Jesus, the author and perfecter of faith, instead of the joy set before Him endured the cross, despising the shame, and has sat down at the right hand of the throne of God**, Hebrews 12:2. He gave up His exalted and joyful position in heaven to become a man, take mankind's sin upon Himself, and to die for man's sins, and then to gain victory over death by His resurrection. As our dread champion, He earned, by right of His heroic victory on earth, that position of glory and honor which was already His by right of His deity. (See the author's commentary on Colossians.)

Then, after all the rebellious angels with their various authorities and powers had been subjected to Him, He went back to His rightful place of honor and authority, as verses 19-20 tell us. Jesus now occupies that exalted place at the Father's right hand. He owned it by right of His deity, and He earned it by right of His victory. So He is doubly honored by the Father. Thus Jesus won by His great victory a people for His own possession.

How could the Father let us fall away and be lost to Jesus when we have been won, fair and square, by His Son's great sacrifice? John 6:39, **And this is the will of Him who sent Me, that of all that He has given Me I lose nothing, but raise it up on the last day.** This is the preservation of the saints. We are the Father's gift to the Son. That's why we **are protected by the power of God through faith for a salvation ready to be revealed in the last time. In this you greatly rejoice, even though now for a little while, if necessary, you have been distressed by various trials**, I Peter 1:5f. Incidentally, the Father uses those trials to polish us up before presenting us to Jesus.

Now here is the point of verses 18-22: Jesus gained these victories for the Father by subjecting Himself to the unjust persecutions of sinful men. It looked, and probably felt, like the way to defeat. But it was, in fact, the way to victory. It's like that for us, too. We fight the good fight. We go through the unjust persecutions because that's the way to victory, in more ways than one. As I Corinthians 1:27f says, **God has chosen the weak things of the world to shame the things which are strong, and the base things of the world and the despised, God has chosen, the things that are not, that He might nullify the things that are.**

Christ's victories are to our benefit, of course. But more to the point, we, too, will gain great victories in Gods' redemptive program if we don't shy away from unjust persecutions. Noah was not intimidated by overwhelming odds. He worked for 100 years on the ark, ignoring the mockery and insults of the majority. He was right, because he believed God; they were wrong. They should have listened to him.

In God's program the temporary suffering always comes first, then the eternal glory. It should be obvious that the suffering can't come *after* the eternal glory!

When the posse came to arrest Jesus on the Mount of Olives, Peter drew his sword and started in on the posse, wanting Jesus to get away.

Jesus said to him, "Put your sword back into its place; for all those who take up the sword shall perish by the sword. Or do you think that I cannot appeal to My Father, and He will at once put at My disposal more than twelve legions of angels? How then shall the Scriptures be fulfilled, that it must happen this way?" Matthew 26:52-54.

Jesus intended the sword for self-defense (Luke 22:36), not for insurrection against the authorities established by God, and certainly not for altering God's plan to suit man's preference.

Jesus could have aborted His redemptive mission at any time. At any point in His unjust suffering at the unjust hands of unjust men, He could have said, "Enough is enough." He could have ended His suffering, and left us all to die in our sins as the eternal victims of our own bad choices. Twelve legions of very agitated angels would have been there in a flash to deal with any objections.

Even when He was on the cross, Jesus **[upheld] all things by the word of His power**, Hebrews 1:3. He could have said the word and let all things fall apart in order to save Himself. Instead, He endured the pain and humiliation, fulfilled His commitment to God's plan to the last detail, and gained absolute, unadulterated victory. Jesus left nothing undone. He paid the price of our redemption to the last cent.

His redemptive work is finished. It needs no repetition and cannot be nullified. It is finished and stays finished. He died **once for all**. So Jesus has returned to His former glory at the right hand of the throne of God. So we are on safe ground, going *against* the *majority* opinion. In fact, you could almost say that, in spiritual matters, one is *never* on safe ground going *with* the majority opinion.

The Conclusion, then…

Considering all that God has accomplished through the persecution of His righteous ones, starting with Jesus, we should not shy away from persecution. We flee it if God says to flee it, and we stand it if God says to stand it. He knows how to direct us. But we never waver in our faithfulness in order to avoid it.

Jesus is the ark of salvation for the whole world. God provided no other means to be saved from the flood in Noah's day, and He provides no other means to be saved from the wrath to come. Even if we don't have any more converts than Noah had, we still have to warn people about God's coming judgment and encourage them to get into Jesus, the ark of salvation, before God closes the door.

The victorious example of Jesus Christ is all the authority and all the motivation we need to speak up for God, even if we should suffer persecution for doing so. We don't need the world's permission to serve God in any that way He commands. Jesus has overcome the world. He told His disciples, **In the world you have tribulation, but take courage; I have overcome the world**, John 16:33. And I John 5:4 tells us, **whatever is born of God overcomes the world; and this is the victory that has overcome the world-- our faith.**

Jesus has gained total victory over the forces of darkness. **You are from God, little children, and have overcome them; because greater is He who is in you than he who is in the world,** I John 4:4. He has gained total victory over sin and death. So **do not be overcome by evil, but overcome evil with good**, Romans 12:21.

Chapter 18

4:1-6, Armed with an Excellent Attitude

¹ **Therefore, since Christ has suffered in the flesh, arm yourselves also with the same purpose, because he who has suffered in the flesh has ceased from sin,**
² **so as to live the rest of the time in the flesh no longer for the lusts of men, but for the will of God.**
³ **For the time already past is sufficient *for you* to have carried out the desire of the Gentiles, having pursued a course of sensuality, lusts, drunkenness, carousals, drinking parties and abominable idolatries.**
⁴ **And in *all* this, they are surprised that you do not run with *them* into the same excess of dissipation, and they malign *you*;**
⁵ **but they shall give account to Him who is ready to judge the living and the dead.**
⁶ **For the gospel has for this purpose been preached even to those who are dead, that though they are judged in the flesh as men, they may live in the spirit according to *the will of* God.**

Attitude is not everything, but it is extremely important. Other things being equal, it's often the determining factor between winning and losing, or between winning and whining. Most people realize that. What they don't know is how to change their attitude long-term. All but the sourest individuals can "turn that frown upside down," at least until the next setback arrives.

What actually forms a person's real attitude? What determines our way of thinking? For many it's desire or emotion—wanting or feeling. For others it's mostly reactionary--will and emotion both. It's not something they've really thought through.

I think the only legitimate and sustainable basis for our attitude is our perspective on where we fit in the grand scheme

278

of things—our understanding of our place and purpose. If you live for yourself, it's hard to keep an excellent attitude, because things don't always go your way. And when things don't go your way, your attitude becomes less agreeable. And if your attitude becomes less agreeable, other people become less cooperative, causing more things not to go your way. It's a downward spiral that you can't get out of by continuing to live for yourself. So if you live for yourself, you are living against your own best interests. That results in a bad attitude.

In fact, if you're living for yourself, you aren't even starting off with a good attitude! In this chapter we will consider attitude as a weapon, not to use against people but against situations. I'm sure you've known people who use their bad attitude as a weapon for evil (to get what they want). We are considering the excellent attitude of Christ as a weapon against evil (to get what God wants). Good attitude is a spiritual weapon, designed to be very effective in spiritual warfare.

Peter has been urging his readers to follow the example set by our Lord Jesus Christ. And that example starts with an attitude. Matthew 20:28 points out that **the Son of Man did not come to be served, but to serve, and to give His life a ransom for many.** He came to live for others. In our text, Peter applies the example of Christ to the situation of those who are about to experience a more severe persecution than they have faced heretofore. Perhaps the biggest test of attitude comes when we are subjected to unjust treatment. How we respond to persecution reveals where our head is and where our heart is.

And this is where we either help or hinder the cause of Christ. In I Corinthians 9:12, Paul wrote: **we endure all things, that we may cause no hindrance to the gospel of Christ.** And in II Timothy 2:10: **For this reason I endure all things for the sake of those who are chosen, that they also may obtain the salvation which is in Christ Jesus and with it eternal glory.**

The Christian's attitude either helps or hinders the reception of the gospel. Peter is still describing what it means to keep our behavior excellent among the Gentiles so they will glorify God in the day of visitation (2:12). So let's think through the issue of what kind of attitude we should maintain toward suffering.

Again, Peter's outline is simple (even if the content is not). Here is what he is saying in the first six verses of chapter 4:

Arm Yourself with Christ's Purpose, 1

Separate Yourself from Sin, 2-3

Entrust Yourself to the Righteous Judge, 4-6.

Arm Yourself with Christ's Purpose, 1

¹ **Therefore, since Christ has suffered in the flesh, arm yourselves also with the same purpose, because he who has suffered in the flesh has ceased from sin,**

This is the key to the passage, and the only command. The word *therefore* points us back to the tremendous victory Christ gained, and specifically to how He gained that victory by subjecting Himself to unjust suffering, 3:17-22. Great victories don't come cheap. Jesus was willing to subject Himself to persecution at the hands of sinners in order to accomplish the Father's redemptive purpose. It was His purpose that determined His attitude toward suffering. If we are to have the same winning attitude, we must adopt the same purpose. That's all these verses are saying; the rest is just support.

And so it was with Moses. Hebrews 11:24-26 gives us some added insight into the attitude behind his choices:

By faith Moses, when he had grown up, refused to be called the son of Pharaoh's daughter; choosing rather to endure ill-treatment with the people of God, than to enjoy the passing pleasures of sin; considering the reproach of Christ greater riches than the treasures of Egypt; for he was looking to the reward.

The writers of the book of Hebrews recalled how the earliest Christians in Jerusalem endured persecution:

But remember the former days, when, after being enlightened, you endured a great conflict of sufferings,

partly, by being made a public spectacle through reproaches and tribulations, and partly by becoming sharers with those who were so treated. For you showed sympathy to the prisoners, and accepted joyfully the seizure of your property, knowing that you have for yourselves a better possession and an abiding one. Therefore, do not throw away your confidence, which has a great reward. For you have need of endurance, so that when you have done the will of God, you may receive what was promised, Hebrews 10:32-36.

Those believers had the same attitude that Christ had. This world is not the goal. It is the preparation for eternity. If we forget that, everything gets confusing. Remember how powerful the gospel was in the early chapters of Acts and how many came to Christ at that time. The excellent attitude of those Christians had a lot to do with that. Arm yourself with the same perspective and purpose that made Jesus willing to suffer, and you will be arming yourself with the same excellent attitude toward suffering that Jesus had. And that will go a long way toward making you as successful as He was.

The Greek word translated *purpose* literally means same thinking, consideration, intent, purpose, or design. It's an attitude formed by purpose. Football players willingly (more or less) suffer for many days in order to accomplish their purpose, which is to play a few games. Job found it hard to suffer because he didn't see God's purpose in it. He wasn't considering what God had considered and didn't have the same intent.

It would be very helpful to Christians to be eager students of God's word and specifically, in this regard, to be students of God's purpose and methods. I find a paradox—that the more you study God's word, the hungrier you get to study it more. God salts His word. It both satisfies our hunger and makes us hungrier for more. Fortunately, it's not junk food; it builds muscle, not fat, if we apply it.

Students of God's word learn from all the Biblical examples and principles that a wise and just God never does anything without a purpose. And He never buys high and sells low. He always gets an excellent return on investment. If our suffering is the currency of His investment, we can be sure that He is not spending our pain foolishly. God never makes a bad deal for His children.

God isn't stupid, that He should do things the hard way, nor unreasonable that He should make *us* do things the hard way. He is not lazy that He should do things the easy way, nor so careless of our spiritual health that He should be slack in our training.

God does things the right way, the smart way, the best way, the way that achieves His purposes. I say purpos*es* because it's rare that God accomplishes only a single purpose by the methods He chooses. He usually accomplishes several purposes at once, as He did with the suffering that Job went through. He developed Job's spiritual understanding, taught his friends some valuable lessons, and added power to Job's witness among his neighbors. God is very efficient. There is literally no limit to God's energy or resources, so He could be wasteful if He wanted to be. Yet God is also wise; therefore He is efficient. If God killed two birds with one stone, that would be below par for Him.

We have already discussed many reasons why God uses or permits suffering in the world, and in the church. It foreshadows and therefore warns of God's judgment, it provides reproof and discipline, it adds power to the gospel, it develops our perseverance and commitment to obey God, it perfects and completes us, it puts us into more intimate fellowship with our Lord, it increases our reward, just to name a few. I'll name one more--a person's reaction to persecution enables unbelievers to discern who is a genuine believer deserving the attention of seekers, and who is an impostor that should be ignored. When you consider all the benefits produced by persecution, we don't wonder that suffering is one of God's favorite tools.

Philippians 2:1-9 says a lot about mind, attitude, and purpose in contrast to selfishness:

If therefore there is any encouragement in Christ, if there is any consolation of love, if there is any fellowship of the Spirit, if any affection and compassion, make my joy

complete by being of the same mind, maintaining the same love, united in spirit, intent on one purpose. Do nothing from selfishness or empty conceit, but with humility of mind let each of you regard one another as more important than himself; do not merely look out for your own personal interests, but also for the interests of others. Have this attitude in yourselves which was also in Christ Jesus, who, although He existed in the form of God, did not regard equality with God a thing to be grasped, but emptied Himself, taking the form of a bond-servant, and being made in the likeness of men. And being found in appearance as a man, He humbled Himself by becoming obedient to the point of death, even death on a cross. Therefore also God highly exalted Him, and bestowed on Him the name which is above every name.

The words *mind, purpose*, and *attitude* in the passage above are all translations of a single Greek synonym (*ennoian*) of the word in I Peter 4:1, which is *phroneo*. This word *ennoian* focuses on what one has *in* the mind, the *content* of one's thinking, whereas the word in I Peter 4:1, *phroneo,* emphasizes the *intent* of the thinking. So both the intent and the content of our thinking should match those of our Lord. **We have the mind of Christ,** I Corinthians 2:16 tells us. And we should **let the word of Christ richly dwell within [us]**, Colossians 3:16.

Of all the people who have ever lived, who would you say had the best attitude? Whose attitude produced the best results? Whose attitude was the most constant, even under duress? Whose attitude found the most favor with God? That's the attitude we should emulate.

It's hard to have the attitude of Christ primarily because of one thing--self-will, the independent desire that Jesus said we must give up if we want to follow Him (Mark 8:34). Self-will is sin. Behind that self-will is the attitude, "I know better than God." And Peter addresses that problem in the second part of verse one, **arm yourselves also with the same purpose, because he who has suffered in the flesh has ceased from sin.**

This points back to the fact that we have been baptized into Christ, which Peter discussed at the end of chapter three. It can't be a reference to those who have been martyred. Martyrs certainly have ceased from sin. But those who have **suffered** and **ceased from sin** in verse 1 are still living **in the flesh** in verse 2.

We have been baptized into Christ's death. **We have died with Christ**, according to Romans 6:8. So we are to **consider ourselves to be dead to sin, but alive to God in Christ Jesus**, Romans 6:11 God never tells us to consider something to be true if it isn't.

I urge you therefore, brethren, by the mercies of God, to present your bodies a living and holy sacrifice, acceptable to God, which is your spiritual [logical] service of worship. And do not be conformed to this world, but be transformed by the renewing of your mind, that you may prove what the will of God is, that which is good and acceptable and perfect, Romans 12:1f.

So the only reasonable attitude for us who have been saved from eternal punishment by Christ's great sacrifice is to see ourselves as living and holy sacrifices to God, knowing how God uses suffering to accomplish His perfect will. If we arm ourselves with that attitude, then momentary, light affliction is not something we would shy away from. When I was a football player, we had some guys who never learned not to shy away from the pain of hard, physical contact. They were known as benchwarmers.

Arm yourselves is from the Greek word for weapons of warfare, *hoplos*. It's the root of *hoplophobia*, the fear of weapons, and *hoplite*, a fighting soldier. We are soldiers of Christ. II Timothy 2:3f commands, **Suffer hardship with me, as a good soldier of Christ Jesus. No soldier in active service entangles himself in the affairs of everyday life, so that he may please the one who enlisted him as a soldier.**

Of all the weapons a soldier trains with and carries into battle, attitude is supreme. That's why military training spends so much time developing the new recruits' attitude. If you give a coward a rifle, he's till a coward. If you give a brave man a stick, he will sharpen it and press the attack.

In Luke 9 Jesus told His disciples,

"If anyone wishes to come after Me, let him deny himself, and take up his cross daily, and follow Me. For whoever wishes to save his life shall lose it, but whoever loses his life for My sake, he is the one who will save it. For what is a man profited if he gains the whole world, and loses or forfeits himself?

Maybe you think, "I'm not up to that!" Neither am I. Neither was Paul. In II Corinthians 4:7 he wrote: **But we have this treasure in earthen vessels, that the surpassing greatness of the power may be of God and not from ourselves.** See also II Corinthians 3:4-6 and 4:8-18. That's cool. That way God gets the glory, and that's what unbelievers need to see.

It's always the cross before the crown. We have, in fact, died in Christ and are therefore dead to sin, as Romans 6 tells us, but we don't always *act* like we are dead to sin. We don't always *consider* **ourselves to be dead to sin.** So Peter takes up that hindrance in verses 2 and 3.

Separate Yourself from Sin, 2-3

² so as to live the rest of the time in the flesh no longer for the lusts of men, but for the will of God. ³ For the time already past is sufficient *for you* to have carried out the desire of the Gentiles, having pursued a course of sensuality, lusts, drunkenness, carousals, drinking parties and abominable idolatries.

The Christian who surrenders to sin puts himself into a position of weakness in many ways. Self-will is a position of weakness because God only helps us to follow His will. He doesn't help us to follow our own. Independent desire is destructive. If we follow self-will, the Holy Spirit stops assisting us and begins to resist us and convict us in order to get us to turn back. The Holy Spirit doesn't help us damage ourselves. If you found your son sitting in the yard hitting himself on the head with his little baseball bat and he asked you for a bigger bat, would you give it to him?

God identifies sin as sin and prohibits it because it has bad consequences. We suffer as a consequence of our sin. Sin undercuts our moral authority and the credibility of our witness. Sin makes us vulnerable to all kinds of attacks. In the minds of God-haters and those who are simply looking on, it justifies actions taken against us.

Sin robs us of our *assurance* of salvation. How would that affect your attitude? It's what Deuteronomy 28:66 says, **So your life shall hang in doubt before you; and you shall be in dread night and day, and shall have no assurance of your life.** And Hebrews 6:11f says, **And we desire that each one of you show the same diligence so as to realize the full assurance of hope until the end, that you may not be sluggish, but imitators of those who through faith and patience inherit the promises.**

And it isn't that sinners disapprove of any particular sin we might commit (unless it's a sin against them). They also sin and are, in fact, shocked and offended that we **do not run with them into the same excess of dissipation.** Part of the offense they take is that we claim to be right with God but act the same way they do. (If they catch us in one sin, they assume we are guilty of more and just haven't been caught yet.) It's that perceived hypocrisy that gets them, even though they might be hypocrites, themselves.

So Christians who sin put themselves in a weak position. They're trying to fight a battle they don't understand while standing on marbles on thin ice with their pants on fire while they're looking in the wrong direction. We have been crucified with Christ so as to live the rest of our time in the flesh no longer for the lusts, the passionate, evil longings, of men. Jesus **gave Himself for us, that He might redeem us from every lawless deed and purify for Himself a people for His own possession, zealous for good deeds,** Titus 2:13.

We were made dead to sin so we could live for the will of God. Mankind was originally created to willingly submit our desires to the will of God, believing that He knows best. We rebelled against God to pursue self-will, making ourselves dead to God and alive to sin. Jesus redeemed us back to live for the will of God, making us alive to God and dead to sin.

286

If you have turned back from your wicked ways to follow God, and have gotten free from sin and death, and have received a glorious future, why would you turn back from turning back? You would be a double-minded man, unstable in all your ways. In that case, you should not expect to receive anything from the Lord (James 1:7f).

Hebrews 10:38f is a stern warning:

BUT MY RIGHTEOUS ONE SHALL LIVE BY FAITH; AND IF HE SHRINKS BACK, MY SOUL HAS NO PLEASURE IN HIM. But we are not of those who shrink back to destruction, but of those who have faith to the preserving of the soul.

I'm dismayed by the casual attitude some Christians have toward sin, even those sins listed in verse 3. Sin is in our sordid past; we must leave it there. Colossians 3:1-7 says,

If then you have been raised up with Christ, keep seeking the things above, where Christ is, seated at the right hand of God. Set your mind on the things above, not on the things that are on earth. For you have died and your life is hidden with Christ in God. When Christ, who is our life, is revealed, then you also will be revealed with Him in glory. Therefore consider the members of your earthly body as dead to immorality, impurity, passion, evil desire, and greed, which amounts to idolatry. For it is on account of these things that the wrath of God will come, and in them you also once walked, when you were living in them.

The time already past is sufficient to have carried out the desire of the Gentiles. How much time have you had? It doesn't matter if it was five years or 50, it was more than enough for self-destructive behavior. If you had spent your life up to a certain point drinking sewer water and then you found the source of pure water, would you want to go back to the sewer water?

Look at these sins that Peter calls his readers away from: **Sensuality** is unrestrained vice of all kinds, excessive indulgence in sensual pleasure. **Lusts** are the sinful passions that drive people into such indulgences. **Drunkenness** is habitual intoxication, debaucheries. It can also refer to narcotic use. **Carousals** mean participating in wild parties or orgies. **Drinking parties** refer to groups gathered for the purpose of getting drunk. **Abominable idolatries** refer to the immoral, debauched worship of false gods.

These certainly are some of the more blatant sins. But how does *any* sin help the cause of Christ, or the condition of the Christian, or the sinner's understanding of God's judgment and the offer of grace? Sins are unsatisfactory substitutes that cause us to miss out on what God has for us. Sins are blessing blockers.

Entrust Yourself to the Righteous Judge, 4-6

⁴And in *all* this, they are surprised that you do not run with *them* into the same excess of dissipation, and they malign *you*;
⁵but they shall give account to Him who is ready to judge the living and the dead.
⁶For the gospel has for this purpose been preached even to those who are dead, that though they are judged in the flesh as men, they may live in the spirit according to *the will of* God.

Sinners malign those who don't join them in their dissipation. (Dissipation refers to that state of mind [attitude] that is so corrupt that it thinks of nothing but evil and how to indulge the sinful passions.) This maligning starts early, with children taunting other children as "Little Miss Goody Two-Shoes." (I don't remember what they called the girls.) Then it proceeds to more severe mockery and accusations of holier-than-thou snobbishness and attempts to thrust Christians into tempting situations.

Lately the bad-mouthing as gotten more aggressively intolerant, saying that Christians should be silenced, and even that they should not be allowed to exist. The news media ignore attacks against Christians as if they weren't happening even while championing the cause of sinners. Hate crime laws often aren't applied if the victims are Christians. Lest you get a persecution complex, they also are not applied equally to others who are politically incorrect.

Why such animosity? Ancient sources, Christian and non-Christian, say that it was the Christians' unwillingness to participate in many conventionally accepted amusements and ungodly civic ceremonies, and their refusal to engage in immoral, idolatrous functions that caused unbelievers to hate and revile them. So Christians were, quite literally, suffering for the sake of their righteousness.

Whatever happened to the live-and-let-live philosophy? Christians who live holy lives are lights to the world. Even if they say nothing, their deeds of righteousness expose the deeds of darkness simply by the stark contrast. Jesus told His followers why sinners might hate them,

"And this is the judgment, that the light is come into the world, and men loved the darkness rather than the light; for their deeds were evil. For everyone who does evil hates the light, and does not come to the light, lest his deeds should be exposed," John 3:19-20.

In a similar vein, Hebrews 10:26f says,

For if we go on sinning willfully after receiving the knowledge of the truth, there no longer remains a sacrifice for sins, but a certain terrifying expectation of judgment, and THE FURY OF A FIRE WHICH WILL CONSUME THE ADVERSARIES.

Sinners can't live comfortably with such terror, and they certainly cannot enjoy their self-indulgence in the knowledge that their momentary pleasure will condemn them to the fury of eternal fire. So they have to live in denial. It is for that reason alone that they deny the very existence of God and cling instead to the scientifically, logically, and theologically goofy theory of evolution.

But our holy lives spoil their game. They hate us because we remind them of what they are trying so desperately to repress. Our holy lives convict sinners and make them extremely uncomfortable. Maybe that's why they refer to the most benign people they know as "dangerous extremists." They believe they have a Constitutional right not to be reminded of God's judgment. Think of how often you hear that some expression of Christian faith is being prohibited by a government entity because it might offend someone. We've never heard the government concern itself that Christians might be offended.

It's predominately Christians who face this discrimination; and not just any so-called Christian, but only those who insist that the Bible is God's word, that it's all true, and who live by it. So our holy lives, threat that they are, become targets for Satan's fiery darts. He's the prince of darkness and he's trying to shoot out the lights.

They will have to give account, verse 5. This is their great fear, the one they deal with by trying to stay in denial. Our lives sound an unwelcome alarm that blares in their ears. You know how annoying it is when gnats won't go away. Our godly lifestyle is like a persistent gnat buzzing around their eyes.

Philippians 1:27f refers to this:

Only conduct yourselves in a manner worthy of the gospel of Christ; so that whether I come and see you or remain absent, I may hear of you that you are standing firm in one spirit, with one mind striving together for the faith of the gospel; in no way alarmed by your opponents-- which is a sign of destruction for them, but of salvation for you, and that too, from God.

I Peter 3:15 says we should be ready to give an account to unbelievers for the hope that is in us. Here we have the same word again. But this time it's the unbelievers who will have to give account. On the day of reckoning they will have to explain to God why they continued in their sin when God has provided salvation and called for all men everywhere to repent. The word for account, *logos*, means a rational expression. Their problem will be that there is no rational explanation for rejecting Jesus Christ. **There is no wisdom and no understanding And no counsel against the LORD**, Proverbs, 21:30.

Think about all that Jesus had to go through to provide salvation. How can sinners present a rationale, that Jesus'

Father will accept, for rejecting His Son and what He did for them? I wouldn't be in their shoes for all the world. I used to be in their shoes; so did you, but there is no way I want to go back. Their Judge is the very one they have been mocking and denying. The targets of their persecutions are the innocent, beloved children of the Judge. And they have rejected the way the Judge provided, at His great personal expense, for their rescue.

Our antagonists presume to judge us as men in the flesh, and in their eyes we are rejects. But they are not our judges. Jesus said **do not fear those who kill the body, but are unable to kill the soul; but rather fear Him who is able to destroy both soul and body in hell,** Matthew 10:28.

Now we come to a difficult saying, **The gospel has been preached even to those who are dead.** What is Peter talking about here? William Barclay, the liberal commentator, thought that this speaks of a second chance for those who have died in their sins. But there is absolutely no biblical support for such an idea. This is not the same announcement that was made in 3:19. That was to spirits and was not good news to them. This is to men and is the good news.

Others think it refers to those who are dead in their sins, but still alive in the flesh. But other men don't have a problem with fellow sinners. They are of the world and the world loves its own.

The context seems to indicate that **those who are dead** are believers who have already died in Christ, some as martyrs. By the time Peter wrote this letter, Christianity had been around for 30 years. Deceased believers had been judged and persecuted while they were in the flesh by the actions of men, but made alive in the spirit by the action of God. Romans 8:33f asks rhetorically, **Who will bring a charge against God's elect? God is the one who justifies; who is the one who condemns?** Sin always involves penalties; penalties from the world of sinners if you don't join in their sin, and penalties from natural consequences and the righteous Judge if you do. Believers who were still alive were afraid that those who had died before the return of Christ had missed out on the glories promised for that time.

Paul dealt with the same concern in I Thessalonians 4:13-18:

But we do not want you to be uninformed, brethren, about those who are asleep, that you may not grieve, as do the rest who have no hope. For if we believe that Jesus died and rose again, even so God will bring with Him those who have fallen asleep in Jesus. For this we say to you by the word of the Lord, that we who are alive, and remain until the coming of the Lord, shall not precede those who have fallen asleep. For the Lord Himself will descend from heaven with a shout, with the voice of the archangel, and with the trumpet of God; and the dead in Christ shall rise first. Then we who are alive and remain shall be caught up together with them in the clouds to meet the Lord in the air, and thus we shall always be with the Lord. Therefore comfort one another with these words.

It might be helpful here to point out that Christians in the first century hoped that Jesus would return in their lifetime. And the New Testament epistles that were written before 70 AD had to leave this possibility open. Even though God knew Israel's hardness and the timing of events--His offer was a valid offer. If the Jews had repented and turned to their crucified Messiah, Jesus could have returned in the first century to set up His promised kingdom on earth. So Paul went "to the Jew first and also to the Greek."

In the same way, Jesus and John the Baptist preached, "Repent, for the kingdom of God is at hand." They did this up until Matthew 12 when official Israel judged that Christ's works were from Satan. After that official rejection, starting in Matthew 13, Jesus began to teach in parables and to refer to the coming of the kingdom as a future event.

In the same way Old Testament predictions of the Messiah speak of both the first and the second advents in the same passage, sometimes in the same verse. Both advents could have happened in the first century, if the Jews had been willing to repent and believe in Jesus as the Messiah. But when Jerusalem and the Temple were destroyed by Titus of Rome in 70 AD, that possibility of a soon return was ended, because prophecy tells us that Jesus will return to the Temple. (Malachi

3:1 refers to both comings but especially to the second coming as the following verses indicate.) The Temple will be rebuilt in the last days before Jesus returns to set foot on the Mount of Olives.

For this purpose, in verse 6, refers back to verse 5 where it says that God **is ready to judge the living and the dead.** We preach the gospel because God really will judge. Our purpose determines our attitude. And the strength of our purpose determines the strength of our attitude. So what is your purpose?

You don't want to go into battle unarmed. And you don't want to go into battle in a weakened state. So we are well-advised to arm ourselves with the same attitude Christ had. It worked for Him in the hardest test imaginable. It will work for us just as well in any test we might face. And we need to know that self-indulgence does not make a ready soldier. So we need to give up self-will. Sin makes us weak. If we arm ourselves with the attitude that got Jesus through His suffering victoriously, then we are well-armed for whatever we must face.

Chapter 19

4:7-11, Excellent Love

7 The end of all things is at hand; therefore, be of sound judgment and sober *spirit* for the purpose of prayer. 8 Above all, keep fervent in your love for one another, because love covers a multitude of sins. 9 Be hospitable to one another without complaint. 10 As each one has received a *special* gift, employ it in serving one another, as good stewards of the manifold grace of God. 11 Whoever speaks, *let him speak,* as it were, the utterances of God; whoever serves, *let him do so* as by the strength which God supplies; so that in all things God may be glorified through Jesus Christ, to whom belongs the glory and dominion forever and ever. Amen.

The Apostle Paul refers to the second coming of Christ as our blessed hope (Titus 2:13). This expression has resonated with believers ever since. It's our motivation for holy living, for perseverance under persecution, for love of the brethren, and for diligent service to God. There is much of interest in this text, so we will get right to it. Our outline:

The End Has Come Near, 7a; Let that affect:

Your Prayers, 7b,

Your Love for One Another, 8-9,

Your Service to One Another, 10-11a, and

Your Motive, verse 11b.

The End Has Come Near, 7a

7 The end of all things is at hand;

Peter is very conscious of time. He's eager for the Lord's return, so he counts time "as a hired man would count," Isaiah 16:14, *et al*. He refers to time and time relationships at least 40 times in his two epistles. Paul also concerns himself with time and how we ought to make wise use of it, in view of the fact that we are in the last days. In Ephesians 5:15-17 he wrote: **Therefore be careful how you walk, not as unwise men, but as wise, making the most of your time, because the days are evil. So then do not be foolish, but understand what the will of the Lord is.**

The whole Bible, in fact, is very conscious of time and kinds of times, like epochs, dispensations, and especially of the end times. God's plan runs on a schedule, and all things happen in due time, when the fullness of time has come. We don't know the schedule, at least the part that is still future. But God has fixed the times. When the disciples asked about God's timing, Jesus answered, **It is not for you to know times or epochs which the Father has fixed by His own authority**, Acts 1:7.

Ephesians 1:9f says that God has

made known to us the mystery of His will, according to His kind intention which He purposed in Him with a view to an administration suitable to the fulness of the times, that is, the summing up of all things in Christ, things in the heavens and things upon the earth.

So Peter says the end of all things has come near. He is speaking of the time when Jesus returns to rule the world, when all things will be put under His authority.

Now, there is an issue here that I think we should address. Did Peter, writing under the inspiration of the Spirit of Truth, mean to say that Jesus would return in a short time? Because I see a problem with that. It has been 2,000 years since Peter wrote those words and Jesus hasn't returned yet. 2,000 years is not a short time--it's 1/3 of the world's history! (Study chapters 5 and 11 in Genesis with careful thought and your calculator.) I know that Peter says in his second letter that with the Lord, one day is as a thousand years and a thousand years is as one day. But I'm not sure that answers the question. That's how time is with the Lord, who lives in the eternal present. But that isn't how it is with us who live day by day.

Note: II Peter 3:8 is written in the context of the timing of the Lord's return. It's quite possible that Peter's words suggest the interpretation that there would be six "days", each lasting 1,000 years, in earth's work week and then a seventh 1,000 year day of sabbath rest, which is called the millennial kingdom. (The term *day* when used metaphorically seems always to refer to a set period of time with a definite beginning and end. Whenever a word is used metaphorically, its figurative meaning is derived from its literal meaning.)

The number seven and especially the seven-day week figure prominently in prophecy, and this interpretation has some biblical data to support it. That would make 2,000 years in which God worked with the whole world, 2,000 with Israel as the special people, and 2,000 with the church as the special people through whom God works.

Several early church fathers held this view, and the present author holds it as his working hypothesis. In this case the "last days" in which we are living might be meant to indicate the last two days before the kingdom, the two days of "man's day." Could the meaning of 666 (Rev. 13:18) be a reference to the conclusion of man's day? So the end of all things is at hand. The sabbath rest, so important in the Old Testament and addressed at some length in Hebrews, is just around the corner. (See Ps. 95:11; Heb. 3:7-- 4:11.)

Most commentators are of the opinion that the early Christians, Apostles included, believed that Jesus would return in their lifetimes. I'm not sure about that, although I can see that some of the people might have had mistaken ideas about it. But I don't see how the Holy Spirit could be mistaken.

These commentators also opine that God used their mistaken expectation as a motivation for holy living and diligent service. It's true that God uses the imminence of Christ's return as a motivation. The point I have a problem with is the suggestion that the Holy Spirit is willing to mislead Christians or even to exploit their misunderstanding.

Some think that maybe He didn't know the exact time, just as Jesus did not know, when He was on earth. But I think He does. I think that Jesus' lack of information had to do with the hypostatic union of the God-man and the fact that Jesus specifically did not use His divinity to "cheat" in His earthly life--to give His humanity an easier time living a sin-free life than His brethren have. It's impossible that God, who is omniscient and unchangeable, doesn't know what time something is going to happen. How could the Holy Spirit lead people to believe that it would happen after a short duration of time, if He didn't know that to be the case? Is there confusion in the Trinity, or intent to deceive in order to accomplish a purpose? Certainly not.

The fact is that Jesus could have returned in the lifetime of New Testament believers if Israel changed its mind, repented of its sin, and received her Messiah. Just as the first and second advents could have come one right after the other if Israel had met the Lord's requirement in the first place. This was discussed in the previous chapter.

Part of the answer may be in the two different ways in which people consider the concept of time. In the Greek language two different words are used to differentiate the two concepts. *Chronos* speaks of the duration of time, as a clock or calendar would mark it off. It's the word Peter used up in verse three.

Kairos considers the kind of time or the nature of that time period, as in seasons, or opportune time, or what we refer to as dispensations or economies. It's the word Thomas Paine would have used, had he been speaking to Greeks, when he said, "These are the times that try men's souls." It's the word Jesus used when He told His brothers, **My time is not yet at hand, but your time is always opportune,** John 7:6.

I Peter 4:7 doesn't use either word for time; it speaks of **the end of all things**. But clearly time is being considered, one way or the other. So we have to discern which idea of time is in Peter's mind. I believe Peter is mainly speaking about the kind of time, without totally ignoring the passage of time, because it's true that the rapture could happen at any time (we say that it is imminent).

The term *telos*, **end**, refers to the termination or limit of an act or state (not to be confused with a cognate, *teleios*, which usually refers to relative spiritual maturity). It refers to the end of man's day and the second coming of Christ. The second coming has a duration aspect, but we mostly think of a unique *kind* of time when we consider the day of the Lord. It will be the time when the **stone cut out without hands crushes all the kingdoms of men** and sets up His everlasting kingdom (Daniel 2).

The church age is the last dispensation or era, the last kind of time, before the day of the Lord. The rapture is the last event in the church age and the first event in the day of the Lord. I Corinthians 10:11 mentions this when it says, **Now these things happened to them as an example, and they were written for our instruction, upon whom the ends of the ages have come.**

So all things considered, I think Peter's point is that we are in the final dispensation, the one at the end of man's reign on earth. That reign has lasted altogether for 6,000 years and has included several dispensations (discernibly different steps by which God administered His plan throughout history). Man's day is almost done. **The end of all things has come near.** Next up is the 1,000-year reign of Christ on earth, followed by the eternal perfect state.

Peter has just written to encourage his readers to have an excellent attitude. The thought of judgment day should motivate them, and us, to love and serve others rather than ourselves. And that's a big part of an excellent attitude. The consummation day of our salvation is a matter of great joy for the redeemed, because we will finally be free from all sin. And sinners will no longer be around to hassle, torment, and persecute us or to spoil our world. But it will be a day of great terror for those who have refused to be separated from their sin. God's righteousness is a two-sided coin--final salvation for believers, judgment for those who won't give up their rebellion.

James 5:7-9 encourages:

Be patient, therefore, brethren, until the coming of the Lord. Behold, the farmer waits for the precious produce of

the soil, being patient about it, until it gets the early and late rains. You too be patient; strengthen your hearts, for the coming of the Lord is at hand. Do not complain, brethren, against one another, that you yourselves may not be judged; behold, the Judge is standing right at the door.

Jesus warned in Mark. 13:35ff:

Take heed, keep on the alert; for you do not know when the appointed time is. It is like a man, away on a journey, who upon leaving his house and putting his slaves in charge, assigning to each one his task, also commanded the doorkeeper to stay on the alert. Therefore, be on the alert-- for you do not know when the master of the house is coming, whether in the evening, at midnight, at cockcrowing, or in the morning--lest he come suddenly and find you asleep. And what I say to you I say to all, 'Be on the alert!'

The kind of time in which you live affects…

Your Prayers, 7b

therefore, be of sound judgment and sober *spirit* for the purpose of prayer.

The kind of time in which we live demands real and relevant communication with God. When a soldier on the smoky battlefield calls up to his commander, it isn't for idle chit-chat. He is appraising the situation with his commander, calling for artillery support or for more ammunition or supplies, or for further instructions, or maybe reinforcements. His communication is focused very sharply on the needs occasioned by the battle.

Prayer is our line of access to all the resources we have in Christ. In reading the Bible I find that God ignores some prayers. The Bible indicates several reasons for this. They die by pocket veto. The prayers that get the most attention from God are the ones from people who know the mind of God and who are actively aligned and engaged with His purpose.

James 4:2f alludes to this principle: **You do not have because you do not ask. You ask and do not receive, because you ask with wrong motives, so that you may spend it on your pleasures.**

If your prayers are all about living a nicer, happier life, then your understanding of God's plan and the purpose of His provision are limited, to say the least.

The kind of time in which we live calls for an alert and focused mindset, as Peter said in his first chapter. It's a time when persecution can happen—our enemy is prowling about like a lion and we could find ourselves in serious danger. Don't be caught unaware. It's a time when we might be called upon to give an account for the hope that is in us—we need to be ready with a reasoned response. Study your Bible. It's the time to work before night comes when no man can work—we need to get down to business. Set aside useless time wasters.

It's a time when the enemy has planted mines and dug pitfalls—we need to be careful how we walk. Let your situation train you to develop situation awareness. This is the last opportunity to lead people to Christ before God closes the door on the church age—we need to warn men of God's wrath and offer them God's grace through Jesus Christ. Take the initiative to share the gospel.

It's the last time period before our Lord returns, an event that might happen at any moment. We should not be caught napping or in any other way derelict in our duties.

Therefore, Peter says, **be of sound judgment**. Be in your right mind, not operating on passion or emotion. Our biblically informed intellect should be calling the shots. Peter already said this in 1:13, **Therefore, gird your minds for action, keep sober in spirit, fix your hope completely on the grace to be brought to you at the revelation of Jesus Christ.**

Peter believed that repetition is the soul of learning. You may have noticed that he repeats himself throughout this letters. We could call him "Peter the Repeater." He is always ready to remind us of what's important. Some say there's no sense beating a dead horse. I disagree. It shows the other horses that you mean business.

Satan's world tries to distract, re-direct, and confuse people's minds, and ultimately to render their minds useless. (Notice how well he has succeeded so far.) Pursuant to that objective, he uses acceptable diversions like video games, music, TV, hanging out with friends, and other entertainment, to which we can devote so much time that we have little time or energy left to be about our Father's business.

Satan gets people to downplay the importance of the intellectual part of their minds, especially as they relate to God. Ironically, he's clever enough to do this in a way that promotes intellectual pride. We call that pseudo-intellectualism. The dumbing down of America is his work. As a teacher I've watched that process for over 40 years. If teachers resist that dumbing down, they risk their jobs. Satan also uses humanistic philosophies and other big lies, and mind-altering chemicals. Some music is not acceptable—it is mind altering in a negative way. Some suicides are influenced by the music that promotes death. All of these tactics separate unwary people from the reality of what lies before them.

God did not create our minds to be formless and void. So we need to be sober in our thinking. I don't mean that we shouldn't laugh. God created our laughter mechanism, and joy is a fruit of the Spirit which often finds expression in grins and laughter. But we can't run around like irresponsible clowns, leaving the important work to someone else.

According to Romans 8:26-27, the Spirit intercedes for us according to His understanding of the mind of God, since He is God. Following His example of effective prayer, we too should pray according to a thorough understanding of God's will. If **we are taking every thought captive to the obedience of Christ,** II Corinthians 10:5, and if we are following up on what II Timothy 3:16f says, **All Scripture is inspired by God and profitable for teaching, for reproof, for correction, for training in righteousness; that the man of God may be adequate, equipped for every good work,** then we will see as God sees. We will have His perspective and want what He wants. God responds to those prayers.

The Bible compares the prayers of the saints to the incense that was burned in the Temple. God prescribed the exact recipe for that incense. They weren't allowed to offer any old incense they might have had on hand. We think that if we are praying at all, then God should be pleased and should jump to give us what we want. He never gives that impression in His word.

Ecclesiastes 5:1f, says,

Guard your steps as you go to the house of God, and draw near to listen rather than to offer the sacrifice of fools; for they do not know they are doing evil. Do not be hasty in word or impulsive in thought to bring up a matter in the presence of God. For God is in heaven and you are on the earth; therefore let your words be few.

A few words, guided by an understanding of the mind of God, are far better than what the pagans do who **suppose that they will be heard for their many words,** Matthew 6:7.

Jude 20f add: **But you, beloved, building yourselves up on your most holy faith; praying in the Holy Spirit; keep yourselves in the love of God, waiting anxiously for the mercy of our Lord Jesus Christ to eternal life.**

Peter really hasn't moved on from the subject of attitude. He's just piling on, another characteristic of his epistles. Besides being "Peter the Repeater," he is also "Peter the Pile Driver." So now he gets to the most important part of our attitude--love. There is no excellent attitude that does not revolve around love.

The kind of time in which we live affects…

Your Love for One Another, 8-9

8 Above all, keep fervent in your love for one another, because love covers a multitude of sins. 9 Be hospitable to one another without complaint.

Here Peter repeats what he said in 1:22, **Since you have in obedience to the truth purified your souls for a sincere love of the brethren, fervently love one another from the heart.**

Jesus was asked which commandment was the greatest. He referred to the *sh_ema,* Deuteronomy 6:4, **Hear, O Israel! The LORD is our God, the LORD is one!** Every conscientious Jew said this verse every morning and every night. In answer to the question about the greatest commandment, Jesus quoted the verse that immediately follows the *shema,* **And you shall love the LORD your God with all your heart and with all your soul and with all your might.** And then He said, **This is the great and foremost commandment. The second is like it, 'YOU SHALL LOVE YOUR NEIGHBOR AS YOURSELF.' On these two commandments depend the whole Law and the Prophets,** Matthew 22:38-40.

We can get so wrapped up in our own lives and in defending the faith and in being vexed by the wickedness we see all around us that we forget the two greatest commandments: to love God and to love our neighbor. If Jesus says that these are the two greatest commandments, then love is the thing that God is most concerned about in our lives. So Peter says **above all**, literally before all things. Love is always the first order of business. Is that how you think? It should be. But if you're like me, then you have to make a conscious effort to think of love before you think of how to act.

And the word **keeping** means that love is the first order of business all the way through, from beginning to end, in everything we do. We are to be like God in every way possible (what are called His communicable attributes). When does God's lovingkindness end? Forty-six times in the Old Testament God says that **His lovingkindness is everlasting.** The fact that **keeping** is in participial form (in the original) ties it back to our prayers in the previous verse, suggesting that our love for one another forms a big part of our prayers.

If we are praying according to sound judgment and sober thinking, that is to say, if we are praying with the mind of Christ, then our prayers won't be directed so much to our brother's physical needs as they are to his spiritual development and his faithfulness to his Christian duties. Physical needs are always secondary. God uses our temporal, physical needs to accomplish His eternal, spiritual objectives, both in our lives and in the lives of those whom we influence. Our prayers should not ask God to undercut His objectives for our loved ones. Instead of focusing our prayers on ease and comfort, we should pray for faithfulness and victory.

Peter says that we are to be **fervent** in our love for one another. He used that word, *fervent*, in chapter 1 also. The adjective means stretched or strained. It means that we are to expend a lot of energy, earnestly, eagerly paying the price for other people's benefit, for that is what *agape* means. We love people unconditionally, faults and all. *Agape* is an act of the will. It's primarily a choice that we make, not just an emotion that we feel. In fact, we may not always feel the affection, but we are always to make the choice.

Agape is independent of the loveliness of its object. Sometimes you're all cute and adorable, and sometimes you're not. Our love is not to be based on how lovable someone is. It's a decision that is motivated by our love for God. And our love for God is based upon His love for us. **We love, because He first loved us**, I John 4:19.

That kind of **love covers a multitude of sins**. Proverbs 10:12 says, **Hatred stirs up strife, but love covers all transgressions.** The people we love make mistakes; they slip up; they say things without considering how others might be affected; they do things that hurt the ones who love them. Some of their sins are purposeful, others are accidental. Some are the result of wrong thinking, others the result of not thinking at all.

Agape love covers those over, conceals them. I Corinthians 13 says that love **does not take into account a wrong suffered.** So we should take no notice of offenses against us. As far as love is concerned, the other person's sins do not enter into the equation. Love **is not provoked**; it **bears all things** and **endures all things**.

The limit of this endurance is somewhere beyond the horizon. **Multitude** means a great number of sins. Jesus told Peter he should forgive, not just seven times, but 70 times seven. To the extent that you take offense or hold grudges or act upon an offense, you neglect this command and choose to operate on the principle of hatred instead of love. Remember the parable that Jesus told Peter about the unmerciful slave in Matthew 18. We are to be patient and long-suffering. It should be very difficult to offend you. And even then you should forgive those who trespass against you just as God has forgiven your trespasses.

Sometimes Christians take up an offense committed against someone else. This is not in keeping with Peter's exhortation. The offended person may have taken no notice of the offense, not being self-absorbed. Or he might have noticed and immediately forgave, so that nothing comes of the offense. The one who takes up the offense ruins the good work of the more mature Christian and causes trouble where it had already been avoided.

Another application of Christian love is hospitality: **be hospitable to one another without complaint,** verse 9. This word literally means "love of strangers." We don't just love those who are in our own little group. Hospitality was a necessity back then when Christians came through town, because the inns were immoral and filthy.

It's also a necessity whenever Christians are displaced or put in a state of need by persecution. Hospitality is a part of bearing one another's burdens. Generosity is a Godly trait, and God loves a cheerful giver. So we should do this without complaint. The providence of God covers the cost of hospitality. We don't submit a bill and receive a check in the mail. But watch and see if that isn't true (II Cor. 9:10).

This takes us to the next way in which a correct understanding of the kind of time in which you live affects your choices. It affects...

Your Service to One Another, 10-11a

[10] **As each one has received a *special* gift, employ it in serving one another, as good stewards of the manifold grace of God. [11] Whoever speaks, *let him speak,* as it were, the utterances of God; whoever serves, *let him do so* as by the strength which God supplies;**

God not only calls us to serve one another, He has also given each one of us a particular blend of spiritual capabilities by which we are equipped to provide the service that is essential to the body of Christ. So you can't say, "I really have nothing to offer. My part is just to sit in the pew and be fed. My job is to be the one who is served." But Peter says, **As each one has received a *special* gift, employ it in serving one another,** 10a.

Every child of God receives, at the time of his spiritual birth, a gift, or perhaps a combination of gifts, that enable him to contribute materially to the building up of the body of Christ. There are to be no idle parts in the body. There are no vestigial organs. Every single believer is to be a functioning part, a contributing member of the body. If you are a foot and you neglect your service, then the body has to hobble around on crutches.

Maybe you think, "Well, I'm just a toenail on the little toe of the church. My part doesn't matter." Yes it does. Toenails form an exoskeleton that supports the end of the toe when walking puts pressure on it. If the toenail didn't do what it was designed to do, then the bone in that little toe would punch through the flesh, or at least keep on bruising it, and a lot of bad things will happen. Without the toenail, the toe will be in trouble. And so will the whole body.

And if that body is going through battles, as in persecution, then the malfunctioning body is put in greater danger because of its weakness. Predators always seek out the weakest member of the herd. It's critical that you know your spiritual gift; that you develop it and employ it, so that, for your part, the body is stronger and not weaker.

Spiritual gifts are listed elsewhere in the New Testament, particularly in Romans 12 and I Corinthians 12. Ephesians 4 lists four man-gifts, two temporary and two long-term. A detailed description of the various gifts is beyond the scope of this book. But Peter gives us terms for the two categories of gifts that are still being given today. These are serving gifts and speaking gifts.

There was a third category—sign gifts. But those were for the infancy of the church. They were the signs of true apostleship (II Corinthians 12:12) and some were transitional, revelatory gifts (I Corinthians 13:9f). According to I Corinthians 13, sign gifts ceased abruptly and the transitional, revelatory gifts, which served as scaffolding, or as an *ad hoc* word of God, before the New Testament was completed, faded away as the church became mature and the permanent New Testament revelation was recorded.

In general, all the permanent spiritual gifts are for serving others, as Peter indicates in verse 10. And we are to use them as good stewards of the manifold grace of God. Have you thought about that? You are a channel of God's grace to others. Don't withhold God's grace by neglecting your gift.

If a church service is just an audience gathered to watch a few people exercise their spiritual gifts, then that church is in trouble. And it's not valid to exalt the showier gifts or the up-front gifts while deprecating the rest, as the Corinthians did. That wears out a few and rusts out everyone else.

The church is not a locomotive, a coal car, and a bunch of passenger cars just being towed along. The church is all locomotive. A locomotive has a variety of parts, and those parts have a variety of functions, some more visible than others. But they are all necessary to the proper functioning of the locomotive. You can't expect a piston to function as a wheel. It isn't designed for that, and if it has to do the wheel's work it won't do it as well as the wheel could, and it will have a hard time doing its own work. Nobody but the engineer appreciates the boiler tubes, but the locomotive is an idle curiosity without them.

What if every part of the locomotive wanted to be the steam whistle because it gets noticed, but no one wanted to be the piston rod? It's easier to do nothing but ride up on top and sound off once in a while. It's hot and heavy work to be the piston rod. God doesn't give us our choice in spiritual gifts. The Holy Spirit distributes to each one according to His will. So whatever part you are, do your part. He has equipped you to do your part.

Stewards are required to be faithful. Faithful stewards serve the church in two ways, besides encouraging faithfulness in general. First they supply the function for which they have been specially equipped—helps or teaching or administration or evangelism or whatever. Second, they serve as training models to the rest of us who don't have that gift but are told to develop that ability. By watching those who have the gift we learn how to do it. I don't have the gift of administration, but I'm a better administrator because I've watched how others have employed that gift.

So we aren't to say, "I don't have the gift of evangelism, so I don't share the gospel." Or, "I don't have the gift of mercy, so don't expect any from me." This is where the body analogy, or my locomotive analogy, breaks down. A hand doesn't have to develop its ability to hear or see or breathe. A locomotive wheel doesn't have to whistle at crossings. But every one of the speaking and serving gifts is a special, heightened ability to carry out a function that all Christians are commanded to do. We are all commanded to share the gospel, to give, to show mercy, to help others, to be leaders, to teach, to encourage, etc. I Peter 3:15 is one example. **We are to grow up in all aspects into Him, who is the head, even Christ**, Ephesians 4:15. By the way, there are no commands that everyone should be learning to do what the sign gifts did.

If you have a speaking gift then you are to **speak, as it were, the oracles of God**. In other words, you are to teach what God has revealed. You aren't to add to or take away from God's word (Deut. 4:2; 12:32; Rev. 22:19), not even if you think your adjustment would make it more powerful or more dynamic or easier to accept.

Paul advised Timothy, **Be diligent to present yourself approved to God as a workman who does not need to be ashamed, handling accurately** [literally, cutting straight] **the word of truth. But avoid worldly and empty chatter, for it will lead to further ungodliness**, II Timothy 2:15f. God's word all fits together into a perfect and precise unity. If we don't cut part of it straight, if we don't interpret it properly, it won't fit.

Utterances (*logia*) is the word Stephen used in Acts 7:38, and Paul used in Romans 3:2 when they spoke of the oracles of God, meaning the Old Testament. Those who speak for God must speak what God has revealed. We can't do as the false prophets did, presenting our own ideas as if they were God's. In Jeremiah 23:32 God said,

"Behold, I am against those who have prophesied false dreams," declares the LORD, "and related them, and led My people astray by their falsehoods and reckless boasting; yet I did not send them or command them, nor do they furnish this people the slightest benefit," declares the LORD.

If you have a serving gift, then you are to serve, not in your own strength, but in the strength that God supplies. The New Testament uses several synonyms to express the idea of strength, might, or power. Ephesians 6:10 uses three of them, **Finally, be strong [*dunamis*] in the Lord, and in the strength [*kratos*] of His might [*ischus*].** Peter uses the word *ischus,* the word that refers to God's might. It speaks of the power to prevail, emphasizing ability. It is power that is effective, capable of producing results. It's a word of more forceful strength or ability than *dunamis* (from which we get the terms dynamo and dynamite).

So there is no reason to be shy about employing your spiritual gift. Nor is there any reason to beg off because of inability. That is false humility. False humility is an excuse for disobedience. God always gauges true humility by how much we believe and obey Him. It is required of a steward that one be found faithful.

The kind of time in which we live also affects…

Your Motive, 11b

so that in all things God may be glorified through Jesus Christ, to whom belongs the glory and dominion forever and ever. Amen.

Being human, there are two pitfalls to avoid when it comes to motives and our use of spiritual gifts. The first is self-preservation. We might neglect to employ our spiritual gift because we are afraid of what other people might think of us, if we don't do as well as others or get results as good as theirs. Or we might want to preserve our time for our own use. Or we might wish not to make ourselves a target of persecution. God gave us spiritual gifts so we can serve and commands us to do so.

The second pitfall is self-promotion or self-gratification. We might employ our spiritual gift in order to pump up our own image. That's why the Corinthians were earnestly desiring the showier gifts. They were in it for their own glory. Spiritual gifts succeed only when we use them in the sphere of love. Some believe that they received a spiritual gift for their own edification. Self-edification might be a by-product of using our gift to serve others, but it isn't the goal God sets for us.

Neither motive is honorable. And both set us up for failure when times get tough. Glorifying yourself does not lead anyone to Christ. And **whoever wishes to save his life shall lose it,** Matthew 16:25.

The glory belongs to God. He alone deserves it. And He can make the best use of it. Our main purpose in life is to glorify God. That's why we were created, so that's where we find the most satisfaction and the most success. Most people don't believe that, but it's true. New Testament writers often break into doxologies, as Peter does here. Their hearts were in it. The better you know God the harder it is not to get excited about His praise and glory.

Peter began this paragraph with the thought of Christ's imminent return when he wrote **the end of all things has come near**. Now he returns to the thought of Christ's second coming, directing our thoughts to His glory and eternal dominion. This refers to Jesus rather than the Father in this case because the nearest antecedent to the pronoun *whom* is Jesus Christ. The Holy Spirit communicates according to grammatical rules because He wants to be understood clearly. Glory and dominion belong to the Father, too, but that isn't the point here.

In John 17:1 Jesus prayed, **Father, the hour has come; glorify Your Son, that the Son may glorify You, even as You**

gave Him authority over all mankind. Daniel 7:14, speaking of the Son of Man, says,

And to Him was given dominion, glory and a kingdom, that all the peoples, nations, and men of every language might serve Him. His dominion is an everlasting dominion which will not pass away; and His kingdom is one which will not be destroyed.

We are living in the last days. They are uncomfortable times if we don't understand the mind of God. But if we are aligned with God's plan and involved in the role He has for us, then they are exciting and hopeful times. It's common to think the most exciting times of history are behind us and we missed them. Not so. The best is yet to come. It's no time for sitting on the sidelines.

Chapter 20

4:12-19, Excellent Faithfulness

¹² **Beloved, do not be surprised at the fiery ordeal among you, which comes upon you for your testing, as though some strange thing were happening to you;**
¹³ **but to the degree that you share the sufferings of Christ, keep on rejoicing; so that also at the revelation of His glory, you may rejoice with exultation.**
¹⁴ **If you are reviled for the name of Christ, you are blessed, because the Spirit of glory and of God rests upon you.**
¹⁵ **By no means let any of you suffer as a murderer, or thief, or evildoer, or a troublesome meddler;**
¹⁶ **but if *anyone suffers* as a Christian, let him not feel ashamed, but in that name let him glorify God.**
¹⁷ **For *it is* time for judgment to begin with the household of God; and if *it begins* with us first, what *will be* the outcome for those who do not obey the gospel of God?**
¹⁸ **AND IF IT IS WITH DIFFICULTY THAT THE RIGHTEOUS IS SAVED, WHAT WILL BECOME OF THE GODLESS MAN AND THE SINNER?**
¹⁹ **Therefore, let those also who suffer according to the will of God entrust their souls to a faithful Creator in doing what is right.**

How do we prove beyond anyone's doubt that the Bible is right and every contradictory idea wrong? Wouldn't you love an overwhelming argument that would unfailingly shame God's critics into silence and convince the undecided to repent and trust God?

I know I would. But upon reflection, I don't think there is such an argument. A perfectly sound argument for repenting and giving one's life to Christ is not difficult to make. But the decision to reject God and keep on sinning is not based upon factual data or sound logic. Sin is a choice based upon will and emotions, neither of which care about sound arguments.

Rejection of God is not based upon intellectual astuteness, even among those who are otherwise intellectually astute.

So an overwhelming number of overwhelming arguments will not overwhelm those who are committed to their sinful way of life. They ignore the consequences, and they ignore the arguments. But the weakness in their plan is that thing about consequences.

God has hard-wired the knowledge of Himself into every human heart. **He has also set eternity in their heart**, Eccl. 3:11. Rom. 1:18f, **the wrath of God is revealed from heaven against all ungodliness and unrighteousness of men, who suppress the truth in unrighteousness, because that which is known about God is evident within them; for God made it evident to them.**

No matter how they harden their hearts and suppress the knowledge of God's righteous judgment, that dread still lies just beneath the surface of their consciousness. They are skating on the thin ice of denial. And they grasp at any arguments or data that sustain them, and push away any truth or logic that would sink them.

When Isaiah 6:10 says, **"Render the hearts of this people insensitive, their ears dull, and their eyes dim, lest they see with their eyes, hear with their ears, understand with their hearts, and return and be healed,"** he doesn't mean that God doesn't want to heal them; it means that they don't want to be healed. If sin is the disease, they don't want the cure. They like their sin and don't want to leave it. So we don't have a silver bullet argument. There is no argument that they can't suppress and ignore. But don't give up. The unreasonableness of sinners does not tie God's hands.

He has other ways to convince those who resist being convinced. And it has to do with the consequences of choices. God can consequence a person to death. He can also consequence a person to life. Isaiah 26:9f say,

For when the earth experiences Thy judgments The inhabitants of the world learn righteousness. ¹⁰ *Though* the wicked is shown favor, He does not learn righteousness; He

deals unjustly in the land of uprightness, And does not perceive the majesty of the LORD.

God gives people a foretaste of consequences by the use of calamities and persecution. He uses the hard times people face to manifest the fundamental difference between those who love and obey God and those who don't. Different responses show different character, and different character shows different destiny.

Throughout Peter's letter, he unites, as allies, two seemingly contradictory concepts. These repeated ideas are suffering and rejoicing. In today's text, the idea of rejoicing occurs six times, one way or another, and suffering nine times. And that's typical of the whole letter.

You understand that Peter is not some old geezer, giving untested, theoretical advice about things he has never experienced. Peter has been the point of the spear for as long as the church has existed and has undergone no small amount of persecution. God preserved him from execution by sending an angel to let him out of jail the night before he was to be beheaded (Acts 12). He learned during that little walk on the beach with Jesus that he will be executed for the name of Christ (Jn. 21:18).

Peter probably suspects that his death might be imminent and will come at the hands of Rome, from which he writes this letter. So when he writes about getting through persecution victoriously, he says, in effect, "Here's how I do it. I do it the way Jesus did it."

In the interest of fostering sound judgment and sober spirit in the end times, Peter encourages his readers regarding:

Fire Proof Joy, 12-13;

Faithful Suffering, 14- 16; and

Fearless Judgment, 17-19.

Fire Proof Joy, 12-13

**[12] Beloved, do not be surprised at the fiery ordeal among you, which comes upon you for your testing, as though some strange thing were happening to you;
[13] but to the degree that you share the sufferings of Christ, keep on rejoicing; so that also at the revelation of His glory, you may rejoice with exultation.**

The first thing Peter says to those who are about to go through some fiery ordeal is that they are beloved, because that's the first thing they will need to know. This is especially the case when the ordeal happens to some Christians and not to others, in a way that seems random and unfair. The Greek word for *happening* normally means to fall by chance.

Suffering won't be uniform; it never has been. God doesn't treat all His children the same because they aren't the same. Some have capabilities that others don't have (put there, perhaps, by previous suffering), and some have needs that others don't have. Some make good choices and some make bad choices. Some suffer because they are faithful and obedient, others because they need to be more faithful. Some have the background, maturity, and frame of mind to be used as champions, as Stephen was, or Martin Luther; others don't.

It's not a question of God's love, but of God's particular purpose in the individual's life. God may want to teach the undiscerning world how to distinguish between a true believer and a false believer. So He may give the false believer a little trouble and the true believer a lot of trouble, and let the difference be manifested by their different responses.

We don't suffer ordeals because God hates us or neglects us. We are His beloved.

When I coached baseball I always wanted my team to win its share of games, plus a good part of the other teams' share. So I taught my players the fundamentals and drilled them in. I made them run laps and sprints. I wanted them to get used to exerting themselves and continuing to perform with focus and to remember the fundamentals even when they were fatigued and uncomfortable. I wanted to develop their endurance and their will to endure.

Some of my teams understood this and did whatever I asked of them. Other teams just wanted to take the game as it came to them, and did not take the training time seriously. I will leave it to you to guess which teams lost more than their share and which teams won more than their share. I will tell you that the teams that won more than their share also got a lot more good out of their experience than the teams that just wanted to have some fun.

Would it surprise you to learn that football practice is rough? Or that infantry training for soldiers is rough? They came up with that saying, "No pain; no gain." Would it surprise you that the game of football is rough or that actual warfare is rough?

Does it surprise you that being an alien operative in Satan's world system is rough? Peter says that we shouldn't be surprised at the fiery ordeal as if it we had no reason to expect it. Being treated unjustly naturally comes as a surprise to those who mean to follow God and love their fellow man—unless they stop to think about it. Then they realize that Satan is the prince of the power of the air (Eph. 2:2), and that the world lies in the lap of the evil one (I Jn. 5:19).

Is it not true that Satan's people have always persecuted God's people unjustly? It started with Cain killing Abel. II Corinthians 2:15f say, **For we are a fragrance of Christ to God among those who are being saved and among those who are perishing; to the one an aroma from death to death, to the other an aroma from life to life**. Christians are a sweet aroma to those who are interested in being righteous, but, like a lily, we are the smell of death to those who want to continue in their sin.

Americans have enjoyed a unique situation, living in a nation that once honored God and recognized the manifold blessings of God. But that's changing. Unless Americans, including Christians, repent *en masse*, I think we can predict fiery ordeals ahead.

Let's consider this fiery ordeal business. The word for fire, *pur*, is used for the fire of hell. It's also the term for the fire used to refine metals. And that's the focus here. I suppose it is easy to confuse one purpose of fire with another when you are going through one.

Shadrach, Meshach, and Abed-Nego were thrown into a fiery furnace. That wasn't a furnace for heating a house. It was a smelting furnace, used for refining metal. So it had to be heated especially hot to melt the metal. This was done by using bellows to force extra oxygen into the firebox. It could be heated hotter by adding more fuel and more bellows and pumping them faster than usual.

The word *testing* in verse 12 is a word used of temptation and the tempter. (I Cor. 10:13, e.g.) It, also, is a term used of the refining process. So the Holy Spirit seems to be indicating that God uses the fires of hell, so to speak, to refine His own people. Satan's world system, which is headed for hell, provides the fire; God turns it to His good use. It's sort of like geo-thermal sanctification. This fiery ordeal, then, comes upon us, with God's permission, for our testing, that is, our refining. It makes us more like Jesus and less like the sinners we used to be.

We are complete in Christ as soon as we are saved (Col. 2:9f). We have everything we need. The problem is that we still have some things that we don't need, things that corrupt the image of Christ in us. We still have impurities, as raw gold ore does. All the gold is there, but the impurities have to come out for the gold to be worth anything to anyone.

The refining process for gold (or any other metal) has always required fire. The non-gold is so intermixed and mechanically bonded to the gold that it can't be separated by any other means. The ore is first crushed into small pieces. Then the fire burns the impurities from the gold and forces them out as slag. They then float to the top of the molten metal and are skimmed off, leaving pure gold. I don't suppose the gold enjoys that process. But I do imagine that the short time in the fire is forgotten when the gold becomes the crown for the king.

If a false believer goes through that fire, his shallow, inadequate response to the gospel is revealed by the heat. As Jesus said in Matthew 13:5f,

[other seed] fell upon the rocky places, where they did not have much soil; and immediately they sprang up, because they had no depth of soil. But when the sun had risen, they were scorched; and because they had no root, they withered away.

Verse 13 considers the end result of suffering and shows why Peter connects suffering with rejoicing. First, they are **the sufferings of Christ**—those who share the sufferings of Christ are properly aligned. *Share* is the word fellowship, a joint participation in a common interest or activity. If the world hates you because it hates Christ, that is an indication to you that you are aligned with Jesus.

Jesus told His disciples in Jn. 15:18f,

If the world hates you, you know that it has hated Me before it hated you. If you were of the world, the world would love its own; but because you are not of the world, but I chose you out of the world, therefore the world hates you.

So if sinners hate God but have no problem with you, something might be amiss.

Second, suffering for Christ is an indication of your eternal destiny. II Thessalonians 1:4f say:

...your perseverance and faith in the midst of all your persecutions and afflictions which you endure... is a plain indication of God's righteous judgment so that you may be considered worthy of the kingdom of God, for which indeed you are suffering.

In other words, the fact that you rejoice in the unjust treatment you suffer because of your relationship to Christ shows that your eternal future is bound up with Christ. Otherwise, you would shrink back from persecution and distance yourself from Christ. Scorched pretenders drop their pretense and run away. If we stand, that reveals the genuineness of our belief that when He is revealed in His glory, then we, too, will be vindicated and glorified.

Our future is one of rejoicing with exultation, endless exultation, nothing negative whatsoever. Some people think heaven will be a boring place; not if there is extreme rejoicing the whole time. Romans 8:16f, **The Spirit Himself bears witness with our spirit that we are children of God, and if children, heirs also, heirs of God and fellow heirs with Christ, if indeed we suffer with Him in order that we may also be glorified with Him,** I Pet. 5:1. II Timothy 2:12 promises, **If we endure, we shall also reign with Him.**

Third, there is a proportional relationship between the degree to which you share the sufferings of Christ and the amount of rejoicing you will do at the revelation of Jesus Christ. Greater suffering brings greater reward. This is made clear to us by the word (*kathos*) which is translated *to the degree*. So our reward is proportional to (greater than, not equal to) our suffering. The suffering is momentary and light, but our reward is eternal and weighty.

The result of understanding how God will reward our suffering is that we become fire resistant. Being fire resistant, we don't scare easily. Any fiery ordeal that comes upon us does not cause us to back away from faithful obedience; it causes us to lean into any trial we face with a greater trust in God and a stronger will to obey.

The principle is not unlike a wealthy man offering to employ you on a hot day. You will have to forego your air-conditioned comfort, and any personal plans you had, in order to do a hot and dirty day's work. But in exchange he will pay you more than you could otherwise earn in a lifetime. Would you decline such an offer? God's good purposes for fiery ordeals far outweigh the cost to us. Knowing that should encourage us to…

Faithful Suffering, 14-16

[14] If you are reviled for the name of Christ, you are blessed, because the Spirit of glory and of God rests upon you.

¹⁵ By no means let any of you suffer as a murderer, or thief, or evildoer, or a troublesome meddler;
¹⁶ but if *anyone suffers* as a Christian, let him not feel ashamed, but in that name let him glorify God.

We are never expected to faithfully suffer persecution on our own. God never allows it. It is impossible to suffer for Christ alone. God has always promised His special grace to those who suffer for His name's sake.

Isaiah 11:1f, says of Jesus,

Then a shoot will spring from the stem of Jesse, and a branch from his roots will bear fruit. And the Spirit of the LORD will rest on Him, the spirit of wisdom and understanding, the spirit of counsel and strength, the spirit of knowledge and the fear of the LORD.

Witnesses actually saw the Spirit descend to rest upon Jesus at the time of His baptism:

And after being baptized, Jesus went up immediately from the water; and behold, the heavens were opened, and he saw the Spirit of God descending as a dove, and coming upon Him, and behold, a voice out of the heavens, saying, "This is My beloved Son, in whom I am well-pleased." Then Jesus was led up by the Spirit into the wilderness to be tempted by the devil, Matthew 3:16ff.

This text shows us that God was pleased with Jesus and that the Holy Spirit was leading Him. So trials do not necessarily indicate God's displeasure or our waywardness.

In Acts 4, after Peter and John were threatened and ordered to stop speaking in the name of Jesus, the church prayed. But they didn't pray for the persecution to cease; they had God's perspective. Rather they prayed for confidence to speak God's word in spite of the persecution. Verse 31 tells us God's answer, **And when they had prayed, the place where they had gathered together was shaken, and they were all filled with the Holy Spirit, and began to speak the word of God with boldness.**

I Peter 4:14 is a promise that the Holy Spirit will be with us the same way. The Spirit, who already indwells every believer, will attend in a special way to those who are suffering for the name of Christ. He will give them supernatural enablement, relief, and good hearts in the midst of their suffering. The Holy Spirit will give them endurance beyond their own strength and courage, and peace that passes understanding. He will give them deliverance, that is, the successful completion of their extreme duty. Aside from all that, there is a divine happiness, a unique joy and thrill in being on the spot and watching God work in a way that is very evident. It's that joy of battle that is known only to those who have known the battle. That alone is worth the price of admission. As Peter wrote in chapter 2: 19f:

For this *finds* favor, if for the sake of conscience toward God a man bears up under sorrows when suffering unjustly. [20] For what credit is there if, when you sin and are harshly treated, you endure it with patience? But if when you do what is right and suffer *for it* you patiently endure it, this *finds* favor with God.

The words **this finds favor,** translated literally are, *this is grace*. If we find ourselves bearing up when suffering unjustly, we can know that we are experiencing the special grace of God.

This promise of grace does not apply if your suffering is the result of your own bad behavior or choices. **By no means let any of you suffer as a murderer, or thief, or evildoer, or a troublesome meddler,** verse 15. Persecution does not justify retaliatory or pre-emptive crimes. There are always people who believe that the end justifies the means. But God doesn't.

Evildoer is a general term for all crimes. But then Peter throws in **troublesome meddler**, meaning one who can't mind his own business; an agitator or troublemaker. Murder, thievery, and being an evildoer will bring the law down on you. Being a troublesome meddler will bring your society down on you. And the law or society will rightly take steps to prevent such actions. And such actions would defame the name of Christ.

Some examples will help clarify the point:

- Marching for the pro-life cause is good, unless it involves civil disobedience; speaking out in defense of the innocent is good if done in a proper forum, but blowing up an abortion clinic is evildoing.

- Preaching that Jesus is the only way to God is good; interfering with a pagan worship service is troublesome meddling. This is what Jesus meant when He said, **do not resist him who is evil** (Mt. 5:39).

- Speaking out against the evils of alcohol is good; throwing rocks through liquor store windows is evildoing.

- Romans 12:17, **Never pay back evil for evil to anyone. Respect what is right in the sight of all men.** They stand justly condemned who say, **"Let us do evil that good may come."** (Rom. 3:8)

- Any Christian who involves himself in evil should be ashamed, whatever his motives, and has only himself to blame if his actions cause him trouble.

But if we suffer at the hands of those who hate Christ simply because we are Christians, there is no reason whatsoever for shame. The very name, Christian, was originally a derisive term meant to shame believers. To be called a Christian was to be persecuted. But believers rightly took the term and its intended derision, as a badge of honor because it identified them with their Lord.

Let's see who should be ashamed: The way of those who hate God leads to murder, violence of all kinds, abortion of millions of innocent children, drug and alcohol abuse, child abuse, crimes of all kinds, corruption, oppression, greed, human trafficking, racial prejudice, and the list goes on. Injustice, lies, social diseases…

The way of Christ produces love, joy, peace, patience, kindness, goodness, faithfulness, gentleness, self-control; people don't write laws against things like that. Christianity has been a great benefit to any society where it gained a foothold. Wherever the gospel goes there generally follow justice, institutions of mercy, prosperity for a broad spectrum of society, domestic peace, foreign respect, and an absence of social ills. And this list could go on too.

The point is that following God has always produced all kinds of good results. Rejecting God has always produced all kinds of evil results. And God-haters think *we* should be ashamed!? Not me! Paul was not ashamed of the gospel. Stephen wasn't; Peter wasn't; neither was John. Why should I be?

Fearless Judgment, 17-19

¹⁷ For *it is* time for judgment to begin with the household of God; and if *it begins* with us first, what *will be* the outcome for those who do not obey the gospel of God?
¹⁸ AND IF IT IS WITH DIFFICULTY THAT THE RIGHTEOUS IS SAVED, WHAT WILL BECOME OF THE GODLESS MAN AND THE SINNER?
¹⁹ Therefore, let those also who suffer according to the will of God entrust their souls to a faithful Creator in doing what is right.

In the last chapter we came to the conclusion that when Peter said, "The end of all things is at hand," (verse 7) he was talking about *kairos*, kind of time, an age or period of time that has distinct characteristics, even though he didn't actually use the word in verse 7. Here he does use the word *kairos*. This is the age when God judges the household of God, the church. He judges it for the purpose of purification. He uses fire to test the quality of each man's work (I Cor. 3). He does this throughout the church age in order to sanctify the church.

The modern church in the western world is largely inattentive to God's word and careless about sin and obedience. It has shown a distressing propensity to compromise, if you can call it compromise when one gets nothing in return. It's like a man confronted by a mugger on the street. The punk demands all his money. The man says, "I'd rather not give it to you." The punk says, "Okay, let's compromise; give me half your money." Not wanting to seem unreasonable, the man compromises. But what kind of a compromise gives something and gets nothing? It's not a compromise; it's a gutless surrender. After a few such compromises, the church has nothing left.

So God judges the impurities in the church, burns them with fire in order to remove them and make the church a holy bride for Christ, without spot or wrinkle. He gives the church a backbone.

Hebrews 12:4-12 describes the judgment that begins with the household of God:

⁴ You have not yet resisted to the point of shedding blood in your striving against sin;
⁵ and you have forgotten the exhortation which is addressed to you as sons, " MY SON, DO NOT REGARD LIGHTLY THE DISCIPLINE OF THE LORD, NOR FAINT WHEN YOU ARE REPROVED BY HIM;
⁶ FOR THOSE WHOM THE LORD LOVES HE DISCIPLINES, AND HE SCOURGES EVERY SON WHOM HE RECEIVES."
⁷ It is for discipline that you endure; God deals with you as with sons; for what son is there whom *his* father does not discipline?
⁸ But if you are without discipline, of which all have become partakers, then you are illegitimate children and not sons.
⁹ Furthermore, we had earthly fathers to discipline us, and we respected them; shall we not much rather be subject to the Father of spirits, and live?
¹⁰ For they disciplined us for a short time as seemed best to them, but He *disciplines us* for *our* good, that we may share His holiness.
¹¹ All discipline for the moment seems not to be joyful, but sorrowful; yet to those who have been trained by it, afterwards it yields the peaceful fruit of righteousness.
¹² Therefore, strengthen the hands that are weak and the knees that are feeble...

That discipline can be severe, because God's love for the church is real, not just show, and His purpose in the world is serious. God takes sin seriously. He is holy. He has to remove all sin from us before He can allow into His presence.

If God disciplines His saints for the purpose of holiness, what will happen to those who refuse to obey God and be separated from their sin? Peter quotes from the Septuagint version of Proverbs 11:31 to make his point in verse 18: **AND IF IT IS WITH DIFFICULTY THAT THE RIGHTEOUS IS SAVED, WHAT WILL BECOME OF THE GODLESS MAN AND THE SINNER?**

We think of our salvation as a free thing. It wasn't free at all, not by a long sight. It is free only to us. Consider the entire plan of salvation, from Genesis 3:15, on. The whole Bible is the record of God working His plan of salvation. Our salvation was difficult! It's only free to us because God did all the work.

The Book of Psalms is the most quoted book in the New Testament. That's because its doctrinal material is so broad and deep, I suppose, even though it is poetry. Psalm 49: 7-9 says, **No man can by any means redeem his brother, or give to God a ransom for him-- for the redemption of his soul is costly, and he should cease trying forever-- that he should live on eternally.** As long as someone is trying for salvation on his own, he won't see the need to receive what Christ has done.

Jeremiah 32:17says, **'Ah Lord GOD! Behold, Thou hast made the heavens and the earth by Thy great power and by Thine outstretched arm! Nothing is too difficult for Thee.** The most difficult work God does is the work of salvation. He made the heavens and earth in six days. It took 4,000 years to bring people to the point where they could understand His plan of salvation. That wasn't due to any weakness on God's part, of course. It was due to man's spiritual rebelliousness and spiritual dimwittedness (he **walks in the darkness,** I Jn. 2:11).

How shall they escape who **neglect so great a salvation,** Heb. 2:3? Those who do not obey the gospel of God have a different judgment than ours. It is one to fear. The judgment of the saints is momentary and light and has exciting results. The judgment of sinners is eternal and heavy and has horrifying results. We should not fear the judgment God sends us, but should welcome it as the weak and sickly patient welcomes the correct diagnosis and cure that will make him stronger and healthier.

But those who reject Christ should be terrified of God's judgment:

For if we go on sinning willfully after receiving the knowledge of the truth, there no longer remains a sacrifice for sins, but a certain terrifying expectation of judgment, and THE FURY OF A FIRE WHICH WILL CONSUME THE ADVERSARIES. ... How much severer punishment do you think he will deserve who has trampled under foot the Son of God, and has regarded as unclean the blood of the covenant by which he was sanctified, and has insulted the Spirit of grace? For we know Him who said, "VENGEANCE IS MINE, I WILL REPAY." And again, "THE LORD WILL JUDGE HIS PEOPLE." It is a terrifying thing to fall into the hands of the living God, Heb. 10:26-31.

So there is a furious consuming fire awaiting those who reject Jesus. Believers may be exposed to refining fire, but never to the consuming fire. The three Hebrews in the book of Daniel who were thrown into the furious, consuming fiery furnace weren't touched by the fire and didn't even smell like smoke. The true believer is fire proof as regards the consuming fire. That's good, because the fiery ordeals will come.

There is a controlled, refining fire, according to I Corinthians 3:11-15:

For no man can lay a foundation other than the one which is laid, which is Jesus Christ. Now if any man builds upon the foundation with gold, silver, precious stones, wood, hay, straw, each man's work will become evident; for the day will show it, because it is to be revealed with fire; and the fire itself will test the quality of each man's work. If any man's work which he has built upon it remains, he shall receive a reward. If any man's work is burned up, he shall suffer loss; but he himself shall be saved, yet so as through fire.

We are also fireproof in this fire, even if we come out smelling like smoke. So v. 10 says, **Let each man be careful how he builds upon the foundation** laid by the Apostles. The less careful you are, or the less diligent you are to build upon that foundation, or the more cheap materials you use, the more you stand to lose when fire tests the quality of your work. Basically, whatever you do on your own gets puffed. Whatever you allow Christ to do through you gets rewarded.

When Paul was stoned and left for dead outside Lystra, his response was to get back up and continue with his work, saying, **"Through many tribulations we must enter the kingdom of God."** (Ac. 14:22)

Paul did what Peter says in v. 19. *Entrust* is a banker's term that means to deposit for safe keeping. There is no safer person to trust yourself to than the God who made you. You're better off in His hands than you are in your own hands. He is faithful. He loves you. His plan for you is eternal glory with His Son. God has all His omni's to call upon for our defense— omniscience, omnipotence, omnipresence, and all. We don't have any omni's. But we do have the righteousness of Christ, so God the Father brings all His omni's to bear on our behalf.

I Pet. 2:23 says that Jesus **kept entrusting Himself to Him who judges righteously.** That's what got Jesus through His ordeal. Certainly it will get us through ours. Our concern is to do what is right and leave the consequences to a loving God who knows His business.

Both the sinner and the saint can be misled by the immediate consequences of their choices, the passing pleasures of sin on the one hand or the passing persecution of a rebellious world on the other. Both the sinner and the saint are put in a weak position if they fail to give due consideration to the eternal consequences of their choices. God always takes the long view. The believer will be strong in his faith if he does, too.

Let's summarize what we have learned in terms of the experience we undergo, the action we should take, and the end result.

1. If we go through the fiery ordeal of testing, we should endure it faithfully, with the result that we will become more like Christ (which is our greatest good).

2. If we share the sufferings of Christ, are reviled for the name of Christ, or suffer as a Christian, then we should keep on rejoicing, not be ashamed, and glory in the name of Christ, with the end result of eternal exultation and rejoicing, being blessed, and experiencing the Spirit assisting us in a special way.

3. When we go through God's judgment as part of the household of God, we should entrust our souls to a faithful Creator in doing what is right, with the end result of enjoying a different eternity than will those who reject Jesus Christ.

So rejoice that you are fire proof, stay faithful in the midst of suffering (and also afterward when the let-down after a victory makes us vulnerable to temptation), and don't fear judgment from God, which is for your good, even if it comes from men. That approach to spiritual warfare is excellent faithfulness. And God knows how to reward faithfulness.

Chapter 21

5: 1-5, Excellent Leadership

¹ Therefore, I exhort the elders among you, as *your* fellow elder and witness of the sufferings of Christ, and a partaker also of the glory that is to be revealed,
² shepherd the flock of God among you, exercising oversight not under compulsion, but voluntarily, according to *the will of* God; and not for sordid gain, but with eagerness;
³ nor yet as lording it over those allotted to your charge, but proving to be examples to the flock.
⁴ And when the Chief Shepherd appears, you will receive the unfading crown of glory.
⁵ You younger men, likewise, be subject to your elders; and all of you, clothe yourselves with humility toward one another, for GOD IS OPPOSED TO THE PROUD, BUT GIVES GRACE TO THE HUMBLE.

One of my favorite teachers of all time was my church history professor in seminary. His name was Dr. Christian, and he was the oldest faculty member at Talbot and one of the most fun. He knew a lot about the history of the church and what it all meant. We thought he might have been an eye-witness. If I'd had twice the time under his teaching it wouldn't have been half enough.

Dr. Christian pointed out to us that every significant movement of God had three things in common. They had the right human leader, the times were right, and the people were ready to follow.

It goes without saying, for example, that Jesus was the right leader. But the Father did not send Him until the fulness of time. And the people were ready and eager to follow the Messiah.

Jon Hus was just as capable and motivated to lead a reformation as Martin Luther was. But he was ahead of his time, and the people weren't quite ready. One hundred years later, all the conditions were right, and God started the Reformation.

God sent Moses, the right man at the right time. And the people were just barely ready to leave Egypt and be led to freedom; probably as ready as they would ever be.

All three of those factors are prominent in Peter's letter. We are in the last days kind of time (4:7); it's the age of grace and the last opportunity for people to be saved and escape God's judgment, that being the next event on God's calendar.

In AD 64, the Apostles were nearing the end of their tenure; Peter and Paul especially were short-timers. Both would die in the fiery ordeal that Nero was setting in motion. Other Apostles were either already gone or soon would be; all except John, who probably lived into the 90's.

Churches, however, always need human leaders. A big part of Jesus' ministry was the development of church leaders. And the Apostles, being good students of the Master, occupied much of their time with the same objective.

In our present text, Peter imparts some principles that will encourage excellent spiritual leadership. Everyone knows that God's sheep have needs. But their shepherds have needs, too. And this is what Peter addresses in our text. His outline is:

Good Leaders Need Good Leaders, 1

Good Leaders Need a Good Attitude, 2-3

Good Leaders Need Good Motivation, 4

Good Leaders Need Good Followers, 5

Good Leaders Need Good Leaders, 1

[1] Therefore, I exhort the elders among you, as *your* fellow elder and witness of the sufferings of Christ, and a partaker also of the glory that is to be revealed

Leaders need good examples, good patterns to follow, good role models. And they need to get their instructions from someone. Spiritual leaders don't originate good information and direction; they pass on what they have received from their leaders.

This rule applied even to Jesus. In John's gospel He said repeatedly, **I can do nothing on My own initiative. As I hear, I judge; and My judgment is just, because I do not seek My own will, but the will of Him who sent Me.** (Jn. 5:30; cf. 8:28, 42; 12:49; 14:10) Jesus passed on what He received from the Father. Following that example, the elders are to pass on what they receive from God's word. II Timothy 2:2 gives the plan, **the things which you have heard from me in the presence of many witnesses, these entrust to faithful men, who will be able to teach others also.**

Moses developed Joshua so he could take over as the leader when Moses was gone. Elijah developed Elisha. Solomon taught his son, Rehoboam (not that it did any good in Rehoboam's case, since he went with the advice of young, unwise counselors). Leaders have to receive the goods from previous faithful men and then pass them on to later faithful men (II Tim. 2:2). And the elders have no authority to make up their own rules or objectives or to change or ignore God's word. Teachers are held strictly accountable to teach God's word, without additions or deletions.

Paul made this point in I Corinthians 4:6:

Now these things, brethren, I have figuratively applied to myself and Apollos for your sakes, that in us you might learn not to exceed what is written, in order that no one of you might become arrogant in behalf of one against the other.

And when John finished the last New Testament book, he issued a warning that serves as the final punctuation mark for the whole Bible. Revelation 22:18f:

I testify to everyone who hears the words of the prophecy of this book: if anyone adds to them, God shall add to him the plagues which are written in this book; and if anyone takes away from the words of the book of this prophecy, God

shall take away his part from the tree of life and from the holy city, which are written in this book. (See also Deut. 4:2; 12:32; Prov. 30:6.)

That's why James warns, **Let not many of you become teachers, my brethren, knowing that as such we shall incur a stricter judgment**, Jam. 3:1. There is a dual focus to that stricter judgment. First, the teacher is to be an example to the flock. A Bible teacher who doesn't live by the Bible seems to refute his own teaching. Paul wrote the Corinthians, **Be imitators of me, just as I also am of Christ**, I Cor. 11:1. Second, the teacher is to be a diligent student of the Word of God so that he gets it right. This is one of the qualifications for being an elder, according to Titus 1:9. He must be able to **hold fast the faithful word which is in accordance with the teaching, that he may be able both to exhort in sound doctrine and to refute those who contradict.**

Some people don't like doctrine because "doctrine divides." Of course it does; that's its purpose. It divides those with sound, biblical doctrine from those with false doctrine. But notice that sound doctrine makes sound minds, sound choices and actions, and sound emotions. Never give up sound doctrine for anything. **Buy truth, and do not sell it,** Prov. 23:23.

Paul addressed both example and doctrine when he told Timothy, **Pay close attention to yourself and to your teaching; persevere in these things; for as you do this you will insure salvation both for yourself and for those who hear you,** I Tim. 4:16.

There is principle that applies here. All authority is delegated authority. People in charge get their authority from the fact that they are under authority. A centurion expressed this principle when he asked Jesus to heal his slave in Luke 7:6-9:

Now Jesus started on His way with them; and when He was already not far from the house, the centurion sent friends, saying to Him, "Lord, do not trouble Yourself further, for I am not worthy for You to come under my roof; for this reason I did not even consider myself worthy to come to You, but just say the word, and my servant will be healed.

For I, too, am a man under authority, with soldiers under me; and I say to this one, 'Go!' and he goes; and to another, 'Come!' and he comes; and to my slave, 'Do this!' and he does it." Now when Jesus heard this, He marveled at him, and turned and said to the multitude that was following Him, "I say to you, not even in Israel have I found such great faith." (Note how Jesus relates faith and understanding.)

Jesus is the Chief Shepherd. All elders and Bible teachers are under-shepherds. They are under Christ's authority. Therefore, they have authority. But it's the Lord's authority, not their own. It comes from being under the authority of God's word. And it's for the sake of His kingdom, not for establishing their own little kingdoms. It is appropriate, therefore, that elders should clothe themselves with humility with regard to their own persons.

But that doesn't mean that they should be wishy-washy when they teach the word of God. They should be correctible but not uncertain. The word of God is to be taught like Jesus did, with authority, not as the scribes of Israel taught (Mt. 7:29). That requires careful, honest, and obedient study to be sure they are interpreting and applying the Bible as God meant it to be understood.

If the bugle produces an indistinct sound, who will prepare himself for battle, I Cor. 14:8? Hebrews 4:12 says, **For the word of God is living and active and sharper than any two-edged sword, and piercing as far as the division of soul and spirit, of both joints and marrow, and able to judge the thoughts and intentions of the heart.** The word of God is a mighty sword with the precision of a scalpel. We shouldn't wield it as if it were a dull and weak thing. Paul told Titus (2:15), **These things speak and exhort and reprove with all authority. Let no one disregard you.** Boldness is not incompatible with humility when it's based upon being under God's authority.

Peter walks this line between personal humility and authoritative teaching masterfully. He learned it from his Master. He doesn't say, "Hey, listen! I'm an Apostle. You'd better do what I say." He doesn't lord it over those under his care. He has Apostolic authority and doesn't shrink away from the duties entailed. But he refers to it obliquely, saying that he is a **witness of the sufferings of Christ**. Jesus called the Apostles to be witnesses.

In Acts 3:14f Peter boldly confronted the audience at Pentecost, saying, **you disowned the Holy and Righteous One, and asked for a murderer to be granted to you, but put to death the Prince of life, the one whom God raised from the dead, a fact to which we are witnesses.**

Peter writes to these elders as a **fellow elder**, rather than as a superior. And just as Peter writes so much in this letter about submission, he himself is submitted to the will of God even concerning when and how he dies. He says that he is **a partaker also of the glory that is to be revealed**. Here he uses the word glory just as he heard Jesus use it when He said, **The hour has come for the Son of Man to be glorified,** Jn. 12:23. Jesus was speaking of His death, of course. And throughout this letter, Peter has united the suffering of the saints with the glory that is to be revealed. So I don't think they would miss this point.

The leaders are the prime targets of the enemy. "Strike the shepherd and the sheep will be scattered." That's why Paul said in I Timothy 3:1, **It is a trustworthy statement: if any man aspires to the office of overseer, it is a fine work he desires to do.** The elders, or overseers, were the first ones persecutors tried to beat down. The "badge" of an elder was a big bull's-eye on his chest. (I wonder if that's another reason that women are not allowed to be elders or teachers or men. God didn't design women for fighting wars.)

Peter was a great leader. And it was precisely because he closely followed a great leader, mimicking what he saw in Christ and obeying what he received from Christ. This letter is full to overflowing with allusions to what Peter saw in Christ. Peter is trying to get everyone, and here especially the elders, to follow Christ's example and teaching. A good leader needs to be following a good leader. So how do you choose a leader? You find out who is the best at following. That's what God looks for and commends in a leader.

By the way, as a point of application, everything Peter writes about elders applies equally well to fathers. Fathers are the elders and shepherds in their family.

Good Leaders Need a Good Attitude, 2-3

² shepherd the flock of God among you, exercising oversight not under compulsion, but voluntarily, according to *the will of* **God; and not for sordid gain, but with eagerness; ³ nor yet as lording it over those allotted to your charge, but proving to be examples to the flock.**

Three different terms are used interchangeably to describe the role of the elder. The term elders (*presbuteroi*) emphasizes the spiritual maturity and experienced wisdom that comes with time spent with Christ (not just how long someone has been a Christian, but "time on task"). This term is always used in the plural when speaking of the leadership of the church. Plurality provides balance, a richer variety of gifts among the leadership, protection for the leaders because they are in a vulnerable position. It also provides continuity of leadership as the church ages, since new elders are added all along as God reveals His choices.

The plurality of elders also prevents dominance by one man, overemphasis on one or two doctrines, or even heretical teaching. It provides a built-in accountability. If a charge is leveled against one elder, other elders of equal authority can investigate and deal with the issue. As I Timothy 5:19 says, **Do not receive an accusation against an elder except on the basis of two or three witnesses. Those who continue in sin, rebuke in the presence of all, so that the rest also may be fearful of sinning.**

The Jewish synagogues had elders who led and taught. This was based upon a very natural practice that went back even before Moses' time and was put in place in Israel by Moses. The church, under the Holy Spirit's guidance, carried over that familiar practice. In the book of Acts, elders were appointed by other elders, not selected by congregational vote.

And elders must meet certain character requirements, as taught in I Timothy 3:1-7 and Titus 1:5-9.

The term overseer is the word *episcopos*. This is the term used in the I Timothy 3 and Titus 1 passages. The word emphasizes the duty to guard the church, to watch over the people, to scope them out.

The term shepherd (Greek *poimen*; Latin *pastor*) emphasizes the priority of feeding the sheep, but also includes leading, applying healing procedures, and protecting, the things a shepherd does for the sheep.

So Peter describes the office pretty well just by using these three terms. But Peter's main concern here is the attitude these leaders need if they are to fulfill their God-given role in the church. And it is a God-given role. In Ephesians 4:11, Paul revealed how leadership in the churches would be transferred as the Apostles and prophets faded from the scene: **And He gave some as apostles, and some as prophets, and some as evangelists, and some as pastor/teachers.**

Apostles and prophets were for the infancy of the church; they were the foundation, as Ephesians 2:20 puts it. I Corinthians 13:8-10 says, **if there are gifts of prophecy, they will be done away. For we know in part, and we prophesy in part; but when the perfect comes, the partial will be done away.** The term translated perfect (*teleios*) means relative spiritual maturity.

As the century progressed the church became a grown-up rather than a child. And the word of God was being completed. So prophecy was gradually done away, according to the verb in I Corinthians 13. (This couldn't happen until divine revelation was complete enough to know what maturity meant. We see the temporary sign gifts fading by the AD 60's.)

And of course, as the century wore on, those who were qualified to be Apostles, according to the requirements specified in Acts 1:21f, died off. Apostleship, by its nature, could not be a continuing office, since no one would be around who had accompanied Jesus from the baptism of John until the ascension. To be an Apostle, one had to be an actual eye-witness of Christ's resurrection.

So the Apostles' leadership in carrying the gospel to the world was taken over by evangelists, and the prophets were replaced by pastors and teachers. And these roles continue throughout the church age.

If your role is a God-given duty, then certain attitudes should govern your work in that role. There are certain ways you must be, and certain ways you must not be. What constitutes a good attitude for a spiritual leader?

First, he must keep in mind that the church isn't his own flock; it is **the flock of God**. Jesus purchased this flock at great cost to Himself. The usual word for flock is *poimne*. But in this case Peter uses the diminutive form, *poimnion,* indicating how dear and precious the flock is to Jesus. Jesus is the Chief Shepherd, so He directs the operation. We are to lead the flock toward Christ-likeness and treat the sheep as He would.

Second, the elders are to rule **not under compulsion, but voluntarily, according to God.** Self-will has no place in spiritual leadership, although I regret to say that I have seen a lot of it. Spiritual leaders must be motivated by God, from within, not by some external compulsion. About the priesthood, we read in Heb. 5:4, **And no one takes the honor to himself, but receives it when he is called by God, even as Aaron was.** In the same way, men don't choose to be pastors. They are chosen and called by God. Not all who have the gift of teaching are called to be pastors. And it may be that not all pastors have the gift of teaching--I'm not sure about that. But they must be apt to teach in order to be an elder.

Third, the elder is to rule **not for sordid gain but with eagerness**. It is right and proper for elders to be given realistic pay for their work.

Let the elders who rule well be considered worthy of double honor, especially those who work hard at preaching and teaching. For the Scripture says, "YOU SHALL NOT MUZZLE THE OX WHILE HE IS THRESHING," and "The laborer is worthy of his wages," I Tim. 5:17f.

The double honor means that he is to be paid well, not given lip-service honor while he is paid meagerly by a miserly, marginally-grateful congregation. Such a practice dishonors and devalues the word of God. This would be a dishonor to God and would hinder the church. It also puts the paid pastor in a difficult situation, since he is required by God to provide for his own family or else be worse than an infidel (I Tim. 5:8; I Cor. 9:11). It divides his attention if he has to worry about providing for his family.

But sordid gain is characteristic of worldly leaders, not Christ's shepherds. Nothing turns the materialistic world off to the gospel like scheming, materialistic spiritual leaders. This prohibition would have in mind things like bribery, embezzlement, deceit, exploiting one's position to fleece the sheep, false teaching for fun and profit, simony (buying and selling church offices for profit), and offering the blessings of God for sale; in short, making merchandise of God's grace. We've seen enough of this in Christendom and in the religions of the world to know how damaging it is. I wonder how much of this disreputable dealing was occasioned by churches that did not consider their teachers worthy of double honor.

Mic.5:11 speaks of this, **Her leaders pronounce judgment for a bribe, her priests instruct for a price, and her prophets divine for money. Yet they lean on the LORD.**

I Timothy 6:9 warns, **those who want to get rich fall into temptation and a snare and many foolish and harmful desires which plunge men into ruin and destruction.**

In II Corinthians 2:17, Paul says, **For we are not like many, peddling the word of God, but as from sincerity, but as from God, we speak in Christ in the sight of God.** If you want to know what God thinks of self-serving shepherds, read Ezekiel 34:1-10.

Those who see themselves as the Lord's under shepherds are not driven by the desire for money. They will do well if their attitude is that expressed in Proverbs 30:8f:

Keep deception and lies far from me, Give me neither poverty nor riches; Feed me with the food that is my portion,
9 Lest I be full and deny *Thee* and say, "Who is the

LORD?" Or lest I be in want and steal, And profane the name of my God.

Pastors shouldn't be accused of greed by ungenerous churches trying to justify their own stinginess. They are driven by love for the sheep and love for and obedience to God. They are to do their work eagerly. Congregations must not exploit this motivation to deprive their pastors of pay that can rightly be called **double honor.**

Fourth, he is not to lord **it over those allotted to his charge.** The quick and dirty method worldlings use for getting compliance is to lord it over people with intimidation and a club of some kind. And many leaders don't trouble themselves beyond that and maybe some underhanded scheming. But the under-shepherd must lead as Jesus directs. And He says,

You know that the rulers of the Gentiles lord it over them, and their great men exercise authority over them. It is not so among you, but whoever wishes to become great among you shall be your servant, and whoever wishes to be first among you shall be your slave; just as the Son of Man did not come to be served, but to serve, and to give His life a ransom for many, Mt. 20:25-28.

How does this square with what we saw earlier about teaching with authority? It is just this: the elder is to teach with God's authority, but it is not his place to beat the sheep into compliance. God knows best how to discipline His children.

Proving to be an example to the flock. This is the third participle describing how the elders are to shepherd the flock of God (the other two were **exercising oversight** and **not lording it over**). Paul wrote in Philippians 3:17, **Brethren, join in following my example, and observe those who walk according to the pattern you have in us.** And in 4:9, **The things you have learned and received and heard and seen in me, practice these things; and the God of peace shall be with you.** In II Thessalonians 3:9 Paul said, [We] **offer ourselves as a model for you, that you might follow our example.**

Paul told Pastor Timothy, **Let no one look down on your youthfulness, but rather in speech, conduct, love, faith and purity, show yourself an example of those who believe,** I Tim. 4:12. You can't very well drive sheep from behind because that's the angle predators take when they are attacking the sheep. You have to lead them from the front, "Follow me as I follow Christ." And then they follow, if they want to, in their own good time. And they are inclined to follow if they trust the leader, especially if they are hungry or thirsty.

Leadership is dangerous, it's a chore, and it requires a good attitude. Why should anyone bother to be a pastor when other occupations are easier, more lucrative, and less hassle? That takes us to verse 4:

Good Leaders Need Good Motivation, 4

⁴ And when the Chief Shepherd appears, you will receive the unfading crown of glory.

We've already seen that bad leaders have bad motives— ego, a desire to make a good showing in the flesh, sordid gain, desire to be domineering, etc. Good leaders are good, in part, because they have good motives. Love for God and for God's people is certainly the strongest motivation. Everyone should be eagerly obeying the two greatest commandments. And given that our service is never up to what God deserves, and we know it, everyone should have the desire to serve God in ever greater ways and to see more fruit.

But God offers a special reward for service as an elder. This will happen when the Chief Shepherd appears. And this reward is based upon the extra effort the under-shepherds have made to tend to the Lord's precious flock in His absence. Because He loves His flock, Jesus amply rewards those who have tended to them.

Our service to Christ is not unlike an investment. The parable of the talents makes that point. In Mark 10:29f, Jesus promised a good return on His followers' investment:

Jesus said, "Truly I say to you, there is no one who has left house or brothers or sisters or mother or father or children or farms, for My sake and for the gospel's sake, but that he shall receive a hundred times as much now in the present age, houses and brothers and sisters and mothers and children and farms, along with persecutions; and in the age to come, eternal life.

A hundred times as much is a 10,000% return on investment. A return like that, backed by the full faith and credit of God Himself, would get anyone's attention, I would think. Normally, you don't get a return on someone else's investment, and others don't get a return on your investment. But an investment counselor could reasonably expect to be compensated for the part he played in guiding his client to a handsome profit. He is justified in expecting a share of that profit.

The elder, or any teacher, invests his time, energy, and expertise in the lives of those under his care. They in turn make their investments, drawing upon what they gained from their teachers. Would God think it fitting to give the teacher some compensation for what the student accomplished for the kingdom? Paul told Timothy, **The hard-working farmer ought to be the first to receive his share of the crops**, II Tim. 2:6.

This isn't a Ponzi scheme, because no one is being gamed. Nor is it some kind of Amway marketing structure, because God doesn't take a share of what you earned to pay someone else. But Hebrews 6:10 says, **God is not unjust so as to forget your work and the love which you have shown toward His name, in having ministered and in still ministering to the saints.** So if any Christian builds into another Christian's life (and we all have that duty, according to Eph. 4)), then it is right in God's eyes for the contributor to be rewarded for the benefits gained by the other person. And God is the one who gives the reward, out of His resources, not out of the student's resources.

So in the case of elders and teachers, under shepherds, the Chief Shepherd, when He returns, will give excellent leaders an **unfading crown of glory**, not an olive branch wreath that will soon fade, but a crown of glory that lasts through all of eternity. Now you may wonder, "What is that good for? That, plus a dollar will buy you a donut." So we should consider what that is good for.

In the parable of the talents, the master said, **'Well done, good and faithful slave; you were faithful with a few things, I will put you in charge of many things, enter into the joy of your master.'** (Mt. 25:21) In the similar parable of the minas He said, **'Well done, good slave, because you have been faithful in a very little thing, be in authority over ten cities.'** (Lk. 19:17) What you do on earth for the kingdom of God determines your position in the kingdom, your station in life for all eternity. This is your investment time; that will be your payday, except that the payday will go on forever.

The honor and glory we experience for the rest of eternity is according to our service on earth. Our service on earth will be reflected in the amount of honor that is given to us in heaven. We will defer to others who have gained more honor for themselves, starting with Jesus, of course, but including also others, many of whose names we already know. Others in heaven, including the angels (Heb. 2:7), will defer to us, to the degree that we have been rewarded with glory by the Chief Shepherd.

Think of how military people differ in their admiration and attention to a Marine colonel in full dress uniform with a chest full of well-earned medals, compared to how they would defer to some private. So if you have the opportunity to make an investment with a minimum 10,000% rate of return, how much would you invest, a little or a lot? How much would you sacrifice in order to get the resources to invest more? And the return is unfading, just as Peter said in chapter 1, verse 4.

We aren't mercenaries in our service to God. Our prime motives are love for God and for His people. But **God is not unjust so as to forget your work.** The government looks for ways to tax us; God looks for ways to reward us.

Now remember Dr. Christian's observation from church history; every significant movement of God has three things in common, the right leader, the right time, and the right people. That brings us to the last need…

Good Leaders Need Good Followers, 5

⁵ You younger men, likewise, be subject to your elders; and all of you, clothe yourselves with humility toward one another, for GOD IS OPPOSED TO THE PROUD, BUT GIVES GRACE TO THE HUMBLE.

You may have heard it said, "You can tell who is a real leader by looking around to see if anyone is following him." That's an obvious measure, but not an accurate one. By that measure, Jeremiah was not a good leader. In fact, most of the prophets would not be considered good leaders if determined by how many people followed them. And this measure is often premature. Jesus would not have been considered a good leader by some, based upon His small initial following.

But God judges leaders by their faithfulness to do what He tells them to do. We often judge, and therefore choose, leaders by their confidence, their charisma, their charm, their forcefulness, their speaking ability, sometimes even because they are tall and good looking, or because they tell us what we want to hear.

God judges leaders by their humility. Do they obey Him? That's God's measure. God chooses His best followers to lead His people. Then it is up to the other followers how well they will listen to God's chosen leaders. God's leaders lead from the front. But the sheep follow only if they want to. The Chief Shepherd said, **My sheep hear My voice, and I know them, and they follow Me**. That's why elders have to be careful to teach God's word. When they speak, the sheep should recognize the Master's voice. God judges followers the same way He judges leaders. Are they humble? Will they set aside their own will to obey God? Or are they stiff-necked and obstinate?

Hebrews 13:17 says, **Obey your leaders, and submit to them; for they keep watch over your souls, as those who**

will give an account. Let them do this with joy and not with grief, for this would be unprofitable for you.

People have a bad habit of judging leadership by all the wrong measures and then justifying their own unwillingness to follow on the basis that the leader wasn't doing things the way they wanted. The Jews did this to Jesus. Others follow begrudgingly and give their leaders a lot of grief. This kind of followership is **unprofitable**.

God has always held His chosen leaders accountable to lead according to His revealed will. And He has always held the people accountable to follow His appointed leaders. He has never held the leaders to blame if the followers refused to follow. In Ezekiel 34 God first takes the leaders to task for feeding themselves and neglecting the flock. Then He goes after the flock for abusing one another.

Peter picks out the young men and tells them to submit, because they would be the most headstrong in wanting to go their own way. And yet, the next generation of elders must come from their number. So they must learn about submission, since spiritual leaders must be good followers.

Peter uses almost the same term for young men that his old fishing buddy, John, uses in I John 2:14, **I have written to you, young men, because you are strong, and the word of God abides in you, and you have overcome the evil one.** These young men have spiritual strength and a heart for sound doctrine, but their relationship with God is not yet mature enough to lead the church. So they should submit to those who are.

Peter returns to the need for submission, one of the central themes of this letter. Christians must submit to governing authorities and to bosses. Wives must submit to their husbands. The household of God must submit to God's cleansing judgment which comes in the form of persecution. And the body of Christ must submit to the leaders God places over them.

All of this submission, from which no one is exempt, requires humility. Humility means being lowly-minded, the opposite of pride and arrogance. Pride is what plunged the race

344

into sin. Pride is obeying our own will, thinking that it's the best. Humility is obeying God's will, knowing that it's the best. It is pride that prevents our submission. It is humility that enables submission. Pride says, "I know, better than God or anyone else, what is best for me."

So Peter tells everyone to gird themselves with humility. The word means to tie on a garment, as a slave would tie on an apron go to work. The noun form of the word means work apron. All who would do God's work, must do so with humility. Here Peter is thinking of an event which left a lasting impression on him at the last supper, when Jesus tied a towel around Himself and washed the disciples' feet, John 13:3-5, 12-17. To bolster his argument, Peter quotes from Proverbs 3:34 (Septuagint version), **GOD IS OPPOSED TO THE PROUD, BUT GIVES GRACE TO THE HUMBLE.** Remember how at the last supper Jesus had to rebuke His men for arguing about who was the greatest.

This is a pretty strong argument. You don't want God setting Himself against you and resisting you in everything you try. The word translated *proud* means arrogant, haughty and disdainful, showing oneself above others. Showing oneself above God caused the fall of man into sin.

God gives grace to the humble. When you are in a state of grace, that's when you are well off. First century Greeks and Romans saw humility as weakness and cowardice, an attitude suitable only for slaves. Many Americans still think that way. But look at what lies in store for them.

So these are the needs of spiritual leaders:

1. Leaders need a good leader to follow. God's leaders are the ones He deems the best followers. Sometimes the best leader available is simply the one who is willing. Those who aren't willing to lead have no business criticizing and resisting the one who is willing.

2. Leaders need a good attitude. They have to be in it for God's glory and the good of others.

3. Leaders need good motivations. The last words of those who give up, and even of those who decline to serve in the first place, are, "It's not worth the trouble."

4. And, in the last analysis, leaders need good followers. Leaders become known as great leaders if they have great followers. Even mediocre leaders can succeed if they have good followers.

Put all these goods together and you get excellent leadership. You really can't leave any of these out and still accomplish anything significant for God's kingdom. What is it we need to do, then? We all need to follow like a leader.

Chapter 22

5:6-14, Stand Firm in the True Grace of God

⁶ Humble yourselves, therefore, under the mighty hand of God, that He may exalt you at the proper time,
⁷ casting all your anxiety upon Him, because He cares for you.
⁸ Be of sober *spirit*, be on the alert. Your adversary, the devil, prowls about like a roaring lion, seeking someone to devour.
⁹ But resist him, firm in *your* faith, knowing that the same experiences of suffering are being accomplished by your brethren who are in the world.
¹⁰ And after you have suffered for a little while, the God of all grace, who called you to His eternal glory in Christ, will Himself perfect, confirm, strengthen *and* establish you.
¹¹ To Him *be* dominion forever and ever. Amen.
¹² Through Silvanus, our faithful brother (for so I regard *him*), I have written to you briefly, exhorting and testifying that this is the true grace of God. Stand firm in it!
¹³ She who is in Babylon, chosen together with you, sends you greetings, and *so does* my son, Mark.
¹⁴ Greet one another with a kiss of love. Peace be to you all who are in Christ.

We began our study of I Peter by comparing it to a survival guide. It doesn't deal with strategies or weapons or uprisings or ways to escape and hide. It deals with mindset, which is widely recognized as the most important element of survival. Certainly for Christians subjected to persecution, attitude is paramount.

God puts His beloved children through ordeals in order to make them like Christ and to harden them up in the faith. Peter's purpose has been to explain how to get through suffering successfully. If you want a victorious life, listen to Peter's closing summary.

His overall outline has been in two parts, the second following logically from the first. Salvation is secured to us by the work of God. Salvation is spread to others by our excellent behavior, which is especially evident when we are suffering for the cause of Christ.

Peter closes his letter with four parting admonitions:

Humble Yourselves, 6-7

Be Sober and Alert, 8-9

Keep God's Perspective, 10-11

Stand Firm in the True Grace of God, 12-14.

Humble Yourselves, 6-7

**6 Humble yourselves, therefore, under the mighty hand of God, that He may exalt you at the proper time,
7 casting all your anxiety upon Him, because He cares for you.**

The word *therefore* points back to the reason to humble ourselves. Verse 5, **GOD IS OPPOSED TO THE PROUD, BUT GIVES GRACE TO THE HUMBLE.** This is how to get God either on your side or else working against you. This seems to me to be the most important information in Peter's whole letter, from a survival standpoint. And it must be the reason he spends so much time on humility, and submission, which comes from humility.

The consequence of humbling ourselves is that God will exalt us at the proper time. We don't know when that proper time will be. What's in view here is the time after the suffering has accomplished God's purpose in our life, as verse 10 says.

Each event of suffering has its purposes. When those purposes are accomplished, and not before, then God ends the suffering, leaving us in better condition for what we have gone through. He doesn't spare for our crying, but makes sure the suffering has time to do its work.

348

Oftentimes, when a believer is going through some uncomfortable situation he will come to his spiritual leader wanting him to put a stop the suffering. If it's a matter of escaping the pain and the benefit, the leader should instead encourage the person through the ordeal. We can comfort others with the comfort with which we have been comforted, but we can't excuse them from God's training. That requires some wisdom and resolve on the part of the leader. Otherwise, he would leave that believer a spoiled child who always expects to get his own way with God. He would never become durable in his faith or useful to his Master.

In Luke 14:11, Jesus said, **For everyone who exalts himself shall be humbled, and he who humbles himself shall be exalted.** So which would you rather have, humbling first, then exaltation ever after, or self-exaltation, which can't be as good as the exaltation God gives us, and then exchange that for suffering? I know what you would choose, the same thing I would choose: I'd like the exaltation forever, starting now, and forget the suffering. But that isn't one of the options, because God wants to make us more like Jesus.

Paul told the Galatians, **I am again in labor until Christ is formed in you,** Gal. 4:19.

In Colossians 1:28 he wrote, **we proclaim Him, admonishing every man and teaching every man with all wisdom, that we may present every man complete in Christ.**

We spoke of the work of the elders in the previous chapter. In Ephesians 4:11-13 Paul wrote:

And He gave some as apostles, and some as prophets, and some as evangelists, and some as pastors and teachers, for the equipping of the saints for the work of service, to the building up of the body of Christ; until we all attain to the unity of the faith, and of the knowledge of the Son of God, to a mature man, to the measure of the stature which belongs to the fulness of Christ.

Being like Jesus is our goal and our glory. Philippians 2:20f say,

For our citizenship is in heaven, from which also we eagerly wait for a Savior, the Lord Jesus Christ; who will transform the body of our humble state into conformity with the body of His glory, by the exertion of the power that He has even to subject all things to Himself.

This passage, like many others, tells us that our greatest good is to be with Jesus and to be like Jesus. That is the leading feature of our exaltation. Everything else follows as the result of being with Jesus and being like Jesus. We will be exalted because Jesus is exalted. We will rule because Jesus will rule. We will have no sin because Jesus has no sin. We will have everything because Jesus owns everything. We will live with the Father forever because Jesus lives with the Father forever. All this comes from being with Jesus and being like Jesus. We are joint heirs with Him.

In God's perfect wisdom, this exalted, eternal goal is worth the temporary sufferings He puts us through. Because God is gracious and loving and has a perfect plan for us, therefore, He leads us through suffering.

So we are to **humble** ourselves **under the mighty hand of God**. The mighty hand of God is God's sovereignty, especially as God uses His strength on behalf of His chosen people. He is strong to prevail, mighty to rule.

The Old Testament repeatedly refers to God's mighty hand and His outstretched arm with regard to taking His people out of Egypt. In Deuteronomy 4:34, for example, we read:

Or has a god tried to go to take for himself a nation from within another nation by trials, by signs and wonders and by war and by a mighty hand and by an outstretched arm and by great terrors, as the LORD your God did for you in Egypt before your eyes?

With regard to the church, God is doing an even more remarkable thing. Jesus came to take for Himself a world system (the kingdom of God) from within another world system (the kingdom of Satan). Jesus referred to this when He said in Matthew 12:28f,

But if I cast out demons by the Spirit of God, then the kingdom of God has come upon you. Or how can anyone enter the strong man's house and carry off his property, unless he first binds the strong man? And then he will plunder his house.

You and I are part of that plunder.

God's sovereign strength is our protection *in* adversity, and our deliverance *out of* adversity. So for a Christian to be in a helpless situation is not necessarily a bad condition, because Peter says, literally, **it matters to God concerning us**. We are the objects of His care.

In Matthew 10:29 Jesus said, **Are not two sparrows sold for a cent? And yet not one of them will fall to the ground apart from your Father. But the very hairs of your head are all numbered. Therefore do not fear; you are of more value than many sparrows.**

That last line, by the way, is an example of humor by understatement. At a half cent per sparrow (the going rate at the time), how many sparrows are you worth? Say 50? That would make you worth 25 cents to God. A thing's value is determined by what someone is willing to pay for it. How much did Jesus pay for you?

If we have humbled ourselves under the mighty hand of God, then we can toss all our anxieties onto Him. No better place exists for taking shelter than "Under the mighty hand of God."

As God turns up the temperature in your fiery ordeals, will you cast all your anxieties upon Him and stand fast, trusting His purpose? Or will you, at some point, run away or surrender to the adversary because you are no longer willing to take the heat? James 1:2-4 was written to encourage the smart choice:

Consider it all joy, my brethren, when you encounter various trials, knowing that the testing of your faith produces endurance. And let endurance have its perfect result, that you may be perfect and complete, lacking in nothing.

The first major battle of the Civil War was at Bull Run on July 21, 1861. The Union came within inches of winning the battle, but when JEB Stuart led a cavalry charge, the Union army panicked and abandoned the battlefield at a full run. General Confusion was the officer in command that day.

At Bull Run again a year later (8/28-30, 1862), the Union army lost another battle, but this time their retreat was calm and orderly. During this battle, Confederate General Longstreet learned that he could disregard General Lee's orders and get away with it. That sowed the seed for their great defeat a year later.

In July of 1863, at Gettysburg, the Union army endured several fiery ordeals. This time, they didn't run or retreat. They were attacked at Little Round Top, the Wheatfield, Devil's Den, the Peach Orchard, Culp's Hill, and Cemetery Hill, all on the second day. On the third and final day of the battle, the Union was attacked again on Culp's Hill and then on Cemetery Ridge by Pickett's famous charge. Everywhere, the Union army repulsed the attacks as they came one at a time. Because of the independence of Lee's generals they were unable to organize a coordinated attack. Lee's shattered army retreated south, and the tide of the war had changed.

What makes armies, or individuals, sturdy and unyielding under fire? The only way to develop that kind of strength is to put them under fire. You can prepare and train to a degree, but it finally comes down to on-the-job training. God wants troops who have been forged under fire.

Peter's source for verse 7 is what the experienced and sturdy soldier, David, said in Psalm 55:22. **Cast your burden upon the LORD, and He will sustain you; He will never allow the righteous to be shaken.**

This doesn't happen automatically, however. So Peter continues.

Be Sober and Alert, 8-9

8 Be of sober *spirit,* be on the alert. Your adversary, the devil, prowls about like a roaring lion, seeking someone to devour.

⁹ But resist him, firm in *your* faith, knowing that the same experiences of suffering are being accomplished by your brethren who are in the world.

Physically, to be sober means to be uncompromised by wine. But metaphorically, it refers to moral alertness and self-control (repeating what Peter wrote in 1:13 and 4:7).

The word translated *alert* means to be awake, to watch, to stand guard. Your own constant vigilance is necessary because you have a personal enemy. It isn't just *the* adversary who prowls around like a roaring lion; it is ***your* adversary** who desperately wants to swallow you up. I wouldn't put too fine a point on this because Satan himself isn't necessarily after you, personally. But some of his evil demons no doubt are. And Satan's schemes are designed to catch individuals, not just the church at large.

In the Roman Coliseum, wild animals, such as lions, were set against victims for the entertainment of the citizens, to keep them distracted from the failures of their government. (Beware of being duped or doped by entertainment.) Peter would have known about this grisly sport, and his day's business might have taken him past the Coliseum so that he heard the lions roaring as they attacked their prey. Some of the coming persecution, Peter knew, would be for the purpose of taking the Roman citizens' minds off the damage done by the fire set by Nero's agents, destroying their homes.

Satan tries to intimidate us into running away from our strong and defensible position so he can get to us. He tries to sneak up on us if he catches us napping at our post. He sets snares to catch us unaware while we're walking around. He tries to entice us into a trap using some attractive sin as bait. He uses all manner of underhanded means, so we need to **be shrewd as serpents and innocent as doves**, Mt. 10:16. Sitting ducks will get eaten up.

The term **adversary** speaks of an opponent in a lawsuit. Satan is our accuser. Our moral alertness will keep him from getting a handle on us. It's not that he can't level charges against us if we're clean. He is the *diabolos*, a malicious slanderer. But the best defense against slanders is to be above reproach.

Our duty is to stand firm against him. Not to attack him. But to withstand his attacks. There's an old tongue-in-cheek army tip that says "Try to look unimportant; the enemy might be low on ammunition." A lot of Christians go this route. But that makes them useless to God. And we weren't saved to be useless.

We are already attacking Satan's kingdom, in effect, when we share the gospel and encourage people to be rescued from his grasp. No other religion does that. They're all working for Satan. That's why the world accepts the ABC principle: anything but Christianity. All religions are products of the evil world system, and the world accepts its own.

The way to resist Satan is to stay firm in our faith. The young men addressed in I John 2:14 had overcame the evil one because the word of God was abiding in them and they were strongly committed to it. The term firm (*stereos*) means hard, firm, solid. We all need to harden up in our faith. As Ephesians 4:14 admonishes, **we are no longer to be children, tossed here and there by waves, and carried about by every wind of doctrine, by the trickery of men, by craftiness in deceitful scheming**.

James 4:7 says, **Submit therefore to God. Resist the devil and he will flee from you.** But when the devil departs it is only to wait **until an opportune time,** Lk. 4:13. So never let down your guard. Don't be on edge, but be alert. Christians are always in a war zone and are always behind enemy lines.

It's also very helpful when under fire to know that we are not alone in the battle. Solomon pointed out, **And if one can overpower him who is alone, two can resist him. A cord of three *strands* is not quickly torn apart**, Eccl. 4:12. When the prophet Elijah was discouraged, he complained to God:

I have been very zealous for the LORD, the God of hosts; for the sons of Israel have forsaken Thy covenant, torn down Thine altars and killed Thy prophets with the sword. And I alone am left; and they seek my life, to take it away, I Kings 19:14.

354

What did God do? He gave Elijah his next assignment. Then He comforted Elijah, telling him that there were still 7,000 in Israel who had not bowed the knee to Baal.

In chapter 4, verse 12, Peter told his readers that suffering was not a strange thing for a Christian. And now he points out that the same experiences of suffering are being accomplished (i.e., successfully completed) by their brethren all over the world. This is positive peer pressure. "If others are standing it, I can, too."

Here are some questions to ask yourself to see how resistant you are to Satan's schemes:

1. Can you distinguish God's truth from Satan's clever lies?

2. Can you stick to the truth when self-will or emotions, or outside pressures try to push you away?

3. Do you have the courage it takes to stick to your convictions?

4. Are you committed to serve God? In other words, has God enlisted you into His service, or have you enlisted Him into yours? That's an important question with eternal ramifications.

5. Do you trust what God says more than you trust what you think, more than you trust what men say, more than you trust the appearance of your situation (cf. II Ki. 6:14-17)?

In II Corinthians 10:4f, Paul says,

the weapons of our warfare are not of the flesh, but divinely powerful for the destruction of fortresses, destroying speculations and every lofty thing raised up against the knowledge of God, and we are taking every thought captive to the obedience of Christ.

These speculations include ideologies, philosophies, pseudo-intellectualism, religions, world-views, and **the opposing arguments of what is falsely called science** [think, for example, of evolutionism] (I Tim. 6:20).

All of these are raised up against the knowledge of God, trying to eliminate the knowledge of God from the world by offering alternatives that appeal to the flesh and to pride. So we must be solid and hardened in the faith, no matter what pressure is exerted against us. It is fire that softens steel so it can be forged into the desired shape, and then it is fire again that hardens and tempers the steel, making it both hard and tough, so it can serve its purpose.

Whenever we are in some situation of suffering, even if it isn't as severe as a fiery ordeal, we tend to get tunnel vision, seeing only what is directly in front of us, here and now. So it is important to…

Keep God's Perspective, 10-11

**10 And after you have suffered for a little while, the God of all grace, who called you to His eternal glory in Christ, will Himself perfect, confirm, strengthen *and* establish you.
11 To Him *be* dominion forever and ever. Amen.**

Suffering is always for a limited time. How much time depends upon what God wants to accomplish in your life and in the lives of those who are watching you.

If we think of the refining process, the amount of time in the fire depends upon how much impurity must be removed and how tightly you hang on to those imperfections. Those who are reluctant to give up their sin can expect more time in the fire or even a hotter fire.

If you think about God's purpose for a particular individual, then you can see that the time in the fire depends upon how hard and tough you have to be to stand up to God's purpose for you. An ax has to be harder than a butter knife. But the ax also gets a greater eternal reward, as we saw in the previous chapter. God uses our trials to forge us into tools useful for His purpose. Or to use another metaphor, the Potter fires the clay pot to make for Himself a vessel for honor.

Without the fire, the clay pot would be very weak and would dissolve to mud when someone put water in it. It is pretty much useless until it has been through the fire. You can't even form the ax without fire. And without the fire the ax would not hold a sharp edge when it was used to chop wood. In fact, if an edged tool hasn't been hardened in the fire, you can't even get a very sharp edge to begin with. That's why you shouldn't buy cheap edged tools; they don't have enough carbon in the steel to respond properly to the fire, so they can't be hardened enough to take a good edge.

This principle totally escapes those who preach a health and wealth doctrine and those who teach that God just wants everyone to be happy. God isn't running a cruise ship. He's running a warship. If you don't realize that, then you are a sitting duck. By the way, there is more genuine love on a warship than there is on a cruise ship, especially if that ship has seen hard service.

The end of verse 10 tells us where God is taking us when He uses suffering in our lives.

The verb **perfect** means to render fit, to mend or repair. It was used of mending fishing nets. Galatians 6:1 translates it *restore*. Luke 6:40 translates it *fully trained*. It is saying that God will adjust us to suit His purpose for us. God takes broken sinners and mends them. Some of that happens at the point of spiritual birth. The rest takes a while. As James 1:4 put it, **the testing of your faith produces endurance. And let endurance have its perfect result, that you may be perfect and complete, lacking in nothing.**

The verb **confirm** has the same root as the word **firm** in verse 9. God uses suffering to make us solid, to solidify our commitment. He uses suffering to make us stronger than we were. According to I John 2, that strength comes from the word of God abiding in us. Not all Christians are concerned to make sure the word of God abides in them. So God may find it necessary to put suffering in their lives to drive them to His word, which they otherwise would neglect. Suffering makes the weak strong and the strong stronger.

Suffering will **establish** us. It puts us on a firm foundation. This word is used in Hebrews 1:10 to speak of the earth's foundation. Imagine the strength of the earth's foundation, even though it's invisible. This is the opposite of being tossed here and there by waves and carried about by every wind of doctrine.

All these put together make us solid, sturdy, and complete Christians, in good repair and firmly established on the Rock. That's a servant God can use for His glory, a soldier for Christ!

All of this is done by **the God of all grace who calls us to His eternal glory in Christ**. It's easier to accept what God is doing in our lives if we trust His motives and know why He is doing it. We have to know that the result is worth the effort. In other words, we need to keep God's perspective. And a big part of that perspective is to recognize His omnipotent ability to rule perfectly. To me there is no greater comfort to be had than the doctrine of God's sovereignty.

If we recognize this, then we praise Him, even in our trials, as Peter does here, instead of complaining to Him and begging for escape. Or as James put it, we **consider it all joy** in the long run. To serve a king who is perfect in every way is a deep and rich joy and a great honor, far surpassing any cost. It makes for a mutual love between God and servant.

Hebrews 12:11f acknowledges:

All discipline for the moment seems not to be joyful, but sorrowful; yet to those who have been trained by it, afterwards it yields the peaceful fruit of righteousness. Therefore, strengthen the hands that are weak and the knees that are feeble.

Christians are not to be spiritual couch potatoes. We may need to get up and get to work, strengthening ourselves where we are weak. If we do, we'll be able to…

Stand Firm in the True Grace of God, 12-14

[12] Through Silvanus, our faithful brother (for so I regard *him*), I have written to you briefly, exhorting and testifying that this is the true grace of God. Stand firm in it!
[13] She who is in Babylon, chosen together with you, sends you greetings, and *so does* my son, Mark.

[14] Greet one another with a kiss of love. Peace be to you all who are in Christ.

Peter is now ready to close his letter. Silvanus, also known by the shortened form, Silas, acted as Peter's amanuensis. He penned the letter as Peter dictated. It was common for the author of the letter to actually take the pen in his own hand to write the closing words of the letter. This is the same Silas who traveled with Paul. Silas was a prophet (Ac. 15:32), and a Roman citizen (Ac. 16:37). He suffered hardship with Paul as a good soldier of Jesus Christ.

Silvanus is a good role model for standing firm in the true grace of God. He's been doing it faithfully for decades. Silas was one of those first-class seconds, serving like a champion under Paul and now also under Peter, both of whom were in Rome when this letter was written.

That second tier of leadership is so important. Think of Joshua serving as Moses' second, Jonathon serving as David's second, Jonathon's armor bearer, Luther's Melanchthon. Blessed is the leader who has a first-class second who is always there for him, ready to assist, a man whom he can send in his own place and know that things will be handled as he would.

John Mark turned out to be a good second. He is there in Rome with Peter. It was Peter, in fact, who led Mark to saving faith. He calls Mark, **my son**, in the same way Paul referred to Timothy. Mark's first attempt at assisting an Apostle was a failure. When things got too rough early in Paul's first missionary journey, he went home. So Paul refused to take him on the next missionary trip. He needed people he could count on. But Barnabas, Mark's cousin, developed him further, and Mark eventually became a useful servant, both to Paul and to Peter. Mark, then, serves as another example who, like Peter, buckled under pressure early on, but then came back stronger and truly useful. I think Peter mentions these two men, who were known to his readers, for the purpose of using them as encouragements.

Silas and Mark are points of contact between Peter, the Apostle to the Jews, and Paul, the Apostle to the Gentiles, who are both in Rome.

Mark's gospel is universally taken to be Peter's perspective on the life of Christ. It wouldn't surprise me if Mark's gospel was written about this time, while Peter and Mark are together, and Peter knows that his time is running out. Peter's buddy John didn't write his gospel until his time was running out. Peter may have quickly guided Mark in the writing of the shortest gospel while writing his two epistles and helping to prepare the Roman Church for the coming persecution, and maybe even collaborating with Paul on the letter to the Hebrews. The abrupt ending of Mark's gospel at Mark 16:8 might have been the result of Peter's death. Mark might have chosen to end it there, in an untimely way that reflected and honored the untimely death of his spiritual father. Mark might have figured that any further work on his gospel would not have apostolic authority after Peter's death. Later someone else, not knowing the story or not willing to leave well enough alone, added verses 9-20. That explanation, I believe, would fit the available data.

This is a time for being shrewd as a serpent, so Peter refers to Rome as **Babylon**. All the New Testament letters were widely circulated. Peter put nothing in this letter that would lead antagonistic authorities back to the Roman church.

This need for caution may be why the letter to the Hebrews is unsigned and yet widely accepted in the canon of New Testament literature. The early church fathers don't mention its authorship. Maybe they understood the need for anonymity and preserved it. The letter to the Hebrews never claims apostolic authority. The Jews would not be impressed by such a claim, since it would amount to begging the question. (If Jesus were not the Messiah, then what authority could He give His designated spokesmen?) The letter's authority depends on its excellent and extensive use of the Old Testament, its tight, logical argument, and the fact that it is in perfect harmony with the rest of the whole Bible.

Also, both Peter and Paul were intensely concerned about the salvation of the Jews, but neither would be welcome in Jerusalem. And since the epistle to the Hebrews was to be distributed widely among Jews who either rejected the Messiah or were vacillating in their commitment to Christ, their names on the letter might have been cause for *prima facie* rejection. The authors could avoid sabotaging their own epistle by leaving the letter anonymous.

This collaboration would explain why in the book of Hebrews we see Pauline style and vocabulary and also the style and vocabulary of a different writer. Both men were steeped in the Old Testament and used it extensively in their known writings, just as Hebrews is full of Old Testament references. There are many clear similarities between I Peter and the book of Hebrews. Silas may also have had a hand in the work. Some have seen enough reasons to propose him as the author.

Consider also the following: Paul's last interaction with the Jews when he was in Rome at the end of the book of Acts, the fact that the church had now become a Gentile movement, that the two apostles were looking at their last days on earth, and that the letter was first known in Rome. Would Hebrews not serve well as Peter and Paul's parting word and final appeal to the Jews?

I didn't find any argument against the possibility in my *New Testament Introduction*. So I continue to entertain the possibility that Hebrews was a collaborative effort between Peter and Paul, and maybe Silas. If so, it is just one more example of the perfect cohesiveness of the Bible and the consequent unity of the leaders of the church. It also means that Peter and Paul were very busy at the end of their lives.

At the end of verse 12, Peter claims that this letter is divinely inspired. He testifies **that this is the true grace of God**. I find that phrase, **the true grace of God**, captivating and inviting. Luke 4:22 says, **And all were speaking well of Him, and wondering at the gracious words which were falling from His lips.** God's word, from Genesis to Revelation, is an outpouring of grace. **For of His fulness we have all received, and grace upon grace. For the Law was given through Moses; grace and truth were realized through Jesus Christ**, Jn. 1:16f.

In 1:23, Peter wrote, **you have been born again not of seed which is perishable but imperishable, that is, through the living and abiding word of God.**

In II Peter 3:2 he wrote, **you should remember the words spoken beforehand by the holy prophets and the commandment of the Lord and Savior spoken by your apostles.** And in II Pt. 1:20f, **But know this first of all, that no prophecy of Scripture is a matter of one's own interpretation, for no prophecy was ever made by an act of human will, but men moved by the Holy Spirit spoke from God.**

That's what Peter is saying when he testifies that this letter he just wrote is **the true grace of God**. It is divinely inspired. It is the word of God

Those who don't understand or believe God's word put forth a lot of false grace; statements such as, "God just wants you to be happy." Or, "If you do your best, God will accept you." Or, "It doesn't matter what you believe, as long as you are sincere." Or, "God is all about tolerance." Or, "If you just keep the faith [whatever that it is], then things will turn out alright." Those are just sweet-tasting poisons from the Deceiver. False grace consists of all the pretty lies Satan publishes in the attempt to get people to live in denial until they are finally overtaken by the consequences.

True grace is truth from **the God of all grace**. He always tells us the truth and then gives us the grace to live in the truth. That's what true grace is. **Stand firm in it**. You can't stand firm in false grace or any other kind of falsehood. Falsehood shifts under your feet. It's like walking on oily marbles.

With a parting encouragement to love one another, Peter closes with the words, **Peace be to all who are in Christ.**

Saying that to people who are already suffering trials and are about to face even tougher trials, is either a mockery or a marvel. If what Peter has written is not the true grace of God, then wishing them peace is a cruel mockery. If what he has written is a true representation of God's grace, then peace under those circumstances is just another example of God's supernatural grace.

Peace comes from humbling ourselves under the mighty hand of God, from being sober and alert, and from keeping God's perspective. This is a peace that passes understanding. It is the peace that enfolds us and shields our spirits when we stand firm in the true grace of God. Peter remembers what Jesus promised at the last supper, recorded for us in John 14:27, **Peace I leave with you; My peace I give to you; not as the world gives, do I give to you. Let not your heart be troubled, nor let it be fearful.**

I hope this study of I Peter has equipped and encouraged you to stand firm in the true grace of God, and that it helps you to understand why God wants to harden you up for the last days. Remember the sovereignty of God and the love of God. And remember that for every trial God has a matching grace. Uppermost in our hearts should be our duty to fulfill the purpose for which God chose us.

Blessed be the God and Father of our Lord Jesus Christ, who according to His great mercy has caused us to be born again to a living hope through the resurrection of Jesus Christ from the dead, to obtain an inheritance which is imperishable and undefiled and will not fade away, reserved in heaven for you, who are protected by the power of God through faith for a salvation ready to be revealed in the last time.

Grace be with you.

Appendix: A Ready Defense for the Gospel

I Peter 3:15 commands us, **sanctify Christ as Lord in your hearts, always being ready to make a defense to everyone who asks you to give an account for the hope that is in you, yet with gentleness and reverence.**

The first step in leading others to the understanding that Jesus should be the Lord of their lives is to **sanctify Christ as Lord in your hearts.** If you don't do that, then defending the faith can easily get personal. Egos get involved, defense mechanisms go up, mouths will not close and ears will not open, and the fight is on. No one wins such fights, especially God.

The word *account* means a reasoned defense. "Here is why I believe in Jesus Christ, and here is what He has done for me since I turned control of my life over to Him." We are to do this **with gentleness and reverence.** So we will begin our discussion with a winning attitude. Arguments against God in general take only a few forms. We will look at four of those and consider some appropriate responses we might make.

A Winning Attitude

Our purpose is to give people reason to repent of their sins and trust in Jesus Christ for salvation. People won't be convinced unless they have reason to trust what you tell them. And they won't trust what you tell them unless they have reason to trust you. They must see you as a worthy witness, one who is reliable and who has their best interests at heart. Any bad character traits will render you untrustworthy in their eyes.

Our Lord's example instructs us to convey the gospel with gentleness and genuine respect. Isaiah 42:1-3 describes Jesus as gentle:

Behold, My Servant, whom I uphold; My chosen one in whom My soul delights. I have put My Spirit upon Him; He will bring forth justice to the nations. He will not cry out or raise His voice, nor make His voice heard in the street. A

bruised reed He will not break, and a dimly burning wick He will not extinguish; He will faithfully bring forth justice.

Jesus Himself said, **Take My yoke upon you, and learn from Me, for I am gentle and humble in heart,** Mt. 11:29. If we have the truth, we have no need to get loud and assertive, as do those who argue weak points. It's good for a grindstone to be abrasive. Its purpose is to remove what is unwanted and to smooth up what remains. But the purpose of the gospel is not to polish up the old sinner. It is to give the Holy Spirit the opportunity to create a new saint.

We can well afford to be gracious. Colossians 4:6 says, **Let your speech always be with grace, seasoned, as it were, with salt, so that you may know how you should respond to each person.** Aggressiveness throws up walls of defense. Graciousness shows that there is no need for a wall. We cannot force anyone to listen to us, nor do we wish to. Jesus told us, **do not throw your pearls before swine, lest they trample them under their feet, and turn and tear you to pieces,** Mt. 7:6. We should beware of trying to convince people who are unwilling to be convinced.

Mark 11:27-33 gives this account:

And as He was walking in the temple, the chief priests, and scribes, and elders came to Him, and began saying to Him, "By what authority are You doing these things, or who gave You this authority to do these things?" And Jesus said to them, "I will ask you one question, and you answer Me, and then I will tell you by what authority I do these things. Was the baptism of John from heaven, or from men? Answer Me." And they began reasoning among themselves, saying, "If we say, 'From heaven,' He will say, 'Then why did you not believe him?' "But shall we say, 'From men'?"-- they were afraid of the multitude, for all considered John to have been a prophet indeed. And answering Jesus, they said, "We do not know." And Jesus said to them, "Neither will I tell you by what authority I do these things."

In other words, they weren't willing to deal honestly with the truth, so Jesus saw no reason to give it to them.

You might question the person who raises arguments against God, "If I could answer all your questions and objections to your satisfaction, would you be willing to repent of your sins and give your life to Jesus?" If the answer is negative, then you are justified in concluding that the person doesn't really have intellectual issues. He just wants to keep on being a sinner. The intellectual objections are either an attempt at self-justification or a smoke screen to fool others.

One excellent way to initiate a conversation about the Lord is to ask a person questions. "What do you think happens to a person after he dies?" Or, "Do you think God will judge the world?" "Do you think it's right that God will judge the world? What do you think will be His basis for judging?" Or, "Do you think Jesus is God?" Always ask the person, "What is your basis for believing that?"

Starting with a question is inviting. It's non-threatening. It opens the way for two-way communication. It's something Jesus often did. And should the conversation start to turn confrontational, asking more questions (not intimidating ones or ones that make the guy think he's being corralled or trapped) calms the nerves and assures the other person that he isn't being rail-roaded. Asking questions expresses appreciation for his mind (which is always well-taken), and challenges him to reconsider the soundness of his views, whether they have any solid basis. Sometimes all you need to do is plant the right question. The conversation will guide you in that respect.

The proper attitude, then, is an attitude of love and concern for the other person's welfare, and a desire for God's glory with no concern for your own. Should your message be rejected, don't take it personally. People rejected the arguments of Stephen, Peter, Paul, Apollos, and even the Lord Jesus.

Remember what God told Samuel, **they have not rejected you, but they have rejected Me from being king over them,** I Sam. 8:7. Jesus told His opponents, **you do not believe, because you are not of My sheep. My sheep hear My voice, and I know them, and they follow Me; and I give eternal life to them,** Jn. 10:26ff.

And keep in mind that immediate rejection is not necessarily final rejection. Jesus doesn't usually knock a guy down and blind him with the light of His glory. More common is the experience of John Mark, who went away grieved when Jesus touched upon his need to abandon materialism. Upon further reflection, Mark later gave his life to Jesus and became a useful servant to God. The fruit might not be ripe yet, so don't bruise it.

The Forms Arguments Take

Arguments against God or His word can be categorized under a few, basic headings. We'll consider four categories: **moral problems**, **factual problems**, **philosophical problems**, and **practical problems**.

Moral Problems

It may seem odd that sinful men should have **moral problems** with God. But some do. They say that God demands perfect adherence to a strict moral code, but violates that code Himself. Therefore, Christians worship an immoral God.

Responding to that, I would say in the first place, that they probably have problems with a strict moral code. They can't abide being restricted in their sin. This is the root of all objections to God. So they construct an argument in which God breaks His own moral code, which means that He has no moral right to hold them accountable.

As an example, they accuse God of genocide for killing people in the flood and for ordering the Hebrews to kill all the men, women and children in Canaan. Most charges that God is immoral are based upon the common element of ignorance concerning what really took place. God did not order the slaughter of everyone in Canaan. Many were given the option of leaving the land. (Challenge their false information. If they are unwilling to deal with facts, you should probably excuse yourself from what has just become a quarrel instead of reasoned discourse.

Concerning the Flood, as we saw in our study of I Peter, in the days of Noah, some demons married women in order to produce an unredeemable mongrel race, called the Nephilim. Had God allowed this demonic plan to continue, the whole human race would eventually become unredeemable and therefore consigned to hell forever. This is due to the principle of the solidarity of the human race, the principle by which Christ's death counts for our sins. At that time, just before the Flood, part of the human race was united with demons, accounting at least in part for the fact that men were excessively violent, immoral, and more evil than the world could tolerate. That unqualified devotion to evil was more than the earth could sustain. So God judged the wicked human race, except for Noah's family. The rest ignored Noah's preaching and chose to continue in their wickedness.

After the flood, and God's promise never again to judge the world by a universal flood, the demons tried to mongrelize the race again in Canaan. If the Canaanites continued in the direction they were headed, they would have corrupted the whole human race and ruined it with their gross immorality. Certainly they would have corrupted the Jews, from which the Savior was to come.

Not knowing the word of God, unbelievers have little idea of the attempts Satan makes to foil the redemptive plan of God. Nor do they consider their own sin to be such a bad a thing. Consequently, they don't see the justice, the wisdom, or the love in what God does. God is perfectly just and righteous. Sinful men are not. They can't even recognize perfect righteousness when they see it. God knows what He is doing. Man does not. So unrighteous men have no business judging a righteous Judge. They will never come out ahead.

As Romans 2:5 warns, **because of your stubbornness and unrepentant heart you are storing up wrath for yourself in the day of wrath and revelation of the righteous judgment of God.** God is the Creator of all, and it is His right to rule over all, which He does in perfect righteousness. The main problem people have with God's morality is that it involves their own judgment. To a sinner, judgment seems unjust and immoral.

Here's another example that is put forth to prove that God does not abide by His own prohibitions. Critics misquote
368

the sixth commandment as, "You shall not kill." (KJV) Again, this is a case of ignorance or misunderstanding. Misunderstandings are common when sinners try to build a case against God. The sixth commandment, as God wrote it, does not say, "You shall not kill." It says, "You shall not murder." Some translations are careless with that distinction, but the Hebrew is not.

They don't need to know the Hebrew. They just need to read the Bible for themselves and let the context help them. Often, they criticize the Bible on the basis of faulty, second-hand information. You've heard of the "straw man" argument. The debater puts forward an argument on behalf of his opponent, but it's a weak argument that is easy to refute. Then he refutes the argument and claims to have refuted his opponent's argument. Many of the moral objections to God are straw man arguments. Opponents misinterpret the Bible and then proceed to find fault with their faulty interpretation and claim that they have refuted the Bible.

But not all moral problems are "straw Bible" misinterpretations. Critics have a moral problem with God because He sends people to hell. This is at the core of their objection to God. They deny that they are sinful and deserve to go to hell. So any God who would send them there must be immoral. In their twisted logic, a moral God would support immorality forever. The fact of the matter is that all men are sinful and in rebellion against God and are deserving of God's righteous judgment. History proves that point and Romans 1-3 presents a strong argument. God is perfectly just to judge any or all sinners any time He pleases.

All of these moral objections arise from man's exalted view of his own state and a woefully inadequate view of God's holy character. So how do we answer the various charges of immorality leveled against God?

Challenge the objector to study the Bible so he can get his facts straight. Tell him that most if not all of his moral challenges would fall away if he just lets the Bible speak for itself. He can't fairly judge God or the Bible on someone else's representation. Hearsay evidence is not admissible in court for good reason.

And you could perhaps answer some of his concerns to demonstrate that there are good answers. You see that done in the Bible often enough that you should have no trouble doing it yourself, especially since the Holy Spirit guides you.

Factual Problems

It may strike you as odd that fallible men disagree with the omniscient God on matters of **factual** knowledge. But they do. Factual issues are ones in which the facts themselves are in dispute. This would include the Biblical text—its authorship and reliability. It would also include the competing, pseudo-scientific theory of evolution, put forth to explain why creation doesn't need a Creator. Also included would be history, geography, etc.

The fact that the Bible doesn't tell us everything is no indication that what it does tell us is wrong. A Bible that answered every question would be bigger than a library. The Bible has proven to be perfectly reliable on everything that can be checked, so we are justified in believing that the Bible is right on the few things that we cannot check, especially given the proven trustworthiness of God Himself.

The fact that an unbeliever has never seen God proves nothing about God's actual existence. Most unbelievers have never seen me, either. But I exist. The Bible says that no man can see God (the Father) and live (Ex. 33:20). A skeptic might say, "Well, that's a convenient way out!" But if that skeptic were taken to court for a crime and told the judge, "I'm innocent," the judge might say, "That's just what a guilty man would say. The court finds you guilty!" Both conclusions would be equally without merit.

People have seen God, the second Person of the Trinity, at various points in history (and the Holy Spirit once, at Jesus' baptism). And they are reliable witnesses. In fact, the God of the Old and New Testaments is the only God who has ever been seen by anyone.

Other religions have to make images and fasten them up somewhere for people to see. Their actual god has never been seen, and in fact has never done anything, giving us good reason to deny his existence. This is an argument from silence,

370

but if a god exists, we are justified in expecting him to make his existence known. The real God has. Other religions (notably Islam and Mormonism) have made the claim that a god secretly revealed his will to one man. This is not something that can be verified. And both of those revelations have been altered as mistakes were found. The Bible has about 40 authors and no alterations. The Bible makes itself objectively verifiable.

Let's consider the authorship and reliability of the Bible. Much has been written about it, and the information is easily obtainable. So let's keep it simple.

The Bible claims to be the inspired word of God. That claim is beyond question, as it is made thousands of times. Now don't allow anyone to accuse you of circular reasoning; we aren't done yet. We're just saying that if the Bible is the word of God, we would expect it to say so. Most of the world's so-called holy writings do not make a claim to be God's word.

That's because such a claim is very easy to refute, if it is false. If the Bible is inspired by God, then it follows that it is infallible in everything it says. In making this claim, the Bible challenges critics to test it. All they have to do is find external inconsistencies between what the Bible really says and known facts from science, or history, or geography, or politics, or whatever (and by science I mean true, empirical science, not theoretical science, since theories don't prove anything). Or they could hunt for internal inconsistencies within the Bible, since truth does not contradict itself. Critics have been desperately searching for internal and external inconsistencies for thousands of years, with zero success.

Some claim that the Bible has been changed down through the centuries. But there is simply too much manuscript evidence that refutes that charge. This information is also readily available if one cares to look. And there are still no inconsistencies. We would reasonably expect that a God who goes to the trouble to reveal Himself would preserve that revelation. Tens of thousands of manuscripts, spanning thousands of years, bear that out.

People will jump on the contradiction thing, since it is widely alleged that the Bible is full of them. But ask them to show you a couple. Usually they have to admit that they have no personal knowledge of any particular contradiction, they just know that the Bible is full of them, because that's what they've heard. Ask them if they've read the Bible themselves and if they found any. Be gentle here, because this puts them on the spot. But don't let them make up arguments. Point out that one's eternal destiny is far too important to be making decisions based on hearsay from biased and unverifiable sources.

You should have no difficulty in answering any supposed contradictions they can name. Most of them come from not knowing the Bible very well. In fact, the longer I study the Bible (more than 45 years now) the more impressed I am with its perfect and intricate consistency, both internal and external.

Furthermore, the Bible does not look like a book written by men. It's not the sort of book they could write, since it is perfectly consistent and since it has a perfect record in the prophetic realm. And it is not the sort of book they would write, if they could, since it condemns mankind and runs contrary to every other religion. They are all based upon man's works and merit. Christianity alone is based upon God's grace, showing that man has no merit of his own.

Let's consider the verification of fulfilled prophecy. In Isaiah God cites prophecy as proof that the Bible is His word. Isaiah 41:21-23:

"Present your case," the LORD says. "Bring forward your strong arguments," the King of Jacob says. "Let them bring forth and declare to us what is going to take place; as for the former events, declare what they were [e.g., the origin of the universe]**, that we may consider them, and know their outcome; or announce to us what is coming. Declare the things that are going to come afterward, that we may know that you are gods."**

"Remember the former things long past, for I am God, and there is no other; I am God, and there is no one like Me, declaring the end from the beginning and from ancient times things which have not been done, saying, 'My purpose

will be established, and I will accomplish all My good pleasure,'" Isaiah 46:9f.

Unlike the writings of the world's religions, the Bible verifies itself, both internally and externally. The others depend upon human reasoning or one human's claimed authority, which is undependable. If you know some of these inconsistencies, you might point them out to your friend.

Biblical prophecy is not like the predictions that men make--some coming true and some not. Anyone with sufficient knowledge and reason can predict some things, such as whether it will rain in the next 24 hours. Even then, man's predictions are prone to failure. Biblical prophecies are always fulfilled to the last detail, without exception. Who could predict the things that God predicts in His word, hundreds of years in advance and in such great detail, even naming names? Prophecy proves that the Bible is God's word. This is such a strong argument that many critics have tried to neutralize it by saying, in spite of the historical evidence, that the prophecies were actually written after the fact. But the prophecies concerning Christ's first coming, for example, were well-known long before Christ was born. The opponent's argument is an *a priori* argument: "True prophecy is impossible, because men don't know the future; therefore Biblical prophecy isn't true prophecy." This assertion assumes that the Bible is nothing more than the work of men. If that sounds like begging the question to you, you're right. It's nothing more than a "because I said so," argument. Fulfilled prophecy is convincing proof that the Old Testament is the word of God.

The prime proof offered in the New Testament is the resurrection of Jesus Christ. And this is one of the best attested events of ancient history. This is the basis for your faith. So you should know why you believe it. You may want to consult Josh McDowell's book, *Evidence That Demands a Verdict*, or Frank Morison's *Who Moved the Stone?*

Here again, the information is easily acquired, as many intelligent men have written extensively about it. And opponents have sought unsuccessfully to refute it for 2,000 years. The New Testament preachers cited the resurrection of Jesus Christ as the proof of their gospel. And they spoke in the time and place where their claim of resurrection could have easily been refuted by Christ's enemies, if it had been false. These enemies were desperate to refute the resurrection. But they could not produce the body or give any reasonable explanation for the empty grave.

One eye witness wrote in I Corinthians 15:3-8:

For I delivered to you as of first importance what I also received, that Christ died for our sins according to the Scriptures, and that He was buried, and that He was raised on the third day according to the Scriptures, and that He appeared to Cephas, then to the twelve. After that He appeared to more than five hundred brethren at one time, most of whom remain until now, but some have fallen asleep; then He appeared to James, then to all the apostles; and last of all, as it were to one untimely born, He appeared to me also.

We have already spoken of the fallacy of evolution, one of the **opposing arguments of what is falsely called "science,"** I Tim. 6:20 Alternative views of the origin of the universe went back before Paul's time. But of concern to us is whether neo-Darwinian evolution is consistent with the scientific method. It is not. Science is the Latin term for knowledge. But in the specialized sense in which we use the term today, science is a method of inquiry that by its nature can deal only with the physical world—what can be observed, measured, repeated, and tested. The origin of the universe cannot be repeated or observed. So science cannot answer the question of how the universe began. We have better tools for determining what happened in the distant past. The legal/historical method, honest logic, and verifiable revelation are all better means of inquiry.

Even forensic science can deal only with what is here now. It is limited in what it can demonstrate of events even in the recent past. It's an illogical leap for a scientist to argue that his scientific method can deal only with the physical world, therefore the metaphysical does not exist. In fact, what we know for sure from operational science demands a metaphysical beginning of the universe. In short, true science logically requires an uncaused, first cause that is outside the natural realm.

Theoretical scientists must assume a closed system in order to proceed with their evolutionary theories, but they cannot have a closed system because empirical science forbids it. And it should be evident that it can't be scientifically proven that the universe is a closed system.

The bottom line is that the origin of the universe is not an issue that empirical science or theoretical science is equipped to solve. They don't have the tools or the methods. The question is in essence an historical and theological issue. Science is out of its field.

Philosophical Problems

It seems awfully arrogant that some people believe they can out-think God. But they do. They have **philosophical problems** with the gospel.

Philosophy is based on logical argument. And logical argument depends upon two elements, complete, factual data and soundness of the argument's form. There are scores of logical fallacies that must be avoided. Honest thinkers often trip over them. And dishonest people often use them purposefully to support desirable false conclusions.

God is omniscient. By comparison, men are ignorant. So they are on dangerous ground attacking God for philosophical reasons. Jeremiah 8:9 says, **The wise men are put to shame, they are dismayed and caught; behold, they have rejected the word of the LORD, and what kind of wisdom do they have?** In other words, having rejected the right answer, all they can do is try to come up with the best wrong answer.

Men are dishonest by nature while God cannot lie, so it is God's revelation that we should trust rather than man's way of thinking. Jeremiah 17:9 points out what is empirically undeniable, **The heart is more deceitful than all else and is desperately sick; who can understand it?** Proverbs 21:30

says, **There is no wisdom and no understanding and no counsel against the LORD.**

One example will suffice, perhaps. Atheistic philosophers have an argument they think is conclusive, "If there is a God who is all-powerful and all-loving, then evil would not exist in the world. But evil does exist in the world. Therefore, an all-powerful and all-loving God does not exist." This is a deductive argument of the form, *If A, then B. Not B. Therefore, not A.* This is called denying the consequent and is a valid form of deductive argument. If the premises were true we would be compelled to accept the truth of the conclusion, because the logical form is unassailable.

But we can easily attack the truthfulness of the major premise. It contains false assumptions. It assumes that God is completely described by the phrase, "all-loving and all-powerful." It leaves out all-knowing, holy, and just. Here, again, the problem is insufficient information on the part of those who argue against the existence of God. Always look for falsehood or incomplete truth in premises used against God.

We can see from Luke 13 and Job 33 that God has good reasons for letting the world experience the consequences of sin. Bad things happen in the world because men are in rebellion against the God who is the source of all good. Calamities are God's tangible and credible warning that He will follow through on His promise to judge sinners. If sinners didn't see plenty of examples of God's judgment, they would dismiss God's warnings and see no reason to repent. A loving God does not set people up for a surprise judgment. He doesn't entrap people.

Practical Problem

Perhaps the biggest problem people have with Christianity is the inconsistent lifestyle of people they believe to be Christians. This **practical problem** must be addressed.

Frederick Nietzsche said, "I might believe in the Redeemer if his followers looked more redeemed." Karl Marx, not one of the Marx Brothers, turned away from his religion when he saw his Jewish father abandon their faith in favor of joining the Lutheran church simply to help his business grow. Think of how much evil can be traced back to these two men.

Many people dismiss God because they have too many acquaintances who claim to be Christians but don't live like Christ. That's why the bulk of Peter's first letter describes how to **keep your behavior excellent among the Gentiles, so that in the thing in which they slander you as evildoers, they may on account of your good deeds, as they observe them, glorify God in the day of visitation.** (2:12)

The opponents of Christianity have a point; though not so fine a point as they think. We must admit that many true Christians aren't very good at living like Jesus. No one is perfect in this world, except Jesus. And Jesus saves sinners. It takes a while to change them into the image of Christ without violating their souls and spirits. And the world system doesn't help with all its pressures to conform to evil.

On the other hand, if someone claims to be a Christian but isn't concerned with following Christ, then there is reason to doubt the genuineness of his faith. Jesus said in Matthew 7:21:

"Not everyone who says to Me, 'Lord, Lord,' will enter the kingdom of heaven; but he who does the will of My Father who is in heaven... I will declare to them, 'I never knew you; DEPART FROM ME, YOU WHO PRACTICE LAWLESSNESS.'"

Jesus has the right to be evaluated on His own merits and not condemned because the sinners He saves don't instantly become perfect. Saving sinners is messy work. And it's certainly wrong to judge Him on the basis of the actions of people who aren't even true Christians.

Our Defense: The Gospel Explained

Sometimes we have to deal with these arguments against God. But our real purpose is to make a reasoned explanation of the gospel. Our job is to demonstrate that the gospel makes perfect sense. And we already have the information we need to do that. I Corinthians 15 contains a concise gospel, several can be found in Acts, and Romans 1-6 is a very complete explanation.

Our explanation must make these points clear:

1. Man's problem is his sinful rebellion against God and the consequent death and judgment. Genesis 3 is a good place to start, also Romans 1-3.

2. God's solution is the judicial satisfaction of God's justice through Christ's death on the cross, and the offer of new life in Christ. You can't do better than Romans as the source of information.

3. What God requires of man is repentance from sin and trust in the Savior God sent us.

No matter how we analyze the problems people have with God, in the final analysis, men really have a single problem. Divine promises and warnings notwithstanding, people are unwilling to give up their sin and yield their lives to God.

They don't have moral problems with actual immorality, especially their own. They don't have factual problems with lies, especially those that support their own desires. They don't have philosophical problems with faulty logic, especially that which justifies their continued rebellion. And they don't have problems with hypocrisy in their ranks, including their own.

They only have problems with God's truth and God's rule. If they insist upon a double standard; if they call good bad and bad good; if they play fast and loose with the facts; if they can't see their own hypocrisy, then they aren't interested in the truth. Don't allow them to draw you into a fight that they will never concede.

You can't win. Nobody wins ego-centered fights. So don't waste your time. Remember the words of Jesus; **No one can come to Me, unless the Father who sent Me draws him... My sheep hear My voice, and I know them, and they follow Me,** Jn. 6:44 and 10:27.

You've hear it said that locks only stop honest people. In the same way, a reasoned defense of the gospel only

378

convinces honest inquirers. In both cases, the others will have to face the judge. So prepare yourself with a well-reasoned explanation of the gospel.

Bibliography

Abbott-Smith, G., *A Manual Greek Lexicon of the New Testament*. Edinburg: T. & T. Clark, 1977.

Alford, Henry, *The New Testament for English Readers: Vol. 4, Hebrews to Revelation*. Grand Rapids: Baker Book House, 1983.

Allen, Dennis L., *I Corinthians 13:10-12: The Maturity of the Church in the Present Age*. Master of Divinity Thesis. La Mirada, CA: Talbot Theological Seminary, 1984.

Christian, James, *Church History Notes*. La Mirada, CA: Talbot Theological Seminary.

Douglas, J. D., *The New Bible Dictionary*. Grand Rapids: Wm. B. Eerdmans Publishing Company, 1979.

Foxe, John, *Foxe's Book of Martyrs*. Grand Rapids: Baker Book House, 1980.

Friberg, Barbara and Timothy, *Analytical Greek New Testament*. Grand Rapids: Baker Book House, 1981.

Holloman, Henry W., *Kregel Dictionary of the Bible and Theology*. Grand Rapids: Kregel, 2005.

MacArthur, John, *The MacArthur New Testament Commentary: I Peter*. Chicago: Moody Publishers, 2004.

Marshall, Alfred, *The Interlinear Greek-English New Testament*. Grand Rapids: Zondervan Publishing House, 1976.

Nicoll, W. Robertson, *The Expositor's Greek Testament: Vol. 5, I Peter - Revelation*. Grand Rapids: Wm. B. Eerdmans Publishing Company, 1983.

Pink, Arthur W., *Eternal Security*. Grand Rapids: Guardian Press, 1974.

Thiessen, Henry C., *Introductory Lectures in Systematic Theology*. Grand Rapids: Wm. B. Eerdmans Publishing Company, 1976.

Walvoord, John F. and Zuck, Roy B, *The Bible Knowledge Commentary, New Testament*. Wheaton: Victor Books, 1984.

Vine, W. E., *An Expository Dictionary of New Testament Words*. Old Tappan, NJ: Fleming H. Revell Company, 1966.